Networks Social Stud...

United States History

Teacher Edition

▲ Cotton

Draw a picture of something made out of cotton.

● A Pueblo Home

Royalty-Free/CORBIS

The Capitol

Bilderbuch/Design Pics/Corbis

Mc Graw Hill Education

PROGRAM AUTHORS

James A. Banks, Ph.D.
Kerry and Linda Killinger Endowed
    Chair in Diversity Studies and
    Director, Center for Multicultural
    Education
University of Washington
Seattle, Washington

Kevin P. Colleary, Ed.D.
Curriculum and Teaching Department
Graduate School of Education
Fordham University
New York, New York

Linda Greenow, Ph.D.
Associate Professor and Chair
Department of Geography
State University of New York at
    New Paltz
New Paltz, New York

Walter C. Parker, Ph.D.
Professor of Social Studies Education,
    Adjunct Professor of Political
    Science
University of Washington
Seattle, Washington

Emily M. Schell, Ed.D.
Visiting Professor, Teacher Education
San Diego State University
San Diego, California

Dinah Zike
Educational Consultant
Dinah-Might Adventures, L.P.
San Antonio, Texas

CONTRIBUTING AUTHORS

James M. Denham, Ph.D.
Professor of History and Director,
    Lawton M. Chiles, Jr., Center for
    Florida History
Florida Southern College
Lakeland, Florida

M.C. Bob Leonard, Ph.D.
Professor, Hillsborough Community
    College
Director, Florida History Internet Center
Ybor City, Florida

Jay McTighe
Educational Author and Consultant
McTighe and Associates Consulting
Columbia, Maryland

Timothy Shanahan, Ph.D.
Professor of Urban Education &
    Director, Center for Literacy
College of Education
University of Illinois at Chicago

ACADEMIC CONSULTANTS

Tom Daccord
Educational Technology Specialist
Co-Director, EdTechTeacher
Boston, Massachusetts

Joe Follman
Service Learning Specialist
Director, Florida Learn & Serve

Cathryn Berger Kaye, M.A.
Service Learning Specialist
Author, *The Complete Guide to
    Service Learning*

Justin Reich
Educational Technology Specialist
Co-Director, EdTechTeacher
Boston, Massachusetts

Send all inquiries to:
McGraw-Hill Education
8787 Orion Place
Columbus, OH 43240

ISBN: 978-0-02-138070-1
MHID: 0-02-138070-8

Printed in the United States of America.

1 2 3 4 5 6 7 8 9 QVS 19 18 17 16 15 14

Common Core State Standards© Copyright 2010. National Governors Association Center
for Best Practices and Council of Chief State School Officers. All rights reserved.

Understanding by Design® is a registered trademark of the
Association for Supervision and Curriculum Development ("ASCD").

Table of Contents

UNIT 1 Geography

BIG IDEA 💡 Location affects how people live.

UNIT 2 Native Peoples of North America

BIG IDEA 💡 Culture influences the way people live.

Notebook FOLDABLES templates can be found on pages R33–R42 at the end of this Teacher Edition.

UNIT ③ The Age of Exploration

BIG IDEA People's actions affect others.

UNIT ④ Colonial America

BIG IDEA Location affects how people live.

Notebook **FOLDABLES** templates can be found on pages R33–R42 at the end of this Teacher Edition.

Table of Contents

Notebook **FOLDABLES** templates can be found on pages R33–R42 at the end of this Teacher Edition.

UNIT 7 Westward Expansion

BIG IDEA 💡 Relationships affect choices.

UNIT 8 Slavery and Emancipation

BIG IDEA 💡 Conflict causes change.

Notebook FOLDABLES templates can be found on pages R33–R42 at the end of this Teacher Edition.

Table of Contents

Skills

Reading Skills

Primary and Secondary Sources

Chart and Graph Skills

Notebook **FOLDABLES** templates can be found on pages R33–R42 at the end of this Teacher Edition.

Maps

Reference

Notebook **FOLDABLES** templates can be found on pages
R33–R42 at the end of this Teacher Edition.

Teacher Planning

Planning pages appear at the beginning of each unit.

• Unit Big Idea

The Big Idea is the major theme that helps students organize and understand information.

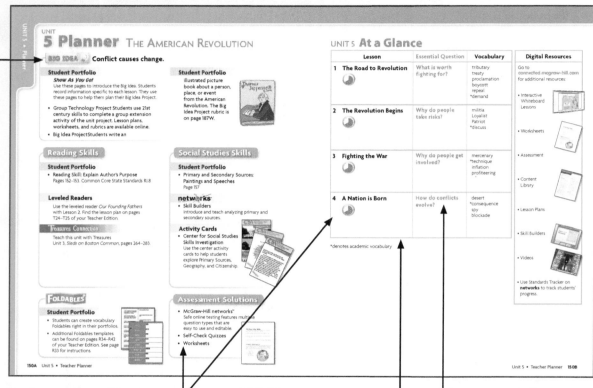

• Resources and Lessons at a Glance

Planning made easy.

NGSS • Standards

Standards are also listed at point of use throughout the student edition.

• Essential Questions

Lesson-specific Essential Questions tie content to the Big Idea.

Start netw⊕rking!

Customizable Model Lesson Plans

The online teacher edition features model lesson plans for each lesson. You can customize each lesson plan to fit your time demands and the needs of your students.

Understanding by Design®

Quality instruction develops and deepens student understanding through the use of carefully crafted learning experiences. The **McGraw-Hill networks™** program focuses on teaching for understanding through on-going, inquiry-based instruction and assessment. This program was created through the Understanding by Design® (UbD) curriculum design model. At the core of UbD lies a focus on what is taught and how it is assessed.

In the **networks** program, each unit is centered on a **Big Idea.** The unit Big Idea focuses student learning through the use of prior knowledge and stimulates deeper understanding.

The end of each unit features a **Big Idea Project.** Through this authentic assessment, students demonstrate the understanding gained within the unit. As a final step, students reflect and explain how what they learned affected their understanding of the Big Idea.

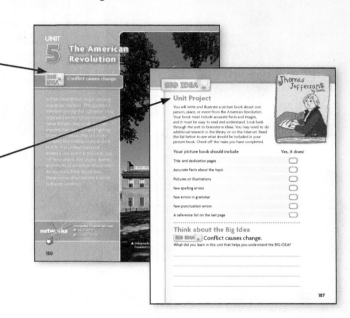

Each lesson focuses on an **Essential Question.** These open-ended questions allow students the opportunity to make connections, view events from different perspectives, and integrate information.

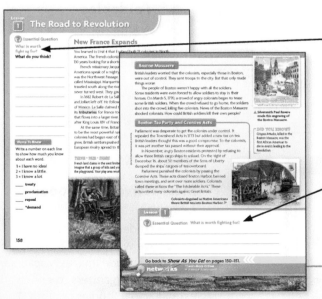

At the end of each lesson, students again respond to the **Essential Question.** This response should reflect a change in student understanding based on their experiences within the lesson.

Contributing Author

Jay McTighe has published articles in a number of leading educational journals and has co-authored ten books, including the best-selling *Understanding by Design®* series with Grant Wiggins. Jay also has an extensive background in professional development and is a featured speaker at national, state, and district conferences and workshops. He received his undergraduate degree from The College of William and Mary, earned a Masters degree from The University of Maryland, and completed post-graduate studies at The Johns Hopkins University.

Student Engagement

Each lesson has activities that stimulate learning and interest.

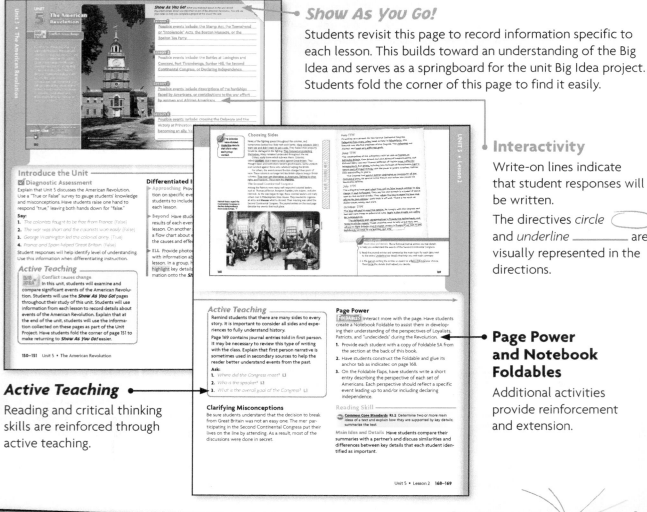

Show As You Go!

Students revisit this page to record information specific to each lesson. This builds toward an understanding of the Big Idea and serves as a springboard for the unit Big Idea project. Students fold the corner of this page to find it easily.

Interactivity

Write-on lines indicate that student responses will be written.

The directives *circle* ⬭ and *underline* _____ are visually represented in the directions.

Page Power and Notebook Foldables

Additional activities provide reinforcement and extension.

Active Teaching

Reading and critical thinking skills are reinforced through active teaching.

Start netw⊛rking!

Interactive Whiteboard Lessons

Engage students with these interactive whiteboard activities. vLessons include images, vocabulary, and graphic organizers to enrich and extend Social Studies content. The vLessons and these additional digital resources motivate students and reinforce Social Studies concepts and skills:

- Interactive Maps
- Videos

Reading Integration

Each unit has skills-based instruction that focuses on Common Core State Standards for English Language Arts: Reading Standards for Informational Text.

Vocabulary Foldable

After constructing the "stay in the book" Vocabulary Foldable, students complete activities that reinforce word meanings.

Vocabulary Instruction

Content and Academic Vocabulary are taught and reinforced through Foldables, graphic organizers, and games.

Graphic Organizers

Each unit has a different graphic organizer to help students gain a deeper understanding of unit vocabulary and concepts.

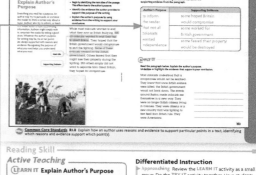

Integrated Reading and Writing Skills

Students learn, try, and apply the skills.

Start netw♦rking!

Interactive Games

Engaging interactive Vocabulary Games help students practice vocabulary and concepts.

The Vocabulary Games and these additional digital resources can be used to introduce and review vocabulary, to reinforce reading skills, and to build comprehension and fluency:

- Vocabulary Flashcards
- Puzzle Maker
- Worksheets
- Graphic Organizers
- Skill Builders
- Audio-Visual Online Student Experience

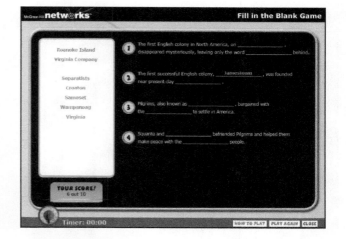

Social Studies Instruction

Skills instruction is spiraled throughout each grade and between grade levels.

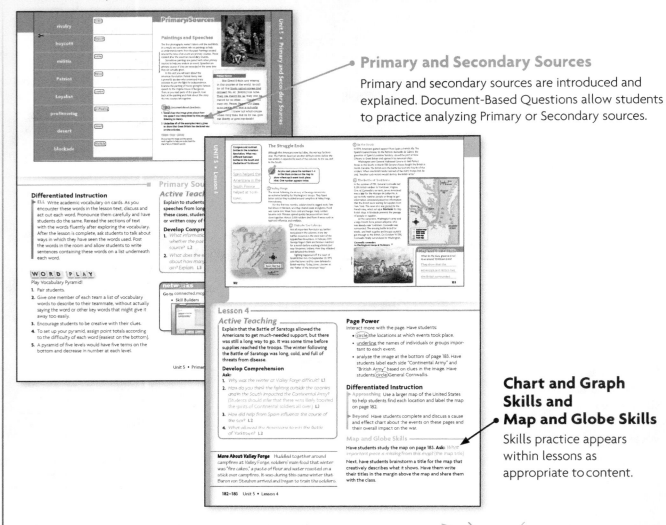

Primary and Secondary Sources

Primary and secondary sources are introduced and explained. Document-Based Questions allow students to practice analyzing Primary or Secondary sources.

Chart and Graph Skills and Map and Globe Skills

Skills practice appears within lessons as appropriate to content.

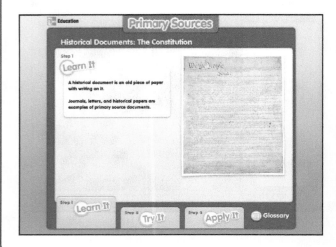

Start networking!

Skill Builders

Interactive learning tools help students use a variety of Social Studies skills. Each tool will allow students to learn, try, and apply each Social Studies skill in an active and engaging way.

- Primary Sources
- Map and Globe Skills
- Chart and Graph Skills

Project and Assessment

Each unit provides a variety of formative and summative assessments, as well as suggested interventions.

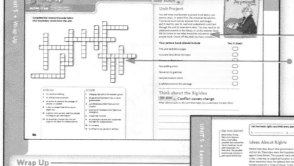

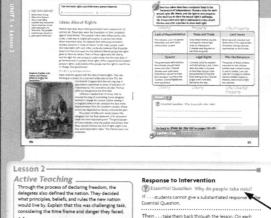

Big Idea Project

Unit performance tasks require students to synthesize information while creating, presenting, and evaluating a project. Students use a checklist as a guide for working through the project. Each project has a reproducible project rubric for scoring.

Unit Wrap Up

Activities review and reinforce unit vocabulary and content.

Formative Assessment

Provides a snapshot of student learning and indicates the need for intervention.

Response To Intervention

This check provides an opportunity to redirect or intervene for struggling students.

Depths of Knowledge

Questions are leveled according to Florida's Depths of Knowledge.

Start networking!

Self-Check Quizzes

Self-Check Quizzes gauge students' level of understanding before, during, or after studying a lesson. The Self-Check Quizzes and these additional resources are available for formative, summative, or project-based assessment.

• McGraw-Hill networks™ Assessment
• Group Technology Project

Differentiated Instruction

Differentiated Instruction activities meet the diverse needs of every student.

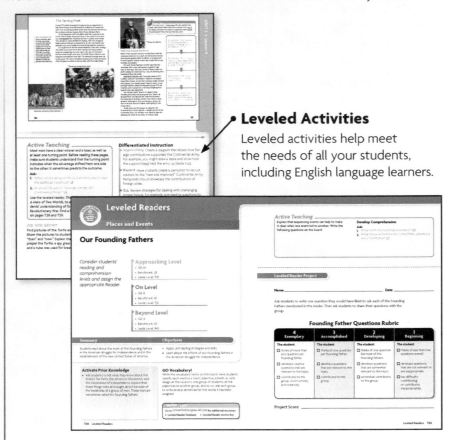

Leveled Activities

Leveled activities help meet the needs of all your students, including English language learners.

Center Card Activities

Students investigate Primary Sources, Geography, and Citizenship.

Leveled Readers

One topic presented at three different reading levels provides an opportunity for your whole class to participate in a discussion about the topic.

Start networking!

- ## Content Library
  There's more to learn in the Content Library! A bank of short articles provides background information about topics covered in each unit. Use the Content Library to enrich or extend student knowledge beyond information presented in the text.

- ## Access Points
  Access Points activities for standards are available in your customizable model lesson plans. Here you will find independent, supported, and participatory activities to meet the needs of your students.

- ## Character Education
  Develop the character of your students with our Character Education curriculum. Students have the opportunity to explain, explore, experience, and exhibit a variety of character traits through cooperative activities and self-reflection.

- ## Service Learning
  Make Service Learning simple and easy with step-by-step guidance to enrich the learning experience of your students. Use hands-on, real-world projects to develop skills, behaviors, and habits of good citizenship.

Levels of Cognitive Complexity

Questions throughout your Teacher Edition are labeled L1 (Level 1), L2 (Level 2), or L3 (Level 3) depending upon their level of complexity.

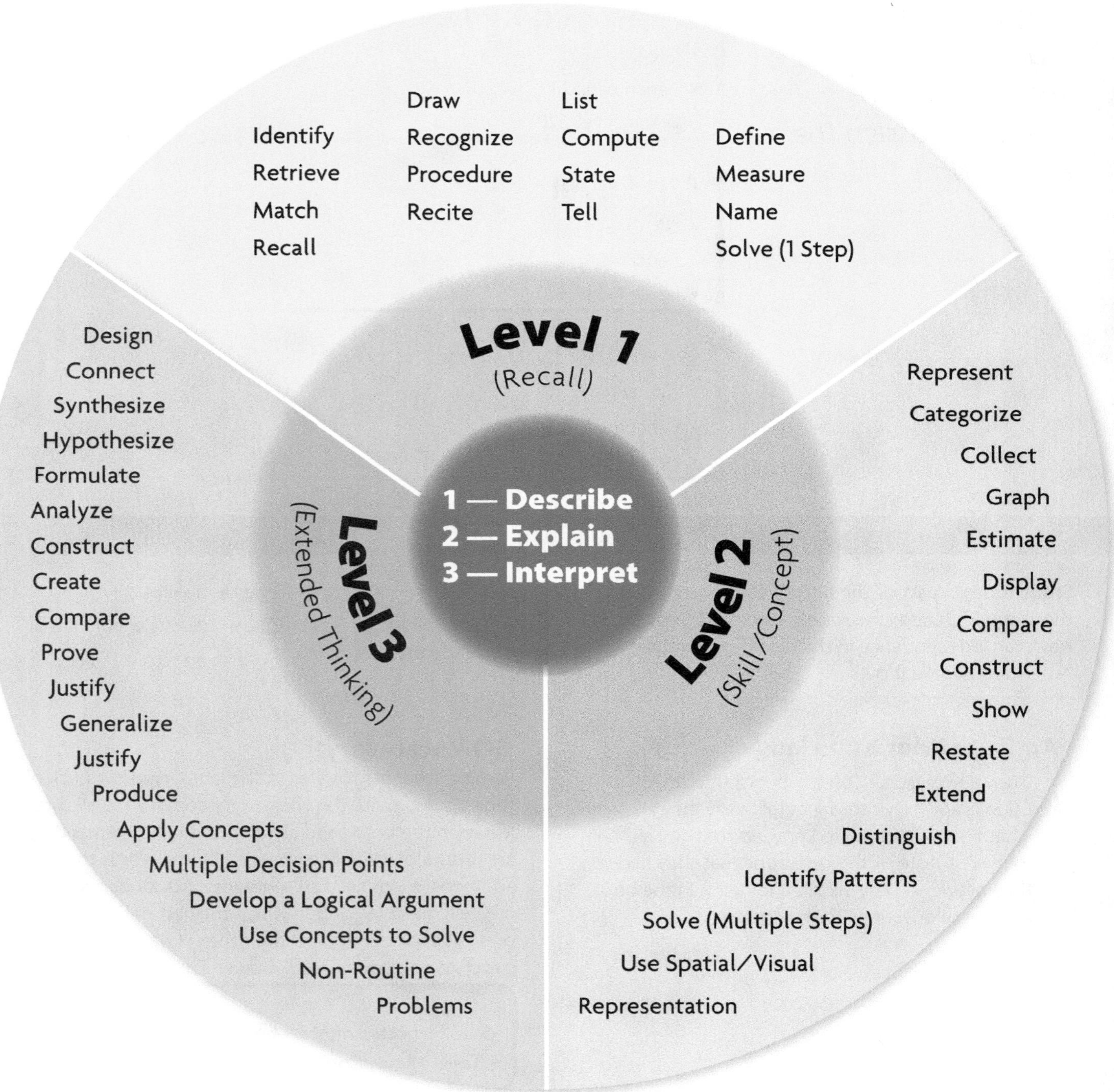

Level 1 (Recall)

Identify
Retrieve
Match
Recall

Draw
Recognize
Procedure
Recite

List
Compute
State
Tell

Define
Measure
Name
Solve (1 Step)

Level 3 (Extended Thinking)

Design
Connect
Synthesize
Hypothesize
Formulate
Analyze
Construct
Create
Compare
Prove
Justify
Generalize
Justify
Produce
Apply Concepts
Multiple Decision Points
Develop a Logical Argument
Use Concepts to Solve
Non-Routine
Problems

1 — Describe
2 — Explain
3 — Interpret

Level 2 (Skill/Concept)

Represent
Categorize
Collect
Graph
Estimate
Display
Compare
Construct
Show
Restate
Extend
Distinguish
Identify Patterns
Solve (Multiple Steps)
Use Spatial/Visual
Representation

Leveled Readers

Biography

Liliuokalani, The Last Queen of Hawaii

Consider students' reading and comprehension levels and assign the appropriate Reader.

▶ Approaching Level
- GR: L
- Benchmark: 24
- Lexile Level: 520

▶ On Level
- GR: Q
- Benchmark: 40
- Lexile Level: 620

▶ Beyond Level
- GR: W
- Benchmark: 60
- Lexile Level: 810

Summary

Students learn part of the history of Hawaii through the story of Queen Liliuokalani, who tried to maintain Hawaiian independence in the face of attempts by Americans to take it over.

Objectives

- Apply unit reading strategies and skills.
- Learn about efforts of Queen Liliuokalani of Hawaii during the late 1800s.

Activate Prior Knowledge

- Draw a K-W-L chart on the board titled "Queen Liliuokalani." Have students tell what they know and what they would like to know about her. Ask them to make a note of the questions that they had as they previewed the visuals and heads in the book. Add these questions to the chart.

GO Vocabulary!

Remind students to refer to the glossary in the back of their books. Write the vocabulary common to all three levels on the board and ask students which terms they are unsure of. With the class, clarify the words through additional examples and sentences. Ask students to create a matching quiz in which they list definitions in one column and terms in the other. Have them exchange papers with a partner and answer each others' quiz.

networks

Go to **connected.mcgraw-hill.com** for additional resources:
- Leveled Reader Database
- Leveled Reader Answer Key

Active Teaching

Explain to students that comparing and contrasting will help them to understand how things or events are similar and how they are different. Write the following questions on the board.

Develop Comprehension

Ask:

1. *How were Queen Liliuokalani and the American plantation owners alike?*

2. *How were they different?*

Leveled Reader Project

Name _____   **Date** _____

Ask students to write a persuasive speech voicing an opinion about the actions of the American plantation owners in Hawaii. The speech should take the side of either Queen Liliuokalani or the American plantation owners.

Persuasive Speech Rubric

4 Exemplary	3 Accomplished	2 Developing	1 Beginning
The speech:	**The speech:**	**The speech:**	**The speech:**
☐ includes many supporting details from the reader.	☐ includes some supporting details from the reader.	☐ includes few supporting details from the reader.	☐ does not include supporting details from the reader.
☐ maintains a consistent point of view.	☐ maintains a mostly consistent point of view.	☐ maintains an inconsistent point of view.	☐ lacks a point of view.
☐ clearly uses persuasive language.	☐ mostly uses persuasive language.	☐ contains little persuasive language.	☐ does not contain persuasive language.

Project Score: _____

The Navajo: Tradition and Change

Consider students' reading and comprehension levels and assign the appropriate Reader.

▶ Approaching Level
- GR: L
- Benchmark: 24
- Lexile Level: 450

▶ On Level
- GR: R
- Benchmark: 40
- Lexile Level: 800

▶ Beyond Level
- GR: V
- Benchmark: 60
- Lexile Level: 940

Summary

Students learn about the history and traditions of the Navajo of the Southwest.

Objectives

- Apply unit reading strategies and skills.
- Learn about the Navajo of the Southwest.

Activate Prior Knowledge

- Draw a K-W-L chart on the board titled "The Navajo." Have students tell what they know and what they would like to know about the Navajo. Ask them to make a note of the questions that they had as they previewed the visuals and heads in the book. Add these questions to the chart.

GO Vocabulary!

Remind students to refer to the glossary in the back of their books. Write the vocabulary common to all three levels on the board and ask students which terms they are unsure of. With the class, clarify the words through additional examples and sentences. As a class, read the list of vocabulary terms and their definitions aloud. This will help auditory learners and those with pronunciation problems.

networks

Go to **connected.mcgraw-hill.com** for additional resources:
- Leveled Reader Database
- Leveled Reader Answer Key

Active Teaching

Explain to students that identifying cause and effect will help them find out what happened and why it happened. Write the following questions on the board.

Develop Comprehension
Ask:

1. *What caused the Navajo to learn to farm?* **L1**
2. *What happened as the result of the discovery of oil on Navajo land?* **L1**

Leveled Reader Project

Name _____ Date _____

Using the book *The Navajo: Tradition and Change,* work with a group to identify five Frequently Asked Questions (FAQ) about The Navajo. Create a pamphlet addressing these FAQs that can be provided for people interested in learning more about the Navajo.

Pamphlet Rubric

4 Exemplary	3 Accomplished	2 Developing	1 Beginning
The pamphlet:	**The pamphlet:**	**The pamphlet:**	**The pamphlet:**
☐ includes 5 FAQ and complete and accurate answers to each.	☐ includes 5 FAQ and mostly complete and accurate answers to each.	☐ includes some FAQ and somewhat complete and accurate answers.	☐ does not include any FAQ or complete or accurate answers.
☐ is interesting and easy to read.	☐ is mostly interesting and easy to read.	☐ is somewhat interesting and easy to read.	☐ is not interesting or easy to read.
☐ contains few errors in spelling and capitalization.	☐ contains some errors in spelling and capitalization.	☐ contains several errors in spelling and capitalization.	☐ contains serious errors in spelling and capitalization.

Project Score: _____

Coronado Searches for Cities of Gold

Consider students' reading and comprehension levels and assign the appropriate Reader.

▶ Approaching Level
- GR: M
- Benchmark: 28
- Lexile Level: 580

▶ On Level
- GR: R
- Benchmark: 40
- Lexile Level: 710

▶ Beyond Level
- GR: V
- Benchmark: 60
- Lexile Level: 890

Summary

Students read about the expedition of Spanish explorer Coronado, and his discovery of the Grand Canyon and the Colorado River, which were previously unknown to Europeans.

Objectives

- Apply unit reading strategies and skills.
- Learn about the adventures of the Spanish explorer Coronado.

Activate Prior Knowledge

- Write **Gold** on the board. Explain to students that people throughout history have been interested in finding gold. Then ask students why they think this might have been the case. Discuss what it means for something to be valuable.

GO Vocabulary!

Before students read the glossary definitions have them find each vocabulary word in the reader. Ask students to write their own definition of the word from the context in which it is used. Then have them compare these definitions with those in the glossary.

networks

Go to **connected.mcgraw-hill.com** for additional resources:
- Leveled Reader Database
- Leveled Reader Answer Key

Active Teaching

Point out that understanding cause and effect can lead to better understanding of the major events in history. Students can learn that one event can cause several effects. Write the following questions on the board.

Develop Comprehension

Ask:

1. *How did the Spanish desire for gold change the lives of Native Americans of the Southwest?* **L1**
2. *How did that same desire increase Europeans' understanding of North America?* **L2**

Leveled Reader Project

Name _____ Date _____

Have students create a list of cause and effect pairs. Using the book *Coronado Searches for Cities of Gold*, ask students to list at least five cause and effect pairs. Invite volunteers to add their cause and effect pairs to a list on the board.

Cause and Effect List

4 Exemplary	3 Accomplished	2 Developing	1 Beginning
The list:	**The list:**	**The list:**	**The list:**
☐ includes more than five cause and effect pairs.	☐ includes five cause and effect pairs.	☐ includes three or four cause and effect pairs.	☐ includes less than three cause and effect pairs.
☐ contains few errors in spelling and capitalization.	☐ contains some errors in spelling and capitalization.	☐ contains several errors in spelling and capitalization.	☐ contains serious errors in spelling and capitalization.
The student:	**The student:**	**The student:**	**The student:**
☐ contributes constructively and creatively to the group.	☐ contributes to the group.	☐ somewhat contributes to the group.	☐ has difficulty contributing or contributes inappropriately.

Project Score: _____

Our Founding Fathers

Consider students' reading and comprehension levels and assign the appropriate Reader.

▶ Approaching Level
- GR: M
- Benchmark: 28
- Lexile Level: 700

▶ On Level
- GR: R
- Benchmark: 40
- Lexile Level: 720

▶ Beyond Level
- GR: X
- Benchmark: 60
- Lexile Level: 940

Summary

Students read about the work of the Founding Fathers in the American struggle for independence and in the establishment of the new United States of America.

Objectives

- Apply unit reading strategies and skills.
- Learn about the efforts of our Founding Fathers in the American struggle for independence.

Activate Prior Knowledge

- Ask students to tell what they know about the Boston Tea Party, the American Revolution, and the Declaration of Independence. Explain that these things were all brought about because of the leadership of a group of men. These men are sometimes called the Founding Fathers.

GO Vocabulary!

Write the vocabulary terms on the board. Have students classify each word as a noun, adjective, adverb, or verb. Assign all the nouns to one group of students, all the adjectives to another group, and so on. Ask each group to write several sentences for the words it has been assigned.

networks

Go to **connected.mcgraw-hill.com** for additional resources:
- Leveled Reader Database
- Leveled Reader Answer Key

Active Teaching

Explain that sequencing events can help to make it clear when one event led to another. Write the following questions on the board.

Develop Comprehension

Ask:

1. *What led to the American Revolution?* **L2**
2. *What happened before the United States adopted a new Constitution?* **L2**

Leveled Reader Project

Name _____ Date _____

Ask students to write one question they would have liked to ask each of the Founding Fathers mentioned in the reader. Then ask students to share their questions with the group.

Founding Father Questions Rubric

4 Exemplary	3 Accomplished	2 Developing	1 Beginning
The student:	**The student:**	**The student:**	**The student:**
☐ thinks of more than one question per founding father.	☐ thinks of one question per founding father.	☐ thinks of one question for most of the founding fathers.	☐ thinks of less than two questions overall.
☐ develops creative questions that are relevant to the topic.	☐ develops questions that are relevant to the topic.	☐ develops questions that are somewhat relevant to the topic.	☐ develops questions that are not relevant or are inappropriate.
☐ contributes to the group constructively and creatively.	☐ contributes to the group.	☐ somewhat contributes to the group.	☐ has difficulty contributing or contributes inappropriately.

Project Score: _____

Leveled Readers

Places and Events

Vote!

Consider students' reading and comprehension levels and assign the appropriate Reader.

▶ Approaching Level
- GR: L
- Benchmark: 24
- Lexile Level: 630

▶ On Level
- GR: R
- Benchmark: 40
- Lexile Level: 780

▶ Beyond Level
- GR: W
- Benchmark: 60
- Lexile Level: 1000

Summary

Students read about the history of voting rights in the United States, from independence through the 2006 Voting Rights Act Amendment..

Objectives

- Apply unit reading strategies and skills.
- Learn about the 200-year struggle to extend the right to vote to all American citizens.

Activate Prior Knowledge
- Write the following dates on the board: 1776 and 2006. Ask: *Who was allowed to vote in the United States in 1776? Who is allowed to vote today?* Elicit students' prior knowledge about voting rights. Review the Civil War and the civil rights movement.

GO Vocabulary!
Write the vocabulary term *suffrage* on the board. Have students look up the other terms in their Leveled Readers. Ask them to explain how each of the other terms relates to this term.

networks
Go to **connected.mcgraw-hill.com** for additional resources:
- Leveled Reader Database
- Leveled Reader Answer Key

Active Teaching

Explain that comparing and contrasting requires students to break down a topic into smaller parts and thus makes the topic easier to understand. Write the following questions on the board.

Develop Comprehension

Ask:

1. *Which group of people was allowed to vote from the early 1800s on?* **L1**
2. *How did voting rights change from 1870 to 1920?* **L1**

Leveled Reader Project

Name _____ Date _____

Ask students to choose one of the groups who won voting rights between the Civil War and 1971. Have them write a speech that a leader from this group might have given. The speech should call for voting rights for the group and give reasons why suffrage should be expanded.

Speech Rubric

4 Exemplary	3 Accomplished	2 Developing	1 Beginning
The speech:	**The speech:**	**The speech:**	**The speech:**
☐ clearly explains many reasons for expanding suffrage.	☐ explains several reasons for the expansion of suffrage.	☐ explains some reasons for the expansion of suffrage.	☐ does not explain reasons for the expansion of suffrage.
☐ maintains a very consistent viewpoint.	☐ maintains a consistent viewpoint.	☐ maintains a somewhat consistent viewpoint.	☐ does not maintain a consistent viewpoint.
☐ contains few errors in capitalization and spelling.	☐ contains some errors in capitalization and spelling.	☐ contains several errors in capitalization and spelling.	☐ contains serious errors in capitalization and spelling.

Project Score: _____

Wagons West!

*Consider students'
reading and
comprehension
levels and assign the
appropriate Reader.*

▶ Approaching Level

- GR: M
- Benchmark: 28
- Lexile Level: 510

▶ On Level

- GR: R
- Benchmark: 40
- Lexile Level: 640

▶ Beyond Level

- GR: X
- Benchmark: 60
- Lexile Level: 850

Summary

Students will read about what it was like to travel on the Oregon Trail—how pioneers prepared for the trip, the dangers they faced along the way, and the rewards that waited for them at the end.

Objectives

- Apply unit reading strategies and skills.
- Learn about the trip west on the Oregon Trail.

Activate Prior Knowledge

- Write "pioneer" on the board. Ask students to name some pioneers they know. Ask students: *What do these people have in common?* Make a list of characteristics that pioneers share.

GO Vocabulary!

Divide students at each level into two groups. Have each group write clues on index cards for a vocabulary term. For example, "These people courageously traveled the Oregon Trail. (pioneers)" When all groups have finished writing their clues, have the groups take turns quizzing the other group using their clues. You may set a timer for 30 seconds and give a point for each correct answer.

networks

Go to **connected.mcgraw-hill.com** for additional resources:

- Leveled Reader Database
- Leveled Reader Answer Key

Active Teaching

Remind students that they should use the facts in the story to draw conclusions. Write the following questions on the board.

Develop Comprehension

Ask:

1. *What was life like on the Oregon Trail?* **L2**
2. *Why did people head west?* **L2**

Leveled Reader Project

Name _____ Date _____

Have students write a shopping list for a family of four waiting in a Missouri town to join a wagon train. They should include at least ten items. They should be able to describe why they need each item for the journey.

Oregon Trail Shopping List Rubric

4 Exemplary	3 Accomplished	2 Developing	1 Beginning
The list:	**The list:**	**The list:**	**The list:**
☐ includes more than ten items.	☐ includes ten items.	☐ includes five to nine items.	☐ includes less than five items.
☐ includes a descriptive reason or purpose for each item.	☐ includes a reason or purpose for each item.	☐ includes a reason or purpose for some items.	☐ does not include a reason or purpose for any items.

Project Score: _____

Riding the Rails to a New Life

Consider students' reading and comprehension levels and assign the appropriate Reader.

▶ Approaching Level
- GR: L
- Benchmark: 24
- Lexile Level: 580

▶ On Level
- GR: Q
- Benchmark: 40
- Lexile Level: 770

▶ Beyond Level
- GR: V
- Benchmark: 60
- Lexile Level: 920

Summary

Students read the story of the orphan trains, which ran from 1854 to 1929, carrying New York City orphans to new homes in the country.

Objectives

- Apply unit reading strategies and skills.
- Learn about the lives of immigrants and orphans in the 1800s.

Activate Prior Knowledge
- Ask students what they know about New York City today. What words would they use to describe the city? What do they think New York City was like in the mid-1800s? Explain that when people came to live in the United States from other countries, many came first to New York City.

GO Vocabulary!

Have students create a crossword puzzle using the terms in the glossary. They will need to write a clue for each term, as well as lay out the puzzle so that all of the words connect.

networks

Go to **connected.mcgraw-hill.com** for additional resources:
- Leveled Reader Database
- Leveled Reader Answer Key

Active Teaching

Point out that looking for the main idea of a story or passage requires students to synthesize information to identify the central message. Write the following questions on the board.

Develop Comprehension

Ask:

1. *What is the story* Riding the Rails to a New Life *about?* **L2**
2. *What facts does the story tell about the lives of orphans in New York City?* **L1**

Leveled Reader Project

Name _____ Date _____

Remind students that Brace and his workers posted ads that told farmers about the orphan trains. Have students create their own ads that include all the information a farm family would need to decide whether they wanted to adopt an orphan.

Poster Rubric

4 Exemplary	3 Accomplished	2 Developing	1 Beginning
The poster:	**The poster:**	**The poster:**	**The poster:**
☐ includes detailed information about how families can adopt an orphan.	☐ includes information about how families can adopt an orphan.	☐ includes some information about how families can adopt an orphan.	☐ does not include information about how families can adopt an orphan.
☐ is very creative.	☐ is creative.	☐ is somewhat creative.	☐ is not creative or is inappropriate.
☐ includes many details from the reader.	☐ includes details from the reader.	☐ includes some details from the reader.	☐ does not include details from the reader.

Project Score: _____

Leveled Readers

Biography

The Gullah: Then and Now

Consider students' reading and comprehension levels and assign the appropriate Reader.

▶ Approaching Level
- GR: L
- Benchmark: 24
- Lexile Level: 580

▶ On Level
- GR: R
- Benchmark: 40
- Lexile Level: 790

▶ Beyond Level
- GR: V
- Benchmark: 60
- Lexile Level: 860

Summary

Students read about the development of Gullah culture and how the Gullah are working to preserve their culture today.

Objectives

- Apply unit reading strategies and skills.
- Learn about the history of the Gullah and the challenges to their culture today.

Activate Prior Knowledge
Draw a K-W-L chart on the board, titled "The Gullah." Have students tell what they know and what they would like to know about the Gullah. Ask them to make a note of the questions that they had as they previewed the visuals and heads in the book. Add these questions to the chart.

GO Vocabulary!
Remind students to refer to the glossary in the back of their books. Write the vocabulary common to all three levels on the board and ask students which terms they are unsure of. With the class, clarify the words through additional examples and sentences. Ask each student to write a sentence for each vocabulary word, in this form: Before the Civil War, many slaves in the South lived and worked on _____. (plantations) After they have completed their sentences, have them trade with a partner and complete the quizzes.

networks
Go to connected.mcgraw-hill.com for additional resources:
- Leveled Reader Database
- Leveled Reader Answer Key

Active Teaching

Remind students that summarizing requires them to restate the text in their own words, including only main ideas and the most important details. Write the following questions on the board.

Develop Comprehension

Ask:

1. *Why did the Gullah culture develop on the Sea Islands?* **L1**
2. *How did the way of life of the Gullah change as a result of the Civil War?* **L2**
2. *How are the Gullah trying to keep their culture alive today?* **L2**

Leveled Reader Project

Name _____ Date _____

Have students each write a news story about the Gullah's efforts to preserve their culture today. Students should include a summary of the history of the Gullah culture as background in the news story.

Gullah News Article

4 Exemplary	3 Accomplished	2 Developing	1 Beginning
The news article:	**The news article:**	**The news article:**	**The news article:**
☐ describes in detail, Gullah efforts to preserve their culture.	☐ describes Gullah efforts to preserve their culture.	☐ briefly describes Gullah efforts to preserve their culture.	☐ fails to describe Gullah efforts to preserve their culture.
☐ extensively and accurately summarizes Gullah culture.	☐ accurately summarizes Gullah culture.	☐ somewhat accurately summarizes Gullah culture.	☐ does not summarize Gullah culture.
☐ contains few errors in capitalization and spelling.	☐ contains some errors in capitalization and spelling.	☐ contains several errors in capitalization and spelling.	☐ contains serious errors in capitalization and spelling.

Project Score: _____

Common Core State Standards

English Language Arts & Literacy in History/ Social Studies, Science, and Technical Subjects

Reading Standards for Informational Text, Grade 4

Standards		Student Pages	Teacher Pages
Key Ideas and Details			
1.	Quote accurately from a text when explaining what the text says explicitly and when drawing inferences from the text.	104–105	104–105, 116–117, 130–131, 174–175, 218–219
2.	Determine two or more main ideas of a text and explain how they are supported by key details; summarize the text.	51, 74–75	74–75, 84–85, 88–89, 92–97, 166–169, 178–179, 216–217, 264–265
3.	Explain the relationships or interactions between two or more individuals, events, ideas, or concepts in a historical, scientific, or technical text based on specific information in the text.	4–5, 192–193	4–5, 84–85, 172–173, 180–181, 192–193, 200–201, 248–249, 262–263
Craft and Structure			
4.	Determine the meaning of general academic and domain-specific words and phrases in a text relevant to a grade 5 topic or subject area.	6–8, 36–38, 76–77, 106–108, 154–155, 194–196, 242–244	6–9, 36–39, 76–77, 106–107, 154–155, 194–195, 242–243
5.	Compare and contrast the overall structure (e.g., chronology, comparison, cause/effect, problem/solution) of events, ideas, concepts, or information in two or more texts.	4–5, 34–35, 45, 52, 61, 65	4–5, 34–35
6.	Analyze multiple accounts of the same event or topic, noting important similarities and differences in the point of view they represent.	240–241	240–241
Integration of Knowledge and Ideas			
7.	Draw on information from multiple print or digital sources, demonstrating the ability to locate an answer to a question quickly or to solve a problem efficiently.	240–241	240–241
8.	Explain how an author uses reasons and evidence to support particular points in a text, identifying which reasons and evidence support which point(s).	152–153	152–153, 162–163
9.	Integrate information from several texts on the same topic in order to write or speak about the subject knowledgeably.	240–241	240–241
Range of Reading and Level of Text Complexity			
10.	By the end of the year, read and comprehend informational texts, including history/social studies, science, and technical texts, at the high end of the grades 4–5 text complexity band independently and proficiently.	*	*

* The McGraw-Hill networks™ program is designed to provide ample opportunity to practice the reading and comprehension of informational texts for history/social studies for grade 5. The use of this book will help students master this standard.

Teacher Notes

UNIT
1 Planner GEOGRAPHY

 **BIG IDEA** **Location affects how people live.**

Student Portfolio

- *Show As You Go!*
  Use these pages to introduce the Big Idea. Students record information specific to each lesson. They use these pages to help them plan their Big Idea Project.

networks™

- **Group Technology Project**
  Students use 21st century skills to complete a group extension activity of the unit project. Lesson plans, worksheets, and rubrics are available online.

Student Portfolio

- **Big Idea Project**
  Students work in a team to research, design, and create a poster about one region of the United States. The Big Idea Project Rubric is on page 29W.

Reading Skills

Student Portfolio

- **Reading Skill: Summarize**
  Pages 4–5. Common Core State Standards RI.3 and RI.5

Leveled Readers

Use the leveled reader *Liliuokalani, The Last Queen of Hawaii* with Lesson 1. Find the lesson plan on pages T18–T19 of your Teacher Edition.

Treasures Connection

Teach this unit with Treasures Unit 1, *Trees for Life*, pages 78–87 and Unit 2, *Seasons in the Tropics*, pages 222–225.

Social Studies Skills

Student Portfolio

- **Primary and Secondary Sources: Graphs**
  Page 9

networks™

- **Skill Builders**
  Introduce and teach analyzing primary and secondary sources.

Activity Cards

- **Center for Social Studies Skills Investigation**
  Use the center activity cards to help students explore Primary Sources, Geography, and Citizenship.

FOLDABLES®

Student Portfolio

- Students can create vocabulary Foldables right in their portfolios.

- Additional Foldables templates can be found on pages R34–R42 of your Teacher Edition. See page R33 for instructions.

Assessment Solutions

- **McGraw-Hill networks™**
  Safe online testing features multiple question types that are easy to use and editable.

- **Self-Check Quizzes**
- **Worksheets**

UNIT 1 **At a Glance**

Lesson	Essential Question	Vocabulary		Digital Resources
1 **The World in Spatial Terms**	How do we show location?	geographers *intersect latitude longitude relative location absolute location		Go to **connected.mcgraw-hill.com** for additional resources: • Interactive Whiteboard Lessons
2 **Geography of the United States**	How do we describe location?	*influence contiguous territories navigable tributary canyon		• Worksheets  • Assessment • Content Library • Lesson Plans • Skill Builders • Videos • Use Standards Tracker on **networks** to track students' progress.

*denotes academic vocabulary

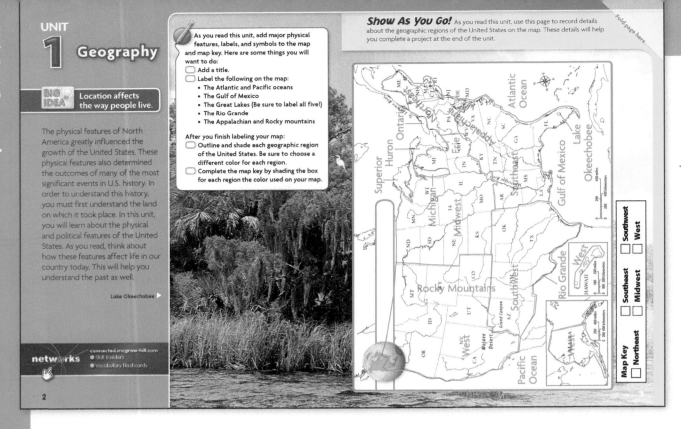

The upper portion shows a magazine-style spread with:

UNIT 1 Geography

BIG IDEA Location affects the way people live.

The physical features of North America greatly influenced the growth of the United States. These physical features also determined the outcomes of many of the most significant events in U.S. history. In order to understand this history, you must first understand the land on which it took place. In this unit, you will learn about the physical and political features of the United States. As you read, think about how these features affect life in our country today. This will help you understand the past as well.

Lake Okeechobee ▶

networks connected.mcgraw-hill.com
● Skill Builders
● Vocabulary Flashcards

2

As you read this unit, add major physical features, labels, and symbols to the map and map key. Here are some things you will want to do:

☐ Add a title.
☐ Label the following on the map:
  • The Atlantic and Pacific oceans
  • The Gulf of Mexico
  • The Great Lakes (Be sure to label all five!)
  • The Rio Grande
  • The Appalachian and Rocky mountains

After you finish labeling your map:
☐ Outline and shade each geographic region of the United States. Be sure to choose a different color for each region.
☐ Complete the map key by shading the box for each region the color used on your map.

Show As You Go! As you read this unit, use this page to record details about the geographic regions of the United States on the map. These details will help you complete a project at the end of the unit.

Fold page here.

Introduce the Unit

✓ Diagnostic Assessment

To pique student interest and gauge prior knowledge, take the class on a treasure hunt! Plan a few routes on your playground. Write descriptive paragraphs that guide small groups of students to a final location. Students should use map skills and teamwork as they follow your directions and create a map of their path. Reward students as they reach their destination with a complete and accurate map. After the activity,

Ask:

1. *What was challenging about following the directions?*
2. *What was challenging about creating the map?*
3. *How well did your group work together? Explain.*

If you don't have time for the activity, provide students with a map and ask a series of questions or provide directions to have students map a path from one location to another on the map.

Student responses and performance in either activity will help identify their level of understanding. Use this information when differentiating instruction.

Active Teaching

BIG IDEA **Location affects the way people live.**
In this unit, students will use a variety of geographic skills to identify and locate physical features, and to construct and interpret maps. Students will use *Show As You Go* pages 2 and 3 throughout this unit. Information from each lesson will help students complete the map and the Unit Project. Have students fold the corner of page 3 to make returning to *Show As You Go* easier.

Differentiated Instruction

Use the following differentiation strategies as students progress through the *Show As You Go* activity.

▶ **Approaching** Provide a copy of the page for students to draft the map. Allow time to compare with a partner before transferring the information to the book.

▶ **Beyond** Have students write 4–5 questions about the map and invite a partner to answer them.

▶ **ELL** Discuss following multi-step directions with students. Review key words such as *first*, *before*, *next*, *then*, *after*, etc. Discuss what clues these words give about sequencing the activity.

Reading Skill

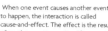

Common Core Standards
RI.3: Explain the relationships or interactions between two or more individuals, events, ideas, or concepts in a historical, scientific, or technical text based on specific information in the text. **RI.5:** Compare and contrast the overall structure (e.g., chronology, comparison, cause/effect, problem/solution) of events, ideas, concepts, or information in two or more texts.

Cause and Effect

When one event causes another event to happen, the interaction is called cause-and-effect. The effect is the result of another event or action. The cause is the action or event that made the effect happen. Connecting causes with effects helps you understand what you read in social studies.

Cause ⟶

Effect ⟶

Mississippi River Basin

(LEARN IT

To identify cause and effect:

- After you read a passage, ask yourself, "What happened?" This is the effect.
- Then ask yourself, "Why did that happen?" This is the cause.
- Look for the clue words *because, so,* and *as a result* to show the cause or effect.

The central part of the United States is sometimes called the Mississippi River Basin. The land in this area is fertile and receives ample rainfall. These conditions make the land of the Mississippi River Basin excellent for farming.

(TRY IT

Use the graphic organizer below to keep track of causes and effects. Fill in the cause and effect from the passage on page 4.

Cause	Effect
Drains more than 1 million square miles of land.	This area is some of the best farmland in country.

(APPLY IT

- Review the steps for identifying cause and effect.
- Read the passage below. Then circle the cause and underline the effect.

As water flows over land, it wears away soil and rock in a process called erosion. Over many millions of years, the waters of the Colorado River wore away soil and rock in the desert of northwestern Arizona. This formed the Grand Canyon—a natural wonder that draws tourists and adventurers from all over the world.

The Grand Canyon ▶

4

5

Common Core Standards RI.3 Explain the relationships or interactions between two or more individuals, events, ideas, or concepts in a historical, scientific, or technical text based on specific information in the text. RI.5 Compare and contrast the overall structure (e.g., chronology, comparison, cause/effect, problem/solution) of events, ideas, concepts, or information in two or more texts.

Reading Skill

Active Teaching

(LEARN IT

Say: *As I read I think, "What happened? Answering this question helps me find the result of an event. This is the effect. Once I know the effect, I can find details that tell me why or how that happened. This is the cause. Understanding the cause/effect relationship helps me understand the event.*

(TRY IT
Encourage students to try the modeled strategy as they complete the **TRY IT** activity.

(APPLY IT
After students have completed the **APPLY IT** activity,

Ask:

1. *What question should you ask yourself to help you find the effect of an event?* **L3**

2. *How do the details of the effect help you find the cause of a historical event?* **L2**

3. *Why is it important to understand cause/effect relationships when you read about history?* **L3**

Differentiated Instruction

▶ **Approaching** Review the **LEARN IT** activity as a small group. Do the **TRY IT** activity together. Have students complete the **APPLY IT** activity independently. Regroup to compare and correct.

▶ **Beyond** Have students choose a fairytale and analyze it for cause/effect relationships.

▶ **ELL** Create a chart with two columns, one labeled "Cause," the other "Effect." Read through the passage together. Ask students to describe what happened. Record the effect on a sticky note and place it in the right column. Ask students to describe why or how the effect happened. Record their response on another sticky note and place it in the left column. Reread the notes. As you do, draw an arrow showing that the cause led to the effect.

networks

Go to **connected.mcgraw-hill.com** for additional resources:

- Skill Builders
- Graphic Organizers

Words to Know

Common Core Standards
RI.4 Determine the meaning of general academic and domain-specific words and phrases in a text relevant to a grade 5 topic or subject area.

The list below shows some important words you will learn in this unit. Their definitions can be found on the next page. Read the words.

geographer (jee • AWG • ruh • fuhr)

latitude (LA • tuh • tood)

longitude (LAHN • juh • tood)

absolute location
(ab • soh • LOOT loh • KAY • shuhn)

relative location
(REH • luh • tihv loh • KAY • shuhn)

contiguous (kuhn • TIH • gyuh • wuhs)

territory (TEHR • uh • tawr • ee)

canyon (KAN • yuhn)

FOLDABLES

The **Foldable** on the next page will help you learn these important words. Follow the steps below to make your Foldable.

Step 1   Fold along the solid red line.

Step 2   Cut along the dotted lines.

Step 3   Read the words and their definitions.

Step 4   Complete the activities on each tab.

Step 5   Look at the back of your Foldable. Choose ONE of these activities for each word to help you remember its meaning:

- Draw a picture of the word.
- Write a description of the word.
- Write how the word is related to something you know.

▲ Lines of Latitude

▲ Lines of Longitude

A **geographer** is someone who studies geography.

Write the root word of *geographer*.

_____ _____

Latitude is an imaginary line on Earth that goes from east to west and shows a location's distance from the Equator.

Circle the key words in the definition of *latitude*. Write those words here:

_____ _____

Longitude is an imaginary line on Earth that goes from north to south and shows a location's distance from the Prime Meridian.

Underline two key words in the definition of *longitude*. Write those words here:

_____ _____

The exact location of a place is its **absolute location**.

Use *absolute location* in a sentence.

_____

The location of a place in relation to other landmarks is its **relative location**.

Circle the words or phrases that can be used to describe *relative location*.

near	across from	at
on	next to	by

Contiguous means to be touching or connected in an unbroken series.

The opposite of *contiguous* is *noncontiguous*. Explain what it means.

A **territory** is an area of land controlled by a nation.

Write the plural form of *territory*.

A **canyon** is a deep valley with steep sides.

Write the definition of a *canyon* in your own words.

6

Common Core Standards RI.4 Determine the meaning of general academic and domain-specific words and phrases in a text relevant to a grade 5 topic or subject area.

Words to Know

Active Teaching

FOLDABLES Have students use the Foldable on these pages to gain a deeper understanding of the vocabulary in this unit.

1. Go to connected.mcgraw-hill.com for flashcards to introduce the unit vocabulary to students.

2. Read the words on the list on page 6 and have students repeat them after you.

3. Guide students as they complete steps 1–5 of the Foldable.

4. Have students use the Foldable to practice the vocabulary words independently or with a partner.

networks

Additional resources are found at connected.mcgraw-hill.com.

- Vocabulary Flashcards
- Vocabulary Games
- Graphic Organizers

GO Vocabulary!

Use the concept map graphic organizer below to help students gain a deeper understanding of the academic vocabulary.

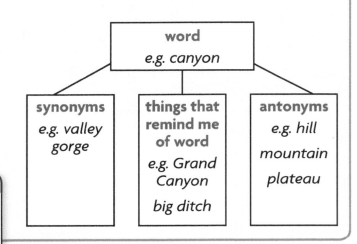

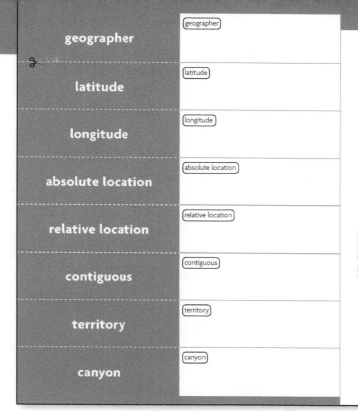

geographer	geographer
latitude	latitude
longitude	longitude
absolute location	absolute location
relative location	relative location
contiguous	contiguous
territory	territory
canyon	canyon

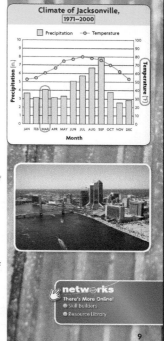

Primary and Secondary Sources

Learn about U.S. history through primary and secondary sources. Primary sources are written or created by someone who witnessed an event. Secondary sources are written or created by someone after an event occurs. Both types of sources teach us about people, places, and events.

Graphs

Graphs show many different types of information. They can show changes over time, differences between groups, or the way parts fit into a whole. A graph can be either a primary or a secondary source. If a graph is made at the time data is collected, it's a primary source. If a graph is made years later with old data, it's a secondary source.

A graph is one tool that you can use to study geography. The graph on this page shows information about the **climate** of a location. Climate is the weather in an area over a long period of time. The climate of an area is a part of its geography. This graph combines a line graph showing the average monthly temperature and a bar graph representing the average amount of precipitation, or rainfall, each month.

DBQ Document-Based Questions

Study the graph. Then complete the following activities:

- In one color, circle the part of the graph that tells how wet it was in March.
- In another color, circle the part of the graph that tells how warm or cold it is throughout the year.
- Put a box around the part of the graph that tells in what years the data was collected.

Climate of Jacksonville,
1971–2000

□ Precipitation —○— Temperature

networks
There's More Online!
● Skill Builders
● Resource Library

9

Differentiated Instruction

▶ **ELL** Use the word web graphic organizer below to help students gain a deeper understanding of the vocabulary. Write the vocabulary word in the center and related words in the other ovals.

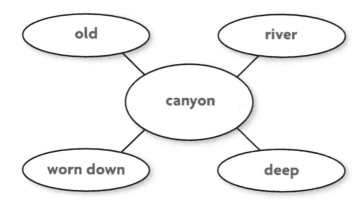

old river

canyon

worn down deep

W O R D   P L A Y

1. Have students place vocabulary words on a 3 x 3 grid.
2. Define the words one at a time. Do not say the words.
3. As students recognize a definition, they should mark or cover it on their card.
4. The first to get a Bingo wins the round.

Primary Sources
Active Teaching

Begin by discussing graphs.

Ask: *What is the purpose of a graph? Have you ever used a graph? When do you use them and why?* **L3**

Explain that there are many types of graphs. Line graphs track changes over time and show how pieces of information are related. Bar graphs show relationships between information. On this page, students will examine a climograph. This type of graph combines line and bar graphs to tell about the climate and weather in an area.

Develop Comprehension

1. *What does this graph show about the climate of Jacksonville? Explain.* **L3**

networks

Additional resources are found at **connected.mcgraw-hill.com**.
- Vocabulary Flashcards
- Vocabulary Games

The World in Spatial Terms

networks
There's More Online!
Content Library • Videos

(?) Essential Question
How do we show location?
What do you think?

Words To Know
Write a synonym for each of
the words below.

*intersect

relative location

absolute location

The Basics of Geography

You've probably looked at a globe or map before. Globes are
models of Earth. Maps are flat representations of Earth. Since
Earth isn't flat, size and distance on a map sometimes are
distorted, or no longer accurate. Both maps and globes use a
grid system to help us locate specific locations on Earth. This
grid is a series of **intersecting** vertical and horizontal lines.

Draw a map of your bedroom from above. Include
a compass rose, map key, and simple grid system
(ABC/123). Write two questions about your map and
have a partner use the map to find the answers.

A

B

C

1 2 3

1. _____

2. _____

Parallels and Meridians

Long ago, **geographers**, or people who study geography, created a
grid system of intersecting lines to help us find places more easily on
maps. Lines of **latitude** go from east to west. Lines of **longitude**
run north to south.

Lines of latitude are called parallels. They are an equal distance
apart. These lines are numbered from 0 degrees (°) at the Equator to
90° North at the North Pole and 90° South at the South Pole.

Lines of longitude, or meridians, circle Earth from pole to pole.
These lines measure distance from the Prime Meridian,
at 0° longitude. Meridians are not parallel. Latitude and
longitude can be used to make observations about
location and generalizations about climate.

Location, Location, Location!

When giving directions, you probably use what is
called **relative location**. This is the location of a place
in relation to landmarks.

Absolute location, on the other hand, is a very
specific way of telling where a place is. Absolute
location is the exact location of any place on Earth. Each
location has a unique number where one line of latitude
intersects a line of longitude. Each spot on Earth has an
absolute location.

Map Skills

1. Label the Prime Meridian, the
Equator, and the unlabeled
continents.

2. Highlight one line of longitude.

3. Circle the degrees for two lines
of latitude.

4. What continent lies southeast of
Africa? Australia

5. Place a star on the continent
that is west of North America.

Prime Meridian

10

11

Lesson 1

Activate Prior Knowledge

Students will create a map of their bedroom. Help them
prepare for this activity by mapping your classroom
together. Be sure to create the map from a birds-eye view,
include a title, and create a map key.

(?) Essential Question How do we show location?

Have students explain what they understand about the
Essential Question. Discuss their responses. Explain that
everything they learn in this lesson will help them to
better understand the Essential Question. Remind them
to think about how the Essential Question connects to
the unit Big Idea: Location affects the way people live.

Map and Globe Skills

Discuss map projections with students. Explain that
maps are flat depictions of the globe. When these
projections are created, the location and size of things
are sometimes distorted. If you have access to a globe,
share it with the class and allow time for the students
to examine it. Discuss any questions or observations the
students have regarding maps, globes, or projections.

Active Teaching

Words To Know After completing the activity,
have students compare their list of synonyms with
a partner.

Ask: *Are there any major differences?* **L3**

Have students share their synonyms aloud. Compile
a list of synonyms for each word. As students share,
discuss the meaning of each and decide as a class
if the synonym fits. Allow students time to change
their responses in their texts.

Develop Comprehension

Remind students that Earth has an imaginary grid
system that allows people to locate places. This
grid is made of lines of longitude and latitude. After
students read the text,

Ask:

1. *Why did geographers create lines of latitude and
longitude?* **L1**

2. *What is the difference between absolute and
relative location?* **L2**

Geography and Technology

Maps have long helped people solve problems at the local, state, and national levels. Today, people also use new technologies. One of these technologies is the Geographic Information System (GIS). GIS uses data to manage, analyze, and share geographic information.

GIS helps people analyze and interpret geographic relationships, patterns, and trends in different ways. This geographic information is shared through maps, graphs, and charts. The information helps people solve problems.

How do people use this information? Take, for example, a fire station that wants to know the fastest emergency routes. Firefighters can see which roads to avoid at busy times of day by placing a map layer showing traffic patterns over a city map. Businesses also use GIS. They might, for example, use GIS to layer data about population, housing, and taxes to find the best location for a new store.

The Global Positioning System (GPS) is a GIS that uses radio signals from satellites to find the absolute location of places on Earth. GPS was originally used by the U.S. military for navigation, map-making, and guiding missiles. Today, many people use GPS devices instead of traditional maps when traveling by car. Cell phone technology even allows people to use GPS when traveling by foot!

> Underline key details about Geographic Information Systems.

GIS combines data to provide information that can be viewed one layer at a time, or all together (below left). This 3-dimensional physical map shows the bottom of the ocean off the west coast of Central America (below right).

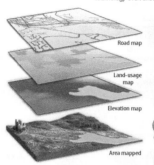

Road map

Land-usage map

Elevation map

Area mapped

> Look at the maps on the next page. Imagine that you and your partner work for the state government. Your job is to analyze GIS data and decide which counties are in need of more elementary schools. Base your decision on population and the number of existing schools.

12

Putting GIS to Use

Florida Population Density

People per Square Mile
- 1,000–3,000
- 250–1,000
- 150–250
- 0–150

Florida Schools per County

Number of Elementary Schools
- 200+
- 100–199
- 25–99
- 1–24

1. Create a bar graph for each map showing the number of counties that fall within each data range. Use the graph frames at the bottom of the page.

2. How many counties have the highest number of elementary schools?

   1

3. How many counties have between 25 and 99 elementary schools? 5

4. How many counties have the largest populations? 5

5. How many counties have both the largest populations and 100 or more elementary schools?

   3

6. Place stars on the counties you think should receive new elementary schools. Explain how you made your decision.

   Answers will vary, but explanations must be supported by data.

Population Density

Number of Counties — People per sq mile
- 0–150: 37
- 150–250: 12
- 250–1000: 13
- 1000–3000: 5

Florida Elementary Schools

Number of Counties — Number of Schools
- 1–24: 45
- 25–99: 16
- 100–199: 5
- 200+: 1

13

Active Teaching

Develop Comprehension
Ask:

1. *How does GIS help people solve problems?* (Allows people to analyze and interpret geographic relationships, patterns, and trends in different ways) **L2**

2. *Which counties did you rule out right away? Why?* **L3**

3. *What criteria did you use when choosing which counties to recommend?* **L3**

Use the leveled reader, *James Franklin: Hurricane Specialist*, to extend and enrich students' understanding of how geographic technologies can help people work together to solve problems. A lesson plan for this leveled reader can be found on pages T18 and T19 of this Teacher Edition.

Differentiated Instruction

▶ **Approaching** Work through the activity with students in a small group. Guide students step-by-step through the analysis of the first map. Ask students to repeat the process for the second map.

▶ **Beyond** Have students prioritize their top 5 recommendations and explain their rationale.

▶ **ELL** Students may confuse the terms used when analyzing the maps. Discuss the relationships between the following words: *largest, highest, most, smallest, lowest,* and *least.*

Clarify Misconceptions

Students may confuse Geographic Information Systems (GIS) with Global Positioning Systems (GPS). Be sure to explain to students that GPS is one type of GIS tool.

After students read page 12, discuss Geographic Information Systems. The activity on page 13 requires students to use GIS information to solve a problem at the state level. After students complete the activity, allow time for students to compare and discuss their recommendations.

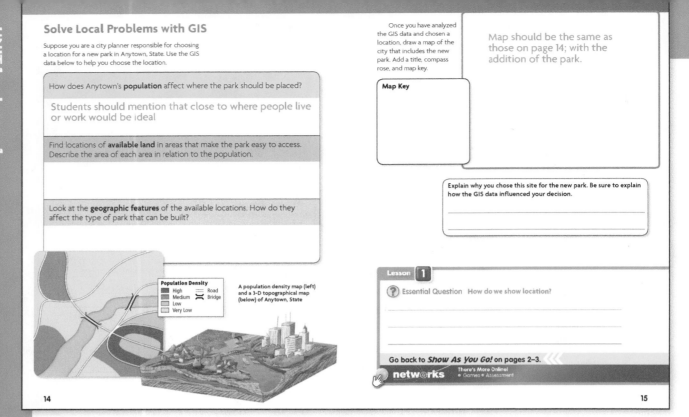

Solve Local Problems with GIS

Suppose you are a city planner responsible for choosing a location for a new park in Anytown, State. Use the GIS data below to help you choose the location.

How does Anytown's **population** affect where the park should be placed?

Students should mention that close to where people live or work would be ideal

Find locations of **available land** in areas that make the park easy to access. Describe the area of each area in relation to the population.

Look at the **geographic features** of the available locations. How do they affect the type of park that can be built?

Population Density
- High
- Medium
- Low
- Very Low
- Road
- Bridge

A population density map (left) and a 3-D topographical map (below) of Anytown, State

Once you have analyzed the GIS data and chosen a location, draw a map of the city that includes the new park. Add a title, compass rose, and map key.

Map Key

Map should be the same as those on page 14; with the addition of the park.

Explain why you chose this site for the new park. Be sure to explain how the GIS data influenced your decision.

Lesson 1

? **Essential Question** How do we show location?

Go back to *Show As You Go!* on pages 2–3.

networks There's More Online!
• Games • Assessment

14   15

Lesson 1

Active Teaching

As an introduction to the activity, visit a park and have students take notes on things they observe in relation to the geography of the park. You may also want to invite someone from the city to speak to the class about park management and planning.

Ask:

1. *Where do people live and work in Anytown?* **L2**

2. *Are there areas of land available that are located close to where people live and/or work?* **L2**

3. *What geographic features exist in these areas?* **L2**

4. *Do any of those geographic features lend themselves to a park more so than others?* **L3**

> *Show As You Go!* Remind students to go back to the Unit Opener and complete the activities for this lesson.

Differentiated Instruction

▶ **Approaching** Work with students to discuss the landscape and population of Anytown. Create the map key together.

▶ **Beyond** Have students design the layout of the park too. Together, brainstorm a list of possible park attractions, such as walking paths, playgrounds, picnic areas, ponds, etc.

▶ **ELL** Review vocabulary related to communities such as *urban*, *suburban*, *rural*, *neighborhood*, *park*, and *country*.

Response to Intervention

? **Essential Question** How do we show location?

If . . . students cannot give a substantiated response to the Essential Question,

. . . .

Then . . . take them back through the lesson. Highlight points in the text that discuss ways people use maps to show or describe location. Discuss how the content relates to the Essential Question.

Ask: *How do maps help us show location?* Following discussion, allow students to respond to the Essential Question again.

Lesson 2 — Geography of the United States

Essential Question
How do we describe location?
What do you think?

_____
_____
_____
_____
_____
_____

Write the definition of each word in your own words.

*influence _____
_____

contiguous _____
_____

navigable _____
_____

tributary _____
_____

16

Think about the area where you live. Are there any hills, plains, lakes, or rivers nearby? Is there a bay, gulf, or ocean? These are all physical features. You may not think about it a lot, but geography affects how your family lives. For example, people living along a lake may fish for a living. They may also boat or swim for fun.

Identify a physical feature near your home. Then explain how it influences your daily life. Draw a picture of this physical feature.

Physical Feature: _____

How it affects my life: _____
_____
_____
_____
_____

The United States

Later in this lesson you will learn about the geographic regions of the United States. But first, let's find out more about our country in general. The United States is the world's third-largest country in size. Forty-eight of the country's fifty states stretch across the middle of North America. Two states lie elsewhere. Alaska lies in the northwestern part of the continent. Hawaii is in the Pacific Ocean.

The western coast of the United States faces the Pacific Ocean. The eastern coast faces the Atlantic Ocean. In the north, the very cold Arctic Ocean borders Alaska. The southern United States enjoys the warm waters of the Gulf of Mexico.

The states located in the central part of North America are **contiguous**, or connected by shared borders. Alaska and Hawaii don't share a border with any other states, so they are noncontiguous. The United States is divided into five regions: the Northeast, Southeast, Midwest, Southwest, and West. Alaska and Hawaii are considered part of the West region.

U.S. Territories
The United States has several **territories**, or areas of land that are under its control and protection. These territories are not part of the country. Puerto Rico and the U.S. Virgin Islands are territories in the Caribbean southeast of Florida. Guam and American Samoa are territories in the Pacific Ocean, west of Hawaii.

U.S. Territories

Locate and circle Puerto Rico, the U.S. Virgin Islands, Guam, and American Samoa on the world map.

17

Lesson 2

Activate Prior Knowledge
Allow time for students to share their drawings with the rest of the class. You may want to tally geographical features to see which most affect the lives of your students. Discuss similarities and differences in student descriptions as they share their drawings. List the major ways that geographic features affect life in your area.

Essential Question
How do we describe location?

Have students explain what they understand about the Essential Question. Discuss their responses. Explain that everything they learn in this lesson will help them to better understand the Essential Question. Remind them to think about how the Essential Question connects to the unit Big Idea: Location affects the way people live.

Active Teaching

Words To Know If students don't have enough space to write the definitions, have them create a Six-Tab Foldable and affix it along the right edge of the words. One word should appear on the front of each tab, with the definition on the back.

Develop Comprehension
Ask:
1. *How many states are contiguous? Noncontiguous?* **L1**
2. *How are states and territories different?* **L2**
3. *Where is your state located in the United States?* **L3**

Map and Globe Skills

Students may notice that Guam and American Samoa are on opposite sides of the world map. Remind them that the earth is round. It may be necessary to make an enlarged copy of this map, cut it, and bend it to demonstrate how the two islands are actually located near each other.

Say:
When looking at maps, it is sometimes helpful to think about travelling around a circle when matching the left side of a map with the right side.

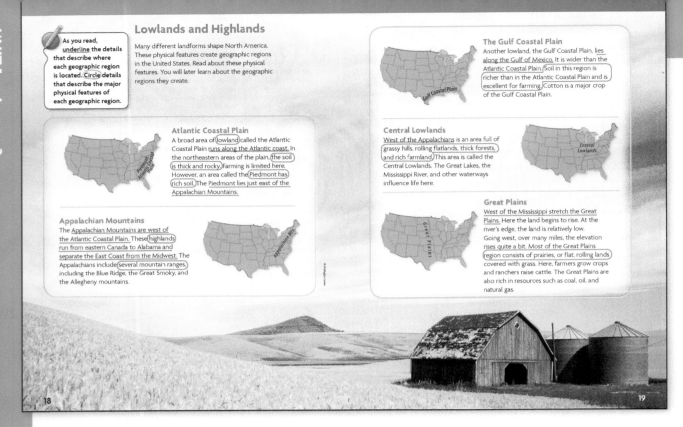

Lowlands and Highlands

As you read, underline the details that describe where each geographic region is located. Circle details that describe the major physical features of each geographic region.

Many different landforms shape North America. These physical features create geographic regions in the United States. Read about these physical features. You will later learn about the geographic regions they create.

Atlantic Coastal Plain

A broad area of lowland called the Atlantic Coastal Plain runs along the Atlantic coast. In the northeastern areas of the plain, the soil is thick and rocky. Farming is limited here. However, an area called the Piedmont has rich soil. The Piedmont lies just east of the Appalachian Mountains.

Appalachian Mountains

The Appalachian Mountains are west of the Atlantic Coastal Plain. These highlands run from eastern Canada to Alabama and separate the East Coast from the Midwest. The Appalachians include several mountain ranges, including the Blue Ridge, the Great Smoky, and the Allegheny mountains.

The Gulf Coastal Plain

Another lowland, the Gulf Coastal Plain, lies along the Gulf of Mexico. It is wider than the Atlantic Coastal Plain. Soil in this region is richer than in the Atlantic Coastal Plain and is excellent for farming. Cotton is a major crop of the Gulf Coastal Plain.

Central Lowlands

West of the Appalachians is an area full of grassy hills, rolling flatlands, thick forests, and rich farmland. This area is called the Central Lowlands. The Great Lakes, the Mississippi River, and other waterways influence life here.

Great Plains

West of the Mississippi stretch the Great Plains. Here the land begins to rise. At the river's edge, the land is relatively low. Going west, over many miles, the elevation rises quite a bit. Most of the Great Plains region consists of prairies, or flat, rolling lands covered with grass. Here, farmers grow crops and ranchers raise cattle. The Great Plains are also rich in resources such as coal, oil, and natural gas.

18

19

Lesson 2

Active Teaching

Explain to students that the United States has five geographical regions. Each of these regions features several physical features that define the area. Some of these features are shared between regions.

Develop Comprehension

Ask:

1. What is a coastal plain? **L2**

2. How do the Gulf and Atlantic coastal plains differ? **L3**

3. What resources are found in the Central Lowlands and Great Plains? **L2**

Differentiated Instruction

▶ **Approaching** Use a blank map to help students identify and label the regions and geographic features of the United States. Note: This differentiated project applies to pages 18–21.

▶ **Beyond** Have students use a blank map to create a topographical map of the United States. Note: This differentiated project applies to pages 18–21.

▶ **ELL** This portion of content deals with a lot of descriptive vocabulary that may be confusing for students. Create picture vocabulary cards to illustrate terms such as *lowland*, *highland*, *valley*, *soil*, *flatland*, *plain*, etc.

More About the Great Plains The lowlands of the Plains between the Appalachian and Rocky Mountains are known as Tornado Alley. Frequent thunderstorms in this region provide conditions perfect for producing tornadoes. The United States averages over 1,000 tornadoes each year, most of which happen in Tornado Alley. May and June have the highest rates of tornadoes due to rapidly changing air temperatures. Texas has the highest average number of tornadoes each year.

Waterways, Mountains, and Plateaus

> Highlight text that describes where each geographic feature is located. Then complete the map below by adding the missing lake and river names.

The United States has many amazing physical wonders, such as the Great Lakes, Rocky Mountains, and Grand Canyon. These physical features shape life in the country.

The Mississippi River

North America has many lakes and rivers. Many of these rivers are **navigable**, or wide and deep enough to allow the passage of ships. One of these rivers, the Mississippi, begins in Minnesota where it is too narrow for ships. As it heads south to the Gulf of Mexico, it enlarges and becomes navigable.

The central part of the United States is sometimes called the Mississippi River Basin. The land in this area is fertile and receives ample rainfall, making it excellent for farming. Over one million square miles of land in this basin drains off into the Mississippi and its **tributaries**. A tributary is a river that flows into another river.

Mississippi River Basin

////// GLUE FOLDABLE HERE //////

The Great Lakes and St. Lawrence Seaway

Giant blankets of ice called glaciers carved out the Great Lakes about 10,000 years ago. Lakes Huron, Ontario, Michigan, Erie, and Superior are located in the central part of North America and are the world's largest group of freshwater lakes. Lake Superior is the largest of the Great Lakes, while Lake Erie is the smallest.

The St. Lawrence Seaway

Canada
United States
St. Lawrence Seaway
○ City
▪ Lock

The Great Lakes drain into the St. Lawrence River, which flows to the Atlantic Ocean. The St. Lawrence was unnavigable due to rapids, waterfalls, and uneven water levels. A series of canals and a system of locks have made the river navigable. A lock is a part of a canal where water is pumped in or out in order to raise or lower ships.

20

Western Mountain Ranges

West of the Great Plains is a group of mountain ranges. The Rocky Mountains begin in Alaska and run south to New Mexico. The Rockies are younger and higher than the Appalachians.

Between the Rockies and the Pacific Coast are the Pacific Coastal ranges. These include several smaller mountain chains, including the Cascade and Sierra Nevada mountains.

> Highlight the text that describes where each geographic feature is located.

The Continental Divide

The Continental Divide runs along the Rocky Mountains. The Divide separates the flow of water in North America. East of the Divide, rivers drain into the Arctic Ocean, the Atlantic Ocean, and the Gulf of Mexico. To the west, rivers flow into the Pacific Ocean and the Gulf of California.

LOVELAND PASS
ELEVATION 11,990
CONTINENTAL DIVIDE
ATLANTIC   PACIFIC

West   East

River

The Plateaus and Canyons

Between the Pacific Ocean and the Rockies is a stretch of dry basins and high plateaus. The Mojave Desert makes up a large part of this area. The Mojave is located in southeastern California, southwestern Utah, southern Nevada, and western Arizona.

In Northwestern Arizona, rivers have worn through rock to create magnificent **canyons**, or deep valleys with steep sides. One of the most beautiful is the Grand Canyon of the Colorado River.

21

Active Teaching

These pages continue the exploration of the physical features of the United States.

Develop Comprehension

Ask:

1. *What makes a river navigable?* **L1**
2. *How does the St. Lawrence Seaway connect the Midwest to the East Coast?* **L2**
3. *How does the Continental Divide affect water flow in North America?* **L2**

Page Power

FOLDABLES Interact more with the page. Have students create a Notebook Foldable to assist them in developing their understanding of geographic features.

1. Provide each student with a copy of Foldable 1A from the Notebook Foldables section at the back of this book.

2. Have students construct the Foldable and glue its anchor tab to page 20 where shown.

3. The front of each tab should be labeled with one geographic features from pages 20–21. The back of each tab should describe the way the feature affects life.

Differentiated Instruction

▶ **Approaching** Pages 18–21 contain a lot of information. Help students organize this information by providing a table or chart that compares major physical features in the five regions.

▶ **Beyond** Have students create a travel brochure for one of the geographic regions or features. This may require them to do additional research in the library or on the Internet.

▶ **ELL** Continue to provide or create picture vocabulary cards to illustrate the difficult geography-related vocabulary. It may also help ELL students to complete a table or chart similar to that in the Approaching activity above.

North America's Temperate Rain Forest The temperate rain forest of the Pacific Northwest stretches from northern California to southern Canada. Warm ocean currents carrying moisture along the coast rise up and cool when they meet inland mountain ranges. The result is a temperate climate with a lot of rainfall. This area is characterized by extremely large old-growth trees, dense vegetation, and a very long, wet season that is followed by a foggy dry season.

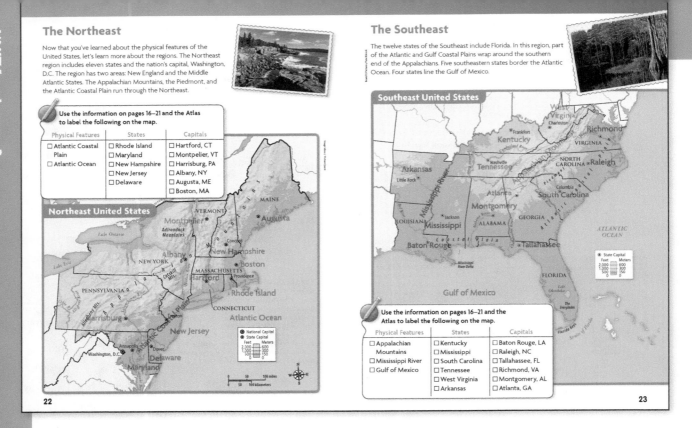

The Northeast

Now that you've learned about the physical features of the United States, let's learn more about the regions. The Northeast region includes eleven states and the nation's capital, Washington, D.C. The region has two areas: New England and the Middle Atlantic States. The Appalachian Mountains, the Piedmont, and the Atlantic Coastal Plain run through the Northeast.

Use the information on pages 16–21 and the Atlas to label the following on the map.

Physical Features	States	Capitals
☐ Atlantic Coastal Plain	☐ Rhode Island	☐ Hartford, CT
☐ Atlantic Ocean	☐ Maryland	☐ Montpelier, VT
	☐ New Hampshire	☐ Harrisburg, PA
	☐ New Jersey	☐ Albany, NY
	☐ Delaware	☐ Augusta, ME
		☐ Boston, MA

Northeast United States

The Southeast

The twelve states of the Southeast include Florida. In this region, part of the Atlantic and Gulf Coastal Plains wrap around the southern end of the Appalachians. Five southeastern states border the Atlantic Ocean. Four states line the Gulf of Mexico.

Southeast United States

Use the information on pages 16–21 and the Atlas to label the following on the map.

Physical Features	States	Capitals
☐ Appalachian Mountains	☐ Kentucky	☐ Baton Rouge, LA
☐ Mississippi River	☐ Mississippi	☐ Raleigh, NC
☐ Gulf of Mexico	☐ South Carolina	☐ Tallahassee, FL
	☐ Tennessee	☐ Richmond, VA
	☐ West Virginia	☐ Montgomery, AL
	☐ Arkansas	☐ Atlanta, GA

22   23

Lesson 2

Active Teaching

On pages 22–26, students will be completing a map for each of the geographic regions. Remind students to refer to the unit or Atlas for information.

As you lead students through these maps, begin by reading the introduction to the region. Then have students label the physical features. To label the states, students may refer to the Atlas. When placing capitals on the map, suggest students locate the state and write the capital on the line.

Differentiated Instruction

▶ **Approaching** Provide a copy of each map or a copy of a map of the United States from the Atlas to allow students to complete the activities on pages 22–26 without flipping back and forth.

▶ **Beyond** Have students compare and contrast the geographic features and topography of two regions. Students may need to do more research in the library or on the Internet.

▶ **ELL** Review text search strategies such as scanning; finding key words; and using images, graphics, and captions to locate information.

✔ Formative Assessment

Prior to teaching pages 22–26, use a chart that shows each of the geographic regions across the bottom and numbers 1–5 up the left side. Have each student place a colored dot on the number that shows how well they know each region. Discuss results and address any content issues before beginning the map activities. Repeat with a different color sticker after the maps on pages 22–26 have been completed.

During the map activity, if students are unable to complete a map, take them back through the lesson. Focus on the physical features and details about the region.

More About the Northeast The Northeast has a humid climate. It has snowy winters, rainy springs, and hot, wet summers. The Northeast gets plenty of precipitation all year. As a result, forests once covered most of the region. As colonists settled in the area, people cleared the land to farm. They also cut forests to make timber products.

More About the Southeast This region has a humid subtropical climate. Rain falls throughout the year but is less heavy during the hot and humid summer months. Humid subtropical winters are generally short and mild. Southern Florida has a tropical climate with hot, dry summers and wet winters.

The Midwest

The Midwest is a region of plains. The twelve states in this region experience extreme weather conditions. From spring through autumn, thunderstorms and tornadoes are a constant danger. During winter, this region experiences low temperatures and snow.

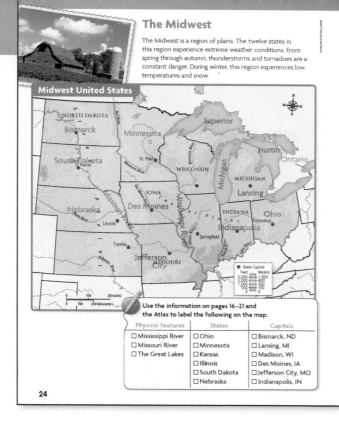

Midwest United States

Use the information on pages 16–21 and the Atlas to label the following on the map.

Physical Features	States	Capitals
☐ Mississippi River	☐ Ohio	☐ Bismarck, ND
☐ Missouri River	☐ Minnesota	☐ Lansing, MI
☐ The Great Lakes	☐ Kansas	☐ Madison, WI
	☐ Illinois	☐ Des Moines, IA
	☐ South Dakota	☐ Jefferson City, MO
	☐ Nebraska	☐ Indianapolis, IN

24

The Southwest

The Southwest has only four states. The Rio Grande separates this part of the United States from Mexico. The region also includes the southern end of the Rocky Mountains.

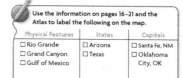

Use the information on pages 16–21 and the Atlas to label the following on the map.

Physical Features	States	Capitals
☐ Rio Grande	☐ Arizona	☐ Santa Fe, NM
☐ Grand Canyon	☐ Texas	☐ Oklahoma City, OK
☐ Gulf of Mexico		

Southwest United States

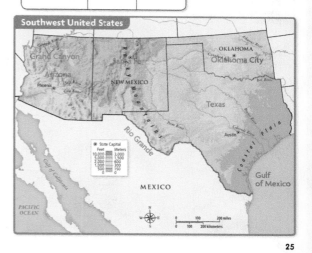

25

Active Teaching

As you lead students through these maps, begin by reading the introduction to the region. Then have students label the physical features. To label the states, students may refer to the Atlas. When placing capitals on the map, suggest students locate the state and write the capital on the line.

netw○rks

Additional resources are found at **connected.mcgraw-hill.com**.

- Interactive Whiteboard Lessons
- Content Library
- Assessments
- Skill Builders

More About the Midwest   The Great Plains receive their moisture from the Gulf of Mexico and the Arctic. The eastern part of this area has a humid climate with cold, snowy winters and hot, humid summers. The western part has light rain. Drought sometimes affects the Great Plains.

Parts of this region are affected by lake effect weather. In the summer, air above the Great Lakes is cooler than the nearby land. Wind crossing the lakes creates a cool breeze. In the winter, these winds pick up moisture and form clouds that cause lake effect snow.

More About the Southwest   Many parts of the Southwestern United States are desert with less than 10 inches of precipitation each year. The Southwest is also closer to the Equator than other parts of the U.S. The heat and dry air affect the region's climate. Plants and animals have adjusted to this harsh climate. Many plants store water from rainfall so they can survive during the dry season.

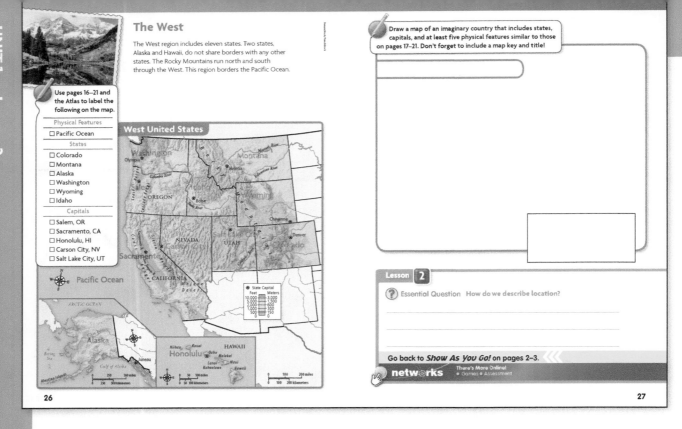

The West

The West region includes eleven states. Two states, Alaska and Hawaii, do not share borders with any other states. The Rocky Mountains run north and south through the West. This region borders the Pacific Ocean.

Use pages 16–21 and the Atlas to label the following on the map.

Physical Features
☐ Pacific Ocean

States
☐ Colorado
☐ Montana
☐ Alaska
☐ Washington
☐ Wyoming
☐ Idaho

Capitals
☐ Salem, OR
☐ Sacramento, CA
☐ Honolulu, HI
☐ Carson City, NV
☐ Salt Lake City, UT

West United States

Draw a map of an imaginary country that includes states, capitals, and at least five physical features similar to those on pages 17–21. Don't forget to include a map key and title!

Lesson 2

? **Essential Question** How do we describe location?

Go back to *Show As You Go!* on pages 2–3.

networks — There's More Online! • Games • Assessment

26

27

Lesson 2

Active Teaching

Before students begin drawing their maps on page 27, read a book about the creation of a new society such as *Weslandia* by Paul Fleischman. As you read, discuss the way people in the story interact with the environment. This activity will introduce the ideas students will need to consider when developing their country maps.

Show As You Go! Remind students to go back to the Unit Opener to complete the project.

More About the West Near the Equator, air and warm water are heated the most. Warm wind and water currents move from the tropics toward the North and South Poles. The Pacific Ocean's warm North Pacific Current keeps this area's climate mild and wet. Evergreen forests, ferns, and mosses are common. By contrast, southern California has a climate of warm, dry summers and mild, wet winters.

Differentiated Instruction

▶ **Approaching** For the activity on page 27, work together as a group to create a basic outline for the map, including borders and geographic features. Students should add this to their book and individually name and label their maps.

▶ **Beyond** Have students write a paragraph explaining how life in their country is affected by its geography.

▶ **ELL** To help students understand the hierarchy of terms, create a flow chart that shows world-continent-country-state-county-city-neighborhood-street-house. Include synonyms for each term to help students see how they all relate to the concept.

Response to Intervention

? **Essential Question** How do we describe location?

If . . . students cannot give a substantiated response to the Essential Question,

Then . . . take them back through the lesson. Highlight examples of description in the text.

Ask: *How do descriptions help us understand and compare the regions of the United States?* Following discussion, allow students to respond to the Essential Question again.

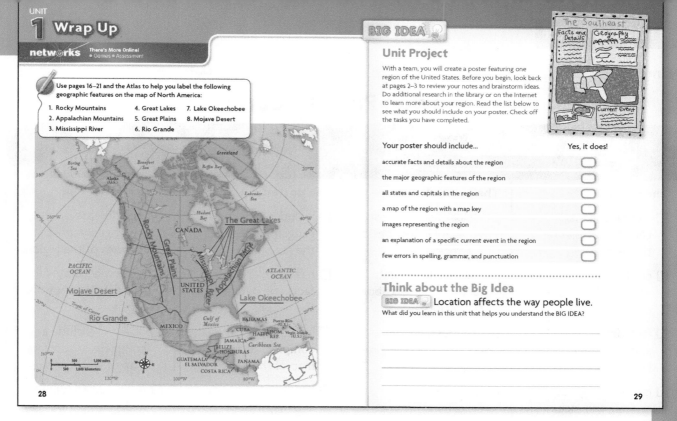

UNIT 1 Wrap Up

Use pages 16–21 and the Atlas to help you label the following geographic features on the map of North America:

1. Rocky Mountains 4. Great Lakes 7. Lake Okeechobee
2. Appalachian Mountains 5. Great Plains 8. Mojave Desert
3. Mississippi River 6. Rio Grande

BIG IDEA

Unit Project

With a team, you will create a poster featuring one region of the United States. Before you begin, look back at pages 2–3 to review your notes and brainstorm ideas. Do additional research in the library or on the Internet to learn more about your region. Read the list below to see what you should include on your poster. Check off the tasks you have completed.

Your poster should include...	Yes, it does!
accurate facts and details about the region	☐
the major geographic features of the region	☐
all states and capitals in the region	☐
a map of the region with a map key	☐
images representing the region	☐
an explanation of a specific current event in the region	☐
few errors in spelling, grammar, and punctuation	☐

Think about the Big Idea

BIG IDEA Location affects the way people live.
What did you learn in this unit that helps you understand the BIG IDEA?

28   29

Wrap Up

Map of North America

Before students begin labeling the map, remind them to revisit Lesson 2 to find the location of each geographic feature.

BIG IDEA Big Idea Project

- Read through the project directions and checklist with students.
- Answer any questions students may have about the project.
- Remind students to use their *Show as You Go* pages to assist them in completing the project.
- To assess the project, refer to the rubric on the following page.

Go to connected.mcgraw-hill.com for additional resources:
- Assessment
- Games
- Group Technology Projects

Differentiated Instruction

▶ **Approaching** Students will complete a modified version of the poster, including only a map with the states, capitals, 2–3 physical features, and 1–2 images.

▶ **Beyond** Students will research to learn more about the current event they chose for their poster. In their summary, they will include an analysis of the role geography plays in the issue.

▶ **ELL** Help students find information about a current event affecting the region. Have students use scanning skills to locate and highlight important information about the issue. These articles or a summary can be included on the students' posters.

Response to Intervention

BIG IDEA Location affects the way people live.

If . . . students cannot give a substantiated response to the Big Idea,

Then . . . take them back to pages 18–21. Discuss how each physical feature affects the lives of people who live nearby. Following discussion, allow students to respond to the Big Idea again.

Name _____ Date _____

Region Poster Rubric

4 Exemplary	3 Accomplished	2 Developing	1 Beginning
The poster: ☐ includes all major geographic features of the region. ☐ contains accurate facts and details about the region. ☐ includes a complete and accurate map of the region. ☐ is interesting, easy to read, and includes images. ☐ contains few, if any, errors in grammar, punctuation, capitalization, and spelling.	**The poster:** ☐ includes most major geographic features of the region. ☐ has mostly accurate facts and details about the region. ☐ includes a mostly complete and accurate map of the region. ☐ is mostly easy to follow and includes some images. ☐ contains some errors in grammar, punctuation, capitalization, and spelling.	**The poster:** ☐ includes a few major geographic features of the region. ☐ has some accurate facts and details about the region. ☐ includes a somewhat complete or accurate map of the region. ☐ is somewhat confusing and may include images. ☐ contains several errors in grammar, punctuation, capitalization, and spelling.	**The poster:** ☐ includes one or no major geographic features of the region. ☐ has few accurate facts and details about the region. ☐ does not include a complete or accurate map of the region. ☐ is difficult to follow and/or does not include images. ☐ contains serious errors in grammar, punctuation, capitalization, and spelling.

Grading Comments: _____

_____

_____

_____

_____

_____

_____

_____

_____

The Climate of the United States

By Gabriel Sanchez

Climate is the weather in a place over a number of years. The weather of a place includes its wind pattern, temperature, and amount of precipitation, or rain and snow, that falls. Climate is mainly determined by latitude. Other factors, such as mountains or bodies of water, also influence climate.

The movement of air and water helps create Earth's climates. The sun's heat is moved around the globe by streaming waters and moving air. In the ocean, the moving streams of water are called *currents*.

Most of the United States is located in a *temperate* climate, which has changing seasons and mild weather that is neither too hot nor too cold. For example, the Northeast experiences snowy winters, rainy springs, and hot, wet summers. The Southeast has mild temperatures due to regular rainfall. The climate in the West varies with elevation.

The warmest parts of the country are nearest the Equator. The air and water here are heated and travel from the tropics toward Earth's poles. Areas near the tropics, such as Florida and Hawaii, are warm all year. The Gulf Stream is one of the strongest, warmest ocean currents in the world. It flows north from the Gulf of Mexico through the cool Atlantic Ocean.

United States and Canada: Climate

❶ What is the theme of this article?

Ⓐ Climate influences the movement of air and water.

Ⓑ The United States has one climate.

Ⓒ Currents have the greatest influence on climate.

Ⓓ Many factors influence the climate of the United States.

❷ Which detail from the article helps show the reasons why areas near the tropics are warm all year?

Ⓕ Frequent rainfall causes mild temperatures.

Ⓖ The air and water near the tropics are heated.

Ⓗ The sun's heat is moved around the globe.

Ⓘ Climate in the West varies by elevation.

❸ The mild temperatures of the Southeast are created by

Ⓐ ocean currents.

Ⓑ moving streams of air.

Ⓒ regular rainfall.

Ⓓ elevation.

❹ By reading the article and looking at the map, you can tell that the climate of Florida is affected by

Ⓕ the Pacific Ocean.

Ⓖ the Gulf Stream.

Ⓗ elevation.

Ⓘ its location in the Northeast.

❺ Read these sentences from the article.

For example, the Northeast experiences snowy winters, rainy springs, and hot, wet summers. The Southeast has mild temperatures due to regular rainfall.

What does the word *mild* mean?

Ⓐ humid

Ⓑ mostly cold

Ⓒ not too hot or too cold

Ⓓ never the same

❻ Which word means *changing seasons and mild weather*?

Ⓕ elevation

Ⓖ climate

Ⓗ current

Ⓘ temperate

30

31

Test Preparation

Test-Taking Tips

Share these test-taking tips with your students:

- Read each question carefully.

- Do not leave any answers blank. If you do not know the answer to a question, skip it and come back to it later.

- Answer the question being asked. Read over the question and your answer. Does your response answer what is being asked?

- Check your answers. Reread each question and make sure your answer makes sense.

- Erase incorrect answers completely.

- Check your answer sheet. For multiple choice questions, fill in each answer bubble completely. Make sure there are no extra marks on the answer sheet.

Answers

1. D **CCS RI.2**

2. G **CCS RI.3**

3. C **CCS RI.1**

4. G **CCS RI.3**

5. C **CCS RI.4**

6. I **CCS RI.4**

UNIT 2 Planner
NATIVE PEOPLES OF NORTH AMERICA

BIG IDEA 💡 **Culture influences the way people live.**

Student Portfolio

- **Show As You Go!**
  Use these pages to introduce the Big Idea. Students record information specific to each lesson. They use these pages to help them plan their Big Idea Project.

netw⊘rks™

- **Group Technology Project**
  Students use 21st century skills to complete a group extension activity of the unit project. Lesson plans, worksheets, and rubrics are available online.

Student Portfolio

- **Big Idea Project**
  Students work in a team to research, design, and create a museum exhibit that features one Native American tribe discussed in the Unit. The Big Idea Project Rubric is on page 69W.

Reading Skills

Student Portfolio

- **Reading Skill: Compare and Contrast**
  Pages 34–35. Common Core State Standards RI.5

Leveled Readers

Use the leveled reader *The Navajo: Tradition and Change* (lesson plan on pages T20–T21) with Lesson 1.

Treasures Connection

Teach this unit with Treasures Unit 5, *The Unbreakable Code*, pages 582–599.

Social Studies Skills

Student Portfolio

- **Primary and Secondary Sources: Artifacts**
  Page 39

netw⊘rks™

- **Skill Builders**
  Introduce and teach analyzing primary and secondary sources.

Activity Cards

- **Center for Social Studies Skills Investigation**
  Use the center activity cards to help students explore Primary Sources, Geography, and Citizenship.

FOLDABLES®

Student Portfolio

- Students can create vocabulary Foldables right in their portfolios.
- Additional Foldables templates can be found on pages R34–R42 of your Teacher Edition. See page R33 for instructions.

Assessment Solutions

- **McGraw-Hill networks™**
  Safe online testing features multiple question types that are easy to use and editable.
- **Self-Check Quizzes**
- **Worksheets**

UNIT 2 At a Glance

	Lesson	Essential Question	Vocabulary
1	**Ancient Cultures**	What makes a civilization?	culture *develop civilization slavery empire irrigation
2	**Native Americans of the Southwest**	How does location affect the way people live?	kachina migrate hogan *translate
3	**Native Americans of the Pacific Northwest**	How does location affect the way people live?	*typically totem pole potlatch
4	**Native Americans of the Great Plains**	How does location affect the way people live?	prairies *characteristic nomads teepee lodge
5	**Native Americans of the Eastern Woodlands**	How does location affect the way people live?	slash-and-burn *conduct *aspect longhouse wampum confederacy

*denotes academic vocabulary

Digital Resources

Go to **connected.mcgraw-hill.com** for additional resources:

- Interactive Whiteboard Lessons

- Worksheets

- Assessment

- Content Library

- Lesson Plans

- Skill Builders

- Videos

- Use Standards Tracker on **networks** to track students' progress.

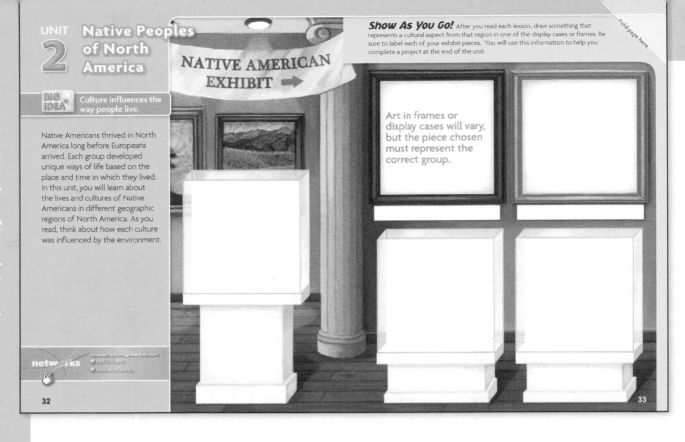

UNIT
2
Native Peoples of North America

BIG IDEA Culture influences the way people live.

Native Americans thrived in North America long before Europeans arrived. Each group developed unique ways of life based on the place and time in which they lived. In this unit, you will learn about the lives and cultures of Native Americans in different geographic regions of North America. As you read, think about how each culture was influenced by the environment.

NATIVE AMERICAN EXHIBIT →

Show As You Go! After you read each lesson, draw something that represents a cultural aspect from that region in one of the display cases or frames. Be sure to label each of your exhibit pieces. You will use this information to help you complete a project at the end of the unit.

Fold page here

Art in frames or display cases will vary, but the piece chosen must represent the correct group.

networks connected.mcgraw-hill.com
● Skill Builders
● Resource Library

32   33

Introduce the Unit

☑ Diagnostic Assessment

Explain to students that Unit 2 discusses Native American cultures. Have students give examples from their own lives for the cultural aspects below.

Ask: *How do these different cultural aspects influence the way you live?*

- clothing
- shelter
- food
- beliefs
- music
- art
- interactions with the environment

Student responses will help identify their level of understanding.

Active Teaching

BIG IDEA **Culture influences the way people live.**
As students read, they will use information from the lesson to complete the **Show As You Go!** pages. Explain to students that at the end of the unit, they will use the information collected on these pages to complete their Unit Project. At this point, have students fold back the corner of this page. This will help them flip back to that page as needed.

Differentiated Instruction

▶ **Approaching** Tell students that each lesson focuses on Native Americans in one region. As lessons are completed, allow students to work in a small group to draw artifacts that represent each region.

▶ **Beyond** As students read each lesson, have them write about different cultural aspects of each group. Their writings can be placed on placards in the museum display.

▶ **ELL** Review the cultures discussed in the unit by discussing food, clothing, shelter, and religion. List details about each topic for each region. Have each student choose one cultural aspect and represent the same aspect for each region in the museum displays.

Reading Skill

Common Core Standards
RI.5: Compare and contrast the overall structure (e.g. chronology, comparison, cause/effect, problem/solution) of events, ideas, concepts, or information in two or more texts.

Compare and Contrast

When you compare, you notice how things are alike. When you contrast, you look at how they differ. Comparing and contrasting helps you understand the people and events you read about in social studies.

LEARN IT

As you read, do the following to compare and contrast:

- To compare two things, note how they are similar. The words *like*, *same*, and *both* are clues to similarities.
- To contrast two things, note how they are different. The words *different*, *however*, and *unlike* show differences.

To protect themselves from enemies, the Creek formed the Creek Confederacy. They divided Creek towns into war towns (red) and peace towns (white). Red towns declared war, planned battles, and held meetings with enemy groups. White towns passed laws and held prisoners. During periods of war, however, even the people in the peace towns joined in the fighting.

This explains how the towns were different. <u>Underline</u> other differences between the towns.

This explains how the towns were similar.

A meeting of the Creek Confederacy ▶

TRY IT

Fill in the diagram below to compare and contrast the information from the passage on page 34.

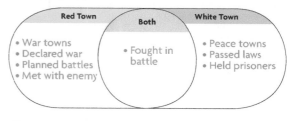

Red Town
- War towns
- Declared war
- Planned battles
- Met with enemy

Both
- Fought in battle

White Town
- Peace towns
- Passed laws
- Held prisoners

APPLY IT

- Review the steps to compare and contrast in Learn It.
- Read the passage below. <u>Underline</u> sentences that compare similarities among groups. Circle sentences that show differences among groups.

In order to survive, the Navajo adapted ideas and practices from their Pueblo neighbors. Unlike the Pueblo, the Navajo built dome-shaped family homes. Like the Pueblo, the Navajo used dry farming to grow crops in the dry land. They also wove cotton to make cloth. However, it is the Navajo who are well known as shepherds. Both the Navajo and the Pueblo are known for their fine silver and turquoise jewelry.

▲ A silver and turquoise ring

Common Core Standards RI.5 Compare and contrast the overall structure (e.g. chronology, comparison, cause/effect, problem/solution) of events, ideas, concepts, or information in two or more texts.

Reading Skill

Active Teaching

LEARN IT Compare and Contrast

Say: *When I make comparisons, I am finding similarities among ideas, objects, or events. I think about how things are the same. When I contrast two ideas, objects, or events, I am finding the differences between them. I think "What about these two things is different?"*

TRY IT Encourage students to try the modeled strategy as they complete the TRY IT activity.

APPLY IT After students have completed the APPLY IT activity, **Ask:**

1. *What key words help you understand how two things are similar?* **L1**

2. *What key words help you understand how two things are different?* **L1**

3. *Why are comparing and contrasting important skills?* (Comparing and contrasting is an important skill because it helps me distinguish between ideas, objects, and events.) **L3**

Differentiated Instruction

▶ **Approaching** Review the **LEARN IT** activity as a small group. Do the **TRY IT** activity together. Have students complete the **APPLY IT** activity independently. Regroup to compare and correct.

▶ **Beyond** Have students complete the following sentences: The Navajo and Pueblo are similar because _____. They are different because _____.

Ask: *Are the Navajo and Pueblo more similar than they are different? Explain your opinion.*

▶ **ELL** After students read each passage, ask them to summarize it in their own words. Using a graphic organizer, work together to compare and contrast the information of the passages.

netw⊕rks

Additional resources are found at **connected.mcgraw-hill.com.**
- Skill Builders
- Graphic Organizers

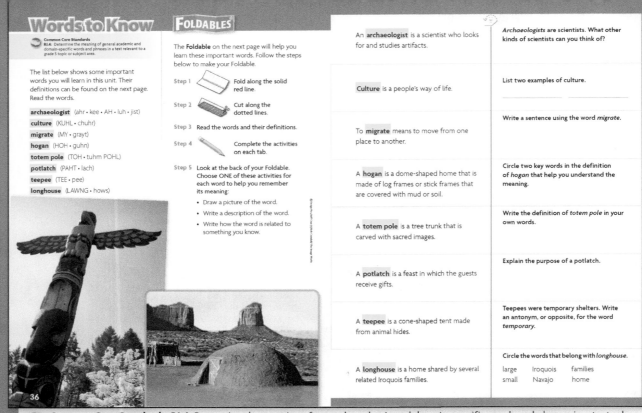

Words to Know

Common Core Standards
RI.4: Determine the meaning of general academic and domain-specific words and phrases in a text relevant to a grade 5 topic or subject area.

The list below shows some important words you will learn in this unit. Their definitions can be found on the next page. Read the words.

archaeologist (ahr • kee • AH • luh • jist)
culture (KUHL • chuhr)
migrate (MY • grayt)
hogan (HOH • guhn)
totem pole (TOH • tuhm POHL)
potlatch (PAHT • lach)
teepee (TEE • pee)
longhouse (LAWNG • hows)

FOLDABLES

The **Foldable** on the next page will help you learn these important words. Follow the steps below to make your Foldable.

Step 1 Fold along the solid red line.

Step 2 Cut along the dotted lines.

Step 3 Read the words and their definitions.

Step 4 Complete the activities on each tab.

Step 5 Look at the back of your Foldable. Choose ONE of these activities for each word to help you remember its meaning:
- Draw a picture of the word.
- Write a description of the word.
- Write how the word is related to something you know.

36

An **archaeologist** is a scientist who looks for and studies artifacts.	*Archaeologists* are scientists. What other kinds of scientists can you think of?
Culture is a people's way of life.	List two examples of culture.
To **migrate** means to move from one place to another.	Write a sentence using the word *migrate*.
A **hogan** is a dome-shaped home that is made of log frames or stick frames that are covered with mud or soil.	Circle two key words in the definition of *hogan* that help you understand the meaning.
A **totem pole** is a tree trunk that is carved with sacred images.	Write the definition of *totem pole* in your own words.
A **potlatch** is a feast in which the guests receive gifts.	Explain the purpose of a potlatch.
A **teepee** is a cone-shaped tent made from animal hides.	Teepees were temporary shelters. Write an antonym, or opposite, for the word *temporary*.
A **longhouse** is a home shared by several related Iroquois families.	Circle the words that belong with *longhouse*. large Iroquois families small Navajo home

Common Core Standards **RI.4** Determine the meaning of general academic and domain-specific words and phrases in a text relevant to a grade 5 topic or subject area.

Words to Know
Active Teaching

FOLDABLES Guide students through the making of their Foldable. Remind students that they are **not** to rip out their Foldable. This will stay in their book as a study guide.

1. Go to connected.mcgraw-hill.com for flashcards to introduce the unit vocabulary to students.

2. Divide the class into pairs and have them work together to discuss the words and their meanings.

3. Initiate a whole-class discussion about the meaning of each word.

4. Have students use the Foldable to practice the vocabulary words independently or with a partner.

GO Vocabulary!
Use the graphic organizer below to help students practice the meanings of the words from the list.

1. Model the graphic organizer using *migrate*.

2. Have students complete the graphic organizer for the other words independently or with a partner

Frayer Model

Definition to move from one place to another	Description (in own words) moving a lot
Examples (from own life) animals that move during different seasons	Non-examples staying put living in one place

(center: **migrate**)

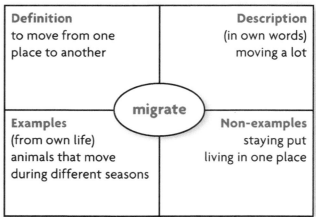

archaeologist	archaeologist
culture	culture
migrate	migrate
hogan	hogan
totem pole	totem pole
potlatch	potlatch
teepee	teepee
longhouse	longhouse

Primary Sources

Artifacts

Objects created by humans long ago are called artifacts. Scientists called **archaeologists** study artifacts to learn about how people lived in the past. To understand artifacts, you must know the geography of the area where it was found. You then need to study the design of the artifact. Next, think about how someone might have used it in the past.

In this unit, you will learn about how different Native American groups lived and expressed their cultures. Examine the Anasazi and Mound Builder artifacts on this page. What clues do they give you about each culture?

▲ Anasazi artifacts

DBQ Document-Based Questions

Study the artifacts. Then complete the activities.

1. Choose an artifact and describe how it was most likely used in the past.

_____

_____

▲ Mound Builder artifact

2. Imagine that scientists in the future are studying our culture. Draw an artifact from your life that would give them clues about how you live.

networks
There's More Online!
● Skill Builders
● Resource Library

39

Differentiated Instruction

▶ **ELL** Have students make a two-column chart. Review each vocabulary word with students. Have students write the word in the left column and write notes or draw pictures to help them remember the meaning of the word in the right column. Students should add notes and pictures to their charts after each word is introduced in a lesson.

W O R D P L A Y

Play WORDO to help students practice the vocabulary

1. Print WORDO cards from **connected.mcgraw-hill.com** and distribute to students.

2. Have students choose eight words from this unit and write one word per square, leaving one square of their choice as the FREE SPACE.

3. Provide each student with nine chips or squares of paper to serve as the game markers.

4. Write the definition for each word on a strip of paper and place the strips in a small container.

5. Pull one definition from the container and read it aloud. Instruct students to cover the word being defined if it appears on their card.

6. A player wins when a horizontal, vertical, or diagonal row is covered. For variation, use each word in a sentence.

Primary Sources
Active Teaching

Explain to students that artifacts are items created by humans. We study artifacts to learn how people lived long ago.

Say: *Did you know there are many types of artifacts? Some artifacts made life easier for people in the past.* Tell them that there are many types of artifacts, including jewelry, clothing, and weapons.

Ask:

1. *What items make your life easier today? Why do you think these items could be considered artifacts in the future?* **L3**

2. *What type of artifacts do you think Native Americans left behind? What do the artifacts tell us about these early peoples?* **L3**

networks

Go to **connected.mcgraw-hill.com** for additional resources:

- Skill Builders
- Resource Library

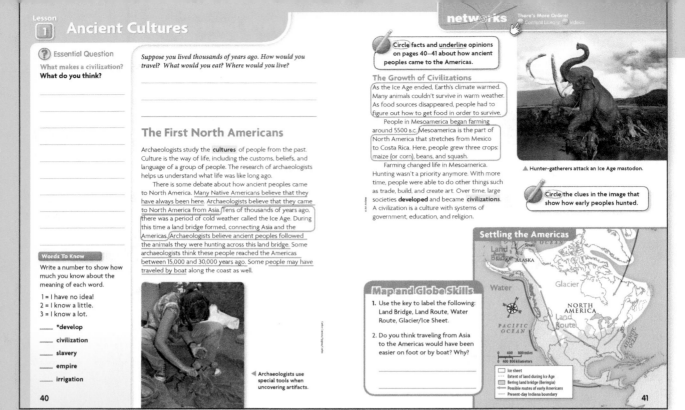

Lesson 1

Ancient Cultures

? Essential Question
What makes a civilization?
What do you think?

Suppose you lived thousands of years ago. How would you travel? What would you eat? Where would you live?

The First North Americans

Archaeologists study the **cultures** of people from the past. Culture is the way of life, including the customs, beliefs, and language of a group of people. The research of archaeologists helps us understand what life was like long ago.

There is some debate about how ancient peoples came to North America. Many Native Americans believe that they have always been here. Archaeologists believe that they came to North America from Asia. Tens of thousands of years ago, there was a period of cold weather called the Ice Age. During this time a land bridge formed, connecting Asia and the Americas. Archaeologists believe ancient peoples followed the animals they were hunting across this land bridge. Some archaeologists think these people reached the Americas between 15,000 and 30,000 years ago. Some people may have traveled by boat along the coast as well.

Words To Know
Write a number to show how much you know about the meaning of each word.

1 = I have no idea!
2 = I know a little.
3 = I know a lot.

____ *develop
____ civilization
____ slavery
____ empire
____ irrigation

◀ Archaeologists use special tools when uncovering artifacts.

40

networks There's More Online!
Content Library Videos

Circle facts and underline opinions on pages 40–41 about how ancient peoples came to the Americas.

The Growth of Civilizations
As the Ice Age ended, Earth's climate warmed. Many animals couldn't survive in warm weather. As food sources disappeared, people had to figure out how to get food in order to survive.

People in Mesoamerica began farming around 5500 B.C. Mesoamerica is the part of North America that stretches from Mexico to Costa Rica. Here, people grew three crops: maize (or corn), beans, and squash.

Farming changed life in Mesoamerica. Hunting wasn't a priority anymore. With more time, people were able to do other things such as trade, build, and create art. Over time, large societies **developed** and became **civilizations**. A civilization is a culture with systems of government, education, and religion.

▲ Hunter-gatherers attack an Ice Age mastodon.

Circle the clues in the image that show how early peoples hunted.

Settling the Americas

Map and Globe Skills
1. Use the key to label the following: Land Bridge, Land Route, Water Route, Glacier/Ice Sheet.
2. Do you think traveling from Asia to the Americas would have been easier on foot or by boat? Why?

Map key:
□ Ice sheet
- - - Extent of land during Ice Age
▨ Bering land bridge (Beringia)
← Possible routes of early Americans
— Present-day Indiana boundary

41

Lesson 1

Activate Prior Knowledge

After students have completed the introductory activity, lead a discussion about other ways they think life in the past was similar to and different from life today. You might choose to use a Venn diagram to record these similarities and differences.

? Essential Question What makes a civilization?

Have students explain what they understand about the Essential Question. Discuss their responses. Explain that everything they learn in this lesson will help them understand the Essential Question. Remind them to think about how the Essential Question connects to the unit Big Idea: Culture influences the way people live.

networks

Go to **connected.mcgraw-hill.com** for additional resources:

- Interactive Whiteboard Lessons
- Worksheets
- Assessment
- Lesson Plans
- Content Library

Active Teaching

Words To Know After completing the Words to Know activity, have students work with a partner to write either a definition (in their own words), an antonym, or a synonym for each vocabulary word. Once pairs have completed their work, have each share their definition, antonym, or synonym for that word with the class. Then record each group's work on the board to create an entire list of associations for each vocabulary word.

Map and Globe Skills

Have students look at the map on page 41.

Ask: *Which present-day state was part of the land bridge?*

The land bridge theory is not the only theory about how people came to North America. As mentioned in the text, Native Americans believe that their peoples have always been here. Some archaeologists believe that people came to the Americas across the Atlantic Ocean.

Ask: *Why do you think there are different ideas about how people came to the Americas?*

The Maya

The development of farming in Mesoamerica led to the growth of some of the first North American civilizations. The Maya were one such group. In about 2500 b.c., the Maya arose in southeastern Mexico and Central America. From about a.d. 250 to 900, they became a powerful civilization. Read about their culture and ways of life.

The Maya
Maya lands,
A.D. 300–A.D. 900

Maya scientists created a 365-day calendar to help with farming and predicting events such as eclipses. The Maya developed a system of mathematics and a form of writing we call hieroglyphs. Hieroglyphs are a series of symbols that represent words.

Maya cities were ruled by kings who claimed to have been chosen by Maya gods. Maya leaders oversaw large building projects and led the military. To form alliances and strengthen trade, Maya royalty often married royalty from other cities.

Religion was at the center of Maya life. The Maya built stone pyramids and temples to honor their hundreds of gods.

Underline different cultural aspects of the Maya including food, shelter, religion, and daily life.

The Decline of the Maya

Maya cities such as Chichén Itzá, Tikal, and Copan had populations of several thousand people. Over time, the population outgrew the food supply. People moved out of the cities in search of food. The Maya lost power by a.d. 900, but the people did not disappear. Today more than 6 million Maya live in Mexico, Belize, and Guatemala.

FUN FACTS
The Maya were one of the first cultures to make chocolate! They made it from the seeds of the cacao tree.

A popular game in Mesoamerica was a ballgame called pok-a-tok. Let me tell you all about it!

This was a dangerous game! Check out all of the protective stuff we had to wear!

The goal of the game was to hit a ball through a stone ring. We passed the ball by using a stick called a manopla, by using our bodies, or by kicking it.

Games drew large crowds. We played to please our gods. Winners were rewarded with clothing and riches. Many times, the losing team was sacrificed to our gods.

Label the pok-a-tok player. Write the number for each item on the lines.
1. **Yugito:** knee guard
2. **Headdress:** head protection
3. **Yoke:** hip protector
4. **Manopla:** used to bat the ball

43

Active Teaching

These pages discuss cultural aspects of the Maya including daily life, architecture, clothing, religion, and recreation.

Ask:

1. *Why did the Maya create a calendar?* **L1**

2. *What were the roles and responsibilities of Maya leaders in their society?* **L2**

3. *Why did the Maya civilization decline?* **L3**

☑ Formative Assessment

After reading pages 42–43, have students summarize what they learned about the Maya through pok-a-tok. Students should compare and contrast pok-a-tok with sports or other games they play today.

Ask: *In what ways are all sports similar? How are they different?*

More About Mayan Writing After the Spanish took over Maya lands, knowledge of how to read Mayan hieroglyphs was lost. Then, a Ukrainian man named Yury Knorosov cracked the code. He realized that the signs were not letters, but syllables. By 1963, he had identified 540 different glyphs. Using his findings, archaeologists were able to translate Mayan writings.

Differentiated Instruction

▶ **Approaching** The page layout may confuse some students. Have them number the panels in the order they should be read. Have students make a sequence chart on a separate piece of paper. This will help them organize the information about Mayan life.

▶ **Beyond** Have students use the illustrations on pages 42–43 to write dialogue to go along with the images. They should use the dialogue to have the characters on the page tell a story. Encourage students to go to the library or use the Internet to find out more about Maya daily life. Their research can aid them in writing the dialogue.

▶ **ELL** Together, read the sections one at a time. After each, summarize the text. Create a chart labeled art/music, clothes, food, shelter, religion, and daily life. Record details in the proper column. After, have students choose one section and restate it in their own words and explain what they learned about the culture through that aspect.

Underline cultural aspects of the Aztec.

The Aztec

To the west of the Maya, the Aztec settled on the shores of Lake Texcoco around A.D. 1325. They built their capital, Tenochtitlán, on an island in the lake. The Aztec connected the island to the surrounding land with wide roads and bridges.

The large markets of Aztec cities were full of excitement. Dancers, musicians, and other performers often entertained the crowd. Other people sold food such as peppers, squash, tomatoes, corn, and beans.

The most highly prized items for sale were the colorful feathers of the quetzal bird. Wealthy Aztec often used quetzal feathers or gold to decorate their clothing. Most Aztec men wore loincloths and cloaks or capes, while women wore simple blouses and skirts.

Religion

The Aztec had many gods and built large temples to honor them. One god they worshipped was Huitzilopochtli, the god of war and the sun. The Aztec believed that the sun god required human blood in order to make the sun rise. Therefore, every day the Aztec would sacrifice slaves or other prisoners to the sun god.

DID YOU KNOW?
Tenochtitlán was built on watery, swampy land. The Aztec developed floating gardens called *chinampas*. They stuck rows of thick posts into the swamp. Then they filled the spaces between the posts with mud.

The Aztec Empire

MEXICO

Gulf of Mexico

Tenochtitlán • Teotihuacan

YUCATAN PENINSULA

VALLEY OF MEXICO

PACIFIC OCEAN

0 100 200 miles
0 100 200 kilometers

Aztec Empire c. A.D. 1500

Map and Globe Skills

1. Shade in the area on the map in which the Maya settled. Tip: Use pages 42–43.

2. What major bodies of water bordered Aztec land to the north and south?

Gulf of Mexico

Pacific Ocean

44

The Aztec and War

War played an important part in the lives of the Aztec. From an early age, Aztec boys were trained as soldiers. In battle, they captured the enemy. Some of these prisoners were forced into **slavery**. Slavery is the practice of owning people and forcing them to work without pay.

The Aztec were often at war with their neighbors. They conquered hundreds of cities in central Mexico. By A.D. 1440, the Aztec had established a powerful **empire**. An empire is a large area of different groups of people controlled by one ruler or government.

Reading Skill

Compare and Contrast Think about different cultural aspects of the Maya and the Aztec. How were they similar? How were they different?

_____

_____

_____

▲ Some Aztec soldiers wore suits made to look like animals that were meant to terrify the enemy.

Tenochtitlán

Ball Court: Like the Maya, the Aztec played ***pok-a-tok.***

The Great Temple: This temple was built to honor the rain god, Tlaloc, and Huitzilopochtli, the god of sun and war.

Chinampas

45

Lesson 1

Active Teaching

As you work through these pages, analyze the culture of the Aztec. Then compare and contrast the cultural aspects of the Maya and Aztec. It may be helpful to use a graphic organizer on chart paper to record student responses. Throughout this unit, students will analyze cultural aspects within and between the geographical regions in North America.

Develop Comprehension
Ask:

1. *How did the Aztec adapt their farming practices to fit their environment?* **L2**

2. *Look at the diagram on page 45. How might having all of the bridges and causeways to the island city be helpful or harmful in the case of an attack?* **L3** (Being built on an island made it difficult to attack as there was only one way in or out. The bridges would have also made it easier to manage battles and prevented enemies from moving farther into the city. This also created limited escape routes.)

3. *How were the religious practices of the Aztec and Maya similar?* **L3**

Page Power

Interact more with pages 44–45. Have students:

- box the date that the Aztec settled on Lake Texcoco.
- write a caption for the image of *chinampas* on page 44.
- identify and circle the main idea in each paragraph on the page.
- draw some of the items found in an Aztec market on the diagram on page 45. These should include peppers, squash, tomatoes, corn, beans, and quetzal feathers.
- label the different pieces of clothing of the Aztec warrior on page 45.

Say: *Explain the materials you think were used to make the warrior's clothing.* **L3**

Map and Globe Skills

Students will use the maps on pages 42 and 44 to compare where the Maya and Aztec lived.

More About the Aztec Origins According to Aztec legends, in the Valley of Mexico, the Aztec came upon an eagle standing on a cactus with a snake in its beak. This was a sign that their search for a homeland was over. It was there that they built their capital, Tenochtitlán.

Early North American Civilizations

The Anasazi

▲ Anasazi bowls

In about A.D. 700, the Anasazi settled in the "Four Corners" area where Utah, Colorado, Arizona, and New Mexico meet. The Anasazi are known as the first "cliff dwellers." They lived in homes that look like large apartment buildings built into the sides of cliffs. Their homes were made of adobe, a sun-baked clay brick. Special underground rooms called *kivas* were used for meetings or religious purposes.

The Four Corners area is a very hot, dry place. As you can imagine, this made farming difficult. The Anasazi adjusted to the heat and dryness by using **irrigation** to bring water to their crops. The Anasazi irrigation system guided rain water through a series of ditches. The Anasazi planted crops such as maize, beans, and squash.

▼ Ruins of an Anasazi dwelling at Mesa Verde

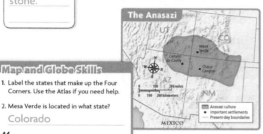

Look at the image of the home on page 47. How is it different than Mesa Verde?

It is made
of ice, not
stone.

The Anasazi

[map showing UT, CO, AZ, NM with Mesa Verde, Canyon de Chelly, Chaco Canyon]

Anasazi culture
■ important settlements
— Present-day boundaries

Map and Globe Skills

1. Label the states that make up the Four Corners. Use the Atlas if you need help.

2. Mesa Verde is located in what state?
   Colorado

46

The Inuit

Living in the desert is certainly difficult. But so is living in the bitterly cold Arctic! The Inuit settled in Alaska and Northern Canada as early as 3000 B.C. They kept warm by building pit houses made of stones covered with earth. On winter hunting trips, men used snow blocks to build temporary shelters called igloos. In warm weather, hunters made tents from wooden poles and animal skins.

The Inuit hunted caribou, walruses, seals, fish, and whales. On land many traveled by dog sled. On water they paddled single-person boats made of sealskin called kayaks.

The Inuit believed that all living things had souls. For this reason, they showed great respect for the animals they hunted by not wasting anything. The meat provided food. Several parts of animals were used for clothing. Boots were made from skin. Animal fur became warm coats called parkas. To sew, the Inuit used bone to create needles. Tools and weapons were carved from bone as well.

Think about the cultural aspects of the Anasazi and the Inuit. Underline similarities and circle differences.

Igloos protect people from the harsh winter weather conditions of the arctic. ▼

The Inuit

[map showing Arctic Ocean, Alaska (U.S.), Canada, Greenland, Victoria Island, Baffin Island, Hudson Bay]

□ Inuit lands, c. A.D. 1500

47

Active Teaching

Before reading the text, discuss how weather affects students' lives.

Ask: *How do you adapt to challenges caused by weather in your daily life?* **L3**

Develop Comprehension
Ask:

1. *What is adobe? What is it used for?* **L1**

2. *What is an igloo?* **L1**

3. *How did living in the cliffs protect the Anasazi?* **L3**

4. *How do the Inuit show respect for animals?* **L3**

5. *Would you rather live in the desert or in the Arctic? What are the positives and negatives of living in each place?* **L3**

Map and Globe Skills

Students will use the map to locate important Anasazi settlements.
Ask:

Using the map, what can you tell about the land where most Anasazi lived? (The Anasazi lived in or around mountains.)

☑ Formative Assessment

After reading pages 46–47, organize the class into pairs. Have pairs role-play as different groups from the lesson meeting each other for the first time. As they interact, they should discuss and compare cultural aspects. After each role play, discuss any details that were inaccurate or incomplete. Use this assessment to monitor student understanding and identify need for intervention.

More About the Decline of the Anasazi The Anasazi population reached into the thousands by about A.D. 900. But in the late 1200s something happened that caused the Anasazi to leave their towns and villages. Many archaeologists believe that a long drought drove them from their homes. Other archaeologists believe that enemy attacks, fighting among the Anasazi, or other reasons may have caused some to leave their homes. By about A.D. 1300 most of the Anasazi towns and villages were empty. Over time, the Anasazi moved or joined other Native Americans in the Southwest. In Lesson 2, students will learn about the Pueblo people, who are believed to be descendents of the Anasazi.

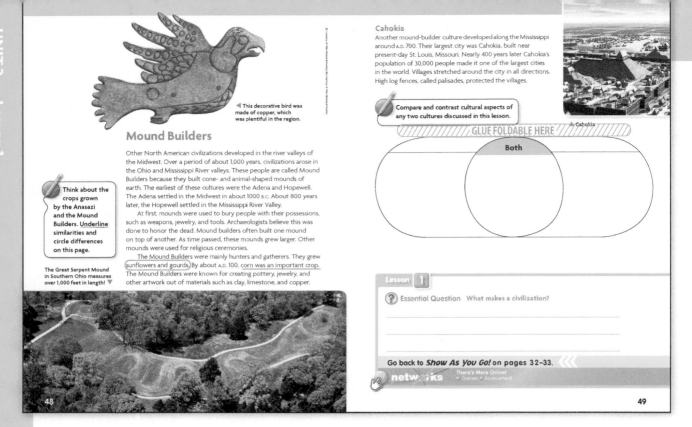

This decorative bird was made of copper, which was plentiful in the region.

Mound Builders

Other North American civilizations developed in the river valleys of the Midwest. Over a period of about 1,000 years, civilizations arose in the Ohio and Mississippi River valleys. These people are called Mound Builders because they built cone- and animal-shaped mounds of earth. The earliest of these cultures were the Adena and Hopewell. The Adena settled in the Midwest in about 1000 B.C. About 800 years later, the Hopewell settled in the Mississippi River Valley.

At first, mounds were used to bury people with their possessions, such as weapons, jewelry, and tools. Archaeologists believe this was done to honor the dead. Mound builders often built one mound on top of another. As time passed, these mounds grew larger. Other mounds were used for religious ceremonies.

The Mound Builders were mainly hunters and gatherers. They grew sunflowers and gourds. By about A.D. 100, corn was an important crop. The Mound Builders were known for creating pottery, jewelry, and other artwork out of materials such as clay, limestone, and copper.

Think about the crops grown by the Anasazi and the Mound Builders. Underline similarities and circle differences on this page.

The Great Serpent Mound in Southern Ohio measures over 1,000 feet in length! ▼

Cahokia

Another mound-builder culture developed along the Mississippi around A.D. 700. Their largest city was Cahokia, built near present-day St. Louis, Missouri. Nearly 400 years later Cahokia's population of 30,000 people made it one of the largest cities in the world. Villages stretched around the city in all directions. High log fences, called palisades, protected the villages.

▲ Cahokia

Compare and contrast cultural aspects of any two cultures discussed in this lesson.

//////// GLUE FOLDABLE HERE ////////

Both

Lesson 1

? Essential Question What makes a civilization?

Go back to *Show As You Go!* on pages 32–33.

networks There's More Online!
• Games • Assessment

48

49

Lesson 1

Active Teaching

Continue to compare and contrast the ancient civilizations in this lesson as a class. Remember to keep students' responses for later comparisons with other regions.

Develop Comprehension
Ask:

1. *Why did Mound Builders bury people with their possessions?* **L1**

Use the leveled reader, *Cahokia: A City of Mystery*, to extend and enrich students' understanding of the ancient Native American cultures of North America. A lesson plan for this leveled reader can be found on pages T20 and T21 at the front of this Teacher Edition.

> *Show As You Go!* Remind students to go back to complete the project on the Unit Opener.

Response to Intervention

? **Essential Question What makes a civilization?**

If . . . students cannot give a substantiated response to the Essential Question, "What makes a civilization?"

....

Then . . . take students back to page 41 and read the definition of *civilization*. Break down the definition into defining its four parts: *culture, government, education,* and *religion*.

Ask: *How do each of the groups from this lesson show each of these different parts? How does that make them civilizations?*

Following discussion, allow students to respond to the Essential Question again.

Page Power

FOLDABLES Interact more with the page.

1. Provide each student with a copy of Foldable 2A from the Notebook Foldables section at the back of this book. Have students construct the Foldable and glue its anchor tab above the chart on page 49.

2. On the Foldable flaps, have students compare and contrast two additional groups discussed in the lesson.

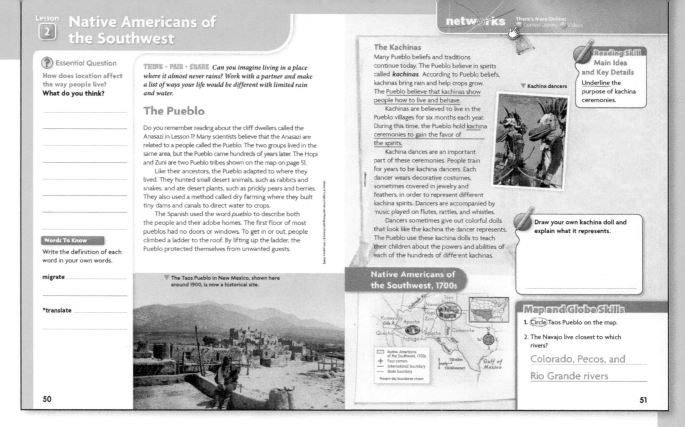

Lesson 2 · Native Americans of the Southwest

Essential Question
How does location affect the way people live?
What do you think?

_____
_____
_____
_____
_____

THINK · PAIR · SHARE _Can you imagine living in a place where it almost never rains? Work with a partner and make a list of ways your life would be different with limited rain and water._

The Pueblo

Do you remember reading about the cliff dwellers called the Anasazi in Lesson 1? Many scientists believe that the Anasazi are related to a people called the Pueblo. The two groups lived in the same area, but the Pueblo came hundreds of years later. The Hopi and Zuni are two Pueblo tribes shown on the map on page 51.

Like their ancestors, the Pueblo adapted to where they lived. They hunted small desert animals, such as rabbits and snakes, and ate desert plants, such as prickly pears and berries. They also used a method called dry farming where they built tiny dams and canals to direct water to crops.

The Spanish used the word _pueblo_ to describe both the people and their adobe homes. The first floor of most pueblos had no doors or windows. To get in or out, people climbed a ladder to the roof. By lifting up the ladder, the Pueblo protected themselves from unwanted guests.

Write the definition of each word in your own words.

migrate _____

*translate _____

▼ The Taos Pueblo in New Mexico, shown here around 1900, is now a historical site.

The Kachinas

Many Pueblo beliefs and traditions continue today. The Pueblo believe in spirits called **kachinas**. According to Pueblo beliefs, kachinas bring rain and help crops grow. The Pueblo believe that kachinas show people how to live and behave.

Kachinas are believed to live in the Pueblo villages for six months each year. During this time, the Pueblo hold kachina ceremonies to gain the favor of the spirits.

Kachina dances are an important part of these ceremonies. People train for years to be kachina dancers. Each dancer wears decorative costumes, sometimes covered in jewelry and feathers, in order to represent different kachina spirits. Dancers are accompanied by music played on flutes, rattles, and whistles.

Dancers sometimes give out colorful dolls that look like the kachina the dancer represents. The Pueblo use these kachina dolls to teach their children about the powers and abilities of each of the hundreds of different kachinas.

▼ Kachina dancers

Reading Skill
Main Idea and Key Details
Underline the purpose of kachina ceremonies.

Draw your own kachina doll and explain what it represents.

Native Americans of the Southwest, 1700s

Map and Globe Skills
1. Circle Taos Pueblo on the map.
2. The Navajo live closest to which rivers?

Colorado, Pecos, and
Rio Grande rivers

50 · 51

Lesson 2

Activate Prior Knowledge

Allow volunteers to share what they wrote with the class. Discuss other difficulties associated with desert life.

Ask: _In what other ways would living in a desert be different from where you live now? What do you think is the most important skill needed to survive in the desert?_

? Essential Question
How does location affect the way people live?

Have students explain what they understand about the Essential Question. Discuss their responses. Explain that everything they learn in this lesson will help them understand the Essential Question better. Remind them to think about how the Essential Question connects to the unit Big Idea.

Active Teaching

Words To Know After students have completed the Words to Know activity, have them locate each word in the text, read its definition, and then use it in a sentence.

Develop Comprehension
Ask:

1. _How is the Pueblo culture connected to the environment?_ **L3**

2. _How were the Pueblo similar to the Anasazi?_ **L3**

Differentiated Instruction

▶ **Approaching** Have students think about any dolls or toys that hold special significance. Have them write about why these items were important.

▶ **Beyond** Have students find images of kachina dolls in the library or on the Internet and research their meaning. They should then present the image and their findings to the class.

▶ **ELL** Students may struggle with terms such as spirits, villages, costumes, and ceremony. Discuss each word and provide synonyms to help them navigate the text.

Reading Skill

Students will analyze the text to identify the main idea of Kachina ceremonies to better understand this part of the Pueblo culture.

Map and Globe Skills

Students will use the map to locate Pueblo and Navajo settlements.

Ask: _Why was it important for Native Americans in the Southwest to settle near rivers?_

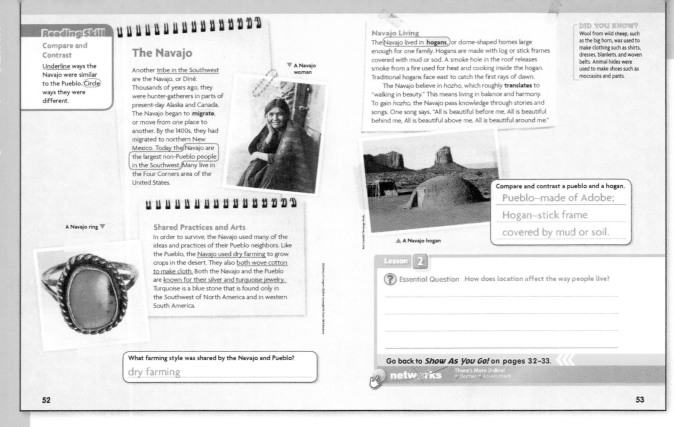

Reading Skill
Compare and Contrast

<u>Underline</u> ways the Navajo were similar to the Pueblo. (Circle) ways they were different.

The Navajo

Another <u>tribe in the Southwest</u> are the Navajo, or Diné. Thousands of years ago, they were hunter-gatherers in parts of present-day Alaska and Canada. The Navajo began to **migrate**, or move from one place to another. By the 1400s, they had migrated to northern New Mexico. Today the Navajo are the largest non-Pueblo people in the Southwest. Many live in the Four Corners area of the United States.

▼ A Navajo woman

▼ A Navajo ring

Shared Practices and Arts
In order to survive, the Navajo used many of the ideas and practices of their Pueblo neighbors. Like the Pueblo, the <u>Navajo used dry farming</u> to grow crops in the desert. They also <u>both wove cotton to make cloth.</u> Both the Navajo and the Pueblo are <u>known for their silver and turquoise jewelry.</u> Turquoise is a blue stone that is found only in the Southwest of North America and in western South America.

What farming style was shared by the Navajo and Pueblo?
dry farming

Navajo Living
The Navajo lived in **hogans**, or dome-shaped homes large enough for one family. Hogans are made with log or stick frames covered with mud or sod. A smoke hole in the roof releases smoke from a fire used for heat and cooking inside the hogan. Traditional hogans face east to catch the first rays of dawn.

The Navajo believe in *hozho*, which roughly **translates** to "walking in beauty." This means living in balance and harmony. To gain *hozho*, the Navajo pass knowledge through stories and songs. One song says, "All is beautiful before me, All is beautiful behind me, All is beautiful above me, All is beautiful around me."

DID YOU KNOW?
Wool from wild sheep, such as the big horn, was used to make clothing such as shirts, dresses, blankets, and woven belts. Animal hides were used to make shoes such as moccasins and pants.

▲ A Navajo hogan

Compare and contrast a pueblo and a hogan.
Pueblo—made of Adobe;
Hogan—stick frame
covered by mud or soil.

Lesson 2

(?) **Essential Question** How does location affect the way people live?

Go back to **Show As You Go!** on pages 32–33.

networks There's More Online! • Games • Assessment

52

53

Lesson 2

Active Teaching

Develop Comprehension
Ask:

1. *What is another name for the Navajo?* **L1**

2. *What did the Navajo learn from the Pueblo?* **L1**

3. *Why would the Navajo have to change when they migrated to the desert?* (Answers should include that the original Navajo home of Alaska had a very different environment than that of the Southwest.) **L3**

Have students complete activities on pages 50–53 of the work text. Before they respond to the Essential Question, summarize the entire lesson with the class.

Show As You Go! Remind students to return to the unit opener and complete the activity with information they have learned from this lesson.

networks
Go to **connected.mcgraw-hill.com** for additional resources.

• Interactive Whiteboard Lessons
• Worksheets
• Assessment
• Content Library

Reading Skill

Students will compare and contrast the lives of Native Americans in the Southwest.

Response to Intervention

(?) **Essential Question**
How does location affect the way people live?

If . . . . students cannot give a substantiated response to the Essential Question, "How does location affect the way people live?"

Then . . . have students create a chart with the following headings: *clothing, shelter, food, art,* and *interactions with the environment.* Have students reread the lesson. As they read, they should fill in the chart. This will help them understand, for example, how the desert affected the lives of Native Americans of the Southwest.

Following discussion, allow students to respond to the Essential Question again.

Lesson 3 · Native Americans of the Pacific Northwest

Essential Question

How does location affect the way people live?

What do you think?

Words To Know

Write the plural form of each word on the line.

totem pole _____

potlatch _____

THINK • PAIR • SHARE *Imagine that it was your birthday party, but YOU had to give gifts to all of your guests! How would you feel? What would you give everyone?*

Life in the Pacific Northwest

Like Native Americans in other regions, those in the Pacific Northwest survived by using natural resources. Food in this region was so plentiful that people there **typically** didn't need to farm. As a result, the Pacific Northwest had one of the highest populations of Native Americans in North America.

The rocky, narrow Pacific coastline and offshore islands provided wild plants, berries, and fish, especially salmon. Every year, millions of salmon return to the rivers of the Pacific Northwest for a few months in order to lay eggs. During this time, it was not uncommon for families to catch hundreds of pounds of fish! People also hunted animals such as deer, elk, beaver, and bears.

Native Americans in the Pacific Northwest used stone axes to cut cedar trees. They hollowed out logs to make canoes as long as 60 feet—perfect for hunting seals and whales in the ocean. Logs were also carved into boxes, dishes, spoons, and masks.

▲ Canoes arriving for a potlatch

54

Totem Poles

Pacific Northwest tribes also used wood to make **totem poles**. Totem poles are logs that are carved and then painted with symbols, called totems, of animals or people. Totem poles often tell stories of important family members or celebrate special events. Totem poles can be very tall. Totem poles can measure 40–60 feet in height. Some are as tall as 150 feet!

Totem Pole ▶

Celebrations

When totem poles were raised, a family sometimes held a **potlatch**. Potlatches are special celebrations at which guests, not hosts, receive gifts. The host might give hundreds of gifts at the potlatch. In return, the host received the respect of the community. These celebrations could sometimes last for days. Potlatches also feature feasts, singing, and dancing. As in the past, potlatches today bring people together for important family events such as the birth, death, or marriage of a family member.

Potlatch dancers ▶

Draw your own totem pole and label each part to explain what it represents. How is your totem pole similar to and different from the kachina doll you made on page 51?

FUN FACTS
Native Americans of the Pacific Northwest wore skirts, loincloths, or blankets made from the soft inner bark of a cedar tree. Jewelry was worn in pierced lips, ears, or noses. Tattoos were also common.

55

Lesson 3

Activate Prior Knowledge

After students complete the activity on page 54,

Ask: *What does generosity say about a group or person?*

? Essential Question
How does location affect the way people live?

Have students explain what they understand about the Essential Question. Discuss their responses. Explain that everything they learn in this lesson will help them understand the Essential Question better. Remind them to think about how the Essential Question connects to the unit Big Idea: Culture influences the way people live.

Differentiated Instruction

▶ **Approaching** Have students draw or create a totem pole with a narrow focus, such as important events of the past year. Before they create their totem, help students brainstorm a list of events.

▶ **Beyond** Have students draw or create a totem pole and write a fictional tale that tells the story of their symbols.

▶ **ELL** Explain that *represent* means to be an example of something. As students draw or create a totem pole, have them write a sentence explaining each level.

Active Teaching

Words To Know After completing the activity, have students complete a word web for *totem pole*.

Develop Comprehension
Ask:

1. *How did Native Americans of the Pacific Northwest use the resources around them to make clothing?* **L1**

2. *Why are salmon important to Native Americans of the Pacific Northwest?* **L2**

Use the leveled reader, *People of the Alaskan Rainforest*, to extend and enrich students' understanding of the Native American cultures of the Pacific Northwest. A lesson plan for this leveled reader can be found on pages T22 and T23 of this Teacher Edition.

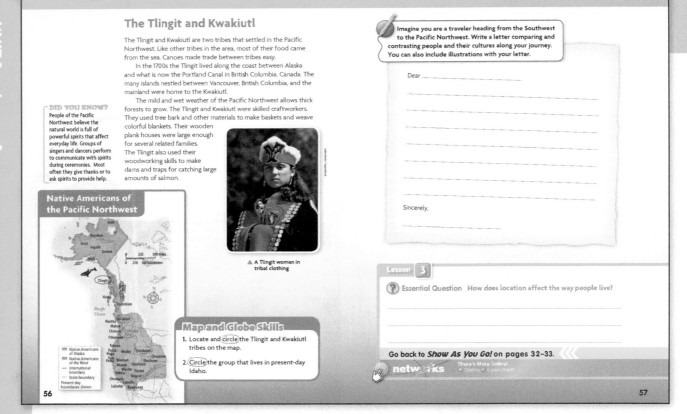

The Tlingit and Kwakiutl

The Tlingit and Kwakiutl are two tribes that settled in the Pacific Northwest. Like other tribes in the area, most of their food came from the sea. Canoes made trade between tribes easy.

In the 1700s the Tlingit lived along the coast between Alaska and what is now the Portland Canal in British Columbia, Canada. The many islands nestled between Vancouver, British Columbia, and the mainland were home to the Kwakiutl.

The mild and wet weather of the Pacific Northwest allows thick forests to grow. The Tlingit and Kwakiutl were skilled craftworkers. They used tree bark and other materials to make baskets and weave colorful blankets. Their wooden plank houses were large enough for several related families. The Tlingit also used their woodworking skills to make dams and traps for catching large amounts of salmon.

DID YOU KNOW?
People of the Pacific Northwest believe the natural world is full of powerful spirits that affect everyday life. Groups of singers and dancers perform to communicate with spirits during ceremonies. Most often they give thanks or to ask spirits to provide help.

Native Americans of the Pacific Northwest

▲ A Tlingit woman in tribal clothing

Map and Globe Skills
1. Locate and circle the Tlingit and Kwakiutl tribes on the map.
2. Circle the group that lives in present-day Idaho.

Imagine you are a traveler heading from the Southwest to the Pacific Northwest. Write a letter comparing and contrasting people and their cultures along your journey. You can also include illustrations with your letter.

Dear _____

Sincerely,

Lesson 3

? **Essential Question** How does location affect the way people live?

Go back to *Show As You Go!* on pages 32–33.

networks There's More Online! • Games • Assessment

56

57

Lesson 3

Active Teaching

Have students outline what they want to include in their letter, including cultural aspects, such as clothing, shelter, food, and major beliefs and practices. Encourage students to find images in the library or on the Internet to include with their letter.

Develop Comprehension
Ask:
1. *How does weather affect life in the northwest?* **L3**
2. *What role did spirits play in the lives of Native Americans?* **L3**

Show As You Go! Remind students to return to the unit opener to complete the activity using information they learned in the lesson.

networks

Go to **connected.mcgraw-hill.com** for additional resources.

- Interactive Whiteboard Lessons
- Worksheets
- Assessment

Map and Globe Skills

Have students analyze the map.

Ask: *What geographic feature had the largest impact on the lives of Native Americans in the Pacific Northwest?*

Response to Intervention

? **Essential Question**
How does location affect the way people live?

If . . . students cannot give a substantiated response to the Essential Question, "How does location affect the way people live?"

....

Then . . . take students back to page 54 and read about the natural resources in the Pacific Northwest.
Ask: *How does having so many resources available affect people in the Pacific Northwest? Is this a positive or a negative? Explain.*

Following discussion, allow students to respond to the Essential Question again.

Lesson 4 Native Americans of the Great Plains

Essential Question
How does location affect the way people live?
What do you think?

_____
_____
_____
_____
_____
_____
_____
_____
_____
_____

THINK · PAIR · SHARE *Imagine that you had to move at a moment's notice. Each time you moved, only a short time would pass before you had to move again. How would it make you feel? What things would you need to bring with you?*

Grass and Sky for Miles

The Great Plains is a vast region made up of **prairies**. A prairie is a flat or gently rolling land covered mostly with grasses and wildflowers. Powerful winds, blistering summer heat, and cold winters are **characteristic** of the region.

Native Americans first settled the Great Plains around A.D. 1300. Some of these people moved constantly as they followed the animals they hunted. These **nomads** had no permanent home and moved in search of food. Hunting on foot with bows and arrows, they chased animals into traps. Other tribes lived permanently near rivers where they farmed.

Taming Wild Horses

By the 1700s, Native Americans had discovered a tool that changed their lives forever: wild horses. Once tamed, horses allowed people to hunt on horseback. Tribes could also travel great distances for trade. As a result, tribes such as the Lakota, Crow, Pawnee, and Cheyenne prospered on the Plains.

Words To Know
Tell a partner what you know about these words.

prairie
nomad
teepee
lodge
*characteristic

58

▼ This painting shows the excitement of a bison hunt.

Different Food, Different Homes

During this time, as many as 100 million bison roamed the Great Plains. They provided plenty of food. Some tribes used bison hides, or skin, to make clothing such as shirts, dresses, robes, and shoes called moccasins.

They also used hides to make **teepees**. Teepees are cone-shaped homes made with long poles covered by animal hides. Teepees were portable and could be put up or taken down quickly. This made it easier for nomadic Native Americans to follow bison or other animals.

Some Great Plains tribes farmed and hunted for food near their permanent communities. Instead of teepees, these groups lived in large earthen **lodges**. Lodges are homes made of logs covered with grasses, sticks, and soil. A fire in a central fireplace provided heat and light.

How are these teepees similar to and different from the Navajo hogan on page 53?

_____
_____

Teepees were decorated in many ways using dyes from plants, animal fur, hooves, and porcupine quills. ▼

DID YOU KNOW?
When the Spanish came to North America in the 1500s, they brought horses with them. Some horses got away and lived in the wild. A few hundred years later, wild horses had spread to the Great Plains.

Native Americans of the Great Plains, 1700s

Blackfoot
Mandan
Crow
Cheyenne
Lakota
Pawnee
Kiowa
Osage
Comanche
Seminole
Natchez

Native Americans of the Plains, 1700s
— International boundary
— State boundary
Present-day boundaries shown

Map and Globe Skills

1. Identify and label the present-day states of the Great Plains. Use your reference atlas if you need help.

2. Most groups settled near what type of geographic feature?
   rivers

59

Lesson 4

☑ Activate Prior Knowledge

Before beginning the lesson, have students draw a teepee and describe how it was used. Student responses will identify their level of understanding.

? Essential Question
How does location affect the way people live?

Have students explain what they understand about the Essential Question. Discuss their responses. Remind them to think about how the Essential Question connects to the unit Big Idea: Culture influences the way people live.

Active Teaching

Words To Know After completing the activity, have students work in groups to create an acrostic poem for one of the vocabulary terms. The first letter of each line of an acrostic poem spells a word. Have groups share their poems with the class.

Map and Globe Skills

Students will use the map to analyze why Native Americans settled where they did on the Plains.

Ask: *How did the geography of the Great Plains influence life in the region?*

Differentiated Instruction

▶ **Approaching** In pairs, students should pick images from the winter count and describe what they think the symbols mean.

▶ **Beyond** Have students draw their own version of a winter count. They should pick a specific period time to write about, such as summer break. Students should also include a description of what each symbol means.

▶ **ELL** Read aloud page 60 with students. As students read along, have them identify and circle new or difficult words. Have students use a dictionary to define these words.

Page Power

FOLDABLES Interact more with the page.

1. Provide each student with a copy of Foldable 2B from the Notebook Foldables section of this book. Have students cut out the Foldable and glue its anchor tabs on page 59 where shown.

2. On the Foldable flaps, have students write: *Shelter, Food, Religion,* and *Art* and details about each aspect of Native American culture.

Life on the Plains

Bison were important to people living on the Plains. In preparation of each bison hunt, they held ceremonies honoring the spirit world and the bison. They believed that without the support of the spirit world, the hunt would be unsuccessful and they could not survive.

FUN FACTS
Spiritual ceremonies often involved drumming, singing, and dancing. Spiritual leaders believed that any mistakes in the performance would prevent the song from reaching the spirits. If performers made any mistakes, they had to start over from the beginning!

Plains Art

The people of the Great Plains often tied their art to everyday life. For example, people decorated everyday items—such as pipes, shields, and clothes—with beads, feathers, and porcupine quills.

Another example of this was the winter count. A winter count was an illustrated calendar that was usually painted on an animal hide. Every year, tribal leaders met to decide the most important events of the past year. These events were painted as picture symbols in a circle on bison hide. The winter count you see below was created by a Lakota named Lone Dog.

Primary Source

Winter Count by Lone Dog, 1800–1871

Examine the artifact and read the translations below. Then complete the activity.

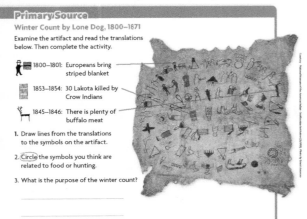

1800–1801: Europeans bring striped blanket

1853–1854: 30 Lakota killed by Crow Indians

1845–1846: There is plenty of buffalo meat

1. Draw lines from the translations to the symbols on the artifact.

2. Circle the symbols you think are related to food or hunting.

3. What is the purpose of the winter count?

_____

60

Learning Responsibilities

Great Plains children were taught about their culture through stories and songs. They also learned skills that prepared them for the tasks of adulthood. Read below to learn about the education of boys and girls.

A Boy's Life

Young boys were taught to hunt and shoot using bows and arrows made especially for children. Older boys took part in shooting contests. During bison hunts and practice battles, boys learned the value of courage.

A Girl's Life

Girls learned to sew by making doll clothes, using sinew from bison as thread. Sinew is the fibers that connect muscles to bone. Girls were also taught to build teepees. Older girls learned to use scraping tools to clean animal hides.

▲ Today, children are still taught traditions at an early age.

Similarities	Differences

Reading Skill
Compare and Contrast

Use the chart to list similarities and differences between religious beliefs of Native Americans of the Great Plains and the Pacific Northwest.

Lesson 4

? **Essential Question** How does location affect the way people live?

_____

_____

Go back to **Show As You Go!** on pages 32–33.

networks
There's More Online!
• Games • Assessment

61

Lesson 4

Active Teaching

Develop Comprehension
Ask:

1. *What does the winter count show about the relationship between the Lakota and other cultures?* **L3** (It shows that they fought with the Crow and traded with Europeans.)

> **Show As You Go!** Remind student to return to the unit opener and complete the activity using information from this lesson.

Primary Source

Students will examine the winter count and make inferences about life on the Great Plains.

Reading Skill

Students will use the chart to compare and contrast the religious beliefs of people in the Great Plains and Pacific Northwest.

Response to Intervention

? **Essential Question**
How does location affect the way people live?

If . . . students cannot give a substantiated response to the Essential Question, "How does location affect the way people live?"

. . . .

Then . . . take students back to pages 59–60. Discuss how the content relates to the Essential Question.

Ask: *In what ways did bison affect the lives of Native Americans of the Great Plains?*

Following discussion, allow students to respond to the Essential Question again.

networks

Go to **connected.mcgraw-hill.com** for additional resources.

• Interactive Whiteboard Lessons
• Worksheets
• Assessment

Lesson 5

Native Americans of the Eastern Woodlands

? Essential Question
How does location affect the way people live?
What do you think?

_____
_____
_____
_____
_____
_____
_____
_____
_____

THINK • PAIR • SHARE *How do you get the things you need to survive? What if you had to find your own food, clothing, and shelter? Where would you get them?*

Living in the Forest

The Eastern Woodlands stretch from the Mississippi River to the Atlantic Ocean. In the past, most of this area was covered in thick forests. People of the woodlands used forest animals, such as deer, bear, and rabbit, for food and clothing.

Farming the Land

The region is divided into two parts: the northeast and the southeast. The southeast is thinly wooded, has a mild climate, and a long growing season, which are all good for farming.

The thicker forests of the northeast made farming more difficult. There, many tribes practiced a type of farming called **slash-and-burn**. They cut down and burned the trees in the forest. Ash from the burned vegetation helped make the soil fertile. In autumn the tribes harvested, dried, and stored the crops for the winter. After the harvest, they let the land rest several years before replanting the crops.

Words To Know

Write a number in each box to show how much you know about each word.

1 = I have no idea!
2 = I know a little.
3 = I know a lot.

___ *conduct
___ longhouse
___ wampum
___ confederacy

▼ The homes of Native Americans of the Eastern Woodlands were often surrounded by the thick forests of the region.

The "Three Sisters"

One Eastern Woodlands group, the Iroquois, includes five tribes: the Cayuga, the Mohawk, the Oneida, the Onondaga, and the Seneca. Each spring most Iroquois planted what they called the "Three Sisters": corn, squash, and beans. These crops were grown together and were often eaten together.

Religion

People in the Eastern Woodlands believed that spirits were involved in everyday life. They believed that good spirits helped those in need, and that evil spirits caused sickness and conflict.

Native Americans **conducted** ceremonies to communicate with spirits. Dancing was important to these ceremonies. People also sang and played instruments, such as wooden flutes and drums. The hope was that these ceremonies would either invite in good spirits or drive out the bad.

Corn
Beans
Squash

Label the "Three Sisters" on the illustration.

Native Americans of the Eastern Woodlands, 1600s

THINK • PAIR • SHARE
Work with a partner to compare and contrast the major beliefs and practices of Native Americans of the Eastern Woodlands and Native Americans of the Great Plains.

Map and Globe Skills

1. Circle the Iroquois tribes on the map.

2. What river forms the western border of the Eastern Woodlands?
   Mississippi River

62

63

Lesson 5

Activate Prior Knowledge

Before reading, ask students how they think living in a dense forest would be different from the locations where other groups they have already learned about lived.

Ask: *How might the lives of those in a forest be different from those in the Southwest, Pacific Northwest, or the Great Plains?*

? **Essential Question**
How does location affect the way people live?

Have students explain what they understand about the Essential Question. Discuss their responses. Explain that everything they learn in this lesson will help them understand the Essential Question better. Remind them to think about how the Essential Question connects to the unit Big Idea: Culture influences the way people live.

More About the Eastern Woodlands This region, which includes the Great Lakes, extends from present-day Virginia into Canada. Its climate is varied, with cold, snowy winters and hot summers.

Active Teaching

Words To Know After completing the activity, have students find the words in the lesson and read their definitions.

Develop Comprehension

Remind students that while Native Americans of the Eastern Woodlands shared many common traits, there were specific differences as well. This was due mostly to the size of the area.

Ask:

1. *How did geography impact culture in this region?* **L3**

2. *Why was farming difficult in the northeast?* **L2**

Map and Globe Skills

Students will use the map to discuss life in the Eastern Woodlands.

Ask: *How would life in the Eastern Woodlands have been similar to that in the Pacific Northwest?*

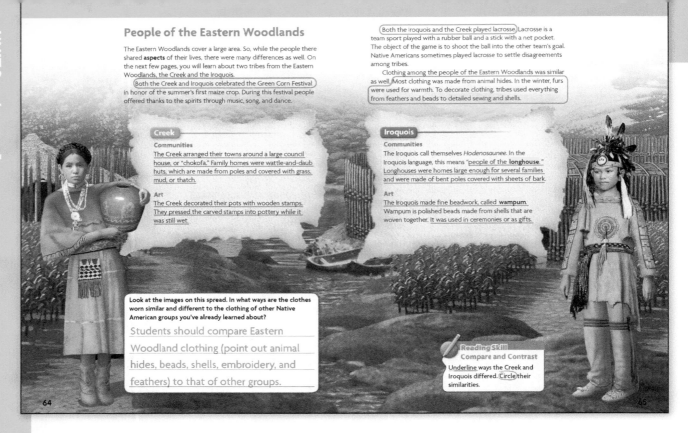

People of the Eastern Woodlands

The Eastern Woodlands cover a large area. So, while the people there shared **aspects** of their lives, there were many differences as well. On the next few pages, you will learn about two tribes from the Eastern Woodlands, the Creek and the Iroquois.

Both the Creek and Iroquois celebrated the Green Corn Festival in honor of the summer's first maize crop. During this festival people offered thanks to the spirits through music, song, and dance.

Both the Iroquois and the Creek played lacrosse. Lacrosse is a team sport played with a rubber ball and a stick with a net pocket. The object of the game is to shoot the ball into the other team's goal. Native Americans sometimes played lacrosse to settle disagreements among tribes.

Clothing among the people of the Eastern Woodlands was similar as well. Most clothing was made from animal hides. In the winter, furs were used for warmth. To decorate clothing, tribes used everything from feathers and beads to detailed sewing and shells.

Creek

Communities
The Creek arranged their towns around a large council house, or "chokofa." Family homes were wattle-and-daub huts, which are made from poles and covered with grass, mud, or thatch.

Art
The Creek decorated their pots with wooden stamps. They pressed the carved stamps into pottery while it was still wet.

Iroquois

Communities
The Iroquois call themselves *Hodenosaunee*. In the Iroquois language, this means "people of the **longhouse**." Longhouses were homes large enough for several families and were made of bent poles covered with sheets of bark.

Art
The Iroquois made fine beadwork, called **wampum**. Wampum is polished beads made from shells that are woven together. It was used in ceremonies or as gifts.

Look at the images on this spread. In what ways are the clothes worn similar and different to the clothing of other Native American groups you've already learned about?

Students should compare Eastern Woodland clothing (point out animal hides, beads, shells, embroidery, and feathers) to that of other groups.

Reading Skill
Compare and Contrast
Underline ways the Creek and Iroquois differed. Circle their similarities.

64   65

Lesson 5

Active Teaching

Have students create a Venn diagram to compare and contrast the Creek and the Iroquois. Ask students to use the details from their Venn diagrams to write a paragraph that summarizes their findings.

Develop Comprehension
Ask:

1. *How are the Creek and the Mound Builders connected?* **L1**

2. *What is lacrosse? Why was it played?* **L2**

3. *In which group did several families live together? Why do you think they lived in that way?* **L3**

Page Power

Interact more with the page. Have students:

- circle and label differences they observe in the images of Creek and Iroquois clothing.
- place a box around the type of home each group used.

Differentiated Instruction

▶ **Approaching** Have students read about the different kinds of houses of Native Americans of the Eastern Woodlands. Have them work in pairs to contrast wattle-and-daub huts with longhouses.

Ask: *How are these types of homes similar to and different from the homes we live in today?*

▶ **Beyond** Have students choose one type of Native American home discussed in this unit and research more about it. What types of materials did they use? How long did they take to build? How many people lived in each home? What were the advantages and disadvantages of the way the home was built? Have them share their findings with the class.

▶ **ELL** Have students look at the images and read the descriptions of one of the different homes discussed in this lesson or the entire unit. Read a description of another home. Then have students draw a picture of it and write a description in their own words.

Reading Skill

Students will compare and contrast the lives of the Creek and Iroquois.

Government in the Woodlands

The people of the Eastern Woodlands worked together to solve their problems. Some tribes formed **confederacies**. A confederacy is a group of people who work together for a common purpose.

Creek Government

To protect themselves from enemies, the Creek formed the Creek Confederacy. They divided towns into war towns (red) and peace towns (white). Red towns declared war, planned battles, and held meetings with enemies. White towns passed laws and held prisoners captive. During periods of war, however, even the people in the peace towns joined in the fighting.

Iroquois Government

When the Iroquois were a small group, they worked together to solve disagreements. But as their numbers began to grow, the Iroquois began arguing among themselves. The Iroquois saw that this fighting was destroying their people. They had to take action.

Around 1570, five Iroquois tribes joined together to form the Iroquois Confederacy, also known as the Iroquois League. Its goal was to maintain peace among the five Iroquois tribes, or nations. The Confederacy later added another tribe, and it was then called Six Nations. The Confederacy is still active today.

Explain the purpose of Native American confederacies.

to maintain peace among tribes

Compare cultural aspects of Native Americans in each region. Use the information from Lessons 2–5 to complete the chart.

Responses may include the following:

Group	Environment	Religion	Food Source	Art and Daily Life
Southwest	hot, dry, desert	Kachina ceremonies hozho-balance	rabbits, snakes, prickly pears, berries	silver and turquoise jewelry; dry farming
Pacific Northwest	coastal forest; rain, mild temperatures	Give thanks to spirits through song/dance	plants, berries, fish, deer, elk, beaver, bear	totems, potlatches, woodwork, and baskets
Great Plains	grassy flatlands; changing seasons	sing & dance for spirits	bison, animals, berries, farming corn, beans, squash	Decorated everyday items; Kids learned responsibilities early
Eastern Woodlands	coastal forests with changing seasons	sing & dance to ask for help or drive bad spirits away	3-sisters, farming, some hunting	Decorated art or beaded; lacrosse

Lesson 5

? **Essential Question** How does location affect the way people live?

Go back to *Show As You Go!* on pages 32–33.

Active Teaching

Have students refer back to Lesson 2 through Lesson 5 to fill in the chart on page 67. Encourage students to use their charts to compare and contrast cultural aspects of groups from different regions of the United States.

Develop Comprehension

Ask:

1. *What is a confederacy?* **L1**

2. *How many tribes were initially in the Iroquois Confederacy?* **L1**

3. *What was the goal of the Iroquois League?* **L1**

4. *How did the Creek protect themselves? Why do you think they were structured that way?* **L3**

> *Show As You Go!* Remind students to return to the unit opener to complete the project using information from this lesson.

Response to Intervention

? **Essential Question**
How does location affect the way people live?

If . . . students cannot give a substantiated response to the Essential Question, "How does location affect the way people live?"

. . . .

Then . . . take students back to pages 62–63 and read about farming in the Eastern Woodlands.

Ask: *How did Native Americans farm in different parts of the Eastern Woodlands? Which farming methods were similar? Which were different?*

Following discussion, allow students to respond to the Essential Question again.

UNIT 2 Wrap Up

Write the name of the tribe in the space provided. Then place the numbers of the tribes in the correct region on the map.

Color in the map key and the corresponding regions on the map.

Key
- ☐ Eastern Woodlands
- ☐ Great Plains
- ☐ Southwest
- ☐ Pacific Northwest

1. This group created a confederacy that is still active today. It is known as the Six Nations. **Iroquois**

2. It is believed that this group is related to the Anasazi. **Pueblo**

3. Lone Dog, a man from this tribe, created a winter count from 1800–1871. **Lakota**

4. These skilled craftworkers lived between Alaska and the present-day Portland Canal in the Pacific Northwest. **Tlingit**

5. Also known as the *Diné*, this tribe was known for being shepherds. **Navajo**

6. The traditional home of this tribe were the islands between Vancouver, British Columbia, and the mainland of Canada. **Kwakiutl**

7. The towns of this tribe were arranged around a large council house called a "chokofa." **Creek**

68

BIG IDEA

Unit Project

Choose a Native American tribe or region you learned about in this unit. Imagine that you have been hired by a museum to create a display about that tribe or region. Draw the layout of your museum exhibit. Before you begin, turn back to pages 32 and 33 to review your illustrations. You may want to use them as part of your display. You should also write a few paragraphs that explain what is in your display, and why. Read the list below to see what you need to include in your display and your writing. As you work, check off each task.

Your museum display should include . . .	Yes, it does!
the name and location of the tribe or region you chose	☐
artifacts from the tribe or region you chose	☐
information about how your tribe or region interacted with their environment	☐
cultural aspects of the tribe or region you chose, including clothing, shelter, food, major beliefs, music, and art	☐
a written summary of what you chose to put in your display	☐

Think about the Big Idea

BIG IDEA Culture influences the way people live.

What did you learn in this unit that helps you understand the BIG IDEA?

69

Wrap Up

Native American Map

Students will complete the map and the map key on the page and use these to complete the statements.

BIG IDEA Unit Project

- Read through the project directions and checklist with students.
- Remind students to use their **Show as You Go** pages to assist them in completing the project.
- To assess the project, refer to the rubric on the following page.
- After students complete their projects, encourage self-reflection

Differentiated Instruction

▶ **Approaching** Students should write an outline for what pieces to include in their museum exhibit. They should draw an exhibit for one group or tribe rather than the region as a whole.

▶ **Beyond** Have students create a pamphlet that contains specific information, details, and facts about their exhibit, displays, or groups included.

▶ **ELL** Encourage students to look back through the unit for key words that describe the artifacts they have included. Allow students to present their exhibit orally rather than in writing.

Response to Intervention

BIG IDEA Culture influences the way people live.

If . . . students cannot give a substantiated explanation of the Big Idea,

Then . . . organize students into pairs. Assign each pair one lesson and have them find examples of how the tribes from different regions lived. Have students present their findings to the other groups in a jigsaw. Be sure to discuss after each presentation.

Following discussion, allow students to respond to the Big Idea again.

net**works**

Additional resources are found at **connected.mcgraw-hill.com**.

- Games
- Assessment
- Group Technology Projects

Name _____ Date _____

Unit 2: Native American Museum Exhibit Rubric

4 Exemplary	3 Accomplished	2 Developing	1 Beginning
The exhibit:	**The exhibit:**	**The exhibit:**	**The exhibit:**
☐ mostly identifies the name and location of the tribe	☐ partially identifies the name and location of the tribe	☐ does not identify the name and location of the tribe	☐ does not include images related to the tribe or region
☐ includes several artifacts that clearly describe the tribe or region	☐ includes at least one artifact that describes the tribe or region	☐ includes one image related to the tribe or region	☐ contains no information about interactions with the environment
☐ contains complete information about how the people interacted with their environment	☐ contains information about interactions with the environment	☐ contains one example of interactions with the environment	☐ does not describe cultural aspects of the tribe or region
☐ clearly describes cultural aspects of the tribe or region	☐ describes cultural aspects of the tribe or region	☐ describes a cultural aspect of the tribe or region	☐ does not have a clearly written summary
☐ includes a clearly written summary of what is in the display and why	☐ includes a written summary	☐ includes a poorly written or incomplete summary	☐ is not interesting to look at
☐ is very interesting to look at and very appealing to visitors	☐ is interesting to look at and appealing to visitors	☐ is somewhat interesting look at	

Grading Comments: _____

_____

_____

_____

_____

_____

_____

_____

Project Score: _____

Read the passage "The Pottery of Nampeyo" before answering Numbers 1 through 8.

The Pottery of Nampeyo

by Elyse Maddox

The Pueblo people live in the American Southwest. In the past, their land stretched into many present-day states, such as Utah, Colorado, California, Arizona, Texas, and New Mexico. The Hopi are a Pueblo people that live in present-day Arizona.

Art has long been an important part of Hopi daily life. The Pueblo are known for their beautiful pottery. Ancient Pueblo pottery often included designs that were tied to nature. Some favorite designs included birds, insects, and water.

One important Hopi potter was a woman named Nampeyo. As a young girl, Nampeyo watched her grandmother make beautiful pottery. Soon, Nampeyo began making her own pottery. In 1895 Nampeyo heard of ancient pottery being uncovered at an archaeological site near her home. When she saw the pottery that had been found there, Nampeyo admired its beauty. She thought the ancient designs were even better than current designs.

At first, Nampeyo used the ancient designs in her work. Later, she created her own designs using the ancient style. Determined to spread interest in the traditional Hopi pottery, Nampeyo taught the skill of pottery making to others. Today, many Hopi potters carry on Nampeyo's work.

1 What is this passage mostly about?

Ⓐ the importance and beauty of Hopi pottery

Ⓑ why traditional pottery is better than modern

Ⓒ the main design elements of Hopi pottery

Ⓓ how archaeologists discover artifacts

2 Read the sentence from the passage.

> When she saw the pottery that had been found there, Nampeyo admired its beauty.

What does the word *admired* mean in this passage?

Ⓕ disliked very much

Ⓖ liked very much

Ⓗ ignored

Ⓘ copied and made your own

3 What happened in 1895?

Ⓐ The Hopi flourished in Arizona.

Ⓑ Nampeyo spread the interest of traditional pottery.

Ⓒ Archaeologists found ancient pottery near Nampeyo's home.

Ⓓ Nampeyo was born.

4 Which two words from the passage have nearly OPPOSITE meanings?

Ⓕ beautiful, nature

Ⓖ ancient, current

Ⓗ favorite, admired

Ⓘ art, pottery

5 Which detail from the passage helps show what influenced Nampeyo to start making pottery?

Ⓐ The Pueblo people lived in the American Southwest.

Ⓑ Today, many Hopi potters carry on Nampeyo's work.

Ⓒ Nampeyo heard of ancient pottery being uncovered at an archaeological site near her home.

Ⓓ As a young girl, Nampeyo watched her grandmother make beautiful pottery.

6 Which of the following was NOT a favorite design item used in Hopi art?

Ⓕ birds

Ⓖ trees

Ⓗ water

Ⓘ insects

7 After Nampeyo saw the ancient pottery found near her home, how did this affect her own pottery designs at first?

Ⓐ She taught others how to make pottery.

Ⓑ She created her own designs using the ancient style.

Ⓒ She copied the designs of the ancient pottery.

Ⓓ She made pottery using current designs.

8 Where do the Hopi traditionally live?

Ⓕ present-day Texas

Ⓖ present-day California

Ⓗ present-day Utah

Ⓘ present-day Arizona

Test Preparation

Test-Taking Tips

Have students use the following steps when comparing and contrasting in a testing situation:

- Read the question and answer choices carefully to learn about the topic. Think about what you know.

- If the question includes other information, find details and clues. This information may be a text passage, a chart, or an image.

- Make connections on how the information is similar to compare.

- Make connections on how the information is different to contrast.

- Identify which answer choice is correct.

Answers

1. A   **CCS RI.2**

2. G   **CCS RI.4**

3. C   **CCS RI.1**

4. G   **CCS RI.4**

5. C   **CCS RI.3**

6. G   **CCS RI.1**

7. C   **CCS RI.3**

8. I   **CCS RI.1**

Teacher Notes

UNIT
3 Planner THE AGE OF EXPLORATION

BIG IDEA 💡 **People's actions affect others.**

Student Portfolio

- *Show As You Go!*
  Use these pages to introduce the Big Idea. Students record information specific to each lesson. They use these pages to help them plan their Big Idea Project.

networks™

- Group Technology Project
  Students use 21st century skills to complete a group extension activity of the unit project. Lesson plans, worksheets, and rubrics are available online.

Student Portfolio

- Big Idea Project
  Students construct a deck of trading cards about the Europeans who explored North and South America. The Big Idea Project rubric is on page 99W.

Vasco Nuñez de Balboa

Reading Skills

Student Portfolio

- Reading Skill: Summarize
  Pages 74–75. Common Core State Standards RI.2

Leveled Readers

Use the leveled reader *Coronado Searches for Cities of Gold!* (lesson plan on pages T22–T23) with Lesson 3.

Treasures Connection

Teach this unit with Treasures Unit 1, *Observing the Night Sky*, pages 72–75 and Unit 5, *Spirit of Endurance*, pages 518–533.

Social Studies Skills

Student Portfolio

- Primary and Secondary Sources: Maps
  Page 79

networks™

- Skill Builders
  Introduce and teach analyzing primary and secondary sources.

Activity Cards

- **Center for Social Studies Skills Investigation**
  Use the center activity cards to help students explore Primary Sources, Geography, and Citizenship.

FOLDABLES®

Student Portfolio

- Students can create vocabulary Foldables right in their portfolios.

- Additional Foldables templates can be found on pages R34–R42 of your Teacher Edition. See page R33 for instructions.

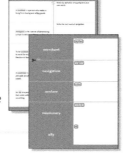

Assessment Solutions

- **McGraw-Hill networks™**
  Safe online testing features multiple question types that are easy to use and editable.

- **Self-Check Quizzes**

- **Worksheets**

UNIT 3 **At a Glance**

Lesson	Essential Question	Vocabulary
1 A Changing World	**Why do people take risks?**	merchant navigation *chart
2 Spanish Exploration and Conquest	**What happens when different cultures meet?**	enslaved *claim missionary
3 French and Dutch Exploration	**What happens when different cultures meet?**	*intent ally

*denotes academic vocabulary

Digital Resources

Go to **connected.mcgraw-hill.com** for additional resources:

- Interactive Whiteboard Lessons

- Worksheets

- Assessment

- Content Library

- Lesson Plans

- Skill Builders

- Videos

- Use Standards Tracker on **networks** to track students' progress.

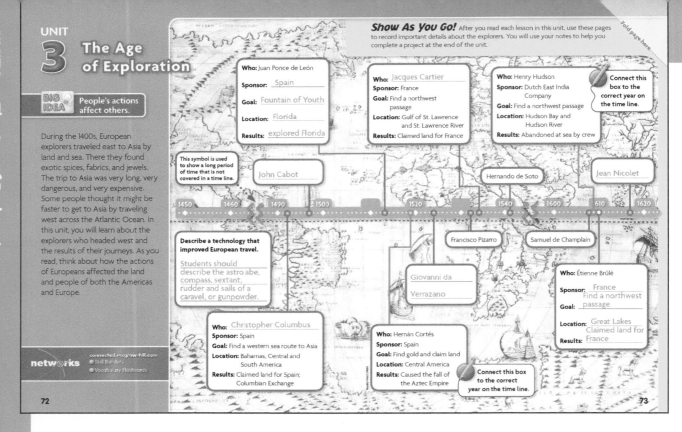

UNIT 3 The Age of Exploration

BIG IDEA People's actions affect others.

During the 1400s, European explorers traveled east to Asia by land and sea. There they found exotic spices, fabrics, and jewels. The trip to Asia was very long, very dangerous, and very expensive. Some people thought it might be faster to get to Asia by traveling west across the Atlantic Ocean. In this unit, you will learn about the explorers who headed west and the results of their journeys. As you read, think about how the actions of Europeans affected the land and people of both the Americas and Europe.

networks connected.mcgraw-hill.com
Skill Builders
Vocabulary Flashcards

Show As You Go! After you read each lesson in this unit, use these pages to record important details about the explorers. You will use your notes to help you complete a project at the end of the unit.

Who: Juan Ponce de León
Sponsor: Spain
Goal: Fountain of Youth
Location: Florida
Results: explored Florida

Who: Jacques Cartier
Sponsor: France
Goal: Find a northwest passage
Location: Gulf of St. Lawrence and St. Lawrence River
Results: Claimed land for France

Who: Henry Hudson
Sponsor: Dutch East India Company
Goal: Find a northwest passage
Location: Hudson Bay and Hudson River
Results: Abandoned at sea by crew

Connect this box to the correct year on the time line.

This symbol is used to show a long period of time that is not covered in a time line.

John Cabot

Hernando de Soto

Jean Nicolet

1450 1460 1490 1500 1520 1540 1600 610 1620

Describe a technology that improved European travel.
Students should describe the astro abe, compass, sextant, rudder and sails of a caravel, or gunpowder.

Francisco Pizarro

Samuel de Champlain

Giovanni da Verrazano

Who: Étienne Brûlé
Sponsor: France
Goal: Find a northwest passage
Location: Great Lakes
Results: Claimed land for France

Who: Christopher Columbus
Sponsor: Spain
Goal: Find a western sea route to Asia
Location: Bahamas, Central and South America
Results: Claimed land for Spain; Columbian Exchange

Who: Hernán Cortés
Sponsor: Spain
Goal: Find gold and claim land
Location: Central America
Results: Caused the fall of the Aztec Empire

Connect this box to the correct year on the time line.

72   73

Introduce the Unit

✓ Diagnostic Assessment

Use a "Fist to Five" survey to gauge students' prior knowledge and misconceptions about European exploration. Have students respond to statements by holding up zero (fist) to five fingers. Displaying a fist means students disagree. Displaying five fingers means they agree.

Say:

1. *Only Great Britain explored in North America.*

2. *Native Americans welcomed all European explorers.*

3. *European exploration began with the search for new lands.*

Student responses will help identify their level of understanding.

Active Teaching

BIG IDEA **People's actions affect others.**
In this unit, students will investigate European exploration. They will use information from each lesson to complete the activities on the Show As You Go pages. Explain to students that at the end of the unit, they will use the information collected on these pages to complete their Big Idea Project. At this point, have students fold the corner of page 73. This will help them flip back to it as needed.

Differentiated Instruction

▶ **Approaching** Provide page numbers where students can find information on specific explorers. After students have identified the required information to complete the time line, allow students to compare answers with a partner.

▶ **Beyond** Have students research 3–4 of the explorers from the time line on the Internet or in the library. Using this information, students should identify additional details about the goals and results of each voyage. They may also find images of the explorers to create flaps that cover boxes on the time line. You may want to share these images with the rest of the class.

▶ **ELL** Provide photocopies of Student Edition pages with information about each explorer. In a group, have students discuss, identify, and highlight information about each explorer. Allow students to copy this information onto the time line or cut and tape it onto the page.

Reading Skill

Summarize

Common Core Standards
RI.2 Determine two or more main ideas of a text and explain how they are supported by key details; summarize the text.

Summarizing is a good way to remember what you read. A summary is a brief statement about the topic of a passage. After you read a paragraph or section in your book, make a summary of it. A summary includes the main ideas of a text. It leaves out minor details and includes only key details.

LEARN IT

To summarize a passage:
- Find its main ideas.
- Include only key details.
- Restate the important points in your summary.

The first people of the Middle Ages to travel to distant regions were the Norse, or "north people," who lived in what are today Denmark, Sweden, and Norway. To gain wealth, they sailed throughout the seas and rivers of Europe trading goods. Some people knew them as Vikings, a Norse word for "raiders."

Around A.D. 1000, Viking explorers were the first Europeans to reach North America. But their settlements there did not last. As a result, the Viking settlements in North America were forgotten for many years.

Detail

Main Idea

TRY IT

Complete the chart. Fill in the top boxes with main ideas and their key details from page 74. Write a summary in the bottom box.

Main Idea and Detail(s)	Main Idea and Detail(s)
Vikings were first Europeans to reach North America. Their settlements did not last.	The Norse were the first in the Middle Ages to travel far distances. They sailed and traded throughout Europe.

Summary

Student summaries should be based on their details.

APPLY IT

- Underline two main ideas. Circle their key details as you read.
- Then summarize the passage on the lines.

In 1095 European soldiers began a long journey to Jerusalem. The city had great religious importance to Jews, Christians, and Muslims. European Christians hoped to capture the city from Muslim Turks who ruled the city at the time. These journeys were called Crusades.

The Crusaders captured Jerusalem but were driven out after about 100 years. Many Europeans returned home with products, such as silk or spices, that were unknown in Europe. Traders soon found that Europeans were willing to pay a lot for these new products such as cotton, pepper, and cinnamon.

74

75

Common Core Standards RI.2 Determine two or more main ideas of a text and explain how they are supported by key details; summarize the text.

Reading Skill

Active Teaching

LEARN IT Summarize

Say: *As I read I think, "What is this about?" Answering this question helps me to find the main idea. Once I know the main idea, I pay attention to sentences that give me more information about the main idea. Those sentences contain key details.*

TRY IT Encourage students to try the modeled strategy above as they complete the **TRY IT** activity.

APPLY IT Have students complete the **APPLY IT** activity.

Ask:

1. *What question should you ask yourself to help you find the main idea?* **L3**
2. *How can you tell which sentences are key details?* **L2**
3. *Why is it important to find the main idea and key details when you are writing a summary?* **L3**

Differentiated Instruction

▶ **Approaching** Review the **LEARN IT** activity as a small group. Do the **TRY IT** activity together. Have students complete the **APPLY IT** activity independently. Regroup to compare and correct.

▶ **Beyond** Have students find a piece of real-world text and write a summary of it. Have them exchange summaries with a partner. Each student should identify the main idea and key details of their partner's summary.

▶ **ELL** Explain the concept of *key details*. Provide an example and discuss. For example, make a statement about something you like to do. Then provide three key details. Ask students to explain how they know you like the thing you described. Encourage them to use the key details in their explanations.

Read the passage one sentence at a time and have students identify key details. List student responses. Then construct the summary as a group.

networks

Go to **connected.mcgraw-hill.com** for additional resources:
- Skill Builders
- Graphic Organizers

Graphic Organizer
Table (Main Idea)

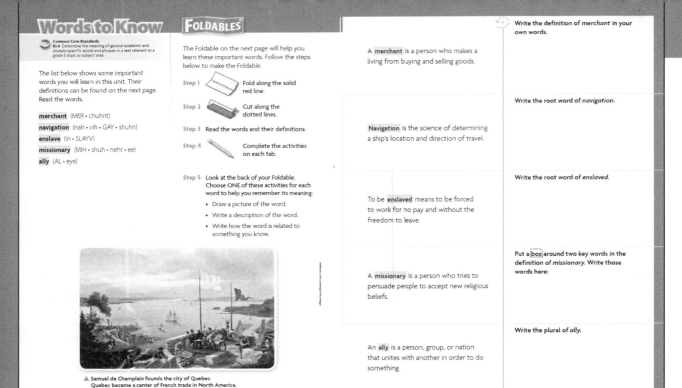

Words to Know

FOLDABLES

Common Core Standards
RI.4 Determine the meaning of general academic and domain-specific words and phrases in a text relevant to a grade 5 topic or subject area.

The list below shows some important words you will learn in this unit. Their definitions can be found on the next page. Read the words.

merchant (MER • chuhnt)
navigation (nah • vih • GAY • shuhn)
enslave (in • SLAYV)
missionary (MIH • shuh • nehr • ee)
ally (AL • eye)

The Foldable on the next page will help you learn these important words. Follow the steps below to make the Foldable.

Step 1 Fold along the solid red line.

Step 2 Cut along the dotted lines.

Step 3 Read the words and their definitions.

Step 4 Complete the activities on each tab.

Step 5 Look at the back of your Foldable. Choose ONE of these activities for each word to help you remember its meaning:
- Draw a picture of the word.
- Write a description of the word.
- Write how the word is related to something you know.

▲ Samuel de Champlain founds the city of Quebec. Quebec became a center of French trade in North America.

76

A **merchant** is a person who makes a living from buying and selling goods.

Write the definition of *merchant* in your own words.

Navigation is the science of determining a ship's location and direction of travel.

Write the root word of *navigation*.

To be **enslaved** means to be forced to work for no pay and without the freedom to leave.

Write the root word of *enslaved*.

A **missionary** is a person who tries to persuade people to accept new religious beliefs.

Put a box around two key words in the definition of *missionary*. Write those words here:

An **ally** is a person, group, or nation that unites with another in order to do something.

Write the plural of *ally*.

Common Core Standards **RI.4** Determine the meaning of general academic and domain-specific words and phrases in a text relevant to a grade 5 topic or subject area.

Words to Know
Active Teaching

FOLDABLES

1. Go to connected.mcgraw-hill.com for flashcards to introduce the unit vocabulary to students.

2. Read the words on the list on page 76 and have students repeat them after you.

3. Guide students as they complete steps 1 through 5 of the Foldable.

4. Have students use the Foldable to practice the vocabulary words independently or with a partner.

networks

Go to connected.mcgraw-hill.com for additional resources:
- Vocabulary Flashcards
- Vocabulary Games
- Graphic Organizers

GO Vocabulary!
Use a word web graphic organizer such as the one shown below to help students gain a deeper understanding of the unit vocabulary. For each term, have students brainstorm other words that relate to the term. Have them complete their graphic organizer with different words from the unit.

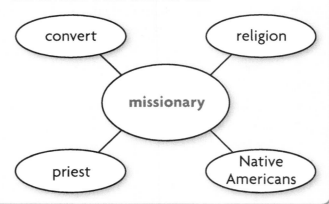

merchant

merchant

navigation

navigation

enslave

enslave

missionary

missionary

ally

ally

Primary and Secondary Sources

Maps

Maps help us examine and understand the geography of a specific area. A map can be a primary source or a secondary source.

If a map was created and used by someone in the past, it is a primary source. Primary source maps show us where people lived and how they saw their world. We also use these maps to learn how people in the past interacted with the geography of an area.

If a map was created and used after the time period it shows, then it is a secondary source. These maps are often called historical maps. They help us understand how the geography of an area influenced people or events in the past.

Spanish Exploration Routes

NORTH AMERICA
ATLANTIC OCEAN
NEW SPAIN
Gulf of Mexico
Bahama Islands
Cuba
Jamaica
Hispaniola
Puerto Rico
PACIFIC OCEAN
Caribbean Sea
CENTRAL AMERICA
SOUTH AMERICA

Lands claimed by 1575
Routes of Exploration
Ponce de León, 1513
Cabeza de Vaca, 1529–1536
de Soto, 1539–1542
Coronado, 1540–1542

0   250   500 miles
0   250   500 kilometers

DBQ Document-Based Questions

Examine the map to answer the questions and complete the activities.

1. Circle one answer to complete the sentence.
   This map is a _____.
   primary source   (secondary source)

2. What events are shown on this map?
   Exploration by the Spanish.

3. How did the early explorers travel? Why?
   Students should support answers
   with sound reasoning.

networks
There's More Online!
• Skill Builders
• Resource Library

79

Differentiated Instruction

▶ **ELL** Have students create a Concept Circle for vocabulary. Ask students to assign a title to their circle and place four related vocabulary words inside it. Have students explain why they chose each word.

Ask: *Why is each of these words related to your title? Could other words have been placed in one of the four sections of the circle?*

WORD PLAY

Play Vocabulary Baseball!

1. Divide the class into two teams.

2. Push the desks to the sides of the room. Set up first, second, and third bases, as well as home plate.

3. Have student take turns "at bat." They must give the correct definition when given a word, state the correct word when given a definition, or supply the correct word for a close-type sentence.

4. Students advance one base with each correct answer.

5. The first team to score 10 runs wins.

Primary and Secondary Sources
Active Teaching

Begin by discussing maps.

Ask: *What is the purpose of a map? Have you ever used a map? When do you use them and why?*

Explain to students that there are many types of maps. In this book, they will use historical maps to learn about United States history. Studying these maps will help them understand how geography influenced the development of our nation.

Develop Comprehension

1. *Is this map a primary or secondary source? How do you know?* **L2**

2. *What does this map tell you about early exploration? Explain.* **L3**

networks

Go to **connected.mcgraw-hill.com** for additional resources:

• Skill Builders

• Resource Library

Lesson 1

A Changing World

? Essential Question

Why do people take risks?
What do you think?

A small number of people have traveled into space. Some have even walked on the moon. But for most people, space is the "great unknown."

THINK • PAIR • SHARE

Imagine you are going to travel into space. Discuss with a partner what you know about space travel. What dangers might you face? What skills, knowledge, and supplies would you need for the trip?

List three items you would need in space and explain the importance of each.

Item you would bring	Reason for bringing it along

Words To Know

Find the definition for each word and write a synonym on the line. A synonym is a word that has the same or almost the same meaning.

merchant _____

navigation _____

*chart _____

Just as space is unknown to you, the oceans were the "great unknown" to Europeans in the 1400s. The idea of traveling too far in any direction scared them. Sailors told tales of mermaids, pirates, sea monsters, and ships sailing right off the edge of the world! Soon, though, Europeans would travel farther than they ever had by sea. Using tools new to them would make Europeans able to explore the unknown.

80

New Trade Routes

European **merchants** were willing to risk everything for the chance to make money. Merchants are people who make their living buying and selling goods. Chinese traders brought goods to western Asia along a trade route called the Silk Road. Here they met European merchants who purchased these goods and then sold them in Europe.

The Silk Road was protected by the Mongolian Empire. In the 1400s, this empire collapsed. Suddenly traveling on the Silk Road became dangerous, and Asian goods became expensive.

Europeans tried new trade routes through the Middle East and in Africa. But Arab merchants controlled these areas and charged high prices for their goods. Europeans found themselves in a tough position. If only there was an easier, faster, and less expensive way to get the goods they wanted!

Trade Routes of the Ancient World

Map and Globe Skills

1. What waterway connected Asian trade routes with Europe?

   Mediterranean Sea

2. Circle the area on the map from which Europeans received silk.

81

Lesson 1

Activate Prior Knowledge

As students complete their charts on page 80, monitor their discussions. Be sure they are staying on topic.

Ask: _Have you ever traveled to a new place? Once you got there, was it different from what you expected?_ **L3**

? **Essential Question** **Why do people take risks?**

Have students explain what they understand about the Essential Question. Explain that everything they learn in this lesson will help them understand the Essential Question better. Remind them to think about how the Essential Question connects to the unit Big Idea: people's actions affect others.

More About Medieval Europe

- In Medieval Europe, a large peasant class lived in cramped, filthy cities. This helped spread the bubonic plague, also known as the "Black Death."
- The smaller upper-classes, who could afford to leave the cities, escaped the plague by moving to the countryside.
- An estimated 200 million people died during the plague. In some countries, 50–80% of the population died.
- The decrease in population caused a shift in the economy. Over time, a large middle class grew, giving bankers, merchants, and tradespeople new customers. This led to the demand for new goods and eventually the Age of Exploration.

Active Teaching

Words To Know After completing the activity, have students compare their lists of synonyms with a partner.

Ask: _How does your list of synonyms compare to your partner's? Are there any major differences?_ **L3**

Have students share their synonyms aloud. Compile a list of synonyms for each word. As students share, discuss the meaning of each and decide as a class if the synonym fits.

Develop Comprehension
Ask:

1. _Why were European merchants willing to risk traveling into dangerous areas?_ (They sold the goods for big profits in Europe.) **L2**

2. _How did trade with Europeans benefit Asian and Middle Eastern traders?_ (Europeans paid a lot for their goods.) **L2**

Map and Globe Skills

Ask students additional questions about the map to encourage further study. **Ask:** _Can you think of another way for Europeans to get to Asia? What items did both India and East Africa trade?_ (cloth, ivory, and spices)

Exploring the Oceans

Europeans still wanted goods from Asia. But they had to find another way to get them. In the 1400s, they turned to the seas. One man did much to encourage travelers to try new routes.

Portugal Sails South

Portugal is a small country on Europe's Atlantic coast. It is close to Africa. In the 1400s, Portugal's enemies controlled land routes to Asia. Portugal's traders had no easy way to get there.

Portugal's leaders and merchants wanted to grow their country's wealth through trade. Prince Henry of Portugal didn't believe the legends about monsters and other dangers lurking in the ocean. He wanted Portuguese ships to sail south along Africa to get to Asia. This route was not well known to European sailors, but Henry encouraged them.

Portuguese sailors were successful in sailing the coasts of Africa, and Portugal grew into a major power. It wasn't alone it its desire to explore. Other European powers wanted to find new routes to Asia as well. The age of exploration had begun.

▲ Prince Henry of Portugal

Primary and Secondary Sources

For centuries, people told tales of Prince Henry's "school for sailors." They did this to explain Portugal's sudden success. Recently, historians have shown that no such school existed. Yet we have paintings of it! How can this be? The paintings, like the one shown, were secondary sources.

How does this story show why it's important to use more than one source when studying history?

Example response: Because

one source may be wrong or

inaccurate.

LAPIS POLARIS MAGNES

82

Improving Navigation

People don't just trade goods. They also trade knowledge, tools, and ideas. **Navigation** tools from other cultures made European exploration possible. Navigation is the science of getting ships from place to place. To navigate, sailors first had to know where they were. Then they had to know which direction to go.

Underline what the astrolabe does and circle what the compass does.

The Astrolabe

In the 1100s, Europeans learned about the astrolabe from Arab traders. This tool <u>measures the height of the stars in the sky.</u> The measurement from the astrolabe was used with a **chart** of the stars. With these two items, sailors could find the ship's latitude. Remember, latitude is a location north or south of the Equator.

An astrolabe ▼

Orienteering Compass

To find where they were going, Europeans used an ancient Chinese invention. The orienteering compass shows the direction of travel. It helps sailors orient, or position, their ships.

Compasses have a magnetic arrow that aligns itself with Earth's magnetic poles. The compass allowed sailors to easily find north and south, so they could turn their ship in the direction they wanted to go.

GLUE FOLDABLE HERE

The Sextant

The astrolabe and compass were important navigation tools for about 300 years. With them, sailors could find direction and latitude. But measuring longitude, or the distance east or west of the Prime Meridian, was still impossible.

That changed in 1759 when John Bird invented the sextant. This tool uses two mirrors and a movable arm to precisely measure the angles of stars in the sky. This was an important piece to the puzzle of how to measure longitude. With the help of the sextant, navigation and mapmaking became more accurate. In fact, sextants are still used today!

▲ The sextant allowed sailors to find their exact longitude.

How did new tools improve navigation?

They made it easier for sailors to

find their location and direction.

83

Primary and Secondary Sources

Engage students in a discussion about why differentiating primary and secondary sources is important to studying history.

Differentiated Instruction

▶ **Approaching** Students may struggle with locating the key details for each invention. Work with a small group and use a graphic organizer to allow students to organize key details. As they work, have them underline or circle these details as directed in the Student Edition.

▶ **Beyond** Have students use a Venn diagram to compare and contrast two of the travel improvements.

▶ **ELL** Work with these words: *direction, location, navigation,* and *invention.* Define each word and discuss its meaning. Explain that *direction* and *location* are part of *navigation.* Show that these inventions made finding direction and location easier.

Active Teaching

Develop Comprehension
Ask:

1. *Explain how the astrolabe and compass worked together to help sailors navigate ships.* (They used the astrolabe to find how far north or south they were of the Equator. This helped them know which direction they needed to go. They used the compass to make sure they traveled in the right direction.) **L3**

2. *Explain how the sextant and astrolabe differ.* **L2**

Page Power

FOLDABLES Interact more with the page. Have students create a Notebook Foldable to assist them in developing their understanding of navigation technology.

1. Provide each student with a copy of Foldable 3A from the section at the back of this book.

2. Have students construct the Foldable and glue its anchor tab to the left of the images on page 83.

3. Have students find and paste or draw their own images of each tool on each flap of their Foldable.

4. On the inside of the Foldable, have students write key words that relate to each piece of technology.

Seaworthy Ships

Sailors now had better tools with which to navigate, but they also needed better ships. They wanted ships to be faster, safer, and easier to control. Sailors also needed more space to store supplies and goods to trade.

Stern Rudder

Navigation tools helped sailors identify their location and the direction they were traveling. But European sailors also needed to be able to steer their ships. The Chinese used an <u>oar that hung off the stern, or back of the boat,</u> to control the direction of a ship. Eventually these "rudders" became a common part of ships. This addition made steering much easier.

The Caravel

The stern rudder helped control a ship, but sailing still wasn't perfect. Sailors needed to be able to catch more wind so they could travel faster. In the late 1400s, the Portuguese developed the caravel. This type of ship had <u>rectangular sails on the front and middle masts. The sail in the middle of the ship was largest and captured a lot of wind,</u> propelling the ship forward. <u>A triangular sail on the stern worked with the rudder to help steer the ship.</u>

Caravels were better in other ways too. They had more room for cargo than earlier ships. They also had flatter bottoms and could float in shallow water. Sailors now could get closer to land to repair ships and make more accurate maps of coastlines.

A stern rudder ▲

Reading Skill

Explain Relationships

Explain how the stern rudder and larger sails made ships more seaworthy.

They made the ships
faster and easier to steer.

Reading Skill
Key Details

<u>Underline</u> the details in the text which describe the sails and rudder on the caravel. Use these details to draw the sails and (circle) the rudder on the ship.

DID YOU KNOW?
One more Chinese invention made European exploration possible: gunpowder. Ship's cannons and explorer's guns were used to protect sailors and conquer peoples. When lit, gunpowder made these weapons fire.

Lesson 1

? Essential Question Why do people take risks?

_____
_____
_____
_____

Go back to *Show As You Go!* on pages 72–73.

networks There's More Online!
• Games • Assessment

84

85

Lesson 1

Active Teaching

Before students read, explain that once sailors had better navigation tools they focused on improving ships. They needed to be able to travel faster, steer easier, and be away from home longer.

> *Show As You Go!* Remind students to go back to the Unit Opener and complete the activities for this lesson.

Differentiated Instruction

▶ **ELL** Review shape words with students. Have them create a guide for the shapes including a picture and labels. Be sure to discuss the suffix –ar.

Reading Skills

Common Core Standards RI.3 Explain the relationships or interactions between two or more individuals, events, ideas, or concepts in a historical, scientific, or technical text based on specific information in the text.

Explain Relationships Have students discuss the role that each development played in operating the ship. Ask: Which invention helped sailors change direction? Which one helped drive the ship forward? Did either development do both?

Reading Skills

Common Core Standards RI.2 Determine two or more main ideas of a text and explain how they are supported by key details; summarize the text.

Once students have completed the activity in their student edition, have them identify and highlight the main idea that each key detail supports.

Response to Intervention

? Essential Question **Why do people take risks?**

If . . . students cannot give a substantiated response to the Essential Question,

. . . .

Then . . . take them back to page 81. Discuss how the content relates to the Essential Question.
Ask: *Why did early merchants and traders take risks? What were the benefits?*

Following discussion, allow students to respond to the Essential Question again.

Spanish Exploration and Conquest

Essential Question

What happens when different cultures meet?

What do you think?

_____

_____

_____

_____

_____

_____

_____

_____

Sailing South and West

Recall that sailors from Portugal were looking for southern water routes to Asia. In 1488 Bartolomeu Dias sailed around Africa's southern tip! He was the first European to do this. Vasco de Gama was another Portuguese explorer. He sailed around Africa all the way to India 10 years later. The voyage south around Africa to Asia took about a year.

Christopher Columbus

An Italian named Christopher Columbus thought sailing west would save time. In August 1492, the king and queen of Spain agreed to pay for the voyage. Two months later, Columbus and his crew sighted land. He believed they had reached the Indies islands in Asia. But they had not. They had landed on an island in North America.

Voyages of Columbus, 1492–1502

NORTH AMERICA
Bahama Islands
San Salvador
Gulf of Mexico
Cuba
Hispaniola
Puerto Rico
Jamaica
ATLANTIC OCEAN
Caribbean Sea
CENTRAL AMERICA
SOUTH AMERICA

— First voyage, 1492
— Second voyage, 1493
— Third voyage, 1498
— Fourth voyage, 1502
Present-day names
Scale varies with perspective

Map and Globe Skills

1. Circle the island where Columbus first landed.

2. On which voyage did Columbus sail along the coast of Central America? _____

   during his fourth voyage

Words To Know

Write another form of each word.

enslaved _____

*claim _____

missionary _____

86

The Columbian Exchange

Columbus called the people who lived on the island "Indios." This is the Spanish word for "Indians." However, the people already had a name—the Taíno.

The Taíno and Columbus offered gifts to each other. Columbus's men explored the island and found plants that they had never seen before. Columbus took the gifts from the Taíno and many plants with him back to Spain. These items excited the king and queen, who sent him back for more. This was the beginning of the Columbian Exchange, or the movement of people, plants, animals, and diseases across the Atlantic Ocean.

New foods from the Americas, such as corn, tomatoes, and potatoes, made European diets healthier. The exchange also introduced European foods and animals to the Americas. Horses changed the way Native Americans hunted. Sheep's wool brought changes to the clothing worn by some people. Unfortunately, Europeans and their animals also brought germs and diseases that were unknown in the Americas. Smallpox, measles, and other diseases from Europe spread quickly. By 1600, millions of native peoples across the Americas had died from those diseases.

DID YOU KNOW?

The Columbian Exchange included a trade in people. Africans and Native Americans were captured and **enslaved**. To be enslaved means to be forced to work for no pay. Traders brought enslaved people to Europe and the Americas.

Chart and Graph Skills

The lists below show items that crossed the Atlantic Ocean. Circle the items that were used for travel. Underline items that were used for food. Put a dot next to items that were used for clothing.

To the Americas:		To Europe:
wheat	goats	tomatoes
bananas	colonists	pineapples
oranges	enslaved Africans	sweet potatoes
horses	onions	hummingbirds
cattle	melons	squirrels
wheels	peaches	enslaved people
honey bees	pigs	potatoes
rice	plows	corn
sugar	diseases	turkeys
coffee	• sheep	diseases

87

Lesson 2

Activate Prior Knowledge

Essential Question
What happens when different cultures meet?

Have students explain what they understand about the Essential Question. Discuss their responses. Explain that everything they learn in this lesson will help them understand the Essential Question better. Remind them to think about how the Essential Question connects to the unit Big Idea: people's actions affect others.

Active Teaching

Words To Know Review suffixes before students complete the activity. Generate a list of as many versions of *missionary* as possible. Have students check a dictionary to make sure their conjugated versions are actually words.

Develop Comprehension

Ask:

1. *Dias and Da Gama were from which country?* **L1**

2. *What was Columbus's motivation for exploring?* **L2**

3. *How did the Columbian Exchange benefit both Europeans and Native Americans?* **L3**

4. *How did it harm both sides?* (Harmful diseases spread to both sides.) **L3**

Clarify Misconceptions

Students may think that the Europeans actually "discovered" the Americas. Explain that native peoples lived in North and South America for thousands of years prior to the arrival of Europeans.

Map and Globe Skill

Students may comment on the round shape of the map. Use this as an opportunity to discuss distortion.

Chart and Graph Skills

Students should use their own judgment to determine whether items not called out in the text were used for travel, food, or clothing. If a student's choice seems odd or implausible, give them an opportunity to explain their reasoning.

The Aztec Empire

Other Spanish explorers came to the Americas after Columbus. If you asked these explorers in 1520 to name the greatest city in the world, chances are that many of them would have said Tenochtitlán. This large city was the capital of the Aztec Empire. Many millions of people lived in the Aztec Empire. Its territory included much of what is now Mexico.

Hernán Cortés was one of these explorers. In 1519 he landed in Central America with more than 500 conquistadors, or Spanish conquerors. The Spanish explorers were very impressed with the city's size, its huge population, riches, and architecture. Native Americans had never seen white skin. They had never heard guns fire. They had never seen horses.

Montezuma II, the Aztec ruler, welcomed the Spanish explorers. But then, Cortés took Montezuma prisoner and demanded gold for the king's freedom. The Aztec refused and drove the Spanish away. Unfortunately, Montezuma was killed in the violence. Later, smallpox killed tens of thousands of Aztec. Cortés came back to destroy Tenochtitlán.

Draw your own graphic novel of the interaction explained above between the Spanish and the Aztec. Make sure to include a title.

The Inca Empire

The Spaniards wanted more gold, so they headed south. They didn't know that the Inca Empire ruled much of South America. It extended more than 2,500 miles along the Pacific coast.

Inca leaders didn't worry when they heard about the Spaniards' arrival. They were busy with their own problems. The Inca Empire was collapsing. It was being torn apart by civil war. Diseases from Central America hurt the empire as well. These diseases spread quickly along a system of stone roads that connected cities within the empire.

In 1532, Francisco Pizarro landed on South America's west coast. He had 168 men and 30 horses with him. They attacked a large Inca city, killing thousands. Pizarro and his men also captured the Inca ruler Atahualpa.

The Inca offered Pizarro a room filled with treasure in exchange for Atahualpa's life. For months gold and silver objects arrived from all over the empire. When the room was filled, Pizarro killed Atahualpa. Then the conquistadors melted the gold and silver items into coins or bars and sent them to Spain.

Aztec and Inca Empires, 1519

Map and Globe Skills

1. Label the Aztec and Inca empires and fill in the map key.

2. Which empire covers these coordinates? 20°S, 70°W

Inca

Reading Skill

Summarize

In the Headlines Write a short description of each event from the point of view of the Spanish, the Aztec, and the Inca.

Fall of the Aztec	Fall of the Inca
Spanish Description:	Spanish Description:
Aztec Description:	Inca Description:

88

89

Lesson 2

Active Teaching

Students may be unfamiliar with graphic novels. Explain that you read a graphic novel just like a comic strip: from left to right, then down the page.

Develop Comprehension

Ask:

1. *What were the Spanish looking for when they arrived in Central and South America?* **L1**

2. *Compare and contrast Cortés and Pizarro.* **L3**

3. *Explain how the Aztec and Inca were affected by the arrival of the Spanish.* **L3**

Use the leveled reader, *The End of an Empire*, to extend and enrich students' understanding of Spanish conquest of the Aztec Empire. A lesson plan for this leveled reader can be found on pages T24 and T25 at the front of this Teacher Edition.

Reading Skill

Common Core Standards RI.2 Determine two or more main ideas of a text and explain how they are supported by key details; summarize the text.

Summarize In order to summarize the events and write headlines, students will have to combine what they know with what they can infer about the various perspectives.

Differentiated Instruction

▶ **Approaching** Tell students the story of Cortés and the Aztec. As you tell the story, allow them to number the boxes showing the order of events. Students should work together to analyze the story and complete the graphic novel.

▶ **Beyond** Have students create a graphic novel to tell the story of Pizarro and the Inca.

▶ **ELL** Tell students the story of Cortés and the Aztec. As you tell the story, have students write a few key words to describe the events of each box. For example: the Spanish scare the Aztec.

Map and Globe Skill

Have students practice using latitude and longitude by having them find the approximate coordinates of the Aztec Empire.

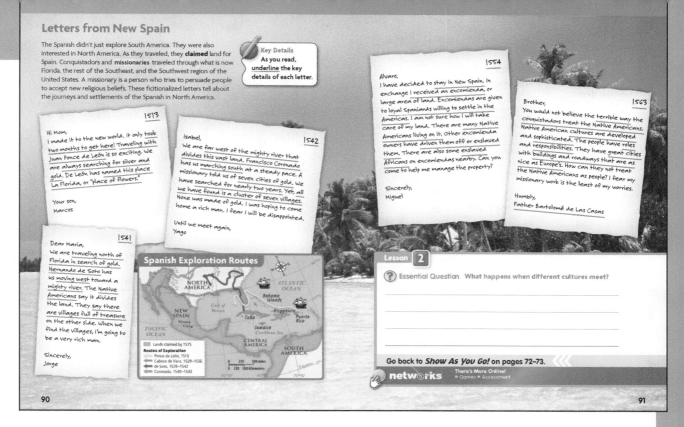

Letters from New Spain

The Spanish didn't just explore South America. They were also interested in North America. As they traveled, they **claimed** land for Spain. Conquistadors and **missionaries** traveled through what is now Florida, the rest of the Southeast, and the Southwest region of the United States. A missionary is a person who tries to persuade people to accept new religious beliefs. These fictionalized letters tell about the journeys and settlements of the Spanish in North America.

Key Details As you read, underline the key details of each letter.

1513

Hi Mom,
I made it to the new world. it only took two months to get here! Traveling with Juan Ponce de León is so exciting. We are always searching for silver and gold. De León has named this place La Florida, or "place of flowers."

Your son,
Marcos

1541

Dear Maria,
We are traveling north of Florida in search of gold. Hernando de Soto has us moving west toward a mighty river. The Native Americans say it divides the land. They say there are villages full of treasure on the other side. When we find the villages, I'm going to be a very rich man.

Sincerely,
Jorge

Isabel,

1542

We are far west of the mighty river that divides this vast land. Francisco Coronado has us marching south at a steady pace. A missionary told us of seven cities of gold. We have searched for nearly two years. Yet, all we have found is a cluster of seven villages. None was made of gold. I was hoping to come home a rich man. I fear I will be disappointed.

Until we meet again,
Yago

Alvaro,

1554

I have decided to stay in New Spain. In exchange I received an encomienda, or large area of land. Encomiendas are given to loyal Spaniards willing to settle in the Americas. I am not sure how I will take care of my land. There are many Native Americans living on it. Other encomienda owners have driven them off or enslaved them. There are also some enslaved Africans on encomiendas nearby. Can you come to help me manage the property?

Sincerely,
Miguel

Brother,

1563

You would not believe the terrible way the conquistadors treat the Native Americans. Native American cultures are developed and sophisticated. The people have roles and responsibilities. They have great cities with buildings and roadways that are as nice as Europe's. How can they not treat the Native Americans as people? I fear my missionary work is the least of my worries.

Humbly,
Father Bartolomé de Las Casas

Spanish Exploration Routes

NORTH AMERICA
ATLANTIC OCEAN
Bahama Islands
NEW SPAIN
Mexico City
Gulf of Mexico
Cuba
Hispaniola
Puerto Rico
Jamaica
Caribbean Sea
PACIFIC OCEAN
CENTRAL AMERICA
SOUTH AMERICA

☐ Lands claimed by 1575
Routes of Exploration
◀── Ponce de León, 1513
◀── Cabeza de Vaca, 1529–1536
◀── de Soto, 1539–1542
◀── Coronado, 1540–1542

0   250   500 miles
0   250   500 kilometers

Lesson 2

? Essential Question What happens when different cultures meet?

_____
_____
_____
_____

Go back to **Show As You Go!** on pages 72–73. ◀◀◀

netw⊙rks There's More Online!
• Games • Assessment

90   91

Active Teaching

Explain to students that this page contains secondary sources written to help them learn about New Spain. These letters show the perspectives of five different men. Three letters describe the travels of men traveling with specific conquistadors. One letter outlines the experience of a Spanish settler. The last letter shows the perspective of a Spanish missionary.

> **Show As You Go!** Remind students to go back to the Unit Opener to complete the activities for this lesson.

Page Power

Interact more with the page. Have students:

• draw an arrow from each letter on page 90 to the explorer's route on the map described by the letter.

• number each letter 1–5 according to the date in which it was written.

Response to Intervention

? Essential Question
What happens when different cultures meet?

If . . . students cannot give a substantiated response to the Essential Question,

. . . .

Then . . . take them back through the lesson. Highlight examples of Spanish and Native American interactions. Discuss how the content relates to the Essential Question.
Ask: _What happened when the Spanish conquistadors met Native Americans?_

Following discussion, allow students to respond to the Essential Question again.

netw⊙rks

Go to **connected.mcgraw-hill.com** for additional resources:

• Interactive Whiteboard Lessons
• Worksheets
• Assessment
• Skill Builders

French and Dutch Exploration

networks There's More Online!
Content Library Videos

Essential Question
What happens when different cultures meet?
What do you think?

_____

_____

_____

_____

_____

_____

Words To Know
Write the definition of each word in your own words.

*intent

_____

_____

ally

_____

_____

_____

Searching for the Northwest Passage

Have you ever used a shortcut to get somewhere fast? Christopher Columbus's **intent** was to find a shortcut to Asia. Instead, he found two large continents! Still, many people believed there must be a shortcut through North America to the Pacific Ocean. They called this waterway the Northwest Passage. Locating and controlling this shortcut would lead to huge profits. The race was on!

English Exploration

John Cabot, an Italian, was one of the first to search for the Northwest Passage. He sailed for England in 1497 and landed on what is now Newfoundland, an island off the coast of Canada. Cabot searched for the passage as he sailed south along the coast.

He didn't find a shortcut. Instead he found an area of the Atlantic Ocean crowded with fish! Sailors scooped them into baskets dropped from the sides of their ships. Colonists who moved to the area built a fishing industry that exported, or sent, dried fish to Europe. Fishing is still important to the economy of this area today.

After Cabot's voyage, England became more concerned with wars at home. Their exploration of North America ended for a long time. When English sailors returned to the continent, they focused on building settlements.

▲ John Cabot

Reading Skill
Key Details Underline the nationalities, dates of travel, and sponsoring country for each explorer.

French Exploration

Another Italian, Giovanni da Verrazano, sailed for the French in 1525. He went from what is now North Carolina north to the mouth of the Hudson River.

Frenchman Jacques Cartier set out in 1535 as well. He traveled around Newfoundland and the Gulf of St. Lawrence. During two other trips he traveled down the St. Lawrence River.

Dutch Exploration

Englishman Henry Hudson sailed south from what is now Maine along the coast of North America in 1609. The Dutch East India Company paid for his voyage. This group of merchants worked together to pay the costs of the voyage in hopes of making money from it.

A second trip in 1610 took Hudson farther north. As winter set in, the ship froze in ice. It was stuck! When spring came, Hudson tried to continue exploring. Tired, hungry, and ready to go home, the crew took over the ship. Hudson, his son, and eight loyal crew were placed on a boat, left behind, and were never seen again.

◄ Giovanni da Verrazano (top), Jacques Cartier (middle), Henry Hudson (bottom)

Map and Globe Skills
How many miles did Verrazano sail up the North American coast?

about 1500 miles

The Search for a Northwest Passage

NORTH AMERICA

Quebec
Montreal
St. Lawrence River
Newfoundland
from England
from England
New Amsterdam (New York)
Plymouth
Atlantic Ocean
Jamestown
Roanoke
from France

Cabot (1497)
Verrazano (1524)
Cartier (1534)
Hudson (1609)
Hudson (1610–1611)
Settlement

0 150 300 miles
0 150 300 kilometers

92

93

Lesson 3

Activate Prior Knowledge

Read aloud these names one at a time: John Cabot, Giovanni de Verrazano, Jacques Cartier, Henry Hudson.

Students should indicate familiarity with each explorer by holding up 1 to 3 fingers.

1 = I know very little about this explorer.

2 = I know some about this explorer.

3 = I know a lot about this explorer.

Student responses will help identify their level of understanding.

Essential Question
What happens when different cultures meet?

Have students explain what they understand about the Essential Question. Discuss their responses. Explain that everything they learn in this lesson will help them understand the Essential Question better. Remind them to think about how the Essential Question connects to the unit Big Idea: people's actions affect others.

Map and Globe Skills

Make sure students know only to measure the length of Verrazano's travels along the coast. They should not include the length of his voyage from France to North America.

Active Teaching

Words To Know Once students have completed the activity, have them share their definitions with the class. Then, based on the definitions students have provided, have students brainstorm examples and non-examples of each word.

Develop Comprehension

The English, French, and Dutch focused their exploration in North America on the search for the Northwest Passage.

Ask:

1. Which explorers sailed for France? **L1**

2. What is a merchant company? **L1**

3. How did weather affect the exploration of Henry Hudson? **L2**

Reading Skill

Common Core Standards RI.2 Determine two or more main ideas of a text and explain how they are supported by key details; summarize the text.

Key Details Students should complete the activity for the paragraphs labeled English, French, and Dutch exploration.

New France

Jacques Cartier claimed the land near the St. Lawrence River for France in 1534. For more than 60 years, France paid little attention to the colony. Then, in 1608, King Henry IV sent Samuel de Champlain to New France as its governor. Champlain built a permanent settlement and fur-trading post called Quebec.

Fur coats and hats were very popular in Europe. Champlain knew that if he managed the colony well, he would make a lot of money. To make it work, he became an **ally**, or political and military partner, with Native Americans in the area. The French provided guns to these allies in exchange for fur, crops, and other goods.

> Write a caption for the picture of Champlain in New France.
>
> _____
>
> _____

Career Opportunities

With the fur trade booming, people rushed to New France with hopes of making a fortune as hunters and trappers. They lived with Native Americans, learned their languages and hunting techniques, and earned their friendship. In exchange, Native Americans received weapons, tools, and money.

French officials feared there were too many hunters exporting fur to Europe. This would lower the price of fur and cause a loss of profit. To control prices, the French government limited the number of people allowed to trap and trade fur in New France.

People who trapped for fur without a permit in New France were known as coureurs de bois, or "runners of the woods." ▼

Reading Skill
Key Details <u>Underline</u> the interactions between Native Americans and the people of New France.

Slow Growth

The French king expanded the colony. He encouraged more people to settle there. He wanted New France to be a Catholic colony. But many people leaving France weren't Catholic and were fleeing religious persecution. They settled in England's colonies, instead.

New France grew slowly because of this. So slowly, in fact, that Native Americans and French colonists didn't compete for land for many years. This helped the French and native peoples build strong alliances at the time.

French Missionaries

French missionaries traveled deep into Native American lands. French missionaries had come to convert the Native Americans, but they didn't try to change native customs. Instead, missionaries lived among Native Americans, learned their languages, and respected their ways.

The Great Lakes

While their fur trade grew, French explorers continued to look for the Northwest Passage. Étienne Brûlé searched for it in 1610. He didn't find the Northwest Passage. But did he became the first European to see Lakes Ontario, Erie, Huron, and Superior.

Seven years later, Jean Nicolet pushed farther west than Brûlé. He became the first European to reach Lake Michigan. Both Brûlé and Nicolet lived with and learned from Native Americans while exploring.

The Great Lakes

> Compare and contrast the interactions of the Spanish and French with Native Americans using the diagram below. Hint: You will have to flip back to pages 86–91 to find information about Spain.

Spanish Interactions
Students should note that they were generally conquerors or adversaries.

In Common
They exchanged items. The Europeans tried to convert Native Americans.

French Interactions
Students should note that they were generally allies or friendly.

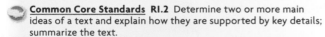

Active Teaching

Life in New France was very different from that in New Spain.

Develop Comprehension

Ask:

1. _How did the French interact with Native Americans?_ **L2**
2. _The economy of New France was based mostly on what good?_ **L1**
3. _What waterway was explored by the French?_ **L1**

Reading Skill

Common Core Standards RI.2 Determine two or more main ideas of a text and explain how they are supported by key details; summarize the text.

Key Details Lead the class in a discussion of whether the interactions they underlined were positive or negative.

Differentiated Instruction

▶ **Approaching** Ask students to find two differences and one similarity to compare and contrast French and Spanish interactions with Native Americans.

▶ **Beyond** Provide a three-way Venn diagram for students to compare and contrast Dutch, French, and Spanish interactions with Native Americans.

▶ **ELL** Discuss these words with students:

- _founding_ = to begin or create
- _career_ = a job
- _interact_ = to talk or do things with others

Have students find one example of each of these ideas for the Spanish and French. Discuss and add each example to the Venn diagram on page 95.

Chart and Graph Skills

Once students have completed the activity, have them write additional details about the geographic locations of the interactions. Students should note that Spanish interactions with Native Americans took place much farther south than French interactions.

New Netherland

While the French settled along the St. Lawrence River, the Dutch settled along the Hudson River. Captain Henry Hudson explored this area for the Netherlands. The newspaper clipping tells about the colony.

Reading Skill

Summarize
Read the newspaper article. Then, write a headline that summarizes the main idea.

FUN FACTS
At this time, 60 Dutch guilders were equal to about $24 today.

DID YOU KNOW?
New Netherland's diverse population included people who were:
- Catholic
- Protestant
- Jewish
- Enslaved Africans
- Native American

Key Details
Underline the benefits of being a patroon in New Netherland.

New Netherland Gazette

Issue 36   September 1653

New Netherland was founded 30 years ago today. In honor of this event, we remember the history of our colony.

Captain Henry Hudson first sailed to North America in 1609. His travels led to the creation of our colony in 1623. We soon built Fort Nassau and Fort Orange along the Hudson River to protect our colonists.

Three years later, Governor Peter Minuit bought the large island in the Hudson River. The Manhattes people sold the land in exchange for goods worth 60 guilders. These goods included cloth and tools.

We named the island New Amsterdam. It soon became the colony's center of trade. This flourishing seaport has allowed all of New Netherland to grow.

As trade increased, so did the number of New Netherland's settlers. Today our colonists are of many backgrounds. They include Dutch, Germans, Swedes, and South Americans.

▲ New Amsterdam

Live Like a King
The Dutch West India Company is offering large estates to anyone bringing at least 50 people to the colony. Come to an informational meeting to hear more. Patroons are people who have received these lands. They will speak about their success. Here is some of what we will discussed:
- The largest estates have their own courts and laws.
- Patroons rule their lands like kings.
- People live and work on the land in exchange for a share of their crops.
- This opportunity is open to all colonists regardless of nationality or religion.

96

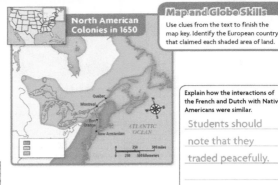

North American Colonies in 1650

Use clues from the text to finish the map key. Identify the European country that claimed each shaded area of land.

Explain how the interactions of the French and Dutch with Native Americans were similar.

Students should note that they traded peacefully.

Lesson 3

? Essential Question What happens when different cultures meet?

Go back to **Show As You Go!** on pages 72–73.

netw⚙rks   There's More Online!
• Games • Assessment

97

Lesson 3

Active Teaching

Explain to students that this page contains a secondary source written to help them learn about New Netherland. This "newspaper" tells the early history of the colony in first person. Explain to students that it was written from the perspective of a newspaper in 1653.

Show As You Go! Remind students to go back to complete the project on the Unit Opener.

netw⚙rks

Go to connected.mcgraw-hill.com for additional resources:

- Interactive Whiteboard Lessons
- Worksheets
- Assessments
- Content Library

Reading Skill

🌐 **Common Core Standards** **RI.2** Determine two or more main ideas of a text and explain how they are supported by key details; summarize the text.

Summarize Students should use details from the article to write their headline.

Response to Intervention

? Essential Question
What happens when different cultures meet?

If . . . students cannot give a substantiated response to the Essential Question,
....

Then . . . take them back through the lesson. Highlight examples of French and Dutch interaction with Native Americans. Discuss how the content relates to the Essential Question.

Ask: *What happened when the French and Dutch met Native Americans?*

Following discussion, allow students to respond to the Essential Question again.

Map and Globe Skills

Once students have completed the activity, have them add further details to the map, based on information from the text. For example, students may draw a line or arrow along the St. Lawerence River to show Jacques Cartier's route.

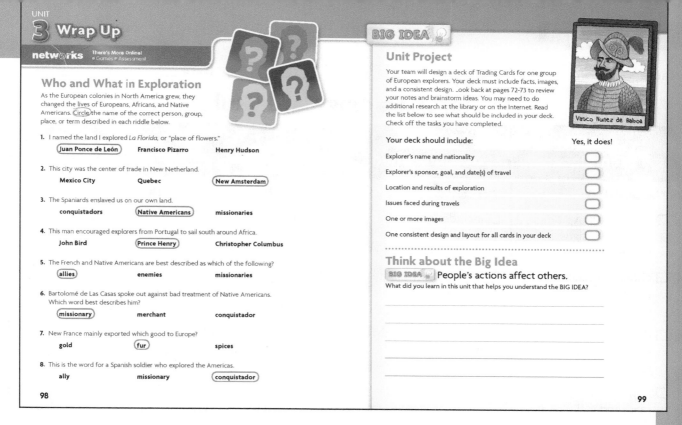

UNIT 3 Wrap Up

networks There's More Online!
• Games • Assessment

Who and What in Exploration

As the European colonies in North America grew, they changed the lives of Europeans, Africans, and Native Americans. Circle the name of the correct person, group, place, or term described in each riddle below.

1. I named the land I explored *La Florida*, or "place of flowers."
   - **(Juan Ponce de León)**   Francisco Pizarro   Henry Hudson

2. This city was the center of trade in New Netherland.
   - Mexico City   Quebec   **(New Amsterdam)**

3. The Spaniards enslaved us on our own land.
   - conquistadors   **(Native Americans)**   missionaries

4. This man encouraged explorers from Portugal to sail south around Africa.
   - John Bird   **(Prince Henry)**   Christopher Columbus

5. The French and Native Americans are best described as which of the following?
   - **(allies)**   enemies   missionaries

6. Bartolomé de Las Casas spoke out against bad treatment of Native Americans. Which word best describes him?
   - **(missionary)**   merchant   conquistador

7. New France mainly exported which good to Europe?
   - gold   **(fur)**   spices

8. This is the word for a Spanish soldier who explored the Americas.
   - ally   missionary   **(conquistador)**

98

BIG IDEA
Unit Project

Your team will design a deck of Trading Cards for one group of European explorers. Your deck must include facts, images, and a consistent design. Look back at pages 72-73 to review your notes and brainstorm ideas. You may need to do additional research at the library or on the Internet. Read the list below to see what should be included in your deck. Check off the tasks you have completed.

Vasco Nunez de Balboa

Your deck should include: **Yes, it does!**

Explorer's name and nationality   ☐

Explorer's sponsor, goal, and date(s) of travel   ☐

Location and results of exploration   ☐

Issues faced during travels   ☐

One or more images   ☐

One consistent design and layout for all cards in your deck   ☐

Think about the Big Idea

BIG IDEA People's actions affect others.
What did you learn in this unit that helps you understand the BIG IDEA?

_____

_____

_____

_____

_____

99

Wrap Up

Who and What in Exploration

Have students complete the activity on page 98 to summarize their understanding of the European exploration.

BIG IDEA Unit Project

- Read through the project directions and checklist with students.
- Answer any questions students may have about the project.
- Remind students to use their **Show As You Go!** pages to assist them in completing the project.
- To assess the project, refer to the rubric on the following page.

After students have completed their projects, encourage self-reflection by asking:

- What did you learn from making your cards?

networks

Go to **connected.mcgraw-hill.com** for additional resources:
- Games
- Assessment
- Group Technology Projects

Differentiated Instruction

▶ **Approaching** Have students complete a modified version of the trading cards, including only the name, employer, and goal for each explorer.

▶ **Beyond** Have students research in the library or on the Internet to learn more about the challenges faced by each explorer. This information should be included on the trading cards.

▶ **ELL** Have students use only the information found on the time line to build their trading cards and complete the assignment in their first language.

Response to Intervention

BIG IDEA People's actions affect others.

If . . . students cannot give a substantiated response to the Big Idea,

. . . .

Then . . . take them back through the unit. Highlight examples of explorers' actions affecting people in the Americas. Discuss how the content relates to the Big Idea. **Ask:** *How did European exploration affect Native Americans?*

Following discussion, allow students to respond to the Big Idea again.

Name _____ Date _____

Explorer Trading Cards Rubric

4 Exemplary	3 Accomplished	2 Developing	1 Beginning
The card deck:	**The card deck:**	**The card deck:**	**The card deck:**
☐ includes all explorers from the assigned nation	☐ includes most explorers from the assigned nation	☐ includes a few explorers from the assigned nation	☐ includes one or no explorers from the assigned nation
☐ contains accurate facts and details about each explorer	☐ has mostly accurate facts and details about each explorer	☐ has some accurate facts and details about each explorer	☐ has few accurate facts and details about each explorer
☐ demonstrates one consistent design and layout	☐ has a mostly consistent design and layout	☐ has some consistent design or layout elements	☐ does not have a consistent design or layout
☐ is interesting, easy to read, and includes an image on each card	☐ is mostly easy to follow and includes an image on most cards	☐ is somewhat confusing and includes an image on some cards	☐ is difficult to follow and does not include images
☐ contains few, if any, errors in grammar, punctuation, capitalization, and spelling	☐ contains some errors in grammar, punctuation, capitalization, and spelling	☐ contains several errors in grammar, punctuation, capitalization, and spelling	☐ contains serious errors in grammar, punctuation, capitalization, and spelling

Comments: _____

_____

_____

_____

_____

_____

_____

_____

Project Score: _____

Read the story "Enslaved Labor in New Spain" before answering Numbers 1 through 8.

Enslaved Labor in New Spain

By Carly Alemu

Life became very harsh for the Native Americans of New Spain. Spain began to settle its new colonies by granting encomiendas to new colonists. An encomienda was an area of land that included Native American towns. The Native Americans on the land had to work for the new owner, and the colonial holder of the encomienda agreed to house and feed them. The system was like slavery, but there were differences. The colonists had to promise to teach the Native Americans new skills and to tell them about Christianity.

Native Americans worked from dawn to dusk. Sometimes they were treated harshly and could even be whipped. Often, they were hungry. When the Spanish found silver in what is now southern Bolivia and central Mexico, they forced Native Americans to work in these mines. The silver helped to make Spain one of the richest and most powerful countries in Europe.

The Native American population suffered under the ecomienda system. Many died from being overworked and from the diseases that came with the Europeans. Soon, the Spanish ecomienda owners needed to find other sources of labor. Their solution was to enslave large numbers of captive Africans.

Not everyone agreed with the ecomienda system. Bartolomé de Las Casas was a Catholic priest who had come to the island of Hispaniola to run an ecomienda. Once he saw the Native Americans dying of disease and overwork, he decided to try to end the system. Eventually, Spanish laws were changed to better govern the ecomiendas. These laws were ineffective, though. Spain was too far away and could not make the landowners obey. Native Americans continued to be mistreated.

1 What is this article mostly about?
Ⓐ life in New Spain
Ⓑ Native Americans in New Spain
Ⓒ encomiendas in New Spain
Ⓓ Spanish exploration in New Spain

2 Read the sentence from the story.

These laws were ineffective, though.

What does the word ineffective mean in this story?
Ⓕ forceful
Ⓖ organized
Ⓗ weak
Ⓘ courageous

3 According to the article, which of the following statements is true?
Ⓐ Colonists had to house and feed Native Americans living and working on their land.
Ⓑ Native Americans were forced to leave all encomiendas.
Ⓒ Native Americans were given encomiendas.
Ⓓ Colonists accepted the religious beliefs of Native Americans.

4 Which sentence best describes Bartolomé de Las Casas?
Ⓕ He was a missionary who worked against the encomienda system.
Ⓖ He was a missionary who ran a successful encomienda.
Ⓗ He was a missionary who started the encomienda system.
Ⓘ He was a missionary who finally ended the encomienda system.

5 What helped Spain become one of the richest and most powerful countries in Europe?
Ⓐ encomiendas
Ⓑ learning new skills
Ⓒ new colonists
Ⓓ silver mines

6 Why did the encomienda owners enslave captive Africans?
Ⓕ because captive Africans lived far away
Ⓖ because captive Africans lived nearby
Ⓗ because the Native American population had greatly declined
Ⓘ because the Native American population had increased too much

7 What key detail supports the author's statement that "life became very harsh for Native Americans"?
Ⓐ Encomiendas included Native American towns.
Ⓑ Colonists agreed to house and feed Native Americans.
Ⓒ Native Americans were sometimes whipped.
Ⓓ Colonists promised to teach Native Americans new skills.

8 The article says Native Americans worked "from dawn to dusk." What does this mean?
Ⓕ They only worked in the morning.
Ⓖ They only worked in the evening.
Ⓗ They didn't each lunch or dinner.
Ⓘ They worked all day long.

Test Preparation

Test-Taking Tips

Share these test-taking tips with your students:

- Read the entire text carefully. As you read, identify the main ideas in the text and their key details. To identify the main ideas, ask yourself, "What is this about?"

- Once you've identified some main ideas, think about how they fit together. Ask yourself, "How are these ideas connected?"

- Then, summarize the main ideas by using key details from the text to support your conclusions.

- Knowing the main ideas and summarizing the text for yourself after you've read can help you understand and answer the questions better.

Answers

1. B CCS RI.2

2. H CCS RI.4

3. A CCS RI.7

4. F CCS RI.7

5. D CCS RI.3

6. H CCS RI.3

7. C CCS RI.2

8. I CCS RI.4

UNIT
4 Planner COLONIAL AMERICA

 **BIG IDEA** **Location affects how people live.**

Student Portfolio

- *Show As You Go!*
  Use these pages to introduce the Big Idea. Students record information specific to each lesson. They use these pages to help them plan their Big Idea Project.

netw⊘rks

- **Group Technology Project**
  Students use 21st century skills to complete a group extension activity of the unit project. Lesson plans, worksheets, and rubrics are available online.

Student Portfolio

- **Big Idea Project**
  Students will construct a pamphlet and make a sales pitch about a colonial region of their choosing. The Big Idea Project rubric is on page 147W.

Reading Skills

Student Portfolio

- **Reading Skill: Draw Inferences**
  Pages 104–105. Common Core State Standards RI.1

Treasures Connection

Teach this unit with Treasures Unit 5, *Weslandia*, pages 546–561.

Social Studies Skills

Student Portfolio

- **Primary and Secondary Sources: Letters**
  Page 109

netw⊘rks

- **Skill Builders**
  Introduce and teach analyzing primary and secondary sources.

Activity Cards

- **Center for Social Studies Skills Investigation**
  Use the center activity cards to help students explore Primary Sources, Geography, and Citizenship.

FOLDABLES®

Student Portfolio

- Students can create vocabulary Foldables right in their portfolios.

- Additional Foldables templates can be found on pages R34–R42 of your Teacher Edition. See page R33 for instructions.

Assessment Solutions

- **McGraw-Hill networks™**
  Safe online testing features multiple question types that are easy to use and editable.

- **Self-Check Quizzes**

- **Worksheets**

UNIT 4 **At a Glance**

Lesson	Essential Question	Vocabulary
1 Early Settlements	Why do people move?	*assume charter persecution Pilgrim
2 Settling New England	How do societies develop?	covenant tyrant tolerate *appropriate
3 Settling the Middle Colonies	How do societies develop?	proprietor diversity *primary
4 Settling the Southern Colonies	How do societies develop?	frontier act profit debt *common
5 Life in the Colonies	How do societies develop?	assembly market economy barter occupation *employ
6 Slavery and the Triangular Trade	How do cultures change?	indentured servant *code

*denotes academic vocabulary

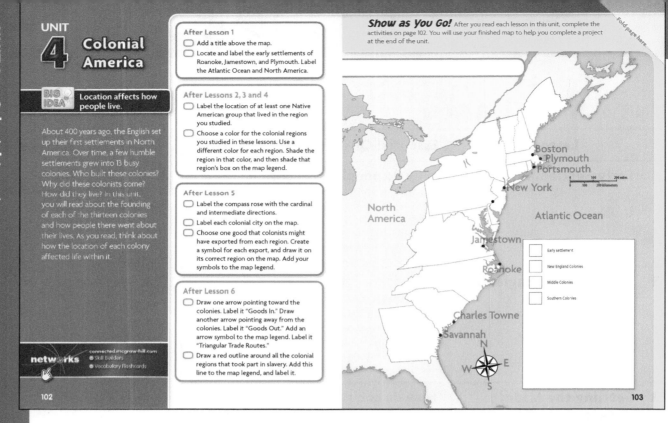

UNIT 4 Colonial America

BIG IDEA Location affects how people live.

About 400 years ago, the English set up their first settlements in North America. Over time, a few humble settlements grew into 13 busy colonies. Who built these colonies? Why did these colonists come? How did they live? In this unit, you will read about the founding of each of the thirteen colonies and how people there went about their lives. As you read, think about how the location of each colony affected life within it.

networks connected.mcgraw-hill.com
● Skill Builders
● Vocabulary Flashcards

102

Show as You Go! After you read each lesson in this unit, complete the activities on page 102. You will use your finished map to help you complete a project at the end of the unit.

After Lesson 1
☐ Add a title above the map.
☐ Locate and label the early settlements of Roanoke, Jamestown, and Plymouth. Label the Atlantic Ocean and North America.

After Lessons 2, 3 and 4
☐ Label the location of at least one Native American group that lived in the region you studied.
☐ Choose a color for the colonial regions you studied in these lessons. Use a different color for each region. Shade the region in that color, and then shade that region's box on the map legend.

After Lesson 5
☐ Label the compass rose with the cardinal and intermediate directions.
☐ Label each colonial city on the map.
☐ Choose one good that colonists might have exported from each region. Create a symbol for each export, and draw it on its correct region on the map. Add your symbols to the map legend.

After Lesson 6
☐ Draw one arrow pointing toward the colonies. Label it "Goods In." Draw another arrow pointing away from the colonies. Label it "Goods Out." Add an arrow symbol to the map legend. Label it "Triangular Trade Routes."
☐ Draw a red outline around all the colonial regions that took part in slavery. Add this line to the map legend, and label it.

103

Introduce the Unit

✓ Diagnostic Assessment

Read aloud the statements below. Students should indicate familiarity with each statement by holding up fingers with:

1 = I know very little about this

2 = I know some about this

3 = I know a lot about this

- English colonists first settled Roanoke, Jamestown, and Plymouth.
- Thirteen British colonies developed in North America.
- The colonies made up three different regions.
- The colonies developed new governments, economies, and ways of life.
- The colonies participated in trade across the Atlantic, including trade in enslaved people.
- Slavery was a part of life early on in the colonies.

Student responses will help identify their level of understanding.

Active Teaching

BIG IDEA Location affects how people live.
In this unit about the growth of the thirteen colonies, students will learn that location affects how people live. Students will use the **Show As You Go!** pages throughout their study of this unit. Students will use information from each lesson to complete the activities.

Explain to students that at the end of the unit, they will use the information collected on these pages to complete their Unit Project. At this point, have students fold back the corner of this page. This will help them flip back to that page as needed.

Differentiated Instruction

▶ **Approaching** Have students read the head above each set of check boxes. Explain that students only need to complete a small portion of their maps at the end of each lesson.

▶ **Beyond** As students read each lesson, have them choose one additional feature to add to their maps.

▶ **ELL** Review each check box with students before they begin each lesson. Help define unfamiliar words in the check boxes. Allow students to write their map labels in their first language.

Reading Skill

Common Core Standards
RI.1: Quote accurately from a text when explaining what the text says explicitly and when drawing inferences from the text.

Draw Inferences

When you read, you often combine new information with what you already know to draw a conclusion. This conclusion is also called an inference. To make an inference, combine the facts you learn from reading with what you already know.

Text Clue

Details

▼ William Penn meeting with the Lenni Lenape.

LEARN IT

To draw an inference:
- Identify text clues and details in the passage.
- Think about what you already know about the topic.
- Draw an inference by combining the text clues and details with what you already know to form a conclusion about what the text is trying to say.

Read the passage below. Think about an inference you could draw.

William Penn did things a little differently than most English settlers. The Lenni Lenape people were Native Americans who lived in Pennsylvania. William Penn paid them for their lands. He welcomed Native American refugees from other colonies, too. The colony was peaceful for a very long time because of this. Penn also granted equality to people of all religions and even to people of other European countries. All of these things helped Pennsylvania grow.

TRY IT

Fill in the chart below in order to draw inferences about good ways to work with people. Use the paragraph on page 104.

Text Clues and Details	What You Know	Inference(s)

APPLY IT

Review the steps for drawing inferences in Learn It. Then, read the passage below. Circle text clues and details that you could use to draw an inference. Draw an inference and explain it on the lines, using details from the text.

The first Jamestown colonists struggled. They didn't want to work, even though they needed to in order to survive. Captain Smith proclaimed, "Those who don't work, don't eat!" He forced them all to work, and things began to look up. But then, Smith was injured in an accident. He had to return to England for treatment. Without his leadership, the colonists quit working. The harsh winter that followed was called the "starving time" because many colonists died.

104

105

Common Core Standards RI.1 Quote accurately from a text when explaining what the text says explicitly and when drawing inferences from the text.

Reading Skill

Active Teaching

LEARN IT Draw Inferences

Say: *As I read I think, "What clues and details are new to me?" Answering this question helps me find information that I didn't yet know. It is important to make sure I read and quote the new information accurately. Once I have completed this step, I think "What do I already know about this topic?" Answering this question helps me recall information I've learned in the past. When I put new information together with information I already knew, I can draw an inference about the text I am reading.*

TRY IT Encourage students to try the modeled strategy as they complete the **TRY IT** activity.

APPLY IT After students have completed the **APPLY IT** activity, **Ask:**

1. *What clues and details did you find?*
2. *Did you make sure you had an accurate understanding of the details?*
3. *What prior knowledge did you apply to the new information to form your inference?*

Differentiated Instruction

▶ **Approaching** Review the **LEARN IT** activity as a small group. Do the **TRY IT** activity together. Have students complete the **APPLY IT** activity independently. Regroup to compare and correct.

▶ **Beyond** Have students evaluate the inference that they drew in the **APPLY IT**. **Ask:** *Is your inference supported by the clues and details in the text? What information would you need to improve your inference?*

▶ **ELL** Have students discuss the image on page 104 and predict what the passage might be about. Explain clues, details, and prior knowledge. Read the **LEARN IT** passage one sentence at a time. Have students discuss the details they discover and their prior knowledge.

net**works**

Go to **connected.mcgraw-hill.com** for additional resources.
- Skill Builders
- Graphic Organizers

Graphic Organizer
Three-Column Chart

Common Core Standards
RI.4: Determine the meaning of general academic and domain-specific words and phrases in a text relevant to a grade 5 topic or subject area.

The list below shows some important words you will learn in this unit. Their definitions can be found on the next page. Read the words.

pilgrim (PIHL • gruhm)

covenant (KUH • vuh • nuhnt)

tolerate (TAH • luh • rayt)

proprietor (pruh • PRY • uh • tuhr)

act (AKT)

assembly (uh • SEHM • blee)

occupation (ah • kyuh • PAY • shuhn)

indentured servant (ihn • DEHN • shuhrd SUHR • vuhnt)

The Pilgrims made a religious journey to find new land in North America. ▼

106

FOLDABLES

The Foldable on the next page will help you learn Foldable these important words. Follow the steps below to make your Foldable.

Step 1 Fold along the solid red line.

Step 2 Cut along the dotted lines.

Step 3 Read the words and their definitions.

Step 4 Complete the activities on each tab.

Step 5 Look at the back of your Foldable. Choose ONE of these activities for each word to help you remember its meaning:
- Draw a picture of the word.
- Write a description of the word.
- Write how the word is related to something you know.

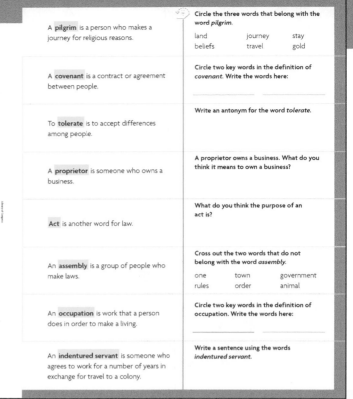

A **pilgrim** is a person who makes a journey for religious reasons.	Circle the three words that belong with the word *pilgrim*. land　　journey　　stay beliefs　　travel　　gold
A **covenant** is a contract or agreement between people.	Circle two key words in the definition of *covenant*. Write the words here: _____　_____
To **tolerate** is to accept differences among people.	Write an antonym for the word *tolerate*. _____
A **proprietor** is someone who owns a business.	A proprietor owns a business. What do you think it means to own a business?
Act is another word for law.	What do you think the purpose of an act is?
An **assembly** is a group of people who make laws.	Cross out the two words that do not belong with the word *assembly*. one　　town　　government rules　　order　　animal
An **occupation** is work that a person does in order to make a living.	Circle two key words in the definition of occupation. Write the words here: _____　_____
An **indentured servant** is someone who agrees to work for a number of years in exchange for travel to a colony.	Write a sentence using the words *indentured servant*.

Common Core Standards **RI.4** Determine the meaning of general academic and domain-specific words and phrases in a text relevant to a *grade 5 topic or subject area*.

Words to Know

Active Teaching

FOLDABLES

1. Go to connected.mcgraw-hill.com for flashcards to introduce the unit vocabulary to students.

2. Read the words on the list on page 106 and have students repeat them after you.

3. Guide students as they complete steps 1 through 4 of the Foldable.

4. Have students use the Foldable to practice the vocabulary words independently or with a partner.

networks

Go to connected.mcgraw-hill.com for additional resources.
- Vocabulary Flashcards
- Vocabulary Games
- Graphic Organizers

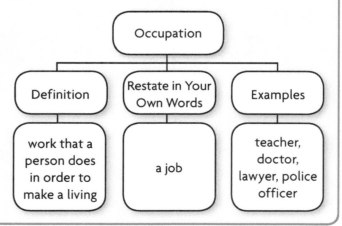

GO Vocabulary!

Use the graphic organizer below to help students gain a deeper understanding of each vocabulary word. Model for students how to complete the graphic organizer using the word *occupation*. Have students complete the graphic organizer for the other words independently or with a partner. For some words, you might want to change the head. For example, instead of having students restate the definition in their own words, you might want students to describe the word.

Occupation
- Definition: work that a person does in order to make a living
- Restate in Your Own Words: a job
- Examples: teacher, doctor, lawyer, police officer

pilgrim	pilgrim
covenant	covenant
tolerate	tolerate
proprietor	proprietor
act	act
assembly	assembly
occupation	occupation
indentured servant	indentured servant

Primary Sources

Letters

Letters are a type of primary source. People send many different types of information through letters. Letters can reveal what it was like to live in a time and place long ago. Without primary sources, such as letters, some of the rich details of history might have been forgotten.

In this unit, you will learn about how settlers from England and other parts of Europe came to North America and made their homes here. A man named John Dickenson lived during this time. On the right is a letter he wrote to his friends and neighbors in England. As you read it, think about the place it describes, and the details that tell you about the writer's life.

DBQ Document-Based Questions

Read the letter. As you read, complete the following activities.

1. Underline details that describe where John Dickenson lived.

2. Circle details that describe his daily life.

3. Put a box around the new vocabulary words in the account.

Primary Source

My Dear Countrymen,
I . . . settled . . . near the banks of the River Delaware in the **province** of Pennsylvania. . . . My farm is small; my servants are few and good; I have a little money. . . . I spend a good deal of [my time] in [my] library . . . I have acquired, I believe, a greater share of knowledge . . . than is generally **attained** by men of my class.

province: a part of a country or settled area

attain: to gain something

networks
There's More Online!
● Skill Builders
● Resource Library

109

Differentiated Instruction

▶ **ELL** Have students select words from each lesson with which they are having difficulty. Help them make flash cards for each word. Write the word in English on one side along with a picture or symbol that students find or create. Write its associated word, phrase, or description in the students' first language on the other side.

WORD PLAY

Have students develop and play a matching game using all of the words in Unit 4.

1. Divide students into six groups.

2. Have each group complete a set of word cards for one lesson. They should make one card for each vocabulary word and one for each definition.

3. Collect the sets and make six copies, so that you have six decks of cards.

4. Have the students divide back into their groups. They should lay all the cards face down. Have the groups play a matching game with the cards.

Primary Sources
Active Teaching

Point out to students that it wasn't just famous people who wrote letters. People from many different walks of life wrote letters. Because so many different people wrote letters, we get a better understanding of how different people lived at different times in history.

Ask:

1. *What is a letter?* **L1**

2. *Why are most letters considered primary sources?* **L2**

3. *How might a letter become a secondary source?* **L3**

4. *What types of information can be learned from letters?* **L2**

networks

Go to **connected.mcgraw-hill.com** for additional resources.

- Primary Sources
- Skill Builders

Lesson 1 Early Settlements

Essential Question
Why do people move?
What do you think?

Have you ever moved to a new home or had a friend who has moved away? In Lesson 1, you'll learn about English colonists who left their homes to move to North America.

Think about how you might feel if you had to move to a new place. Use your thoughts to complete the short story below.

When I was _____ years old, my family moved to

_____. We moved because _____

I felt _____

because _____

In the 1500s, Europeans were excited about new lands in North America. Countries eagerly gobbled up land there, expanding their territories. People **assumed** they would find vast amounts of gold and other riches in North America.

In 1585 Queen Elizabeth I issued a **charter** to settle land in North America. A charter is an official document that gives special rights to its holder. This charter said a man named Sir Walter Raleigh could claim land for England. In this lesson, you will learn about three early English settlements.

Words To Know
Have you heard these words before? Make a guess about what each word means and write it on the lines. Then find it in the lesson.

*assume
_____

persecution
_____

What continent is on this side of the illustration?
North America

Who are these people?
Native Americans

110

Roanoke

Founding date: 1585
Location: present-day North Carolina
Founder: Sir Walter Raleigh
Motivations: Expand England's territory; search for gold and other riches
Settlement Attempts: Two

Life was rough in Roanoke. The land was bad for farming, and those who traveled there were businessmen, not farmers or woodsmen. They weren't fully prepared, and supply ships were few and far between. The first group of settlers survived a long, hungry winter and returned to England in the spring. They had found no riches in Roanoke.

In 1587 John White led a second group to Roanoke. This time women and children came along, too. They had similar troubles as the first group. White returned to England for supplies and help, but he was held up in Europe by a war. When he finally made it back to Roanoke in 1590, all the colonists were gone. No one knows for sure what happened to them. Roanoke became known as the Lost Colony.

▲ In 1585 Queen Elizabeth I gave Sir Walter Raleigh his charter.

What body of water is this?
Atlantic
Ocean

In the empty space of the illustration, draw a ship leaving the port.

Think about the illustration and what you already know about European explorers. Make a prediction about how English settlers and Native Americans will interact.

111

Lesson 1

Activate Prior Knowledge

After students have completed the stories about moving, ask for volunteers to share what they wrote with the class. Discuss the reasons for moving and the associated feelings that students came up with. Explain that in this lesson, students will learn about the excitement and hardships associated with English colonists setting up new homes in an unfamiliar land.

Essential Question Why do people move?

Have students explain what they understand about the Essential Question. Discuss their responses. Explain that everything they learn in this lesson will help them understand the Essential Question better. Remind them to think about how the Essential Question connects to the unit Big Idea, Location affects how people live.

Differentiated Instruction

▶ **Approaching** Review the key words in each of the activity boxes to help students identify what they should be looking for as they read.

▶ **Beyond** Have students create and analyze a time line of events that took place in the early years of English colonization of North America.

▶ **ELL** Have students circle any unfamiliar words. Explain the meaning of these words.

Active Teaching

Words To Know After students have completed the Words to Know activity, have them find and read the definitions in the text. Then, present students with a list of three to five words or phrases that are related to each vocabulary word. Have students identify the word or phrase that does not fit with the rest of the group. Have students explain their choice.

Develop Comprehension

Have students read pages 110 and 111 before completing the activities at the bottom of both pages. Students should draw inferences from the text in order to fill in each blank. Students should use their knowledge from Unit 3 in order to draw a ship leaving port and make a prediction about how English settlers and Native Americans will interact.

networks

Go to **connected.mcgraw-hill.com** for additional resources.
• Interactive Whiteboard Lessons
• Worksheets
• Assessment
• Lesson Plans
• Videos
• Content Library

Early English Settlements

1. Measure the distance between Plymouth and Jamestown.

   Plymouth was about __450__

   miles __North__ of Jamestown.

2. What line of latitude is closest to Plymouth? __42°N__

Jamestown

Founding date: 1607
Location: Inside the Chesapeake Bay, on the James River
Founders: The Virginia Company
Motivations: Expand England's territory; search for gold and other riches; grow cash crops
Folk Hero: John Smith

Jamestown's founders were a group of business owners called the Virginia Company. The first Jamestown colonists struggled just like those at Roanoke. Captain John Smith forced settlers to work hard. He proclaimed, "Those who don't work, don't eat!" Unfortunately, Smith was badly injured and had to return to England. Without his leadership, the colonists quit working. The harsh winter that followed was called the "starving time." Many colonists died.

Besides hunger, disease and injury also threatened colonists' lives. During the early years, only 20 percent of the colonists survived. Eventually, they adjusted. John Rolfe planted the first successful tobacco crop in Jamestown in 1612. The money he made inspired others. Tobacco brought stability and wealth, and as a result, Jamestown began to prosper! It became the first permanent English settlement in North America.

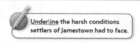

Underline the harsh conditions settlers of Jamestown had to face.

This is what archaeologists think Jamestown may have looked like. ▼

Flymouth

Founding date: 1620
Location: Cape Cod
Founders: The Pilgrims
Motivations: Religious freedom

In England in the 1600s, it was illegal to belong to any church except the Church of England. Those who spoke out against the Church faced **persecution**, or harsh treatment for their religious beliefs. One group who wanted to break away from the Church were the **Pilgrims**. A pilgrim is someone who makes a journey for religious reasons. The Pilgrims thought that the Church would never make the changes they wanted. They decided to head to North America.

A ship called the *Mayflower* left England in September 1620. The 102 men, women, and children aboard faced rough seas, hunger, and disease during their journey across the Atlantic.

When they arrived two months later, a harsh winter was right around the corner. By spring, only half remained—the rest died of disease or starvation. Those who survived set about building a settlement called Plymouth.

▲ In 1620 the first Pilgrims landed in Plymouth.

Native Americans

Native Americans and the settlers at Roanoke and Jamestown competed for food and other resources. Differing languages and cultures made understanding each other very difficult at times. Conflict between the two groups soon became a part of life.

At Plymouth, the Pilgrims found a village abandoned by the Pawtuxet, who had died of European diseases years earlier. One remaining Pawtuxet man lived nearby with the Wampanoag. His name was Squanto, and he spoke some English. The Wampanoag and Squanto helped the Pilgrims survive their first year at Plymouth.

Lesson 1

(?) Essential Question Why do people move?

_____

_____

_____

Go back to *Show As You Go!* on pages 102–103.

netw⊛rks There's More Online! • Games • Assessment

112

113

Active Teaching

Develop Comprehension
Ask:

1. *What were the economic, political, and socio-cultural motivations for the English to come to North America?* **L1**

2. *Who were some important individuals who worked to found the English colonies?* **L1**

3. *Both the Jamestown colonists and the Pilgrims experienced harsh winters. How do you think they adapted in order to survive?* **L3**

4. *Compare the interactions between the English and Native Americans at Jamestown and Plymouth.* **L2**

> **Show As You Go!** Remind students to go back to the Unit Opener and complete the activities for this lesson.

Response to Intervention

(?) **Essential Question Why do people move?**

If . . . students cannot identify the economic, political, or socio-cultural motivations for English settlement

· ·

Then . . . hold a class discussion about what the words *economic, political,* and *socio-cultural* mean and give examples for each. Then, have students examine the text again, looking for one type of motivation at a time. Following discussion, allow students to explain why they think each motivation was important to the settlers.

Map and Globe Skills

Have students create their own may key for the map on page 112. They should use prior knowledge and information from the text to figure out which outlines represent which groups. (green areas: early English settlements; red outline: Powhatan; yellow outline: Wampanoag)

Students will need to use their knowledge of map scales in order to find the distance between each settlement on the map. Help students activate prior knowledge by modeling how to use a scale to find distance on a different map.

Lesson 2 — Settling New England

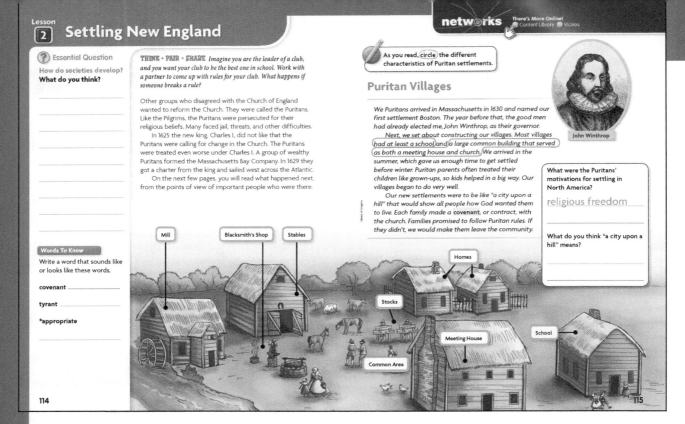

Lesson 2

Activate Prior Knowledge

After students have completed the Think-Pair-Share activity, ask for volunteers to share what they wrote with the class. Discuss the reasons why someone might want to break the rules. Ask: Are there times when breaking the rules is justified? Explain that in this lesson, students will learn about a group of English settlers called Puritans. The Puritans came to North America seeking the freedom to practice their religion in the way they thought was best.

(?) Essential Question How do societies develop?

Have students explain what they understand about the Essential Question. Discuss their responses. Explain that everything they learn in this lesson will help them understand the Essential Question better. Remind them to think about how the Essential Question connects to the unit Big Idea, Location affects how people live.

The Development of Puritanism After the death of King Henry VIII, England experienced a series of religious conflicts. Unlike the Pilgrims—who were separatists—the Puritans wished to transform the Church of England, or "purify" it. The Puritans believed Christianity should be a system of apostles and followers who lived simple, morally strict lives.

Active Teaching

> **Words To Know** After students have completed the Words to Know activity, have them locate each word in the text and read its definition. Then, divide students into groups. Have each group write one sentence for each word.
>
> #### Develop Comprehension
>
> The content that is ***boldfaced and italicized*** on pages 115, 117, and 119 is told in first person from the point of view of the historical figure shown. Students may need to be reminded of what it means to read a first-person point of view.

Other groups who disagreed with the Church of England

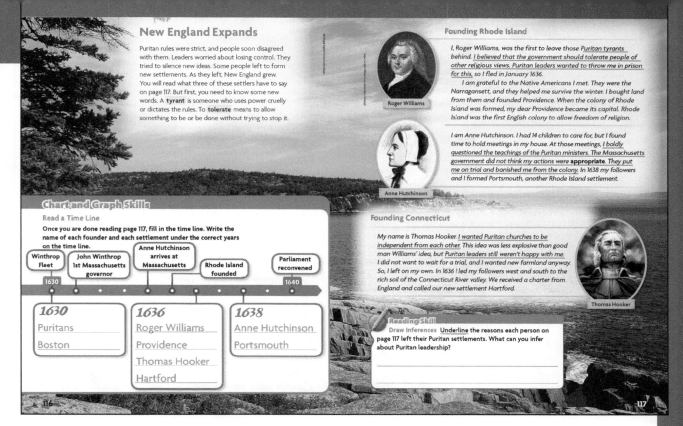

New England Expands

Puritan rules were strict, and people soon disagreed with them. Leaders worried about losing control. They tried to silence new ideas. Some people left to form new settlements. As they left, New England grew. You will read what three of these settlers have to say on page 117. But first, you need to know some new words. A **tyrant** is someone who uses power cruelly or dictates the rules. To **tolerate** means to allow something to be or be done without trying to stop it.

Founding Rhode Island

I, Roger Williams, was the first to leave those Puritan tyrants behind. I believed that the government should tolerate people of other religious views. Puritan leaders wanted to throw me in prison for this, so I fled in January 1636.

I am grateful to the Native Americans I met. They were the Narragansett, and they helped me survive the winter. I bought land from them and founded Providence. When the colony of Rhode Island was formed, my dear Providence became its capital. Rhode Island was the first English colony to allow freedom of religion.

Roger Williams

I am Anne Hutchinson. I had 14 children to care for, but I found time to hold meetings in my house. At those meetings, I boldly questioned the teachings of the Puritan ministers. The Massachusetts government did not think my actions were **appropriate**. They put me on trial and banished me from the colony. In 1638 my followers and I formed Portsmouth, another Rhode Island settlement.

Anne Hutchinson

Chart and Graph Skills

Read a Time Line

Once you are done reading page 117, fill in the time line. Write the name of each founder and each settlement under the correct years on the time line.

Winthrop Fleet	John Winthrop 1st Massachusetts governor	Anne Hutchinson arrives at Massachusetts	Rhode Island founded	Parliament reconvened

1630 — 1640

1630
Puritans
Boston

1636
Roger Williams
Providence
Thomas Hooker
Hartford

1638
Anne Hutchinson
Portsmouth

Founding Connecticut

My name is Thomas Hooker. I wanted Puritan churches to be independent from each other. This idea was less explosive than good man Williams' idea, but Puritan leaders still weren't happy with me. I did not want to wait for a trial, and I wanted new farmland anyway. So, I left on my own. In 1636 I led my followers west and south to the rich soil of the Connecticut River valley. We received a charter from England and called our new settlement Hartford.

Thomas Hooker

Reading Skill

Draw Inferences Underline the reasons each person on page 117 left their Puritan settlements. What can you infer about Puritan leadership?

116 / 117

Active Teaching

Have students read pages 116–117 before completing the time line on page 116.

Differentiated Instruction

▶ **Approaching** Review with students the parts of a time line and how to read one. Have them identify the parts of the time line they will need to fill in. Allow students to work as a group to complete the time line.

▶ **Beyond** Have students write a short description of the events on the time line, showing how one event led to or influenced another. Students may need to do some independent research to draw appropriate inferences or conclusions.

▶ **ELL** Make sure students understand that they are matching three sets of data: the founder, the settlement, and both of those pieces of information to the date on the time line. It may help students to approach this activity as they would a word search.

Chart and Graph Skills

Read a Time Line Point out to students that they will need to place two founders and two settlements for 1636.

Page Power

Interact more with the page.

- After students read the account of Roger Williams, have students underline words in the text that describe his interactions with Native Americans. As a class, discuss what students can infer about relations between the English and Native Americans at this time and in this region. **Ask:** *Would your inference apply to all places where English and Native Americans interacted at this time, or could relations be different from place to place?*

- After students read all accounts, have them locate and circle the motivations of each historical figure for founding his or her own settlement. As a class, identify each circled text as an economic, political, or socio-cultural motivation.

Reading Skill

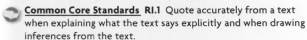

Common Core Standards RI.1 Quote accurately from a text when explaining what the text says explicitly and when drawing inferences from the text.

Draw Inferences If students have trouble making an inference, refer them to the first paragraph on page 116 that describes Puritan rules and leaders.

New Englanders and Native Americans

FUN FACT
Maine and Vermont were never separate colonies. Settlers did live in those areas, but Maine was part of Massachusetts. And England and France fought over Vermont. Even some nearby colonies wanted it! Maine and Vermont became states much later.

Do you remember reading about how Native Americans helped the Pilgrims survive? This kindness led to a long peace between them. Not all New Englanders got along with all Native American tribes, though. Many experienced conflict, especially as settlements continued to expand.

The Pequot War
As Puritan towns grew, settlers needed more land and resources. This increased competition for resources with Native Americans nearby, especially with the Pequot. Tensions exploded into warfare. In 1637 Connecticut settlers attacked the Pequot. The settlers killed or captured hundreds of Pequot, and by 1638, they had defeated them. Pequot survivors joined other Native American villages nearby. English settlers then moved north into what became the colony of New Hampshire.

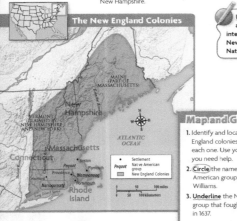
The New England Colonies

MAINE (PART OF MASSACHUSETTS)
VERMONT (CLAIMED BY NEW HAMPSHIRE AND NEW YORK)
New Hampshire
Massachusetts
Boston
Pequot
Plymouth
Hartford
Providence
Wampanoag
Connecticut
Narragansett
Portsmouth
Rhode Island
ATLANTIC OCEAN

Settlement
Native American group
New England Colonies

50   100 miles
50   100 kilometers

Underline positive and circle negative interactions between New Englanders and Native Americans.

Map and Globe Skills
1. Identify and locate the four New England colonies on the map. Label each one. Use your reference atlas if you need help.
2. Circle the name of the Native American group that helped Roger Williams.
3. Underline the Native American group that fought with the settlers in 1637.

King Philip's War
Even colonists and Native Americans who had been friends, such as the Pilgrims and the Wampanoag, soon viewed each other as enemies. Read what happened next from the point of view of one Native American leader.

Metacomet

I am Metacomet. I was called King Philip by the colonists. My father was Massasoit, the Wampanoag leader who helped the Pilgrims. He had kept peace with the Pilgrims for 40 years. After my father died in 1661, I became the new leader of our people. And soon, the colonists began taking our lands. I was angry that these people, who had been our friends, now had so little respect for us.

Protecting our lands was my duty. Over the years I made plans and convinced other Native American groups to fight with us. In 1675 our warriors attacked more than 50 settlements and killed hundreds of colonists. They fought back, attacking and burning many of our towns.

King Philip's War lasted more than a year, until Metacomet was trapped and killed by rival Native American forces that helped the English settlers. His death ended the war and marked the end of Native American power in the region.

DID YOU KNOW?
Why did the colonists call Metacomet "king"? The colonists often misunderstood the governing systems of Native Americans. To the colonists "leader," "elder," "chief," and "sachem" were the same as "king."

Why did colonists call Metacomet "Philip"? Massasoit had asked the governor of the Pilgrims to give his sons English names. Metacomet received the name Philip.

Lesson 2

(?) **Essential Question** How do societies develop?

Go back to *Show As You Go!* on pages 102–103.

netw⊙rks There's More Online!
• Games • Assessment

118

119

Lesson 2
Active Teaching

Develop Comprehension
Ask:
1. *What happened in 1637? Where did this event take place?* **L1**
2. *Why did peaceful relations between the English and Native Americans change?* **L2**
3. *Imagine that you are a mediator between colonists and Native Americans. How would you get them to compromise in order to prevent future conflicts?* **L3**

Use the leveled reader, *King Philip's War*, to extend and enrich students' understanding of colonial conflicts with Native Americans. A lesson plan for this leveled reader can be found on pages T26–T27 at the front of this Teacher Edition.

Show As You Go! Remind students to go back to the Unit Opener and complete the activities for this lesson.

Map and Globe Skills
Say: *Two areas on the map, Maine and Vermont, were settled by the English, but never became formal colonies.*

Response to Intervention
(?) **Essential Question How do societies develop?**

If . . . students cannot identify and locate the four New England colonies on the map on page 118 using clues from the text
. . . .
Then . . . have students refer to the United States political map in the Reference Atlas. Explain to students that the thirteen colonies later became the first thirteen states and that they're all located in the eastern United States. First, identify the general area of the New England colonies. Next, identify Massachusetts and Cape Cod. Then, have students find Rhode Island and Connecticut, respectively. Correct students if they identify Rhode Island as an island in error. Finally, have students use their finger to trace north from Massachusetts to find New Hampshire.

netw⊙rks
Go to **connected.mcgraw-hill.com** for additional resources.
• Interactive Whiteboard Lessons
• Worksheets
• Assessment

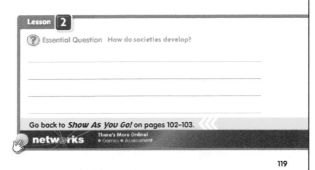

Lesson 3 · Settling the Middle Colonies

Essential Question
How do societies develop?

What do you think?

_____
_____
_____
_____
_____
_____
_____

When you were little, you probably played with blocks or other building toys. You may have had to defend your creations against others.

Think about a time when you had a conflict like this. Write about it on the lines below.

_____
_____
_____
_____
_____

A group of settlers in North America had to defend their settlement in 1664. They worked very hard building their colony, only to have someone declare that he was taking over! The settlers didn't have anyone nearby to go to for help. Think about this as you read their story.

Words To Know

Find the definition for each word and write a synonym on the line. A synonym is a word that has the same or almost the same meaning.

proprietor _____

*primary _____

Traders arrive in New Amsterdam. ▼

120

networks — There's More Online! Content Library • Videos

England Takes New Netherland

Here's how the story began. Remember that the Dutch had settled New Netherland in 1621. Its largest and most important settlement was New Amsterdam. Settlers to New Netherland came for the opportunity to own land and make a better life. As the colony flourished, England took notice.

> Read the story panels below, then complete the activity.

New Amsterdam, 1664

Meanwhile in England, King Charles II is feeling greedy.

I want to increase our colonies.

There is New Netherland…

Taking it over would make trade easier.

To my brother, the Duke of York, I give a gift. All the land between the Charles and Delaware Rivers!

"You'll have to take it by force."

We hereby claim this land for England. Surrender at once!

The English ships came armed and ready to fight. The Dutch colonists knew they couldn't win. They convinced their governor to surrender to the English. New Netherland became the English colony of New York. The settlement of New Amsterdam became New York City.

The Duke of York shared a small part of the land with his friends. They named their share New Jersey. Like Virginia, New York and New Jersey were run by **proprietors**, another word for business owners. The proprietors' main goal was to make money. They promised settlers land, religious freedom, and a voice in government. In return, settlers paid a tax.

What would you do? Draw yourself as a member of the crowd in the last scene. Then, explain what you would do on the lines below.

_____
_____
_____
_____

121

Lesson 3 —

Activate Prior Knowledge

Before beginning the lesson, divide the class into two or three teams. Lead them in a relay game in which they recall what they learned in Unit 3 about New Netherland. Have ready on the board two identical charts containing missing information about the colony. Teams will send one student at a time to the board to fill in one missing piece of information. Teammates may correct incorrect answers. The first team to correctly complete their chart wins. Student responses will help identify their level of understanding.

? Essential Question How do societies develop?

Have students explain what they understand about the Essential Question. Discuss their responses. Explain that everything they learn in this lesson will help them understand the Essential Question better. Remind them to think about how the Essential Question connects to the unit Big Idea: Location affects how people live.

networks

Go to connected.mcgraw-hill.com for additional resources.

- Interactive Whiteboard Lessons
- Worksheets
- Assessment

Active Teaching

Words To Know After students have completed the Words to Know activity, have students pair up and share the synonyms they wrote. Have partners then come up with antonyms for the words.

Develop Comprehension

Students should read the paragraph at the top of page 121 before reading the comic panels. Then, students should read the comic panels and complete the activity before reading the bottom paragraph.

Differentiated Instruction

▶ **Approaching** Remind students that when New Netherland changed from Dutch to English control, the names of the colony and the main city changed: New Netherland (the colony) became New York; New Amsterdam (the city) became New York City.

▶ **Beyond** Have students compose a piece of creative writing that dramatizes the story of New Netherland's transition from Dutch to English hands.

▶ **ELL** Read the passages one sentence at a time and have students identify details. Have students create connections between the details they identified and the images on the page.

A Patron for Pennsylvania

The rest of the Middle Colonies were founded by a man named William Penn. He came from a wealthy and powerful English family. They belonged to the Church of England. Penn, however, joined another religious group called the Quakers. The Quakers were tolerant of other religions. They believed that everyone was equal. Like other religious groups, the Quakers were persecuted in England.

Penn's father had loaned money to the king. When his father died, William asked King Charles II to pay this debt with land in North America. The king gave William a large piece, west of New Jersey and southwest of New York. William named this land Pennsylvania, which means "Penn's Woods." He founded a colony where Quakers—and everyone else—could worship freely.

THINK • PAIR • SHARE
Underline the religious beliefs of the Quakers. Work with a partner to discuss how these beliefs differed from those of the Puritans.

This painting shows William Penn (second from the left) meeting with the Lenni Lenape to pay for their lands and negotiate peace. ▶

Describe how William Penn interacted with the Lenni Lenape.

Peace and Diversity

William Penn interacted with Native Americans differently than most English settlers. He signed a peace treaty with the Lenni Lenape and paid them for their lands. Penn welcomed Native American refugees from other colonies, too. The colony was peaceful for a very long time because of this.

Penn also granted equality to people of all religions and even to people of other European countries. Pennsylvania soon had as much ethnic and religious **diversity** as New York and New Jersey. Diversity is the condition of having people who are different in some way living or working together in the same place.

Philadelphia

William Penn's **primary** motivation for founding Pennsylvania was religious freedom. He also wanted to make money, just like the proprietors of New York and New Jersey! He picked the location for the first capital of Pennsylvania and carefully planned it out himself. He called it Philadelphia, which means "city of brotherly love." Philadelphia grew to become the busiest city in the colonies.

Delaware

Pennsylvania was mostly shaped like a box, but it had a little piece of land hanging off its southeastern corner. This piece of land was called the Three Lower Counties. Before the English and the Dutch came, this region had been colonized by people from Sweden.

In 1704 they asked William Penn for the right to make their own laws. He granted their request. The land was still part of Pennsylvania, but the people who lived there called it Delaware. Over time, Delaware came to be thought of as its own colony.

The Middle Colonies

Map and Globe Skills

1. **Identify and locate** the four Middle Colonies on the map. Label each one. Use your reference atlas if you need help.
2. **Circle** the city that used to be called New Amsterdam.
3. **Underline** the "city of brotherly love."

Lesson 3

(?) **Essential Question** How do societies develop?

Go back to **Show As You Go!** on pages 102–103.

netw⊙rks There's More Online!
• Games • Assessment

122

123

Lesson 3

Active Teaching

Lead a class discussion in which students compare and contrast the motivations for founding the Middle Colonies with the motivations for founding the New England Colonies.

Develop Comprehension
Ask:

1. *What was England's motivation for taking over New Netherland?* **L1**

2. *Was William Penn's motivation for founding Pennsylvania an example of an economic, a political, or a socio-cultural reason?* **L2**

3. *Did William Penn have a second motive for founding Pennsylvania? What was it?* **L1**

4. *What were the Three Lower Counties? Who settled there?* **L1**

5. *Describe the relative location of Delaware.* **L2**

6. *What might have happened if William Penn and the Lenni Lenape had not signed a treaty?* **L3**

Show As You Go! Remind students to go back to the Unit Opener and complete the activities for this lesson.

Response to Intervention

(?) **Essential Question** **How do societies develop?**

If . . . students cannot identify and locate the four Middle Colonies on the map on page 123 using clues from the text

Then . . . have them refer to the United States political map in the Reference Atlas. Remind students that the thirteen colonies later became the first thirteen states and that they're all located in the eastern United States. First, locate the New England Colonies and identify the general area of the Middle Colonies as being west and south of New England. Next, identify New York. Correct students if they identify only Manhattan Island as New York in error. Then, have students use their finger to trace south and west from New York to find New Jersey, Pennsylvania, and Delaware.

Map and Globe Skills

Use this additional question with the map on page 123.
Ask:

1. *Which Native American group lived in present-day Pennsylvania? (Lenni Lenape)* **L1**

Lesson 4
Settling the Southern Colonies

Essential Question
How do societies develop?
What do you think?

_____
_____
_____
_____
_____

Imagine that you are looking for a new house. Make a short list of some things you want.

_____
_____

Is a big back yard or nearby playground on your list? If so, you have something in common with many who came to the Southern Colonies! You both want land.

You remember reading about Jamestown's first successful tobacco crop, right? Virginia's climate was perfect for growing it. Tobacco was grown on plantations, or large farms that often grow just one crop. Each new harvest earned a lot of money. People flooded Virginia to either start their own farms or work on existing plantations. This caused Virginia to grow and expand each year. Soon, the colonists needed more room.

Words To Know
Look at the words below. Discuss with a partner what you think they mean.

frontier

act

profit

*common

▼ A painting of a Virginia plantation

124

Virginia and Maryland

As Virginia grew, settlers pushed west, north, and south into new lands. At the same time, English leaders issued new colonial charters. The Southern colonies began to take shape.

George Calvert

Cecilius Calvert

The Algonquians

By now you know that Native Americans already lived on the land that Virginians wanted. Relations between the Jamestown settlers and the Algonquians had never been easy. As colonists claimed more land, conflict became more frequent.

The colonists had advantages, including guns and resistance to the diseases that came with them from Europe. These and other factors wore the Algonquians down year by year. In 1646 a Jamestown settler killed the leader of the Algonquians. This ended most of the major fighting, but smaller conflicts continued on the **frontier**. This is the edge of land settled by colonists. Virginia's growth was unstoppable, however.

1. Underline the motivations for founding Maryland.

2. How was this similar to the reasons for founding colonies in New England?

They wanted to get away from the Church of England.

Founding Maryland

As you read in Lesson 1, in England in the 1600s it was illegal to belong to any church except the Church of England. Even so, at that time King Charles I was friends with a man named George Calvert, a Catholic.

Calvert hatched a plan to found a colony where Catholics could have religious freedom. King Charles agreed and in 1632 wrote up a colonial charter that founded Maryland. Unfortunately, Calvert died before the first settlers arrived. His son Cecilius took over.

Most of the settlers who came to Maryland from England were Catholic. However, many of Maryland's settlers came from Virginia and were members of the Church of England. Soon, Catholics were outnumbered. They might have faced persecution, but Maryland's charter protected them. In 1649 the Toleration **Act** made religious freedom the law for Christians in Maryland. Act is another word for law.

125

Lesson 4

Activate Prior Knowledge

Before beginning the lesson, administer a short quiz about the founding of Virginia and the settlements of Roanoke and Jamestown. Student responses will help identify their level of understanding of the foundation of the Southern colonies.

Essential Question How do societies develop?

Have students explain what they understand about the Essential Question. Discuss their responses. Explain that everything they learn in this lesson will help them understand the Essential Question better. Remind them to think about how the Essential Question connects to the unit Big Idea: Location affects how people live.

Active Teaching

Words To Know After students have completed the Words to Know activity, have students use the glossary to find the definitions of the vocabulary words. Have them write this beneath their own definition.

Develop Comprehension
Ask:
1. Who were the Algonquians? **L1**
2. Why do you think conflicts between settlers and Native Americans continued on the frontier? **L3**

Differentiated Instruction

▶ **Approaching** Explain to students that because of England and Scotland merging into Great Britain in 1707, both the names Britain and England are used to refer to that country. Similarly, citizens of Great Britain are called either *British* or *English*.

▶ **Beyond** As students read about the founding of each Southern colony, have them circle the motivations by which each colony was founded. Then, have students write the motivations on the correct colony next to the map on page 126 and evaluate each motivation as economic, political, or socio-cultural.

▶ **ELL** Read aloud the lesson with students. As students read along, have them identify and circle new or difficult words. Have students use a dictionary to find out what each word means, and then write the definition in the margins.

networks
Go to **connected.mcgraw-hill.com** for additional resources.
• Interactive Whiteboard Lessons
• Worksheets
• Assessment

The Carolinas, North and South

Underline who settled Carolina. Circle their motivations.

England kept adding to its colonies. A new king, Charles II, set his sights on land south of Virginia. In 1663 he gave a charter for the colony of Carolina to eight proprietors. Seven years later, they founded their first settlement, the port city of Charles Towne.

Carolina's settlers established large plantations. They grew crops, such as tobacco and rice, for **profit**. Profit is the money left over after a business has paid all of its bills. They also sold forest products such as timber and tar. Soon Charles Towne prospered.

New settlers continued to arrive, lured by promises of religious freedom and land. Before long, farms and small settlements dotted Carolina's coast.

Carolina was a large piece of land—so large that its northern and southern parts developed differently. The northern part grew slowly because it didn't have a good port. The southern part grew rapidly because of Charles Towne. In 1729 the colonists decided to split their colony in two—North Carolina and South Carolina.

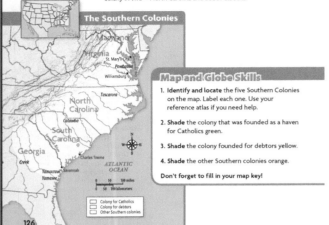

The Southern Colonies

Maryland
Virginia
St. Mary's City
Powhatan
Williamsburg
Tuscarora
North Carolina
Catawba
South Carolina
Georgia
Creek
Yamacraw Savannah
Yamasee
Charles Towne
ATLANTIC OCEAN
0   50   100 miles
0   50 100 kilometers

☐ Colony for Catholics
☐ Colony for debtors
☐ Other Southern colonies

126

Map and Globe Skills

1. **Identify and locate** the five Southern Colonies on the map. Label each one. Use your reference atlas if you need help.

2. **Shade** the colony that was founded as a haven for Catholics green.

3. **Shade** the colony founded for debtors yellow.

4. **Shade** the other Southern colonies orange.

Don't forget to fill in your map key!

Founding Georgia

As the colonies continued to bloom in the early 1700s, life back in Great Britain was pretty bad. Many families were poor and in **debt**, which means they owed money to others. It was **common** for debtors to be thrown in prison if they failed to pay. The British needed a solution to the misery.

A Colony for Debtors

James Oglethorpe had an idea. Why not create a new colony and send debtors there? They could work off their debt and make the colony rich! King George II liked the idea. He named the new colony after himself. In 1733 the first families sailed for Georgia.

Hundreds of poor came to Georgia. But in the end, Georgia didn't attract as many debtors as Oglethorpe had hoped. Other groups filled the gap. People from Germany and Switzerland came to Georgia. Promises of religious freedom and land lured them there. Once in the colonies, they fell under British rule. The founding of Georgia made Britain's set of thirteen colonies complete.

Native Americans and Georgia

Oglethorpe worked with Native Americans. Before building a settlement, he met with Tomochichi, the leader of the Yamacraw. The Yamacraw lived in the area where the settlers wanted to build. Oglethorpe obtained land for the settlement of Savannah, and Tomochichi became a friend to the settlers. He helped the settlers keep peace with Creek tribes nearby.

James Oglethorpe

Draw or describe James Oglethorpe's plan in the thought bubble.

Lesson 4

? **Essential Question** How do societies develop?

Go back to *Show As You Go!* on pages 102–103.

networks   There's More Online!
• Games • Assessment

127

Lesson 4

Active Teaching

Follow these steps to guide students through page 127.

- Have students read the first two paragraphs before completing the activity.

- Once students have completed the activity, have them read the third paragraph.

- Then, lead students in a discussion about the motivations for settling Georgia, and whether or not Oglethorpe's plan was successful.

Show As You Go! Remind students to go back to the Unit Opener and complete the activities for this lesson.

Map and Globe Skills

As students fill in their maps, note that Maryland should be shaded green, Georgia should be shaded yellow, and Virginia, South Carolina, and North Carolina should be shaded orange.

Response to Intervention

? **Essential Question** How do societies develop?

If . . . students cannot identify and locate the five Southern Colonies on the map on page 126 using clues from the text

. . . .

Then . . . have them refer to the United States political map in the Reference Atlas. Remind students that the thirteen colonies later became the first thirteen states and that they're all located in the eastern United States. First, locate Virginia and identify the general area of the Southern Colonies. Next, have students use their finger to trace north from Virginia to find Maryland. Then, return to Virginia and have students use their finger to trace south to find the Carolinas and Georgia.

Lesson
5 Life in the Colonies

networks There's More Online! Content Library • Videos

? Essential Question

How do societies develop?
What do you think?

_____

_____

_____

_____

_____

In 300 years, your community may look very different from today. Pretend that someone from the future is describing your community. What facts would they need to know?

_____

_____

_____

In Lesson 5 we'll explore what communities looked like in the thirteen colonies. As you will see, communities 300 years ago were very different from those we live in today.

Words To Know

Write the plural form of each word on the lines.

assembly _____

barter _____

occupation _____

*employ _____

Colonial Settlement by 1760
- Settled by 1750
- ⚓ Colonial city
- ⚓ Major port

MAINE (PART OF MA)
NH, Boston
NY, MA
Hartford CT, RI Newport
PA, NJ Trenton, New York
MD, Philadelphia
DE, Dover
VA, St. Marys City, Williamsburg
ATLANTIC OCEAN
NC
SC
GA, Charles Towne, Savannah

What can you infer about the colonies based on this map?

_____

_____

How Did Colonists Live?

By the mid-1700s, English colonists had settled the East Coast from Massachusetts to Georgia. They had set up new communities with governments, economies, and ways of life. While each colonial region had similarities, they also had characteristics that set them apart.

As you read this lesson, come back to this page and fill the chart below with the different characteristics of the colonies.

///// GLUE FOLDABLE HERE /////

	New England Colonies	Middle Colonies	Southern Colonies
Government			
Economy			
Social Aspects			

128

129

Lesson 5

Activate Prior Knowledge

After students have completed the activity, have volunteers discuss their responses. Make a list on the board. Then, point out that a lot had changed in the colonies since they were initially settled. Ask a series of questions about the founding of the thirteen colonies such as: _Do you remember the names of the New England Colonies?_ Students should indicate their level of recall with each question by holding up fingers with:

1 = I know very little about this

2 = I know some about this

3 = I know a lot about this

Student responses will help identify their level of understanding.

? Essential Question How do societies develop?

Have students explain what they understand about the Essential Question. Discuss their responses. Explain that everything they learn in this lesson will help them understand the Essential Question better. Remind them to think about how the Essential Question connects to the unit Big Idea: Location affects how people live.

Active Teaching

Words To Know Once students have completed the Words to Know activity, have them identify the part of speech to which each vocabulary word belongs. Next, have students come up with one or more synonyms or antonyms for each word.

Page Power

FOLDABLES Interact more with the page. Have students create a Notebook Foldable to assist in developing their understanding of the political, economic, and social aspects of daily colonial life as they apply to each of the regions.

1. Provide students with a copy of Foldable 4A from the Notebook Foldables section at the back of this book.

2. Have students construct the Foldable and glue its anchor tab just above the chart on page 129.

3. On the Foldable flaps, have students write additional details about each region as they read Lesson 5.

4. On the backs of the flaps, students should write down which colonies were in each region. They should also take notes about any of the details on the chart (Government, Economy, Social Aspects) that are specific to each colony.

Governing the Thirteen Colonies

Settlers typically formed their own governments soon after they arrived. Many colonial charters guaranteed the colonists' right to form an **assembly**, or lawmaking body. The assembly represented the people of its colony. Members gathered to discuss important issues and to make laws based on the needs and wants of their colonists. Each colony also had a governor, who represented the needs and wants of Great Britain. While many things about government in the colonies were the same, there were also some differences. The chart shows ways colonial governments were similar and different.

Characteristics of Colonial Governments

All Colonial Governments

- Each colony had an assembly, a governor, and judges.
- Only white males could vote or hold office.
- Britain's government could reject any law proposed by the colonies.
- Governors and assemblies appointed judges to answer questions about laws and settle disputes.
- The king or colonial proprietors appointed colonial governors.
  - Except in Rhode Island and Connecticut! There colonists could choose their own governors.

Local Governments in New England and the Middle Colonies

- Local government was based around cities and towns.
- Colonists held town-hall meetings where they:
  - discussed important issues.
  - elected local officials.
  - elected their representatives.
  - settled disputes.

County Governments in the Southern Colonies

- Local government was county-wide, instead of city-wide.
- County officials were appointed by the colonial governor.
- People met at the county court house once a month to do business, discuss issues, and hear speeches.

130

▲ Reenactors recreate Virginia's colonial assembly every year in Williamsburg.

Participating in Colonial Politics

Colonial governments were the early beginnings of our government today, but they were far different from what we're used to. One difference is that there was no national government! Each colony was separate from the others. Everyone was subject to the will of Great Britain.

Another difference is that only a few colonists were allowed to participate. Only white males were allowed to vote. And there were other restrictions. In some colonies, people had to own land or belong to a certain church. If you didn't meet all of an area's requirements, you couldn't vote or hold office.

Colonists often made their needs and wants known to their assembly members and governors. They did this through writing and speaking about political ideas. You'll learn more about these actions in the coming units. For now, just remember this: through their actions, colonists set up the political traditions that we carry on today.

 Turn back to page 129. Fill in the "Government" row of your chart.

Reading Skill

Draw Inferences

Using the picture above and the chart on page 130, make an inference about who was NOT allowed to participate in government.

women and

non-whites

DID YOU KNOW?

Writing down all the rules of government is a time-honored tradition! Here's a short list of some of the government documents written during the colonial period.
- Mayflower Compact
- Fundamental Orders of Connecticut
- Frame of Government of Pennsylvania

131

Lesson 5

Active Teaching

After students have finished reading page 131, explain that participating in politics is another way of saying participating in government. So, when students read about or hear people discussing politics, it's a "safe bet" that the topic relates in some way to government. Have students return to page 129 and complete the "Government" row of the chart.

Clarify Misconceptions

Because the thirteen colonies are taught as a group, students may infer that settlers in each colony thought of themselves as unified with the other colonies. In reality, settlers thought of themselves as British subjects first and citizens of their colony second. There was no unity among the thirteen colonies until the Revolution. Students will learn more about the disunity of British colonists/Americans in Units 5 and 6, so it may help to clarify this misconception now.

Page Power

Interact more with the page. Have students:

- underline details that describe political relationships between the thirteen colonies and Great Britain.
- circle details that show who could vote and hold office in the colonial era.

Differentiated Instruction

▶ **Beyond** Have students brainstorm a list of reasons why forming colonial governments was important. Then, have them imagine how life in the colonies would be different without colonial governments.

Reading Skill

🔵 **Common Core Standards RI.1** Quote accurately from a text when explaining what the text says explicitly and when drawing conclusions from the text.

Draw Inferences Remind students that when drawing an inference, they combine the facts they learn from the reading with what they already know.

netw⊙rks

Go to connected.mcgraw-hill.com for additional resources.

Interactive Whiteboard Lessons
- Worksheets
- Assessment
- Lesson Plans
- Videos

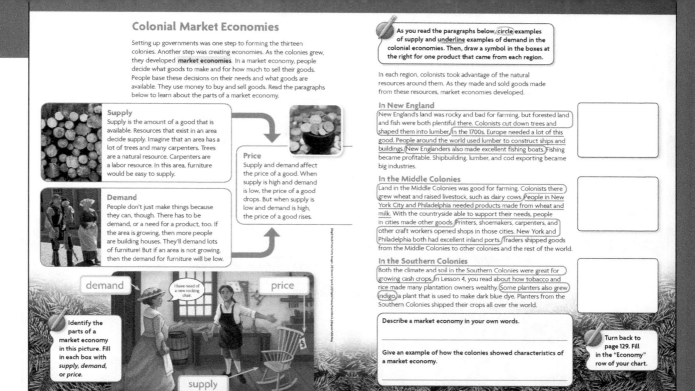

Colonial Market Economies

Setting up governments was one step to forming the thirteen colonies. Another step was creating economies. As the colonies grew, they developed **market economies**. In a market economy, people decide what goods to make and for how much to sell their goods. People base these decisions on their needs and what goods are available. They use money to buy and sell goods. Read the paragraphs below to learn about the parts of a market economy.

Supply
Supply is the amount of a good that is available. Resources that exist in an area decide supply. Imagine that an area has a lot of trees and many carpenters. Trees are a natural resource. Carpenters are a labor resource. In this area, furniture would be easy to supply.

Demand
People don't just make things because they can, though. There has to be demand, or a need for a product, too. If the area is growing, then more people are building houses. They'll demand lots of furniture! But if an area is not growing, then the demand for furniture will be low.

Price
Supply and demand affect the price of a good. When supply is high and demand is low, the price of a good drops. But when supply is low and demand is high, the price of a good rises.

Identify the parts of a market economy in this picture. Fill in each box with *supply, demand,* or *price.*

demand

I have need of a new rocking chair.

price

supply

As you read the paragraphs below, circle examples of supply and underline examples of demand in the colonial economies. Then, draw a symbol in the boxes at the right for one product that came from each region.

In each region, colonists took advantage of the natural resources around them. As they made and sold goods made from these resources, market economies developed.

In New England
New England's land was rocky and bad for farming, but forested land and fish were both plentiful there. Colonists cut down trees and shaped them into lumber. In the 1700s, Europe needed a lot of this good. People around the world used lumber to construct ships and buildings. New Englanders also made excellent fishing boats. Fishing became profitable. Shipbuilding, lumber, and cod exporting became big industries.

In the Middle Colonies
Land in the Middle Colonies was good for farming. Colonists there grew wheat and raised livestock, such as dairy cows. People in New York City and Philadelphia needed products made from wheat and milk. With the countryside able to support their needs, people in cities made other goods. Printers, shoemakers, carpenters, and other craft workers opened shops in those cities. New York and Philadelphia both had excellent inland ports. Traders shipped goods from the Middle Colonies to other colonies and the rest of the world.

In the Southern Colonies
Both the climate and soil in the Southern Colonies were great for growing cash crops. In Lesson 4, you read about how tobacco and rice made many plantation owners wealthy. Some planters also grew indigo, a plant that is used to make dark blue dye. Planters from the Southern Colonies shipped their crops all over the world.

Describe a market economy in your own words.

Give an example of how the colonies showed characteristics of a market economy.

Turn back to page 129. Fill in the "Economy" row of your chart.

132   133

Active Teaching

Once students have read the introductory paragraph, check for students' understanding of a market economy.

Develop Comprehension
Ask:

1. *What is a market economy?* **L2**
2. *Do we have a market economy today?* **L2**
3. *What goods do people buy and sell today?* **L1**
4. *What goods are made or grown in our area?* **L1**

Students should read the headings "Supply," "Demand," and "Price" in that order. Students should complete the activities on both pages. Then, have students return to page 129 and complete the "Economy" row of the chart.

Teach pages 132–133 in conjunction with page 134 (Trade With Native Americans).

Page Power
Interact more with the page. Have students use prior knowledge and context clues from the paragraphs to come up with additional examples of products that might have been made, grown, or caught in each of the colonial regions. Students should write their examples next to each region's paragraph.

Differentiated Instruction

▶ **Approaching** Make the concept of a market economy more accessible to students by using the example of a farmer and a market. Explain to students that the farmer is a producer. The crops he grows are his goods. The farmer and his crops are the supply in a market economy. The people who shop at the market are consumers. They are the demand in a market economy. Find real-life images to illustrate these concepts and have students use them to identify the parts of a market economy.

▶ **Beyond** Have students find real-life images of people producing, buying, or selling goods. Have students label the parts of a market economy shown in their image and write image captions that explain a market economy.

▶ **ELL** Have students define the terms "supply," "demand," and "price" in their own words. Then, have students come up with examples from everyday life that fit the concepts. They may want to draw these examples on a separate sheet of paper and glue it into the book.

Trade With Native Americans

Settlers in the thirteen colonies also traded with Native Americans. Think back to what you learned about trade between Native Americans and European explorers.

> Use what you know to finish this sentence.
>
> Native Americans traded _____ for _____
>
> with explorers from _____ .

As you read the paragraphs on page 134, show that you recognize the positive and negative effects of this trade. Highlight positive effects of trade. Underline negative effects of trade.

Native Americans and British colonists traded for many years as well. Native Americans usually didn't use British money, so traders would often **barter**, or exchange goods for other goods. Bartering was also a common practice among European colonists.

This trade affected how colonists and Native Americans interacted with each other. Native Americans and British traders made important business connections and friendships. Sometimes they even married into each other's families.

Trade changed Native American ways of life. They began to hunt for profit, instead of just for what they needed. Trade made them more dependent on British goods, such as clothing and tools.

Settlers benefited by selling furs and other North American goods in Europe for a high price. This brought money into the colonies and created growth, which the colonial proprietors welcomed. But land disputes and arguments over trading practices often turned violent between colonists and Native Americans. The animal populations suffered, as well. For example, beavers became almost extinct in parts of the colonies.

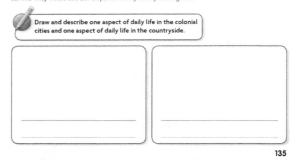

Colonists traded many things with Native Americans. ▶

134

Daily Life

In the 1700s, shipping goods over water was the easiest way to transport them. So colonists typically landed, stayed, and built settlements where there were good, deep harbors. Over time, many of these settlements grew into bustling port cities.

In Colonial Cities

Men in the cities had many different **occupations**, or jobs. Many worked at a trade or craft, such as brick laying or shoe making. Others were **employed** as doctors, lawyers, and ministers. They performed services for people in the cities and countryside.

Women in the cities mostly took care of the home and children. Children helped out as soon as they were old enough. There were many chores to do, like cooking, cleaning, washing laundry, and sewing.

In the Countryside

Many settlers came to the colonies for the chance to own land. As a result, most colonial families lived in the countryside on farms. New England farms were typically small and only supported one family. Farms in the Middle Colonies were a little larger. Plantations in the Southern Colonies were the largest of the colonial farms.

Farm life was full of hard work. Men planted crops and hunted. Women did household chores such as cooking, cleaning, and weaving cloth. Children helped take care of farm animals.

Families could often make or grow much of what they needed to survive. They would also sell crops for money to buy other goods.

Draw and describe one aspect of daily life in the colonial cities and one aspect of daily life in the countryside.

135

Lesson 5

Active Teaching

Page 134: Teach in conjunction with pages 132–133. Once students have read the pages and completed the activities,

Ask: *How did you decide which effects were positive and which ones were negative?*

Then, tie the discussion of trade with Native Americans into the larger discussion about colonial market economies.

Say: *As Native Americans and European settlers traded goods, they also traded aspects of their cultures. One aspect Europeans traded to Native Americans was the concept of a market economy.*

☑ Formative Assessment

Page 134: Have students summarize what they have learned about market economies in the thirteen colonies by writing a short story or expository essay that tells how a market economy works and gives examples from one colonial region. Students should also mention trade interactions between settlers and Native Americans. Use this assessment to monitor student understanding and identify the need for intervention.

Active Teaching

Page 135: Teach separately from page 134. Teach in conjunction with pages 136–137.

Develop Comprehension
Ask:
1. *What occupation did many colonists do in the countryside?* **L1**
2. *What is an occupation? What occupations did men do in the cities?* **L1**
3. *What kinds of work did women and children do?* **L1**
4. *Did most colonists live in the cities or on farms in the countryside? Why do you think that was?* **L2**
5. *Why were cities built near deep harbors?* **L2**
6. *What was life like in colonial communities? How does it compare to life today?* **L3**

Education in the Colonies

Schools in the thirteen colonies were very different from what you're used to! The first schools began in New England towns. Children learned in private homes or in small "writing schools." Students learned to read, write, and do basic math. Around the age of eight, though, formal education ended for most girls and many boys. At this age, children were expected to learn how to do things around the home. They also helped with the family farm or business.

In the Middle and Southern Colonies, most children didn't go to school. Most families taught their children at home. Only the largest cities had public schools, anyway.

Throughout the colonies, wealthy families sent their children to private schools, or had them tutored at home. Eventually, wealthy students could go on to colleges in New England or Great Britain.

Children of middle class families had another option. They could become apprentices and learn a trade. An apprentice learns a trade or craft from someone who is already skilled at it. After studying and practicing, an apprentice might become a silversmith or carpenter. At first, only boys were allowed to be apprentices. Later, girls began to learn some trades too. This system offered poorer children a way to move up in society.

FUN FACTS
Benjamin Franklin started out as an apprentice printer. He later became a famous inventor! Two of his inventions were the Franklin stove and bifocals. The Franklin stove was a metal fireplace that used less wood and provided more heat than other stoves at that time. Bifocals are glasses that help people see things both up close and far away.

▲ A young apprentice furniture maker learns his trade.

Imagine you are part of a colonial family. Choose a role by circling one word from each column. Then describe how you might get an education.

My family is:
poor
middle class
wealthy

We live in:
Boston, Massachusetts
Delaware
South Carolina

Colonial Recreation

Of course colonial children and adults alike wanted to have some fun too! When they were not helping at home or studying, children played with wooden toys, marbles, hoops, and dolls. Women gathered in small groups to sew, knit, cross-stitch, and quilt. Board games, such as chess and checkers, were common. Colonists also liked ninepin, a game similar to bowling.

Events, such as feasts and dances, drew community members out to sing, dance, tell stories, and eat. Colonists sometimes staged competitions based on who could do ordinary tasks the fastest or with the most skill. Activities varied from colony to colony and reflected the cultures of the people who settled there.

▲ Colonial children played many games.

Make a list of some social aspects of daily colonial life. (Hint: These are ways colonists interacted with each other.) Then, circle an item on your list that you do today or an item that you'd like to try.

Turn back to page 129. Fill in the "Social Aspects" row of your chart.

Lesson 5

(?) **Essential Question** How do societies develop?

Go back to *Show As You Go!* on pages 102–103.

networks There's More Online!
● Games ● Assessment

Active Teaching

Develop Comprehension

Ask:

1. *What aspects of colonial life are discussed on these pages?* **L1**

2. *Why were children in the Middle and Southern colonies less likely to go to a formal school?* **L2**

3. *The first schools in America began in New England towns. Use this clue to guess which group of settlers cared a great deal about education. (Puritans)* **L3**

4. *How did colonists have fun?* **L1**

5. *What kinds of community events did colonists hold?* **L1**

Have students return to page 129 and complete the "Social Aspects" row of the chart.

>>> ***Show As You Go!*** Remind students to go back to the Unit Opener and complete the activities for this lesson.

Response to Intervention

(?) **Essential Question** How do societies develop?

If . . . students are unable to compare characteristics (political, economic, and social) of the colonial regions, begin by identifying the actual issue. For example, are they missing a particular characteristic or region? Once you have identified the specifics of the misunderstanding,

. . . .

Then . . . take students back to the pages that cover the topic(s) with which students are having the most difficulty. As students reread each section of text, discuss the key details. It may be helpful to have students record their findings. After all sections are completed, discuss the similarities and differences in the key details. Have students glue or tape their notes into the book for future reference.

Lesson 6 Slavery and the Triangular Trade

? Essential Question

How do cultures change? **What do you think?**

_____

_____

_____

_____

Words To Know

Write the definition of each word in your own words.

indentured servant

_____

_____

*code

_____

_____

_____

When something interesting, exciting, or sad happens to you, what do you do? Do you often tell others about your experience? If you do, you're not alone. Most people tell stories! Sometimes stories are just for fun, but other times stories are serious. In this lesson, you'll learn about someone who had a very important story to tell.

Olaudah Equiano

My name is Olaudah Equiano. I lived at a very interesting and very sad time in history. I was born in Africa in the 1740s, and I traveled the world. Look for me as you read. I'll tell you what I saw.

In 1619 these enslaved Africans arrived in Jamestown, Virginia aboard a Dutch ship. ▼

How Slavery Was Introduced

Growing cash crops requires a lot of labor—more labor than colonial planters could do themselves. Planters needed workers. At first, the planters hired **indentured servants** to do the work. An indentured servant agreed to work for a number of years in exchange for travel to a colony. Not enough indentured servants came, though. Planters looked for other sources of labor.

To meet the demand for labor, traders began purchasing captives (people!) in West Africa. Most captives were taken from their homes and families.

This is what happened to me, Olaudah. I was around your age when I was kidnapped and taken from my home. I never saw my mother again.

Traders shipped the captives across the Atlantic Ocean to colonies that needed labor. Tobacco planters brought the first African captives to Jamestown in 1619. As the colonies grew, a system of slavery developed. Recall that slavery is the practice of treating people as property and forcing them to work. By 1750, all thirteen colonies had made slavery legal.

DID YOU KNOW?

Some of the first Africans in the colonies were treated more like indentured servants than enslaved people. After years of labor, they gained their freedom. Later, colonial assemblies passed laws against setting captive Africans free. This meant that most were enslaved for life.

Reading Skill

Sequencing

Put these events in the correct order to describe the introduction of slavery to the colonies.

3 Proprietors hire indentured servants.

1 Colonists settle Jamestown.

5 Africans are captured and shipped to the colonies.

2 Jamestown settlers begin growing tobacco.

6 Captive Africans are sold in the colonies.

4 Planters look for other people to help grow cash crops.

7 Slavery is made legal.

Lesson 6

Activate Prior Knowledge

After students have read the introductory paragraphs on page 138, **Ask:**

1. *Can you give an example of a story that people tell just for fun? How about an example of a serious story?*

2. *Why do you think people tell serious stories?*

Explain to students that Equiano's story is a serious one. It is a first-person account of a dark chapter in American history. First-person accounts of all kinds of events (positive and negative) are an important part of preserving history for future generations.

? Essential Question How do cultures change?

Have students explain what they understand about the Essential Question. Discuss their responses. Explain that everything they learn in this lesson will help them understand the Essential Question better. Remind them to think about how the Essential Question connects to the unit Big Idea: Location affects how people live.

Active Teaching

Words To Know Once students have completed the Words to Know activity, explain to students that *code* is a word with multiple meanings. Have students use a dictionary to write down all of the meanings of *code*. Ask them to circle the meaning that applies in this lesson.

Develop Comprehension

The content that is ***boldfaced and italicized*** throughout the lesson is told in first person from the point of view of Olaudah Equiano and is based on facts as presented in his memoir. Students may need to be reminded what it means to read a first-person point of view in order to understand the lesson.

Reading Skill

Sequencing Remind students that when they are sequencing, they are placing events in the order that they occurred. **Say:** *Sequencing helps you deal with a lot of information in a way that is more understandable. When we study history, sequencing events can help us understand causes and effects.*

The Triangular Trade

During the 1700s, a system of shipping routes developed as trade grew across the Atlantic Ocean. The routes linked Europe and Africa with the West Indies and the thirteen British colonies. Traders exchanged goods and resources. They also brought enslaved Africans to the colonies. This system became known as the Triangular Trade. The groups were each responsible for something different. This is called specialization.

Follow my journey on the map. I was born in Africa. When I was kidnapped, I was put on a ship bound for the West Indies. Later, I was sold to a man in Virginia. Can you imagine being a whole ocean away from your home?

A Very Important Trade

As the Triangular Trade developed, it promoted economic growth in the colonies. In fact, some colonists grew very rich from it, especially in New England.

At this time, British rulers wanted the colonists to trade only with Great Britain. The British government, called Parliament, passed laws to try to control colonial trade. Parliament couldn't control the colonists, though. British taxes cut into merchants' profits. Merchants began secretly importing and exporting goods with traders from other countries. This was an early step on the long road to independence.

The Triangular Trade had another effect. It quickly increased the number of enslaved Africans in the colonies. Traders and planters became dependent on slavery to do business. They were interdependent, or relied on each other to meet needs and wants.

Explain the importance of the Triangular Trade.

140

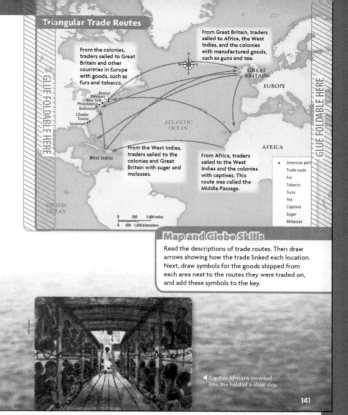

Triangular Trade Routes

From Great Britain, traders sailed to Africa, the West Indies, and the colonies with manufactured goods, such as guns and tea.

From the colonies, traders sailed to Great Britain and other countries in Europe with goods, such as furs and tobacco.

From the West Indies, traders sailed to the colonies and Great Britain with sugar and molasses.

From Africa, traders sailed to the West Indies and the colonies with captives. This route was called the Middle Passage.

American port
Trade route
Fur
Tobacco
Guns
Tea
Captives
Sugar
Molasses

Map and Globe Skills

Read the descriptions of trade routes. Then draw arrows showing how the trade linked each location. Next, draw symbols for the goods shipped from each area next to the routes they were traded on, and add these symbols to the key.

◀ Captive Africans crowded into the hold of a slave ship.

141

Active Teaching

Have students read page 140 and study the map and images on page 141. Then have students complete the map on page 141. You might further develop students' understanding by having them:

- circle details that show how the Triangular Trade promoted economic growth in North America.
- underline details that show how the Triangular Trade promoted slavery.
- write a caption for the image on page 141 that describes the emotions evoked by the image.

Differentiated Instruction

▶ **ELL** Students may confuse the terms Triangular Trade and Atlantic slave trade. Explain that *Triangular Trade* refers to the exchange of all goods and resources across the Atlantic Ocean during this time period. *Atlantic slave trade* refers only to the exchange of captive Africans. Give students the opportunity to translate each of these terms in their own words to reinforce understanding.

Page Power

FOLDABLES Interact more with the page. Have students create a Notebook Foldable to assist in developing their understanding of the geography and economics of the Triangular Trade.

1. Provide students with a copy of Foldable 4B from the Notebook Foldables section at the back of this book.

2. Have students construct the Foldable and glue its anchor tabs to the left and right of the map on page 141.

3. On the Foldable flaps, have students write the names of: 1) the thirteen colonies, 2) European countries, 3) African countries, and 4) islands of the West Indies that were major participants in the Triangular Trade. Students may need to refer to their Reference Atlas for names of the islands.

4. Finally, have students do research to discover one additional item that was traded on each leg of the route. Students should write a description of their items on the inside of each flap.

Map and Globe Skills

Use this additional question with the map on page 141.
Ask:

1. *What kinds of goods were sent out from the West Indies?* (sugar and molasses) **L1**

Slavery's Role

You just learned that slavery started in North America because planters needed laborers to plant and harvest cash crops.

That's not all we did though. There were many different jobs to do, and they varied by region. Some of us were skilled laborers, such as carpenters, blacksmiths, and cooks. Others worked in the homes of slaveholders. I was a sailor on a ship.

In New England and the Middle Colonies, many enslaved Africans worked as servants in wealthy households, in shipyards, on small farms, or at a trade. New York had a large enslaved population. In New York City, some enslaved people were brick layers. They built the wall that gave Wall Street its name. Some colonists in the New England and Middle Colonies owned slave ships. Before the 1770s, many ships full of African captives sailed to Rhode Island. From there, the captives were sold throughout the colonies. Ship owners, traders, and merchants grew rich from the capture and sale of enslaved people. The New England and Middle Colonies benefitted from slavery. The Southern colonies, however, benefitted a great deal more.

▲ This is a reenactment of a young enslaved apprentice learning to weave a basket.

Underline the role ship owners played in the slavery system.

> **Describe the roles of enslaved people in the New England and Middle Colonies.**
>
> Enslaved Africans worked as servants.
>
> Some worked as brick layers.

142

◄ This image shows a reenactment of enslaved field work.

Slavery on Plantations

Recall that many farms in the Southern Colonies grew cash crops. Both rice and tobacco plants required many workers to plant, tend, and harvest them. Enslaved Africans did most of this labor. Most farms were small and had just a few enslaved Africans. However, the Southern Colonies became known for their large, stately plantations. These plantations sometimes used hundreds of workers. In fact, many plantations in the Southern Colonies couldn't operate without enslaved workers.

Owners of these plantations hired poor whites, or forced enslaved Africans, to act as overseers. Overseers watched the workers in the fields. They made sure that work continued, dawn to dusk. Plantation owners grew rich from the crops grown by enslaved people. As a result, they enjoyed comfortable lives, free of hard work.

The owners also enriched the economies of their colonies, which benefited traders and other merchants. From Maryland to Georgia, settlers in the Southern Colonies viewed slavery as very important to their way of life.

Highlight the ways plantations relied on slavery.

> **Describe the roles of enslaved people in the Southern Colonies.**
>
> They did most of the labor on
>
> plantations. Some worked as overseers.

143

Lesson 6

Active Teaching

As students read, have them pay attention to similarities and differences in the role of enslaved people in the colonies. Have them take notes in the margins.

Develop Comprehension
Ask:

1. *What were some skilled jobs that enslaved Africans did in North America?* (carpenters, blacksmiths, cooks, and brick layers) **L1**

2. *Which region do you think had the largest number of enslaved Africans? Why?* (the South; there was a greater need for labor on large plantations) **L2**

Clarify Misconceptions

Students may associate slavery only with the South, when in reality slavery took place in all of the thirteen colonies. Students may also think that enslaved people only worked in unskilled jobs, when many enslaved individuals actually were skilled laborers.

Differentiated Instruction

▶ **Approaching** Simplify the questions on pages 142–143 for approaching students. Replace words such as "role" and "rely" with "jobs" and "depend on." Then have students underline and circle words in the text that provide clues to help them answer each question.

▶ **Beyond** Invite students to broaden their knowledge of slavery in the colonies by choosing a specific region, colony, trade, or historical figure to research. Students may work individually or in groups or pairs to develop a novel way to present their research findings to the class.

▶ **ELL** Have students work in groups to identify key words in the reading. Help define unfamiliar words. Provide or create visuals to represent any words that students still struggle with.

netw⊙rks

Go to **connected.mcgraw-hill.com** for additional resources.

- Interactive Whiteboard Lessons
- Worksheets
- Assessment

Slavery's Impact

Enslaved people suffered greatly, starting with our kidnapping in Africa. Captains of slave ships chained hundreds of us together in the ship's cargo area. Conditions were terrible, and many died along the way. Once in the colonies, traders sold us at auction.

Laws called slave **codes** set the rules of slavery. Under these laws, slave holders had total power over enslaved workers, whom they often treated brutally. Enslaved people could be beaten, sometimes without reason.

Slave holders only barely provided for workers' needs. Most enslaved people lived in simple cottages with dirt floors. They were cold in the winter and hot in the summer. Children of enslaved mothers were often taken away and sold to another slave holder. An enslaved person who tried to run away could be killed. This almost happened to Olaudah Equiano.

Slavery and Colonists

By the mid-1700s, slavery was a part of daily life. Whole economies required slave labor to keep them running.

Slavery also had other negative affects on colonists. Colonists developed false ideas about the intelligence and value of enslaved people in order to justify their actions. Today we call these ideas racism.

Colonists constantly feared violent revolts as well. Revolts were rare, but they sometimes happened as people struggled to be free. The false ideas and fears they held encouraged whites to reinforce slavery. As time passed, slave codes became harsher.

After you read, write a sentence about the impact of slavery for each topic below.

Enslaved Africans

_____

_____

_____

Colonists

_____

_____

_____

American Culture

_____

_____

_____

◀ At slave auctions, people were traded and sold like livestock.

144

Slavery and American Culture

Despite facing brutal hardships, enslaved Africans kept their cultures alive in the colonies. They contributed words from their native languages, such as *banjo* and *gumbo*, to American English. Enslaved people were not allowed to read or write, so they told stories to teach their children about their culture and life. Spirituals, the religious songs of enslaved Africans, have influenced American music.

Slavery was a miserable system and most enslaved people never escaped it. Despite all that I endured, I was able to save enough money to buy my freedom. This was a rare event, indeed. Very few enslaved people could earn money, much less save it up. After I bought my freedom, I sailed for Great Britain, where I wrote a book about my experiences.

Olaudah Equiano spoke out against slavery. People who came after him spoke out against it, too. Over time, movements against slavery grew in Great Britain and America. Even so, slavery would not end for a long time. It left lasting effects on our country.

▲ The influence of songs of enslaved Africans can be heard in gospel songs today.

Lesson 6

? Essential Question How do cultures change?

_____

_____

_____

_____

_____

Go back to *Show As You Go!* on pages 102–103. ◀◀◀

netw⊙rks There's More Online! • Games • Assessment

145

Active Teaching

Develop Comprehension
Ask:

1. *What was the purpose of slave codes?* **L1**
2. *Explain what the lives of enslaved people were like.* **L2**
3. *In what ways did enslaved people resist their captivity?* **L1**
4. *What impact did slavery have on the colonies?* **L2**
5. *What were some of the cultural contributions made by enslaved Africans?* **L1**
6. *Slavery was woven into the fabric of colonial economies. Why do you think it took "a long time" for slavery to end in America?* **L3**

⟪ *Show As You Go!* Remind students to go back to complete the project on the Unit Opener

Response to Intervention

? Essential Question How do cultures change?

If . . . students cannot describe the introduction, impact, and role of slavery in the colonies,

. . . .

Then . . . take students back to the pages that cover the topic(s) with which students are having the most difficulty. Check that students understand what is meant by "introduction," "impact," or "role" (whichever the students are struggling with). Direct students to the parts of the text which cover the aspect of slavery that needs reinforced. Ask students specific questions about points made in the text to help develop their understanding. Have students write their responses in the margins on the page(s).

UNIT 4 Wrap Up

Draw a line from each date in the list to its correct spot on the time line. Then, fill in each blank with the correct answer about the founding of the 13 colonies.

1600
1610
1620
1630
1640
1650
1660
1670
1680
1690
1700
1710
1720
1730
1740

• **1607:** The Virginia Company founds <u>Jamestown</u>, Virginia.

• **1619:** The first enslaved <u>Africans</u> arrived this year.

• **1620:** The <u>Pilgrims</u> found Plymouth, Massachusetts.

• **1632:** King Charles I gives a charter to Cecilius <u>Calvert</u>

• **1636:** Thomas Hooker leaves the Puritans and founds <u>Hartford</u>

• **1664:** England takes over New Netherland and renames it <u>New York</u> and <u>New Jersey</u>.

• **1681:** William Penn founds <u>Pennsylvania</u>, a colony where Quakers and others could worship freely.

• **1729:** The colony of <u>Carolina</u> splits into North and South.

• **1733:** James Oglethorpe founds the colony of <u>Georgia</u> for debtors.

146

BIG IDEA

Unit Project

Choose a colonial region you learned about in this unit. Imagine that you are a sales person, and you are trying to convince Europeans to move to your colonial region. Create a sales pitch and a pamphlet to promote your region. Before you begin, turn back to pages 102 and 103 to review your map. Read the list below to see what you need to include in your sales pitch and pamphlet. As you work, check off each task.

Your sales pitch and pamphlet should include . . .	Yes, it does
facts about the founding of the colonies in your region	◯
facts about the government in your colonial region	◯
facts about the economy of your colonial region	◯
facts about trade in your colonial region	◯
facts about daily life in your colonial region	◯
facts about slavery in your colonial region	◯
ideas about what your region can offer Europeans who settle there	◯
at least two illustrations	◯

Think about the Big Idea

BIG IDEA Location affects how people live.

What did you learn in this unit that helps you understand the BIG IDEA?

147

Wrap Up

Time Line

Have students fill in the blanks, then draw a line from each entry to the appropriate spot on the time line. Explain that the answers come from information throughout the unit.

BIG IDEA Big Idea Project

- Read through the project directions and checklist with students.
- Answer any questions students may have about the project.
- Remind students to use their **Show As You Go!** pages to assist them in completing the project.
- To assess the project, refer to the rubric on the following page.

Differentiated Instruction

▶ **Approaching** Student pamphlets may highlight one fact about each bullet point. Students may or may not present a sales pitch to the class.

▶ **Beyond** Have students include in their sales pitch an explanation of what the colonies had to gain by encouraging more people to settle.

▶ **ELL** Allow students to work in pairs or groups to create their pamphlet. Students may give their sales pitch to only their instructor.

Response to Intervention

BIG IDEA Location affects how people live.

If . . . students cannot give a substantiated explanation of how location affects how people live

Then . . . send students on a scavenger hunt through the unit. Break students into teams and give them a set amount of time in which they must find five examples of geography or location affecting how the colonists lived. Once time is up, have teams share their answers and discuss each answer with the class.

netw⊕rks

Go to **connected.mcgraw-hill.com** for additional resources.
- Games
- Assessment
- Group Technology Projects

Name _____ Date _____

Colonial Sales Pamphlet and Pitch Rubric

4 Exemplary	3 Accomplished	2 Developing	1 Beginning
The pamphlet: ☐ includes all of the colonies in the student's chosen region. ☐ contains accurate facts and details appropriate to the region. ☐ demonstrates one consistent design and layout. ☐ is interesting, easy to read, and includes two or more illustrations of the colony. ☐ contains none or few errors in grammar, punctuation, capitalization, and spelling. **The pitch:** ☐ includes information and details consistent with the pamphlet. ☐ is interesting and dynamic. ☐ The student "stays in character" and truly tries to "sell" the class on his or her region.	**The pamphlet:** ☐ includes most of the colonies in the student's chosen region. ☐ has mostly accurate facts and details appropriate to the region. ☐ has a mostly consistent design and layout. ☐ is mostly easy to read, and includes two illustrations. ☐ contains some errors in grammar, punctuation, capitalization, and spelling. **The pitch:** ☐ includes information and details that are mostly consistent with the pamphlet. ☐ is interesting. ☐ The student mostly "stays in character."	**The pamphlet:** ☐ includes at least two of the colonies in the student's chosen region. ☐ has some accurate facts and details appropriate to the region. ☐ has some consistent design or layout elements. ☐ is somewhat confusing and includes only one illustration. ☐ contains several errors in grammar, punctuation, capitalization, and spelling. **The pitch:** ☐ includes information and details that are somewhat consistent with the pamphlet. ☐ is flat but stays focused. ☐ The student "falls out of character."	**The pamphlet:** ☐ includes one or none of the colonies in the student's chosen region. ☐ has few accurate facts and details appropriate to the region. ☐ does not have a consistent layout or design. ☐ is difficult to follow and lacks an illustration. ☐ contains serious errors in grammar, punctuation, capitalization, and spelling. **The pitch:** ☐ includes information and details that are inconsistent with the pamphlet. ☐ is unfocused. ☐ The student never takes on the sales-person character.

Grading Comments: _____

_____

_____

_____

Project Score: _____

Read the passage "Free African Americans in the Colonies" before answering Numbers 1 through 8.

Free African Americans in the Colonies

by James B. Clark

Not all African Americans in the colonies were enslaved. About 5 percent were free. Some had been indentured servants or were the children of indentured servants. They never had been enslaved. Some free African Americans had been emancipated by their slave holders. Others risked their lives by escaping. Still others had bought their freedom by working paid jobs.

Free African Americans lived in both cities and towns in the New England, Middle, and Southern colonies. There were also small communities of free African Americans on the frontier. Many of them lived in friendship with Native Americans in the eastern foothills of the Appalachian Mountains.

Few laws protected free African Americans. Even though they had freedom, they remained in danger of being forced into slavery. Some formed organizations to help protect free African Americans. One was the Brown Fellowship Society of South Carolina. It was founded in 1790. Churches were also among the earliest and most important organizations to help free African Americans. By 1787 there were African American Baptist, Methodist, Presbyterian, and Episcopalian churches in the colonies.

1 What is the author's MAIN purpose for writing "Free African Americans in the Colonies"?
Ⓐ to tell how enslaved people escaped
Ⓑ to tell about African Americans in Florida
Ⓒ to tell when the Brown Fellowship Society was founded
Ⓓ to tell about African Americans who were not enslaved

2 Where did free African Americans live in the colonies?
Ⓕ only in the New England Colonies
Ⓖ only on the frontier
Ⓗ throughout the colonies, in the cities and countryside
Ⓘ only in the foothills of the Appalachian Mountains

3 How many African Americans lived in the colonies as free men and women?
Ⓐ about 5 percent of all African Americans in the colonies
Ⓑ about 5 percent of all people in the colonies
Ⓒ about 5 percent of enslaved African Americans
Ⓓ none

4 What happened in 1790?
Ⓕ The Brown Fellowship Society was founded.
Ⓖ The first African American churches were founded.
Ⓗ Laws began to protect free African Americans.
Ⓘ A small African American community was founded on the frontier.

5 Read the sentence from the passage.

Some free African Americans had been emancipated by their slave holders.

What does the word *emancipated* mean in this passage?
Ⓐ enslaved
Ⓑ given freedom
Ⓒ held captive
Ⓓ allowed to travel

6 Which two words from the passage have nearly OPPOSITE meanings?
Ⓕ enslaved, emancipated
Ⓖ cities, towns
Ⓗ foothill, mountain
Ⓘ friendship, freedom

7 Read the sentences from the passage.

Few laws protected free African Americans. Even though they had freedom, they remained in danger of being forced into slavery. Some formed organizations to help protect free African Americans.

Why did free African Americans turn to churches and other organizations for help?
Ⓐ because they needed money
Ⓑ because they needed food
Ⓒ because they needed work
Ⓓ because they needed protection

8 What was the purpose of the Brown Fellowship Society of South Carolina?
Ⓕ It protected enslaved people.
Ⓖ It protected free African Americans.
Ⓗ It set up African American churches.
Ⓘ It helped build friendships with Native Americans.

Test Preparation

Test-Taking Tips

Share these test-taking tips with your students:

- Read the passage carefully before looking at the question. Identify the main idea.
- Think about what you already know about the topic.
- Read each question carefully. Examine how the question relates to the text and your prior knowledge.
- Reread the title and the text. Look for text clues that relate to the question being asked.
- Choose the answer choice that best answers the question being asked based on what you read and what you already know.

Answers

1. D CCS RI.2

2. H CCS RI.3

3. A CCS RI.7

4. F CCS RI.7

5. B CCS RI.4

6. F CCS RI.3

7. D CCS RI.2

8. G CCS RI.2

Teacher Notes

UNIT
5 Planner THE AMERICAN REVOLUTION

 **BIG IDEA** **Conflict causes change.**

Student Portfolio

Show As You Go!
Use these pages to introduce the Big Idea. Students record information specific to each lesson. They use these pages to help them plan their Big Idea Project.

- Group Technology Project Students use 21st century skills to complete a group extension activity of the unit project. Lesson plans, worksheets, and rubrics are available online.

- Big Idea ProjectStudents write an

Student Portfolio

illustrated picture book about a person, place, or event from the American Revolution. The Big Idea Project rubric is on page 187W.

Reading Skills

Student Portfolio

- Reading Skill: Explain Author's Purpose
  Pages 152–153. Common Core State Standards RI.8

Leveled Readers

Use the leveled reader *Our Founding Fathers* with Lesson 2. Find the lesson plan on pages T24–T25 of your Teacher Edition.

Treasures Connection

Teach this unit with Treasures Unit 3, *Sleds on Boston Common*, pages 264–283.

Social Studies Skills

Student Portfolio

- Primary and Secondary Sources: Paintings and Speeches
  Page 157

networks

- Skill Builders
  Introduce and teach analyzing primary and secondary sources.

Activity Cards

- Center for Social Studies Skills Investigation
  Use the center activity cards to help students explore Primary Sources, Geography, and Citizenship.

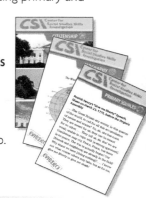

FOLDABLES

Student Portfolio

- Students can create vocabulary Foldables right in their portfolios.

- Additional Foldables templates can be found on pages R34–R42 of your Teacher Edition. See page R33 for instructions.

Assessment Solutions

- McGraw-Hill networks™
  Safe online testing features multiple question types that are easy to use and editable.

- Self-Check Quizzes

- Worksheets

UNIT 5 **At a Glance**

Lesson	Essential Question	Vocabulary
1 The Road to Revolution	What is worth fighting for?	tributary treaty proclamation boycott repeal *demand
2 The Revolution Begins	Why do people take risks?	militia Loyalist Patriot *discuss
3 Fighting the War	Why do people get involved?	mercenary *technique inflation profiteering
4 A Nation is Born	How do conflicts evolve?	desert *consequence spy blockade

*denotes academic vocabulary

Digital Resources

Go to **connected.mcgraw-hill.com** for additional resources:

- Interactive Whiteboard Lessons

- Worksheets

- Assessment

- Content Library

- Lesson Plans

- Skill Builders

- Videos

- Use Standards Tracker on **networks** to track students' progress.

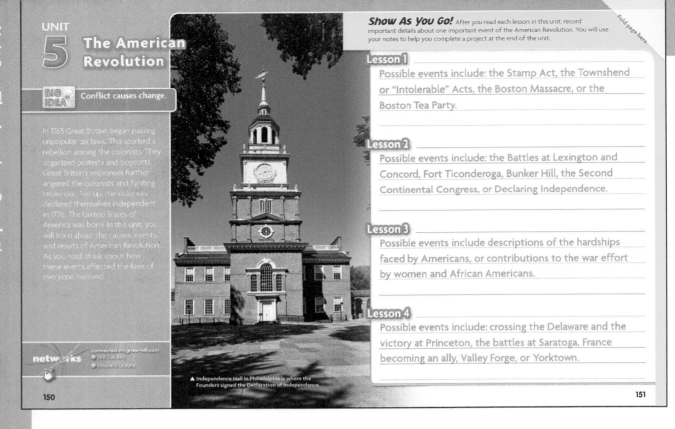

UNIT 5 — The American Revolution

BIG IDEA Conflict causes change.

In 1765 Great Britain began passing unpopular tax laws. This sparked a rebellion among the colonists. They organized protests and boycotts. Great Britain's responses further angered the colonists and fighting broke out. Fed up, the colonists declared themselves independent in 1776. The United States of America was born! In this unit, you will learn about the causes, events, and results of American Revolution. As you read, think about how these events affected the lives of everyone involved.

networks connected.mcgraw-hill.com
- Skill Builders
- Resource Library

150

▲ Independence Hall in Philadelphia is where the Founders signed the Declaration of Independence.

Show As You Go! After you read each lesson in this unit, record important details about one important event of the American Revolution. You will use your notes to help you complete a project at the end of the unit.

Fold page here.

Lesson 1
Possible events include: the Stamp Act, the Townshend or "Intolerable" Acts, the Boston Massacre, or the Boston Tea Party.

Lesson 2
Possible events include: the Battles at Lexington and Concord, Fort Ticonderoga, Bunker Hill, the Second Continental Congress, or Declaring Independence.

Lesson 3
Possible events include descriptions of the hardships faced by Americans, or contributions to the war effort by women and African Americans.

Lesson 4
Possible events include: crossing the Delaware and the victory at Princeton, the battles at Saratoga, France becoming an ally, Valley Forge, or Yorktown.

151

Introduce the Unit

✓ Diagnostic Assessment

Explain that Unit 5 discusses the American Revolution. Use a "True or False" survey to gauge students' knowledge and misconceptions. Have students raise one hand to respond "true," leaving both hands down for "false."

Say:

1. *The colonists fought to be free from France.* (False)
2. *The war was short and the colonists won easily.* (False)
3. *George Washington led the colonial army.* (True)
4. *France and Spain helped Great Britain.* (False)

Student responses will help identify level of understanding. Use this information when differentiating instruction.

Active Teaching

BIG IDEA Conflict causes change.
In this unit, students will examine and compare significant events of the American Revolution. Students will use the **Show As You Go!** pages throughout their study of this unit. Students will use information from each lesson to record details about events of the American Revolution. Explain that at the end of the unit, students will use the information collected on these pages as part of the Unit Project. Have students fold the corner of page 151 to make returning to **Show As You Go!** easier.

Differentiated Instruction

▶ **Approaching** Provide page numbers where information on specific events can be found. Require students to include only one detail for each event in each lesson.

▶ **Beyond** Have students research details about the results of each event they chose to write about for each lesson. On another sheet of paper, have students create a flow chart about events of the Revolution, based on the causes and effects they wrote about.

▶ **ELL** Provide photocopies of Student Edition pages with information about one significant event in each lesson. In a group, have students discuss, identify, and highlight key details. Allow students to copy this information onto the **Show As You Go!** pages.

Reading Skill

Common Core Standards
RI.8 Explain how an author uses reasons and evidence to support particular points in a text, identifying which reasons and evidence support which point(s).

Explain Author's Purpose

Everything you read has a purpose. An author may try to persuade, or convince the reader to think a certain way about a topic. Authors also try to inform, or teach the reader about a topic by providing information. Authors might simply wish to entertain the reader by telling a good story. Whatever the author's purpose for writing may be, his or her points are always supported with reasons and evidence. Recognizing the purpose of what you read helps you understand what you read.

LEARN IT

To find and explain the author's purpose:

• Begin by identifying the main idea of the passage. This offers clues to the author's purpose.

• Identify the evidence the author provides to support the purpose of the writing.

• Explain the author's purpose by using evidence from the writing to support your conclusions.

While most colonists wanted to end what they saw as British bullying, not all colonists wanted to end their ties to Great Britain. They hoped that the British government would compromise to end the fighting. Some of these colonists worked for the British government. Others feared that they might lose their property during the fighting. Still others simply did not want to separate from Great Britain; they hoped for compromise.

Main Idea

Supporting Evidence

152

TRY IT

Complete the chart by stating the author's purpose and supporting evidence from the paragraph.

Author's Purpose	Supporting Evidence
to inform the reader that not all colonists wanted independence	some hoped Britain would compromise
	some worked for British government
	some feared their property would be destroyed

APPLY IT

Read the paragraph below. Explain the author's purpose.
Underline or highlight the evidence that supports your conclusion.

Most colonists understood that a compromise would not be reached. They knew that once British soldiers were killed, the British government would not back down. The events around Boston made colonists see themselves in a new way. They were no longer British citizens living in colonies. They were citizens of a new country that was fighting to free itself from British rule. They were Americans.

_____

_____

_____

_____

_____

_____

_____

153

Common Core Standards RI.8 Explain how an author uses reasons and evidence to support particular points in a text, identifying which reasons and evidence support which point(s).

Reading Skill

Active Teaching

LEARN IT Explain Author's Purpose

Say: As I read I think, "What is the author trying to tell me?" Answering this question helps me to find the author's purpose. Understanding the author's purpose helps me focus on the main topic and the evidence provided to support it.

TRY IT Encourage students to try the modeled strategy as they complete the TRY IT activity.

APPLY IT After students have completed the APPLY IT activity, **Ask:**

1. What information can you use to help you locate the author's purpose? **L3**

2. Why is it important to be able to identify the author's purpose and supporting evidence when you read? **L3**

Differentiated Instruction

▶ **Approaching** Review the LEARN IT activity as a small group. Do the TRY IT activity together. Have students complete the APPLY IT activity independently. Regroup to compare and correct.

▶ **Beyond** Have students read a newspaper article and explain the author's purpose using supporting evidence from the article in their explanation.

▶ **ELL** Explain that *evidence* is *proof,* or the details authors use to explain what they want you to learn. Read the passage one sentence at a time and have students identify key details in each sentence. List student responses. Read the list and discuss to identify the author's purpose. From this list, have students decide which details on their list support the author's purpose.

networks

Go to **connected.mcgraw-hill.com** for additional resources:

• Skill Builders

• Graphic Organizers

Words to Know FOLDABLES

Common Core Standards
RI.5.4 Determine the meaning of general academic and domain-specific words and phrases in a text relevant to a grade 5 topic or subject area.

The list below shows some important words you will learn in this unit. Their definitions can be found on the next page. Read the words.

rivalry (REYE • vuhl • ree)
boycott (BOY • kaht)
militia (muh • LIH • shuh)
Patriot (PAY • tree • uht)
Loyalist (LOY • uh • lihst)
profiteering (prah • fuh • TIHR • ihng)
desert (DEH • zuhrt)
blockade (blah • KAYD)

The **Foldable** on the next page will help you learn these important words. Follow the steps below to make your Foldable.

Step 1   Fold along the solid red line.

Step 2   Cut along the dotted lines.

Step 3   Read the words and their definitions.

Step 4   Complete the activities on each tab.

Step 5   Look at the back of your Foldable. Choose ONE of these activities for each word to help you remember its meaning.
- Draw a picture of the word.
- Write a description of the word.
- Write how the word is related to something you know.

The Boston Tea Party took place in 1773. Similar events happened in other American cities, too. ▶

154

A **rivalry** is when two or more people or groups compete to become the best at or have the most of something.	Write the plural form of *rivalry*.
To **boycott** means to refuse to do business or have contact with a person, group, company, country, or product.	Write the definition of *boycott* in your own words.
A **militia** is a group of volunteers who fight in times of emergency.	Write two words that are related to the word *militia*.
A **Patriot** was a colonist who supported the fight for independence.	Write a synonym for the word *Patriot*.
A **Loyalist** was a colonist who supported Great Britain in the American Revolution.	Describe the opposite of a *Loyalist*.
Profiteering means making excess profits from goods that are in short supply.	Write the root word of *profiteering*.
To **desert** means to go away and leave a person or thing that should not be left.	Circle words that mean the same as *desert*. leave wet dry join quit stay
A **blockade** is a barrier that prevents the movement of troops and supplies.	Explain how the root word of *blockade* helps you remember the definition.

Common Core Standards RI.4 Determine the meaning of general academic and domain-specific words and phrases in a text relevant to a grade 5 topic or subject area.

Words to Know
Active Teaching

FOLDABLES

1. Go to **connected.mcgraw-hill.com** for flashcards to introduce the unit vocabulary to students.

2. Read the words on the list on page 154 and have students repeat them after you.

3. Guide students as they complete steps 1 through 5 of the Foldable.

4. Have students use the Foldable to practice the vocabulary words independently or with a partner.

GO Vocabulary!
Write one vocabulary word in each section of a grid like the one below. Have students write a sentence for each set of vocabulary words in a line (across the middle, down the middle, and diagonally). Tell students they are not permitted to write two sentences and connect them with the word *and*. For variation, divide the class into four groups and arrange the words differently for each group. Have the groups share their sentences with the class.

rivalry	treaty	blockade
inflation	Patriot	boycott
		Loyalist

networks

Go to connected.mcgraw-hill.com for additional resources:
- Vocabulary Flashcards
- Vocabulary Games
- Graphic Organizers

rivalry

rivalry

boycott

boycott

militia

militia

Patriot

Patriot

Loyalist

Loyalist

profiteering

profiteering

desert

desert

blockade

blockade

Primary Sources

Paintings and Speeches

The first photographs weren't taken until the mid-1800s. As a result, we sometimes rely on paintings to help us understand events from the past. Paintings created around the time of an event are primary sources. Those created after the event are secondary sources.

Sometimes paintings are paired with other primary sources to help you analyze an event. Speeches are primary sources if they are recorded at the same time they are actually given.

In this unit you will learn about the American Revolution. Patrick Henry was a powerful speaker who convinced many colonists to join the fight for independence. Examine the painting of Henry giving his famous speech to the Virginia House of Burgesses. Then, as you read parts of this speech, look back at the painting and think about the story the two sources tell together.

DBQ Document-Based Questions

1. Circle clues the image gives about how the speech was interpreted by the people listening to Henry.

2. Underline all of the examples Henry gives to show that Great Britain has declared war on the colonies.

THINK · PAIR · SHARE
Discuss how the image and the speech work together to help you understand the importance of Henry's speech.

Primary Source

. . . Has Great Britain any enemy, in this quarter of the world, to call for all this [build up] of navies and armies? No, sir, [Britain] has none. They are meant for us; they can be meant for no other. . . . Gentlemen may cry, Peace, Peace, but there is no peace. The war is actually begun! . . . I know not what course others may take; but as for me, give me liberty or give me death!

netw☉rks
There's More Online!
• Skill Builder
• Resource Library

157

Differentiated Instruction

▶ **ELL** Write academic vocabulary on cards. As you encounter these words in the lesson text, discuss and act out each word. Pronounce them carefully and have students do the same. Reread the sections of text with the words fluently after exploring the vocabulary. After the lesson is complete, ask students to talk about ways in which they have seen the words used. Post the words in the room and allow students to write sentences containing these words on a list underneath each word.

W O R D   P L A Y

Play Vocabulary Pyramid!

1. Pair students.

2. Give one member of each team a list of vocabulary words to describe to their teammate, without actually saying the word or other key words that might give it away too easily.

3. Encourage students to be creative with their clues.

4. To set up your pyramid, assign point totals according to the difficulty of each word (easiest on the bottom).

5. A pyramid of five levels would have five terms on the bottom and decrease in number at each level.

Primary Sources

Active Teaching

Explain to students that electronic recordings of speeches from long ago may not be available. In these cases, students need to examine a transcript, or written copy of the speech.

Develop Comprehension

1. *What information would you need to determine whether the painting is a primary or secondary source?* **L2**

2. *What does the excerpt of Henry's speech tell you about how many colonists felt about Great Britain? Explain.* **L3**

netw☉rks

Go to **connected.mcgraw-hill.com** for additional resources:
• Skill Builders
• Resource Library

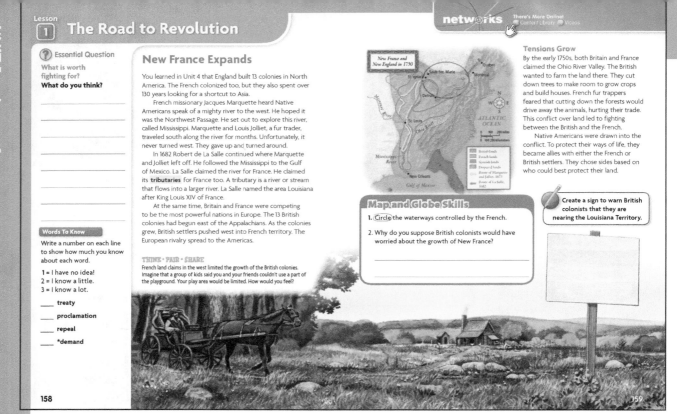

Lesson 1 The Road to Revolution

networks There's More Online! Content Library • Videos

? Essential Question
What is worth fighting for?
What do you think?

Words To Know
Write a number on each line to show how much you know about each word.

1 = I have no idea!
2 = I know a little.
3 = I know a lot.

____ treaty

____ proclamation

____ repeal

____ *demand

New France Expands

You learned in Unit 4 that England built 13 colonies in North America. The French colonized too, but they also spent over 130 years looking for a shortcut to Asia.

French missionary Jacques Marquette heard Native Americans speak of a mighty river to the west. He hoped it was the Northwest Passage. He set out to explore this river, called Mississippi. Marquette and Louis Jolliet, a fur trader, traveled south along the river for months. Unfortunately, it never turned west. They gave up and turned around.

In 1682 Robert de La Salle continued where Marquette and Jolliet left off. He followed the Mississippi to the Gulf of Mexico. La Salle claimed the river for France. He claimed its tributaries for France too. A tributary is a river or stream that flows into a larger river. La Salle named the area Louisiana after King Louis XIV of France.

At the same time, Britain and France were competing to be the most powerful nations in Europe. The 13 British colonies had begun east of the Appalachians. As the colonies grew, British settlers pushed west into French territory. The European rivalry spread to the Americas.

THINK • PAIR • SHARE
French land claims in the west limited the growth of the British colonies. Imagine that a group of kids said you and your friends couldn't use a part of the playground. Your play area would be limited. How would you feel?

Tensions Grow
By the early 1750s, both Britain and France claimed the Ohio River Valley. The British wanted to farm the land there. They cut down trees to make room to grow crops and build houses. French fur trappers feared that cutting down the forests would drive away the animals, hurting their trade. This conflict over land led to fighting between the British and the French.

Native Americans were drawn into the conflict. To protect their ways of life, they became allies with either the French or British settlers. They chose sides based on who could best protect their land.

New France and New England in 1750

Map and Globe Skills
1. Circle the waterways controlled by the French.
2. Why do you suppose British colonists would have worried about the growth of New France?

Create a sign to warn British colonists that they are nearing the Louisiana Territory.

158

159

Lesson 1

Activate Prior Knowledge

After students have responded to the activity, have them extend the discussion to the historical scenario.
Ask: *Why would the colonists be upset about not being allowed to move west?*

? Essential Question What is worth fighting for?

Have students explain what they understand about the Essential Question. Discuss their responses. Explain that everything they learn in this lesson will help them understand the Essential Question better. Remind them to think about how the Essential Question connects to the unit Big Idea: Conflict causes change.

Map and Globe Skill

Ask: *Based on the map, where in North America could a war between Britain and France take place?* (in the red and green shaded area marked "disputed")

networks

Go to **connected.mcgraw-hill.com** for additional resources:

- Interactive Whiteboard Lessons
- Worksheets
- Assessments
- Videos

Active Teaching

Words To Know Use the verbal-visual word association graphic organizer to help students gain a deeper understanding of the lesson vocabulary.

Write the word	Draw a picture that represents the word
Write the definition	Describe a person, situation, or characteristic that reminds them of this word

Develop Comprehension

- Show students a map of the United States on an overhead or whiteboard. Have students identify the 13 colonies, the Appalachian Mountains, the Mississippi River, and the Great Lakes. Shade or label these areas.
- Add the Louisiana Territory to the map. Shade this differently to show French control.

Ask:

1. *What major geographic features divided the British colonies from Louisiana?* (The Appalachian Mountains and the Mississippi River) **L2**

2. *Why might it have been easy for France to control disputed territories west of the Appalachians?* (The British army was too far away, and it took a long time to get there.) **L3**

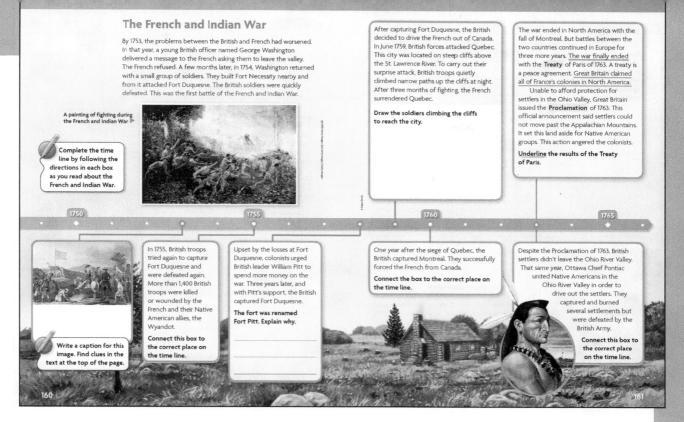

The French and Indian War

By 1753, the problems between the British and French had worsened. In that year, a young British officer named George Washington delivered a message to the French asking them to leave the valley. The French refused. A few months later, in 1754, Washington returned with a small group of soldiers. They built Fort Necessity nearby and from it attacked Fort Duquesne. The British soldiers were quickly defeated. This was the first battle of the French and Indian War.

A painting of fighting during the French and Indian War ▶

Complete the time line by following the directions in each box as you read about the French and Indian War.

After capturing Fort Duquesne, the British decided to drive the French out of Canada. In June 1759, British forces attacked Quebec. This city was located on steep cliffs above the St. Lawrence River. To carry out their surprise attack, British troops quietly climbed narrow paths up the cliffs at night. After three months of fighting, the French surrendered Quebec.

Draw the soldiers climbing the cliffs to reach the city.

The war ended in North America with the fall of Montreal. But battles between the two countries continued in Europe for three more years. The war finally ended with the **Treaty** of Paris of 1763. A treaty is a peace agreement. Great Britain claimed all of France's colonies in North America.

Unable to afford protection for settlers in the Ohio Valley, Great Britain issued the **Proclamation** of 1763. This official announcement said settlers could not move past the Appalachian Mountains. It set this land aside for Native American groups. This action angered the colonists.

Underline the results of the Treaty of Paris.

1750 — **1755** — **1760** — **1765**

Write a caption for this image. Find clues in the text at the top of the page.

In 1755, British troops tried again to capture Fort Duquesne and were defeated again. More than 1,400 British troops were killed or wounded by the French and their Native American allies, the Wyandot.

Connect this box to the correct place on the time line.

Upset by the losses at Fort Duquesne, colonists urged British leader William Pitt to spend more money on the war. Three years later, and with Pitt's support, the British captured Fort Duquesne.

The fort was renamed Fort Pitt. Explain why.

_____
_____
_____

One year after the siege of Quebec, the British captured Montreal. They successfully forced the French from Canada.

Connect the box to the correct place on the time line.

Despite the Proclamation of 1763, British settlers didn't leave the Ohio River Valley. That same year, Ottawa Chief Pontiac united Native Americans in the Ohio River Valley in order to drive out the settlers. They captured and burned several settlements but were defeated by the British Army.

Connect this box to the correct place on the time line.

160   161

Active Teaching

Begin by walking the students through the time line.

Ask:

1. *What is shown on the time line?* (the events of the French and Indian War) **L1**

2. *How many years are covered by this time line?* (15 years) **L2**

As students work through the time line activities, stop to monitor progress and comprehension.

✓ Formative Assessment

Have students explain the French and Indian War by summarizing the beginning, middle, and end of the war in writing. Summaries should include some of the following: the British asked the French to leave and they refused; the British won many early battles but failed to capture key forts; the French enlisted the help of Native American allies; the British invaded Canada and drove the French from Quebec and Montreal; the Treaty of Paris (1763) ended the war.

Differentiated Instruction

▶ **Approaching** Students may struggle when reading the time line. Guide students through the dates in each text box. Have them label each box sequentially to show the order of events.

▶ **Beyond** To help students understand the events that drove the French from North America, have them research the invasions of Quebec and/or Montreal. Have students present the details of the events and prepare a list of questions to ask classmates after their presentations.

▶ **ELL** A few concepts on the time line may be confusing for students: *capture* (to get control of something); *drive out* (to force someone to leave); *siege* (to surround and attack a place); and *surprise attack* (to act with force without warning). Define these terms and phrases for students. Together, write sample sentences using each. Have students pair and act them out.

Colonists Protest New Taxes

Wars are expensive! British leaders needed to find a way to pay for the French and Indian War. Many people in Great Britain thought the colonists should have to pay for the war since it was fought to protect them.

The colonists disagreed. Before the 1760s, only the colonial legislatures had taxed the colonists. Colonists accepted those taxes because they had voted for, and were represented by, the members of colonial legislatures. But the colonists couldn't vote for members of Parliament. When Parliament passed taxes on the colonies to pay for the war, many colonists saw this as taxation without representation. They felt their rights as British citizens were being violated.

The Stamp Act

In 1765 Parliament passed the Stamp Act. This tax forced colonists to buy stamps for everything made of paper. This included newspapers, wills, journals, and playing cards. Colonists weren't happy about this tax, passed without their consent, or agreement.

In response, a group of colonists called the Sons of Liberty planned to **boycott** British goods. To boycott means to refuse to buy goods or services. The Sons of Liberty organized protests and threatened tax collectors across the colonies.

Leaders called "Patriots" emerged against the British government. Samuel Adams led the fight against the Stamp Act in Massachusetts. In Virginia, Patrick Henry spoke out about the tax. His many speeches inspired others to protest. The protests worked! In 1766 the British government **repealed**, or canceled, the tax.

Colonists protested in the streets. ▼

The Townshend Acts

Parliament raised taxes another way, though. In 1767 it passed the Townshend Acts, which taxed goods such as tea, glass, and paint.

Colonists **demanded** that the British repeal the hated Townshend Acts and organized another boycott. This boycott included taxed goods and any colonial businesses selling or using them too.

Boston Massacre

British leaders worried that the colonists, especially those in Boston, were out of control. They sent troops to the city. But that only made things worse.

The people of Boston weren't happy with all the soldiers. Some residents were even forced to allow soldiers to stay in their homes. On March 5, 1770, a crowd of angry colonists began to tease some British soldiers. When the crowd refused to go home, the soldiers shot into the crowd, killing five colonists. News of the Boston Massacre shocked colonists. How could British soldiers kill their own people?

▲ Silversmith Paul Revere made this engraving of the Boston Massacre.

Boston Tea Party and Coercive Acts

Parliament was desperate to get the colonies under control. It repealed the Townshend Acts in 1773 but added a new tax on tea. British leaders thought this was a good compromise. To the colonists, it was yet another tax passed without their approval.

In November, angry Boston residents protested by refusing to allow three British cargo ships to unload. On the night of December 16, about 50 members of the Sons of Liberty dumped the ships' cargoes of tea overboard.

Parliament punished the colonists by passing the Coercive Acts. These acts closed Boston Harbor, banned town meetings, and sent over more soldiers. Colonists called these actions "The Intolerable Acts." These acts united many colonists against Great Britain.

DID YOU KNOW?
Crispus Attucks, killed in the Boston Massacre, was the first African American to die in events leading to the Revolution.

Colonists disguised as Native Americans threw British tea into Boston Harbor. ▶

Lesson 1

(?) Essential Question   What is worth fighting for?

Go back to **Show As You Go!** on pages 150–151.

networks   There's More Online!
• Games • Assessment

Lesson 1

Active Teaching

Explain that the British colonists had fees placed on things they used every day. They weren't happy about these fees, and in some cases, were mad enough to fight over them.

Develop Comprehension
Ask:

1. *Why did the British continue to repeal one tax but add another?* (They needed to make the colonists happy but still pay for the war.) **L3**

2. *How were the Townshend Acts and tea tax the same?* (Both taxed tea.) **L2**

3. *What caused the Boston Massacre?* **L3**

Show As You Go! Remind students to go back to the Unit Opener and complete the activities for this lesson.

Differentiated Instruction

▶ **Beyond** Have students write a summary of these events from the perspective of a patriotic colonist and that of a British soldier in Boston.

▶ **ELL** Read each section of text with students and discuss the problem. Have students work together to restate each event using their own words.

Reading Skill

Common Core Standards RI.8 Explain how an author uses reasons and evidence to support particular points in a text, identifying which reasons and evidence support which point(s).

Explain Author's Purpose Once students have completed the activity, have them actually write a paragraph that might be included in such a pamphlet. They should pull reasons and evidence for their points from any of the pages in the lesson.

DID YOU KNOW?

Crispus Attucks was the first to die in the Boston Massacre, so he is commonly regarded as the first casualty of the American Revolution. Not much else is known about him.

Response to Intervention

(?) **Essential Question** What is worth fighting for?

If . . . students cannot give a substantiated response to the Essential Question,

....

Then . . . take them back to pages 162–163. Discuss how the content relates to the Essential Question.
Ask: *What events are discussed on these pages? How do the colonists' reactions to them show their feelings?* **L1, L3**

Following discussion, allow students to respond to the Essential Question again.

Lesson 2 — The Revolution Begins

Lesson 2

Lexington and Concord

? Essential Question

Why do people take risks?
What do you think?

The British decided that capturing colonial leaders might stop colonial protests. When the Sons of Liberty heard of this plan, they sent two important leaders, Samuel Adams and John Hancock, to Lexington, a town outside Boston. The colonists also hid weapons in Lexington and another town, Concord.

On April 18, 1775, General Thomas Gage sent about 700 soldiers from Boston to seize the weapons stored in Lexington and Concord. The soldiers were also ordered to arrest Adams and Hancock. When colonists learned of Gage's plan, they sent two men, Paul Revere and William Dawes, to warn the people of Lexington and Concord. As a result, the colonists were able to hide most of the weapons, and Adams and Hancock escaped.

THINK · PAIR · SHARE

Revere and Dawes warned the colonists and ruined the "element of surprise" for the British. Why might surprise have made a difference? Why did it help the colonists to know the British were coming?

Minutemen, shown wearing blue jackets, fought off an attack by British soldiers, shown wearing red coats, on the Old North Bridge in Concord, Massachusetts. ▼

Words To Know

Tell a partner what you know about each word:

militia

Loyalist

Patriot

*discuss

164

Routes to Concord

networks There's More Online! Content Library Videos

Map and Globe Skills

1. Which American rode the longest distance to warn colonists that the British were coming?

   William Dawes

2. Use the scale to measure the distance from:

   Boston to Lexington — about 18 miles

   Lexington to Concord — about 7 miles

In Lexington, a **militia** of 70 men called minutemen were waiting for the British. Militias are groups of volunteers who fight only in an emergency. No one knows who fired first, but many shots rang out. Eight minutemen were killed, and the British marched on to Concord.

A larger militia waited just outside Concord. The British never made it into town and instead retreated toward Boston. The minutemen followed and continued shooting along the way. More than 90 British soldiers were killed. The Revolutionary War had begun.

DID YOU KNOW?
Paul Revere never completed his famous Midnight Ride. Here's what happened: As Revere and Dawes left Lexington headed for Concord, Dr. Samuel Prescott joined them. Outside Lexington they were stopped by British guards. Prescott and Dawes escaped, but Revere was held for questioning and his horse was taken away. Revere walked back to Lexington. In the meantime, Prescott reached Concord and warned the militia.

165

Lesson 2 ⟶

Activate Prior Knowledge

Engage students in a discussion about surprise. Ask them to give examples of good and not-so-good kinds of surprises. Have them brainstorm ways surprise can be used in a game, such as tag or capture the flag.

? Essential Question Why do people take risks?

Next, have students explain what they understand about the Essential Question. Discuss their responses. Explain that everything they learn in this lesson will help them understand the Essential Question better. Remind them to think about how the Essential Question connects to the unit Big Idea: Conflict causes change.

More About Revolutionary War Communication *Secret military information was often written in code. Over time, both sides learned each other's codes. This led to messengers memorizing information and reciting messages in person. Even then, not all secrets were safe because each side found ways of making people talk. As a result, not much was a secret during the war. At many points, both sides knew exactly what the other was planning.*

Active Teaching

Words To Know Have each pair of students create definitions for the words based on what they know. Discuss and compare as a class.

Develop Comprehension

Have students look back to their map of the 13 colonies on page 103 and locate New England. Discuss its major cities, location, and importance. Have students examine the map on page 165.

Ask: *What colony is this? How do you know?* **L2**

Next, begin a discussion about the battles at Lexington and Concord.

Ask: *Why did the British want Adams and Hancock?* **L3**

Map and Globe Skill

Engage students in a discussion about why Patriot leaders sent two riders. Have students look to the map to find clues that support their reasoning.

Early Battles

Underline or highlight the results of each battle described on these pages.

The battles at Lexington and Concord were the beginning of the Revolutionary War. Battles in New York and Boston quickly followed. As militias began to work together, a colonial army took shape.

Fort Ticonderoga

Three weeks after Lexington and Concord, a man from New England named Benedict Arnold led a small militia toward Fort Ticonderoga in New York. News traveled slowly in the 1700s, so the British soldiers there had no idea about the battles in Lexington and Concord. Arnold planned to attack the fort and take its cannons for the colonial army. On May 10, 1775, another militia led by Ethan Allen joined Arnold in the surprise attack. Amazingly, they captured the fort without firing a single shot.

It took teams of oxen nearly eight months to drag the heavy canons from Fort Ticonderoga to Boston. ▼

DID YOU KNOW?
Benedict Arnold wanted to be a famous war hero. After years of fighting with the colonial army, Arnold felt he wasn't respected by colonial leaders. As a result, he planned to surrender the fort at West Point to the British. His betrayal shocked the colonists. Arnold got his wish: he is remembered but as a traitor. In fact, even today, people who betray others are sometimes called a "Benedict Arnold."

166

The Battle at Bunker Hill

At the same time, the British were losing control of the Boston area. General Gage decided to attack the hills around Boston. Taking them would give the British a strategic advantage. But the colonists learned of the plan. A colonial militia was sent to protect Bunker Hill across the Charles River from Boston. Instead, the militia decided to protect Breed's Hill, which was closer to the river. The colonists worked all night to build earthen walls for protection.

▲ This painting shows colonists fighting British soldiers at the Battle of Bunker Hill.

On June 17, British soldiers crossed the Charles River by boat and marched up Breed's Hill. The militia waited, hidden behind earthen walls. The Americans didn't have much ammunition, or musket balls and gunpowder. Officers told them not to waste ammunition by firing at soldiers that were too far away. Historians say that either Colonel William Prescott or General Israel Putnam said, "Don't shoot until you see the whites of their eyes."

Twice the British charged up the hill, only to be stopped by the militia. Finally, the Americans ran out of ammunition. After a third try, the British won what became known as the Battle of Bunker Hill. More than 400 colonists were killed or wounded. The victory was costly for the British as well. More than 1,000 soldiers were killed or wounded in the battle.

Reading Skill

Summarize Suppose you are a member of a Committee of Correspondence. You are responsible to report one of these events to another colony. Summarize the information you think needs to be shared.

_____

_____

_____

167

Lesson 2

Active Teaching

Two separate battles are discussed on these pages. Be sure to clarify this for students.

Develop Comprehension
Ask:

1. *What made Benedict Arnold and Ethan Allen able to capture Fort Ticonderoga?* **L1**

2. *Why would capturing the hills around Boston, and not Boston itself, be an advantage for the British?* **L3**

3. *Explain why the militia generals wanted their soldiers to wait as long as possible before firing.* **L2**

DID YOU KNOW?

Arnold's treasonous reputation followed him forever, even to Britain where he emigrated after the war.

Reading Skill

Common Core Standards RI.2 Determine two or more main ideas of a text and explain how they are supported by key details; summarize the text.

Summarize Students should base their answers on text clues found on pages 166 and 167. Have students circle the key details that they wish to include before they begin writing their summaries.

Differentiated Instruction

▶ **Approaching** Provide students with a map of the colonial regions. As they progress through this unit, track the location of each battle. Discuss where the events took place and how location may have affected the outcome of each battle.

▶ **Beyond** Have students create a map of the colonies. As they progress through the unit, they should code the map to show the major battles of the war and the winner of each battle. The maps should include a key, several geographic features, and be accurate.

▶ **ELL** Students may be unfamiliar with some of the words used to describe the battles of the war. Describe these words in the context of war: *winner, loser, side,* and *charge*.

networks

Go to **connected.mcgraw-hill.com** for additional resources:

- Interactive Whiteboard Lessons
- Worksheets
- Assessments
- Skill Builders

Choosing Sides

The colonies were divided. Underline details that show what each group wanted.

News of the fighting spread throughout the colonies, and compromise looked less likely with each battle. Many colonists didn't want war and didn't want to pick a side. They feared their property would be damaged in the fighting. They focused on protecting themselves. Many remained undecided throughout the war.

Others easily knew which side was theirs. Colonists called **Loyalists** didn't want to rebel against Great Britain. They thought taxes and restrictions weren't good reasons. Some Loyalists even worked against those who rebelled, helping the British.

For others, the events around Boston changed their point of view. These colonists no longer felt like British citizens living in British colonies. They now saw themselves as Americans, fighting for their rights and freedom. These were the **Patriots**.

The Second Continental Congress

Among the Patriots were many well-respected colonial leaders, such as Thomas Jefferson, Benjamin Franklin, John Adams, and John Hancock. As the war began to rage, these colonial leaders and many others met in Philadelphia's State House. They needed to organize an army and **discuss** what to do next. Their meeting was called the Second Continental Congress. The journal entries on the next page describe key events that took place.

Patrick Henry urged the Continental Congress to declare independence from Great Britain. ▼

GLUE FOLDABLE HERE

168

May 1775

I'm working as a servant for the Second Continental Congress. Delegates from every colony have arrived in Philadelphia. John Hancock was elected president of the Congress. The delegates are divided and have very different goals.

June 1775

The conversations of the delegates could be seen as treason, or betraying Britain. Sam Adams and John Adams of Massachusetts, and Richard Henry Lee and Thomas Jefferson of Virginia have called for independence. But others, including John Dickinson of Pennsylvania, hope to remain part of Great Britain, with the power to govern ourselves. Neither side seems willing to give in.

The Congress has named George Washington as commander of the Continental Army. His service in the French and Indian War proved his leadership abilities.

July 1775

The delegates have sent what they call an "olive branch petition" to King George III and Parliament. They say the olive branch is a symbol of peace used by the ancient Greeks. They asked the king to repeal his laws and policies for the colonies. I don't think it will work. There is too much at stake—power, money, and pride.

October 1775

The king refused to read the petition. He is angry with the Congress and has sent more troops to enforce his rules. People in the streets are calling for independence.

The delegates sent representatives to France, the Netherlands, and Spain to ask for support. These countries want to help us, but they are afraid to fight Britain—the strongest country in Europe. If we hope to get assistance, we need to win battles, and soon!

Reading Skill
Main Idea and Details These fictional journal entries use real details to help you understand the events of the Second Continental Congress.

1. Read the journal entries and summarize the main topic for each date next to the entry. Underline key details that help you with each summary.

2. Is the person writing the entries a Loyalist or a Patriot? Circle your choice. Then circle the details that helped you decide.

169

Active Teaching

Remind students that there are many sides to every story. It is important to consider all sides and experiences to fully understand history.

Page 169 contains journal entries told in first person. It may be necessary to review this type of writing with the class. Explain that first person narrative is sometimes used in secondary sources to help the reader better understand events from the past.

Ask:

1. *Where did the Congress meet?* **L1**
2. *Who is the speaker?* **L1**
3. *What is the overall goal of the Congress?* **L3**

Clarifying Misconceptions

Be sure students understand that the decision to break from Great Britain was not an easy one. The men participating in the Second Continental Congress put their lives on the line by attending. As a result, most of the discussions were done in secret.

Page Power

FOLDABLES Interact more with the page. Have students create a Notebook Foldable to assist them in developing their understanding of the perspectives of Loyalists, Patriots, and "undecideds" during the Revolution.

1. Provide each student with a copy of Foldable 5A from the section at the back of this book.

2. Have students construct the Foldable and glue its anchor tab as indicated on page 168.

3. On the Foldable flaps, have students write a short entry describing the perspective of each set of Americans. Each perspective should reflect a specific event leading up to and/or including declaring independence.

Reading Skill

Common Core Standards **RI.2** Determine two or more main ideas of a text and explain how they are supported by key details; summarize the text.

Main Idea and Details Have students compare their summaries with a partner's and discuss similarities and differences between key details that each student identified as important.

List two basic rights you think every person deserves.

1. _____   2. _____

Ideas About Rights

Patriots had ideas about what governments were supposed to do and not do. These ideas were the foundation of their complaints against Great Britain. The colonists' ideas were influenced by John Locke. Locke was an English philosopher, or person who thinks about important ideas. He believed that without governments, humans existed in a "state of nature." In this state, people could deal reasonably with each other. Locke also believed that all people were born free and equal. He also believed that all people had rights given to them by nature. Three of these rights were life, liberty, and the right the own property. Locke wrote that the main duty of government was to protect these rights. When a government violated people's rights, Locke believed the people had the right to overthrow, or change, that government.

Declaring Independence

Many colonists agreed with the idea of natural rights. They saw the king as a tyrant, or a cruel and unfair ruler. In June 1776, the Continental Congress took the next, big step. It appointed a committee to write a Declaration of Independence. The committee decided Thomas Jefferson should write the first draft.

Jefferson included a list of crimes that he accused the king of committing. Some delegates wanted to change this section before sending it to England. Jefferson also attacked the slave trade. Representatives from the Southern colonies, whose economies depended on slavery, removed this part.

The power of Jefferson's words inspired the delegates. But the final statement of his document made the most important point: "The good people of these colonies, solemnly publish and declare, that these United Colonies are, and of right ought to be free and independent states." The Patriots were now Americans.

Benjamin Franklin, John Adams, and Thomas Jefferson writing the Declaration ▼

Each box below describes a complaint listed in the Declaration of Independence. Choose a color for each natural right: life, liberty, and the right to own property. Color each box to show the natural right it addresses. *Tip: If more than one right is addressed in a box, divide the box and color a portion to show each right.*

Liberty   Property   Life/Property

Lack of Representation	Taxes and Trade	Land Issues
The colonists could not govern themselves and were taxed without their consent.	Great Britain limited imports and exports and set high taxes on these goods. Colonists were required to pay taxes on goods.	Britain ignored colonists' land claims west of the Appalachian Mountains, leaving colonists unprotected on the frontier.
Tyranny	**Legal Rights**	**War-like Behaviors**
The government enforced laws the colonists thought were severe and unfair. Colonial charters were taken away. Great Britain refused to make laws necessary to protect the colonists. Colonial legislatures were suspended.	Colonists could be arrested and held without a trial. Some were also taken to Europe to face false charges. New laws prevented immigrants from coming to the colonies. Judges were controlled directly by the king.	Thousands of British soldiers were sent to the colonies. Soldiers took colonial homes to use for shelter. Laws and rules did not apply to soldiers. German soldiers, known as Hessians, were hired to fight the colonists.

Liberty   Liberty   Life/Liberty/Property

Lesson 2

❓ **Essential Question** Why do people take risks?

_____
_____
_____

Go back to *Show As You Go!* on pages 150–151.

networks There's More Online!
• Games • Assessment

170   171

Lesson 2

Active Teaching

Through the process of declaring freedom, the delegates also defined the nation. They decided what principles, beliefs, and rules the new nation would live by. Explain that this was challenging task, considering the time frame and danger they faced.

Ask:

1. *What are "natural" rights? Explain.* **L3**
2. *What basic rights are outlined in the Declaration of Independence?* **L2**

Show As You Go! Remind students to go back to the Unit Opener and complete the activities for this lesson.

Response to Intervention

❓ **Essential Question** Why do people take risks?

If . . . students cannot give a substantiated response to the Essential Question,

Then . . . take them back through the lesson. On each spread, identify and discuss examples of risks taken by colonists.

Ask: *What risks were the colonists willing to take? What risks were the British willing to take? Why?*

Following discussion, allow students to respond to the Essential Question again.

More About the Declaration of Independence The ideas of the Declaration of Independence were inspired by many philosophers, including John Locke, to whom Thomas Jefferson gave much credit. In addition to Locke's philosophies, much of the Declaration was based on the Virginia Statute of Religious Freedoms.

? Essential Question
Why do people get involved?
What do you think?

Everyone has strengths and weaknesses. Strengths are things you do well, and weaknesses are things that you could improve. What are your strengths and weaknesses?

Strengths	Weaknesses

Ready for War?

Patriot soldiers, now called the Continental Army, were eager to fight. But at first they were no match for the British Army. Many British military leaders believed the war would end quickly. Instead, it would last eight years. The British had not counted on the Americans' strengths. And they didn't recognize their own weaknesses.

The British didn't understand that the Patriots were willing to suffer a great deal to gain their freedom. Many Americans gave everything they had to win their independence.

Reading Skill
Compare and Contrast Use the information on these pages to compare the two armies.

	Strengths	Weaknesses
British	many soldiers; well-trained soldiers; mercenaries; bayonets; help from Loyalists	muskets were less accurate than rifles; red coats—made them easy targets; no support from British citizens
Americans	fought protect homes; attacked by surprise; rifles more accurate than muskets; help from Patriots	fewer soldiers; untrained soldiers; lack of uniforms and shoes

Words To Know
Add a suffix to each word.
mercenary _____
*technique _____
inflation _____
profiteering _____

172

BRITISH ARMY

GLUE FOLDABLE HERE
RED COATS

Strengths and Weaknesses
Army Soldiers and military supplies had to be shipped across the Atlantic Ocean. The British had as many as 60,000 soldiers in the American colonies. They included many **mercenaries**, professional soldiers from other countries. Most were Hessians from Germany.

Training British soldiers were well-trained fighters who joined the army for life. Soldiers were only trained to fight in open battlefields.

Equipment Each soldier carried a gun called a musket tip that had a sharp blade, or bayonet, on the front. Uniforms included red coats, which made soldiers easy targets.

Support British soldiers were helped by Loyalists. Many British citizens didn't support the war because it raised taxes.

AMERICAN ARMY

Strengths and Weaknesses
Army Patriots fought to protect their homes, families, and a new nation. General Washington never had more than 19,000 soldiers at any time during the war.

Training Soldiers signed up for six months. This was not enough time to train to fight using traditional military **techniques**. Some Patriots attacked by surprise, firing from well-protected spots.

Equipment Many Patriot soldiers used long rifles, which were more accurate than muskets. A lack of uniforms, especially shoes, was a constant problem.

Support Patriot citizens supported the army by making musket balls or blankets. Farmers gave food to soldiers. Some Americans hid supplies or sold food to the army at high prices.

GLUE FOLDABLE HERE

173

Lesson 3

Activate Prior Knowledge

Use the strengths/weaknesses activity to encourage students to set an academic goal. Create a chart to monitor students' progress. Celebrate accomplishments.

? Essential Question Why do people get involved?

Have students explain what they understand about the Essential Question. Discuss their responses. Explain that everything they learn in this lesson will help them understand the Essential Question better. Remind them to think about how the Essential Question connects to the unit Big Idea: Conflict causes change.

Active Teaching

Words To Know Discuss how suffixes can change the meaning of a word or make it plural.

Develop Comprehension
In order to compare the battles and military campaigns of the war, students must understand the armies. Pages 172 and 173 examine the strengths and weaknesses of the British and Continental armies.

Ask:
1. *Which army had easier access to supplies? Why? (The British; they controlled ports and access to supplies from Europe.)* **L2**

✔ Formative Assessment

Ask a series of true/false questions about the two armies. Ask students to raise their hands for true statements and keep them down for false. Use this assessment to monitor student understanding and identify need for intervention.

Reading Skill

Common Core Standards RI.3 Explain the relationships or interactions between two or more individuals, events, ideas, or concepts in a historical, scientific, or technical text based on specific information in the text.

Compare and Contrast Students may have difficulty identifying which characteristics were strengths and which were weaknesses. Have the students work in pairs initially, then discuss their answers as a class.

Page Power

FOLDABLES Interact more with the page.

1. Provide each student with a copy of Foldable 5B from the section at the back of this book.

2. Have students construct the Foldables and glue their anchor tabs above the images on page 173.

3. On the Foldable flaps, have students explain each army's greatest strength on the front and each army's greatest weakness on the back.

Supporting the War Effort

My name is Martha. You probably know my husband, General George Washington of the Continental Army. These are turbulent times for us all. We are divided by our ideas and the war. Though I don't fight in battle, I do what I can to support our brave soldiers. I gather supplies such as clothing, food, and blankets for the troops. Read below to see the many ways others at home support the fight for independence.

Support at Home

American women supported the war in many ways. When the men left for war, some women became carpenters, blacksmiths, or shipbuilders. Others took over family farms or businesses.

Some women gave hope to Americans through writing. Mercy Otis Warren recorded the events of the Revolution. This helped everyone know what was happening. Phillis Wheatley, a free African American, wrote poetry which inspired many people.

Other women, like Abigail Adams, greatly influenced the work of their husbands. Abigail and her husband John Adams discussed issues being debated by the Continental Congress. She asked her husband to remember women's rights as the Congress planned the new government.

FUN FACT
Women had already played an important role in the events leading up to the war. Groups called Daughters of Liberty gathered to spin cloth during the boycotts. This allowed Americans to keep the boycotts going.

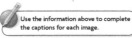
Use the information above to complete the captions for each image.

▲ Freed from slavery at the age of 20,
Phillis Wheatley
wrote poetry about freedom.

▲ Abigail Adams and her husband John discussed
women's rights

▲ Mercy Otis Warren wrote about the events of the
Revolution

174

The snow and bitter winds of winter make battle difficult. This is why troops on both sides remain in camps during the winter months. I spend this time with George. So many men are tired, hungry, injured, and homesick. The other officers' wives and I do what we can to comfort them and keep their spirits high. At night we knit socks and scarves to help keep them covered. I've never seen so many shoeless men! Read below to see other ways our brave soldiers are supported on the battle field.

Support in the Field

Many women helped on the battlefields. Some traveled to military camps to cook or care for wounded soldiers. Sybil Ludington is called the "female Paul Revere" because she warned colonists in Connecticut about a British attack. Deborah Sampson disguised herself as a man to join the army.

At this time, most African Americans were enslaved. As the war continued, many joined the army to support the fight for independence. About 5,000 African Americans served with the Continental Army. The words "all men are created equal" from the Declaration of Independence gave African Americans hope that the new nation would treat all people equally.

In 1777 Rhode Island's African American soldiers formed their own unit called the First Rhode Island Regiment. These soldiers fought in many battles of the Revolution, including the final battle at Yorktown. ▼

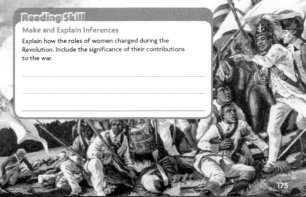

Reading Skill

Make and Explain Inferences

Explain how the roles of women changed during the Revolution. Include the significance of their contributions to the war.

_____

_____

175

Lesson 3

Active Teaching

On pages 174 and 175, students will learn about support for the Continental Army at home and on the battlefield. The text on each page begins with a first person narrative, then switches to third person text.

Develop Comprehension
Ask:

1. *What does Martha mean when she says, "We are divided by our ideas and the war"?* **L3**

2. *How did each woman support the war?* **L1**

3. *What motivated many African Americans to join and support the Continental Army?* **L2**

☑ Formative Assessment

Have students summarize what they know about the challenges faced by the Continental Army and the support it received by writing three facts they learned. Use this assessment to monitor student understanding and identify need for intervention.

Differentiated Instruction

▶ **Approaching** Work with a group to identify the overall contributions of women at home and on the battlefield.

▶ **Beyond** Have students research more about the contributions of women to the war effort. Have them share this information with the rest of the class.

▶ **ELL** Explain to students that women in the United States were not always considered equal to men. In fact, like African Americans, many women hoped the phrase "all men are created equal" from the Declaration of Independence included them as well. Have students look for evidence of women equaling the efforts of men in the text.

Reading Skill

 Common Core Standards **RI.1** Quote accurately from a text when explaining what the text says explicitly and when drawing inferences from the text.

Make and Explain Inferences It may help students to choose the contribution(s) of one woman and focus on how that behavior was different from what was normally expected from women of that era. Students will have to draw on knowledge gained in Unit 4, Lesson 5. Refer students back to the pages that discuss women's roles if they need help.

The Problems of War

Funding the Revolution was a major problem. The Continental Congress had no power to raise money through taxes. State treasuries sent some money. Some foreign governements, who wanted to see the British defeated, sent money as well. But it wasn't enough.

Some Americans loaned their own money to the government. Merchants Robert Morris and Hyam Salomon loaned the government money to buy gunpowder, food, and supplies. Other Americans helped by keeping businesses open, while their owners went off to fight.

To pay for the war, the Congress printed paper money called "Continentals." But, the treasury did not have enough gold to back up their value. As more Continentals were printed, their value decreased. Continentals became worthless. The drop in the value of Continentals led to **inflation**, or a rapid rise in prices.

▲ Continental dollars

Wartime Shortages

All trade was cut off at the start of the war. Like Patriot soldiers, most Americans soon faced shortages. Food became scarce, as did items such as cloth, kettles, and tools.

Americans caused shortages as well. Hoarding, or hiding away goods such as flour, molasses, and manufactured items, was a serious problem. Hoarding made these products hard to get—and raised their price. Some farmers and merchants became wealthy by **profiteering**, or charging high prices for goods they hoarded.

The Costs of Loyalty

Loyalists lived in every state. Many Loyalists, however, fled the American colonies during the Revolutionary War. They packed their belongings and sold whatever they could. Some left quickly for England. Others moved to Florida, Canada, or to the frontier beyond the Appalachian Mountains.

Loyalists who stayed in the United States faced many challenges. Their neighbors treated them badly, and some became victims of violence. Loyalist property often was taken or destroyed. Some Loyalists helped the British by spying on the Patriots. If caught, they were arrested by the Continental Army and tried as traitors.

> Underline personal hardships faced by Americans during the war.

Chart and Graph Skills

Read a Bar Graph

Bar graphs use bars to show information in a way that is easy to read. Study the graph and answer the questions.

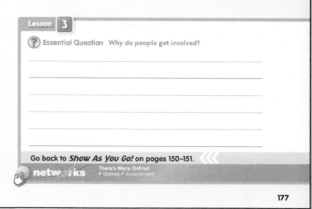

WARTIME SHORTAGES
Paper Dollars Equaling One-Dollar Coin, 1777–1781

1. In 1779, about how many Continental dollars would you need to by an item worth a one-dollar coin?

about 45

2. Describe how the value of Continental dollars changed from 1777 to 1781.

The value fell quickly.

3. Explain why inflation was a problem.

People could no longer afford the things they needed.

Lesson 3

? **Essential Question** Why do people get involved?

Go back to **Show As You Go!** on pages 150–151.

networks There's More Online!
＊ Games ＊ Assessment

176

177

Active Teaching

Explain that the war caused many problems for Americans. Most of these were due in part to complications caused by being a new nation.

Ask:

1. *How did the Continental Congress pay for the war?* **L1**

2. *How did hoarding cause problems for some while benefitting others?* **L2**

3. *What were the consequences of remaining loyal to Great Britain? Why do you think this was so?* **L3**

Chart and Graph Skills

Read a Bar Graph Students may have trouble understanding how the value of money can change over time. Explain this concept by using an analogy involving the cost of buying toys or another item of interest to students. Next, apply this concept to data shown on the graph. If students continue to struggle with this concept, work through the activity as a class.

Response to Intervention

? **Essential Question** Why do people get involved?

If . . . students cannot give a substantiated response to the Essential Question,

....

Then . . . take them back through the lesson. Highlight examples of people becoming involved in the war effort, discussing both the British and American sides. For each example,

Ask: *Why did this person get involved?*

As the discussion progresses make a list of reasons students provide. At the end of the discussion, have students summarize the list and respond to the Essential Question again.

networks

Go to **connected.mcgraw-hill.com** for additional resources:

- Interactive Whiteboard Lessons
- Worksheets
- Assessments
- Content Library

Lesson 4 · A Nation is Born

Essential Question

How do conflicts evolve?
What do you think?

Think about a time when you tried to do something difficult. What happened? Did you give up, or did you keep trying until you succeeded?

Fighting the War

As you read in Lesson 2, the Americans had some early successes. But by October of 1776 they had lost several battles and control of New York City. People began to question George Washington's leadership.

By late December many Patriots had left the army. Some chose to **desert**, or run away. Many who remained had no shoes or supplies. Without a victory to give Americans hope, Washington believed the Revolution would fail. The Americans needed a win, and they needed it fast.

> Think back to what you have learned about the problems caused by the war. What personal hardships might have led people to desert the Continental Army? Explain why you agree or disagree with the decision to desert.

Words To Know

Write a synonym for each of the words below.

desert _____

*consequence _____

spy _____

blockade _____

Crossing the Delaware

Washington decided that a sneak attack on the Hessian soldiers in Trenton, New Jersey, was the best option. On December 25, an icy storm blew into the area. This made traveling across the Delaware River from Pennsylvania to New Jersey difficult. The Patriots finally reached the shore at 4 A.M. The plan worked! The surprised Hessians quickly surrendered. Washington lost only two men in the battle, and both had frozen to death.

On January 3, 1777, the Patriots defeated the British at Princeton, New Jersey, and captured badly needed supplies. Now Patriot soldiers had food, weapons, shoes—and hope.

Main Idea

By December 1776, the Revolution was near failure.

Key Details

Americans had lost many battles. Some soldiers had deserted. Others lacked supplies and hope.

Washington and his soldiers crossed the Delaware and caught the Hessians by surprise.

The American win at Princeton in January 1777 gave the soldiers food, weapons, shoes, and hope.

▲ Washington led Patriots across the icy Delaware River.

Reading Skill

Main Idea and Key Details
After reading these pages, complete the graphic organizer. Underline information in the text that helps you identify the main idea and key details.

178   179

Lesson 4

Activate Prior Knowledge

In pairs, have students share their stories about a time when they tried to do something difficult. Afterward, they should list the words they used to describe their hardship and its conclusion. Have each pair share their list and compile a tally of these words. As you progress through the lesson, revisit this list and discuss how the Continental Army and General Washington may have felt.

Essential Question How do conflicts evolve?

Have students explain what they understand about the Essential Question. Discuss their responses. Explain that everything they learn in this lesson will help them understand the Essential Question better. Remind them to think about how the Essential Question connects to the unit Big Idea: Conflict causes change.

netw⚇rks

Go to **connected.mcgraw-hill.com** for additional resources:

- Interactive Whiteboard Lessons
- Worksheets
- Assessments
- Content Library

Active Teaching

Words To Know After students have listed a synonym for each word, challenge them to identify antonyms as well.

Develop Comprehension

Explain that the Continental Army had a few early successes but then had many losses in the middle of the war. Morale was low, and it looked doubtful that they could win.

Ask:

1. _Why did soldiers desert the Continental Army?_ **L2**
2. _How did crossing the Delaware help revive the Continental Army?_ **L3**

Reading Skill

Common Core Standards RI.2 Determine two or more main ideas of a text and explain how they are supported by key details; summarize the text.

Main Idea and Key Details Once students have completed the graphic organizer on page 179, have them revisit page 178 and 179, searching for an alternative main idea. Once students have identified a new main idea, have them identify and explain the key details that support it. As a class, combine both main ideas to form a summary of the text.

The Turning Point

In June 1777, British General John Burgoyne saw an opportunity to trap Patriot forces. He led thousands of soldiers from Canada into New York. He believed another British force would march North from the Southern colonies, trapping Patriot forces between them.

At first Burgoyne's army was able to push the Americans south. But the British supply wagons got stuck on the muddy forest roads. As a **consequence**, the Americans had time to gather more troops. They decided to stand and fight at Saratoga, New York. Burgoyne finally reached Saratoga on September 16. By then the Patriots had gathered many more soldiers and had built dirt walls for protection.

On September 19, the two armies battled at a farm near Saratoga. The British won control of the farm, but they lost many soldiers. Burgoyne needed help, but none was on the way. On October 7, the two armies fought once more. The British had no chance to win. Burgoyne surrendered 10 days later. The battles at Saratoga were the turning point. The victory boosted American spirits. It also convinced other European countries to become allies with the United States.

DID YOU KNOW?
The first submarine, called the Turtle, was invented and used in 1776. American inventor David Bushnell designed the one-man sub to place bombs on British ships. Unfortunately, the Turtle didn't successfully place a bomb. But another of Bushnell's inventions did work. His floating mines exploded on contact and destroyed many British ships.

▼ Reenactors portray Patriot militia

Reenactors portray the British Red Coats ▲

180

◀ Marquis de Lafayette

Help from Around the World

News of the American victory convinced France that the Americans could win. As a result, the French and American governments signed a treaty of alliance, or an agreement to work together. Several months later, France sent troops, warships, and supplies.

For years, France had been secretly supporting the Americans with money and supplies shipped through Haiti. At that time, Haiti was a center of French trade and profit. Helping the Americans was a way of protecting their investments from the British.

Individuals helped as well. During the winter of 1777, a military instructor named Baron Friedrich von Steuben arrived from Prussia. He saw that American soldiers needed strict training. Von Steuben taught them to march in rows and fight together instead of separately. By June 1778, the American army had become a well-trained fighting force ready for the open battlefield.

Von Steuben wasn't alone in his desire to help. Thaddeus Kosciuszko was an engineer from Poland. He designed forts, including the dirt walls that protected the Americans at Saratoga. Another Pole, Casimir Pulaski, served in Washington's army and became a general. He died of wounds received in battle while fighting for the young nation.

Finally, there was the Marquis de Lafayette. This 19-year-old from France became a valuable member of the Continental Army. You will learn more about his plans for defeating the British at the Battle of Yorktown later.

 Reading Skill
Sequence Events Using pages 178–181, identify four events significant to the Americans' success in the war. In the boxes, describe the events in sequential order. Circle the information from the text that you used.

> Details about the crossing of the Delaware River and/or the attack on the Hessians at Trenton.

> Details about British supply wagons getting stuck which allowed the Patriots time to prepare for battle.

> Details about the Battle of Saratoga and how the Americans won.

> Details about help from foreign powers such as France and /or individuals such as Baron von Steuben.

181

Active Teaching

Most wars have a clear winner and a loser, as well as at least one turning point. Before reading these pages, make sure students understand that the turning point indicates when the advantage shifted from one side to the other. It sometimes predicts the outcome.

Ask:

1. *What events allowed the Continental Army to win the Battle of Saratoga?* **L1**

2. *How did the win at Saratoga change the Continental Army?* **L3**

Use the leveled reader, *Thaddeus Kosciuszko: A Hero of Two Worlds*, to extend and enrich students' understanding of foreign influences on the Revolutionary War. Find a lesson plan for this reader on pages T28 and T29.

DID YOU KNOW?

Find pictures of the *Turtle* and of modern submarines. Show the pictures to students and have them compare "then" and "now." Explain that foot pedals were used to propel the *Turtle*, a spy glass was used to aid in steering, and a tube was used for breathing.

Differentiated Instruction

▶ **Approaching** Create a diagram that shows how foreign contributions supported the Continental Army. For example, you might draw a table and show how the support (legs) held the army up (table top).

▶ **Beyond** Have students create a pamphlet to recruit soldiers to the "new and improved" Continental Army. Pamphlets should showcase the contributions of foreign allies.

▶ **ELL** Review strategies for dealing with challenging proper nouns. For example, pre-reading questions to identify important people and places is one strategy. Also, encourage students to use substitution techniques, such as replacing difficult names with initials, so they can focus on the content.

Reading Skill

 Common Core Standards RI.3 Explain the relationships or interactions between two or more individuals, events, ideas, or concepts in a historical, scientific, or technical text based on specific information in the text.

Sequence Events Once students have completed the activity, have them explain why each event belongs in a certain place in the sequence and why it could not have come earlier or later. Have them evaluate how removing one event would change the course of history.

The Struggle Ends

Although the Americans now had allies, the war was far from over. The Patriots faced yet another difficult winter. Before the war ended, it expanded to west of the colonies, to the sea, and to the South.

> **Compare and contrast battles in the American Revolution. What was different between battles in the South and the Battle of Yorktown?**
>
> Spain helped the Americans in the South. France helped at Yorktown.

As you read, place the numbers 1–4 in the blank circles on the map to show where each event took place. **Hint: One number appears twice.**

① Valley Forge

The winter following the victory at Saratoga turned into an extreme hardship for Washington's troops. They faced bitter cold as they huddled around campfires at Valley Forge, Pennsylvania.

For the first two months, soldiers lived in ragged tents. Few had shoes or blankets, and they shared coats and gloves. Food was scarce too. Weak from cold and hunger, many soldiers became sick. Diseases spread quickly because soldiers lived close together. Almost 2,000 soldiers died from illnesses such as typhoid, influenza, and smallpox.

② Outside the Colonies

Not all important Revolutionary battles took place in the colonies. Many key battles occurred in the areas west of the Appalachian Mountains. In February 1779, George Rogers Clark and his men marched for a month before reaching a British fort near Vincennes, Indiana. Here they attacked and defeated the British.

Fighting happened off the coast of Great Britain too. On September 23, 1779, John Paul Jones and his crew defeated a British warship. Today, Jones is known as the "father of the American Navy."

③ In the South

In 1779, Americans gained support from Spain, a French ally. The Spanish loaned money to the Patriots. Bernardo de Gálvez, the governor of Spain's Louisiana Territory, closed the port at New Orleans to Great Britain and opened it to American ships.

Washington sent General Nathanael Greene to lead Patriot forces in the South. In March 1781 Greene's forces fought the British in North Carolina. The British won the battle but lost one-fourth of the soldiers. When one British leader learned of the many troops lost, he said, "Another such victory would destroy the British army."

④ The Battle of Yorktown

In the summer of 1781, General Cornwallis led 8,000 British soldiers to Yorktown, Virginia. One of Cornwallis's servants, James Armistead, was a **spy** for the Marquis de Lafayette. A spy secretly watches people or things to get information. Armistead passed on information that the British were waiting for supplies from New York. This news also was passed to the French navy, which set up a **blockade** to stop British ships. A blockade prevents the passage of people or supplies.

At the same time, Washington's army and a large French force joined Lafayette, who was already near Yorktown. Cornwallis was surrounded. The ensuing battle lasted for weeks, and fresh supplies and troops couldn't get through to the British. On October 19, 1781, Cornwallis finally surrendered to Washington.

Cornwallis surrenders to Washington's troops at Yorktown. ▼

Map and Globe Skills

What do the blue, green and red lines around Yorktown show?

They show that the Americans and French had the British surrounded.

182   183

Lesson 4

Active Teaching

Explain that the Battle of Saratoga allowed the Americans to get much-needed support, but there was still a long way to go. It was some time before supplies reached the troops. The winter following the Battle of Saratoga was long, cold, and full of threats from disease.

Develop Comprehension

Ask:

1. *Why was the winter at Valley Forge difficult?* **L1**

2. *How do you think the fighting outside the colonies and in the South impacted the Continental Army? (Students should infer that these wins likely boosted the spirits of Continental soldiers all over.)* **L3**

3. *How did help from Spain influence the course of the war?* **L2**

4. *What allowed the Americans to win the Battle of Yorktown?* **L2**

More About Valley Forge   Huddled together around campfires at Valley Forge, soldiers' main food that winter was "fire cakes," a paste of flour and water roasted on a stick over campfires. It was during this same winter that Baron von Steuben arrived and began to train the soldiers.

Page Power

Interact more with the page. Have students:

- (circle) the locations at which events took place.

- underline the names of individuals or groups important to each event.

- analyze the image at the bottom of page 183. Have students label each side "Continental Army" and "British Army" based on clues in the image. Have students (circle) General Cornwallis.

Differentiated Instruction

▶ **Approaching** Use a larger map of the United States to help students find each location and label the map on page 182.

▶ **Beyond** Have students complete and discuss a cause and effect chart about the events on these pages and their overall impact on the war.

Map and Globe Skills

Have students study the map on page 183. **Ask:** *What important piece is missing from this map?* (the map title)

Next, have students brainstorm a title for the map that creatively describes what it shows. Have them write their titles in the margin above the map and share them with the class.

The Results of the War

Fighting continued after Yorktown. But the British recognized they could not afford to continue the war. After Cornwallis's surrender, the British government began peace talks. The Americans, France, and Spain all took part. In 1783 the Treaty of Paris ended the American Revolution.

Under the agreement, Great Britain recognized American independence. The Mississippi River became the country's new western border. The treaty also opened the Mississippi River to ships from France, Spain, Britain, and the United States.

The American Revolution was over. The 13 colonies were now known as the United States. In his farewell orders to the Continental Army, Washington wrote that the determination of the troops "through almost every possible suffering and discouragement for the space of eight long years, was little short of a standing miracle."

> **Many people were injured or killed during the war. How do you think these casualties and losses affected life after the war?**
>
> _____
>
> _____
>
> _____

Primary and Secondary Sources

The illustration at the bottom of the page was drawn in 1906. What does it show? Is it a primary or secondary source? Circle your answer.

_____

_____

184

Several years after the revolution, John Adams was asked about the war. He said that there had been two revolutions. One was the war itself. The other was "in the minds and hearts of the people." The United States had won independence. But not all of the hearts and minds of the people had been changed. For some groups, this was due to the personal and political hardships they faced long after the end of the war.

> Complete the chart by writing the name of the group being described and by describing the result of the hardships.

Group	Personal and Political Hardships	Result
Women	They lost husbands and sons in the war.	Took on new roles
African Americans	The new government needed the support of slave-holding Southern plantation owners.	Slavery continued.
Loyalists	They were forced to give up their homes and property because they supported Great Britain.	Left colonies; fled to Britain, Canada, Florida, and the Bahamas
Native Americans	They fought alongside the British to protect their homelands.	Americans considered them enemies and took their lands.

Lesson 4

? **Essential Question** How do conflicts evolve?

_____

_____

Go back to **Show As You Go!** on pages 150–151.

netw⊙rks There's More Online!
• Games • Assessment

185

Active Teaching

After Yorktown, British forces still controlled major cities, including New York. They remained in the United States while the Treaty of Paris was negotiated. The last British troops finally departed from New York in November 1783.

Develop Comprehension
Ask:

1. *What were the results of the Treaty of Paris of 1783?* **L2**

2. *Were all Patriots satisfied with the results of the war? Explain.* **L3** (Have students use their completed chart on page 185 to help them decide.)

3. *How were the hardships of Loyalists after the war different than those of Patriots?* **L2**

Primary and Secondary Sources

Have students practice analyzing the secondary source. Provide them with a larger version of the image. Divide students into three groups and have each group analyze one third of the illustration. Have them look for clues that answer the questions "Who, What, When, Where, Why, and How?"

Response to Intervention

? **Essential Question** How do conflicts evolve?

If . . . students cannot give a substantiated response to the Essential Question,

. . . .

Then . . . take them back through the lesson. Highlight examples that illustrate change leading up to, during, and following the American Revolution. It may be helpful to track these examples on a flow chart. Discuss how this content relates to the Essential Question.

Ask: *What was the American Revolution like in the beginning, in the middle, and in the end? What generalizations can you make about the ways in which it changed?*

Following discussion, allow students to respond to the Essential Question again.

UNIT 5 Wrap Up

networks There's More Online! • Games • Assessment

Complete the crossword puzzle below with vocabulary words from this unit.

Crossword answers:
- repeal
- proclamation
- blockade
- tributary
- spy
- Loyalist
- treaty
- profiteering
- patriot
- inflation
- mercenary
- militia
- deserter

ACROSS
3 to cancel something
7 an official announcement
8 an action to prevent the passage of people or supplies
11 a river or stream that flows into a larger river
13 a person who secretly watches people or things to get information
14 an American colonist who did not support the fight for independence

DOWN
1 charging high prices for hoarded goods
2 an agreement between two or more governments
4 a professional soldier from another country
5 an army of volunteers who fight in an emergency
6 a rapid rise in prices
9 an American colonist who supported the fight for independence
10 to run away
12 to refuse to buy goods or services

186

BIG IDEA — Unit Project

You will write and illustrate a picture book about one person, place, or event from the American Revolution. Your book must include accurate facts and images, and it must be easy to read and understand. Look back through the unit to brainstorm ideas. You may need to do additional research in the library or on the Internet. Read the list below to see what should be included in your picture book. Check off the tasks you have completed.

Your picture book should include	Yes, it does!
Title and dedication pages	◯
Accurate facts about the topic	◯
Pictures or illustrations	◯
Few spelling errors	◯
Few errors in grammar	◯
Few punctuation errors	◯
A reference list on the last page	◯

Think about the Big Idea

BIG IDEA Conflict causes change.
What did you learn in this unit that helps you understand the BIG IDEA?

_____

_____

_____

187

Wrap Up

Crossword Puzzle

Before students begin the puzzle, lead them in making a class word bank by having them recall unit vocabulary words from memory.

BIG IDEA Big Idea Project

- Read through the project directions and checklist with students.
- Answer any questions students may have about the project.
- Remind students to use their *Show As You Go!* pages to assist them in completing the project.
- To assess the project, refer to the rubric on the following page.

After students complete their projects, encourage self-reflection by asking:

- How did you plan your picture book?

networks

Go to connected.mcgraw-hill.com for additional resources:
- Games
- Assessment
- Group Technology Projects

Differentiated Instruction

▶ **Approaching** Have students complete a pamphlet, instead of an entire book. Students should still include an image and accurate facts and details about a person, place, or event from the American Revolution.

▶ **Beyond** Have students complete an expanded picture book about an event from the American Revolution, including facts and details about the event's location and a key individual involved. Students should complete a detailed bibliography for their books.

▶ **ELL** Allow students to complete the assignment in their first language.

Response to Intervention

BIG IDEA Conflict causes change.

If . . . students cannot give a substantiated explanation of how or why conflict causes change,

. . . .

Then . . . highlight examples of people's actions affecting others in the unit and discuss each one.

Ask: *How did the conflicts of the American Revolution bring change to the former colonies?*

Following discussion, allow students to respond to the Big Idea again.

Name _____ **Date** _____

Revolution Picture Book Rubric

4 Exemplary	3 Accomplished	2 Developing	1 Beginning
The picture book:	**The picture book:**	**The picture book:**	**The picture book:**
☐ explains in detail how the person, place, or event chosen is associated with the American Revolution.	☐ explains generally how the person, place, or event chosen is associated with the American Revolution.	☐ does not explain how the person, place, or event chosen is associated with the American Revolution.	☐ describes a person, place, or event that is not associated with the American Revolution.
☐ contains accurate facts and details about the topic chosen.	☐ contains mostly accurate facts and details about the topic chosen.	☐ contains some accurate facts and details about the topic chosen.	☐ contains inaccurate facts and details about the topic chosen.
☐ demonstrates one consistent design and an organized layout.	☐ demonstrates mostly consistent design elements and has a layout that is mostly organized.	☐ demonstrates inconsistent design elements and has a layout that is somewhat organized.	☐ lacks a design and organized layout.
☐ is interesting, easy to read, and includes multiple images.	☐ is easy to read and includes multiple images.	☐ is somewhat easy to read and includes an image.	☐ is difficult to read and lacks an image.
☐ contains few, if any, errors in grammar, punctuation, capitalization, and spelling.	☐ contains a few errors in grammar, punctuation, capitalization, and spelling.	☐ contains many errors in grammar, punctuation, capitalization, and spelling.	☐ contains errors in grammar, punctuation, capitalization, and spelling that make it difficult to understand.

Grading Comments: _____

_____

_____

_____

_____

_____

_____

_____

Project Score: _____

Read the passage "Thomas Jefferson" before answering Numbers 1 through 8.

Thomas Jefferson

By Lamar Peterson

Thomas Jefferson was one of the most influential men in the history of the United States. He was born in 1743 on his family's plantation in what is now Albemarle County, Virginia. He went to school at the College of William and Mary in Williamsburg, Virginia. Later he practiced law. Jefferson played the violin and studied history, science, and architecture.

Jefferson designed Monticello, his home near Charlottesville, Virginia. He also designed the Virginia Capitol building and the University of Virginia.

In 1775 the Second Continental Congress met in Philadelphia to discuss the recent events in Massachusetts. In June 1776, the Continental Congress named Jefferson, John Adams, Benjamin Franklin, Roger Sherman, and Robert Livingston to a committee to write a statement of independence. Jefferson received the support of John Adams to draft the document. Adams said, "You can write ten times better than I can."

Jefferson was well-prepared to write the Declaration. He had heard Patrick Henry speak against the Stamp Act. He had read Thomas Paine's *Common Sense*. He studied the ideas of John Locke, an English philosopher from the late 1600s. Locke wrote that all people are born with certain rights, including life, liberty, and the right to own property. Locke believed that it was the responsibility of governments to protect these rights.

Using the ideas of these philosophers, the 33-year-old Jefferson wrote his draft in two days and then showed it to Franklin and Adams. They made a few changes and then decided to bring it to the Congress.

Jefferson was a man of many talents, interests, and skills. He served the United States in many ways and at different levels, including his two terms as the third President of the United States.

1 What is the author's purpose?

Ⓐ to tell about Jefferson as President

Ⓑ to describe Jefferson's many talents

Ⓒ to describe Jefferson's designs for Monticello

Ⓓ to tell about Jefferson writing the Declaration of Independence

2 To whom did Jefferson show the first draft of the Declaration?

Ⓕ Adams and Paine

Ⓖ Franklin and Locke

Ⓗ Sherman and Livingston

Ⓘ Franklin and Adams

188

3 Who wrote *Common Sense*?

Ⓐ Thomas Jefferson

Ⓑ Thomas Paine

Ⓒ John Locke

Ⓓ Patrick Henry

4 Read this sentence from the article.

"You can write ten times better than I can."

What did John Adams mean by his statement?

Ⓕ He was a better writer than Jefferson.

Ⓖ Jefferson was good at solving math problems.

Ⓗ Jefferson could write more than Adams.

Ⓘ He trusted Jefferson to write the draft alone.

5 Which information from the article supports the author's statement that Jefferson was well-prepared to write the Declaration?

Ⓐ He had designed both his home and the Virginia Capitol building.

Ⓑ He was a good writer.

Ⓒ He had heard Patrick Henry speak and studied the ideas of John Locke.

Ⓓ He was chosen by the Congress to be on the committee.

6 Which sentence below BEST explains the author's view of Jefferson?

Ⓕ Thomas Jefferson was one of the most influential men in the history of the United States.

Ⓖ Jefferson was well-prepared to write the Declaration.

Ⓗ Jefferson played the violin, and studied history, science, and architecture.

Ⓘ Jefferson designed Monticello, his home near Charlottesville, Virginia.

7 Which two words from the passage have nearly OPPOSITE meanings?

Ⓐ influential, philosopher

Ⓑ talents, interests

Ⓒ support, against

Ⓓ rights, changes

8 Read these sentences from the article.

Locke wrote that all people are born with certain rights, including life, liberty, and the right to own property. Locke believed it was the responsibility of governments to protect these rights.

What is the meaning of *responsibility* as used in the above sentence?

Ⓕ a job or duty

Ⓖ a change

Ⓗ a disagreement

Ⓘ a choice

189

Test Preparation

Test-Taking Tips

Share these test-taking tips with your students:

- Begin by reading the title of the excerpt. This title may provide clues to help you answer questions about the author's purpose.

- Read each paragraph in the excerpt carefully, noting information that seems more important and less important.

- Read the question carefully, identifying what it is asking for. Some answer options may contain true information but will not answer the question asked. The correct answer will be true and answer the question.

- Check your answers against the text excerpt. Do they agree?

Answers

1. B **CCS RI.2**

2. I **CCS RI.7**

3. B **CCS RI.7**

4. I **CCS RI.3**

5. C **CCS RI.8**

6. G **CCS RI.8**

7. C **CCS RI.4**

8. F **CCS RI.4**

Teacher Notes

UNIT
6 Planner FOUNDING THE NATION

 **Rules provide order.**

Student Portfolio

- **Show As You Go!**
  Use these pages to introduce the Big Idea. Students record information specific to each lesson. They use these pages to help them plan their Big Idea Project.

net**w**rks™

- **Group Technology Project**
  Students use 21st century skills to complete a group extension activity of the unit project. Lesson plans, worksheets, and rubrics are available online.

Student Portfolio

- **Big Idea Project**
  Students will be instructed to participate in a mock U.S. government. They will create a new classroom rule. The Big Idea Project rubric is on page 235W.

Reading Skills

Student Portfolio

- **Reading Skill: Analyze Information**
  Pages 192–193. Common Core State Standards RI.3

Leveled Readers

Use the leveled reader *Vote!* with Lesson 2. Find the lesson plan on pages T26–T27 of your Teacher Edition.

Treasures Connection

Teach this unit with Treasures Unit 3, *Everybody Can Serve,* pages 390–391, and Unit 4, *Getting Out the Vote,* pages 452–455.

Social Studies Skills

Student Portfolio

- **Primary and Secondary Sources: Diaries**
  Page 197

net**w**rks™

- **Skill Builders**
  Introduce and teach analyzing primary and secondary sources.

Activity Cards

- **Center for Social Studies Skills Investigation**
  Use the center activity cards to help students explore Primary Sources, Geography, and Citizenship.

FOLDABLES®

Student Portfolio

- Students can create vocabulary Foldables right in their portfolios.

- Additional Foldables templates can be found on pages R34–R42 of your Teacher Edition. See page R33 for instructions.

Assessment Solutions

- **McGraw-Hill networks™**
  Safe online testing features multiple question types that are easy to use and editable.

- **Self-Check Quizzes**

- **Worksheets**

UNIT 6 At a Glance

Lesson	Essential Question	Vocabulary
1 Struggles of a New Nation	What is the purpose of government?	constitution ratify *conclusion delegate
2 Writing the Constitution	What are the functions of government?	*persuade veto appeal impeach federalism amendment
3 Convincing the People	How do people make decisions?	*debate guarantee submit
4 Protecting and Expanding Rights	How do we protect our rights?	fundamental press due process jury *defend
5 Active Citizenship	How do citizens participate?	responsibility politics *inform

*denotes academic vocabulary

Digital Resources

Go to **connected.mcgraw-hill.com** for additional resources:

- Interactive Whiteboard Lessons

- Worksheets

- Assessment

- Content Library

- Lesson Plans

- Skill Builders

- Videos

- Use Standards Tracker on **networks** to track students' progress.

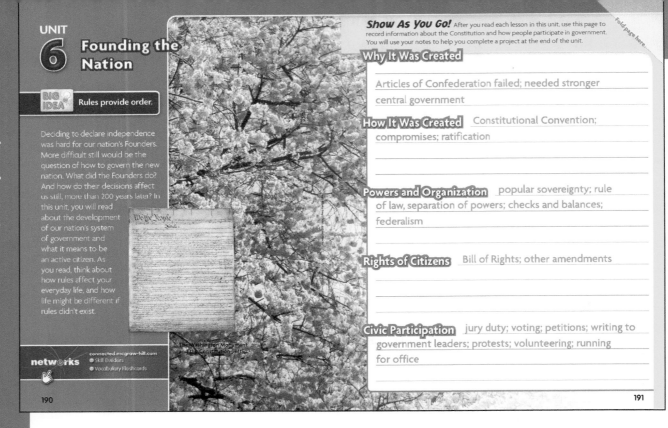

UNIT 6 Founding the Nation

BIG IDEA Rules provide order.

Deciding to declare independence was hard for our nation's Founders. More difficult still would be the question of how to govern the new nation. What did the Founders do? And how do their decisions affect us still, more than 200 years later? In this unit, you will read about the development of our nation's system of government and what it means to be an active citizen. As you read, think about how rules affect your everyday life, and how life might be different if rules didn't exist.

networks connected.mcgraw-hill.com
● Skill Builders
● Vocabulary Flashcards

The Washington Monument and the Constitution (left)

190

Show As You Go! After you read each lesson in this unit, use this page to record information about the Constitution and how people participate in government. You will use your notes to help you complete a project at the end of the unit.

Why It Was Created

Articles of Confederation failed; needed stronger central government

How It Was Created Constitutional Convention; compromises; ratification

Powers and Organization popular sovereignty; rule of law, separation of powers; checks and balances; federalism

Rights of Citizens Bill of Rights; other amendments

Civic Participation jury duty; voting; petitions; writing to government leaders; protests; volunteering; running for office

191

Introduce the Unit

✓ Diagnostic Assessment

On a separate sheet of paper have students write these four sentences, one in each corner of the paper:

1. I know this about the United States government.
2. I know this about the United States government, too.
3. This confuses me about the United States government.
4. I have this question about the United States government.

Have students write statements or questions underneath each sentence. Student responses will help identify their level of understanding.

Active Teaching

BIG IDEA Rules provide order.
In this unit, students will learn about how and why the United States Constitution was written.

Students will use the ***Show As You Go!*** pages throughout this unit. As they read each lesson, students will use information from it to complete these pages. Explain to students that at the end of the unit, they will use the information on these pages to complete their Unit Project. Have students fold back the corner of page 191. This will help them flip back to this page as needed.

Differentiated Instruction

▶ **Approaching** Review the text of each prompt with students. Have them identify key words which tell what information the text is asking for. Then have students brainstorm words that are similar. They should stay alert for these words as they read each lesson, to help them find the information they need.

▶ **Beyond** As students complete each lesson, have them include in their notes one thing they would have done differently than the Founders and give a short explanation why. If students need additional space to write, have them attach a half sheet of paper to the page on which to record their thoughts.

▶ **ELL** As students complete each lesson, allow them to work together in pairs or groups to respond to the prompts. Help students define unfamiliar words.

Reading Skill

Common Core Standards
RI.3: Explain the relationships or interactions between two or more individuals, events, ideas, or concepts in a historical, scientific, or technical text based on specific information in the text.

Analyze Information

Analyzing information can help you better understand a particular topic. Start by collecting information about the topic. It's important to gather facts from many sources. For example, if you are analyzing information about an event, it's important to have more than one account of the event. Next, look closely at the information you collected to find patterns, relationships, or trends. Patterns are pieces of information that appear more than once. Relationships are the way two or more things interact. Trends are the way things change over time.

It took almost 200 years for African Americans to gain full voting rights. ▼

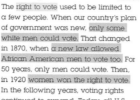

192

LEARN IT

To analyze information:

- Identify the topic that the information is about.
- Break the information into smaller pieces, called details.
- Examine each piece of information and look for patterns, relationships, or trends.

> **Topic**

The right to vote used to be limited to a few people. When our country's plan of government was new, only some white men could vote. That changed in 1870, when a new law allowed African American men to vote too. For 50 years, only men could vote. Then, in 1920 women won the right to vote. In the following years, voting rights continued to expand. Today, all U.S. citizens 18 years or older can vote.

> **Details**

TRY IT

You can use a graphic organizer like the one below to keep track of the topic and details. Fill in the chart with the topic and details from page 192. Then answer the question below.

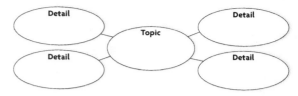

Detail · Detail · Topic · Detail · Detail

What pattern, relationship, or trend do you notice? _____

APPLY IT

Read the paragraph below. Circle text clues and details that you could use to help you analyze the information. Describe the pattern, relationship, or trend that you notice on the lines.

The Founders were fed up with the powerful British government. They came up with a new plan of government for the United States. The first plan they tried did not make the government powerful. It didn't work well, and over time this caused many problems. The next plan made the government more powerful. But the American people feared it was too powerful! People demanded that the Founders include a list of rights for their protection. Today, our government still works according to this second plan of government created by the Founders. It is powerful, but not too powerful.

_____
_____
_____
_____
_____

193

Common Core Standards RI.3 Explain the relationships or interactions between two or more individuals, events, ideas, or concepts in a historical, scientific, or technical text based on specific information in the text.

Reading Skill

Active Teaching

LEARN IT Analyze Information

Say: *As I read I think, "What is this information about? And, what kinds of questions can I ask about this information?" Identifying the topic and coming up with a set of questions helps me focus on the parts of the information that I need to find. Once I have completed this step, I think "What sorts of patterns, relationships, or trends can I find that will help me answer my questions?" To answer this question, I look for pieces of information that match, repeat, form a cause and effect, or form a series of events. Answering this question helps guide my search for links between pieces of information.*

TRY IT Encourage students to try the modeled strategy as they complete the **TRY IT** activity.

APPLY IT After students have completed the **APPLY IT** activity, **Ask:**

1. *What topic or question was this information about?* **L1**

2. *How did you identify which details mattered to the topic or question?* **L2**

3. *What additional question might you ask based on the pattern, relationship, or trend that you noticed?* **L3**

Differentiated Instruction

▶ **Approaching** Review the **LEARN IT** activity as a small group. Do the **TRY IT** activity together. Have students complete the **APPLY IT** activity independently. Regroup to compare and correct.

▶ **Beyond** Have students evaluate their analysis from **APPLY IT. Ask:**
Is your analysis supported by the facts as presented in the text? In order to improve your analysis, what additional information would you need to answer an additional question?

▶ **ELL** Have students work in pairs or groups to discuss the passage and come up with a series of questions about it. Then, have them create a flow chart, placing each event in its correct location on the chart. Have students describe their chart orally or in writing.

networks

Go to **connected.mcgraw-hill.com** for additional resources.
- Skill Builders
- Graphic Organizers

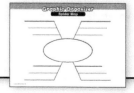

Graphic Organizer
Spider Map

Words to Know FOLDABLES

Common Core Standards
RI.4: Determine the meaning of general academic and domain-specific words and phrases in a text relevant to a grade 5 topic or subject area.

The list below shows some important words you will learn in this unit. Their definitions can be found on the next page. Read the words.

constitution (kahn • stuh • TOO • shuhn)
ratify (RAT • uh • feye)
veto (VEE • toh)
impeach (ihm • PEECH)
amendment (uh • MEHND • muhnt)
guarantee (gehr • uhn • TEE)
fundamental (fuhn • duh • MEHN • tuhl)
responsibility (rih • spahn • suh • BIH • luh • tee)

The Foldable on the next page will help you learn these important words. Follow the steps below to make your Foldable.

Step 1 Fold along the solid red line.

Step 2 Cut along the dotted lines.

Step 3 Read the words and their definitions.

Step 4 Complete the activities on each tab.

Step 5 Look at the back of your Foldable. Choose ONE of these activities for each word to help you remember its meaning:
- Draw a picture of the word.
- Write a description of the word.
- Write how the word is related to something you know.

◀ The Constitutional Convention was held in Independence Hall in Philadelphia.

194

A **constitution** is a plan for government.	Write a sentence using the word *constitution*.
To **ratify** is to approve and adopt an official document.	Circle the three words that belong with the word *ratify*. accept reject document wrongdoing adopt addition
To **veto** is to reject a bill.	Write an antonym for the word *veto*.
To **impeach** is to put an official on trial for wrongdoing.	What do you think is the purpose of impeaching someone?
An **amendment** is a change or addition to an official document.	Circle two key words in the definition of *amendment*. Write the words here: _____ _____
A **guarantee** is a promise that something will be provided.	What does it mean to give someone a guarantee?
Fundamental is a word that means basic or essential.	Write a sentence using the word *fundamental*.
A **responsibility** is something people do because it is their job or duty.	Write a synonym for the word *responsibility*.

Common Core Standards **RI.4** Determine the meaning of general academic and domain-specific words and phrases in a text relevant to a grade 5 topic or subject area.

Words to Know
Active Teaching

FOLDABLES

1. Go to connected.mcgraw-hill.com for flashcards to introduce the unit vocabulary to students.

2. Read the words on the list on page 214 and have students repeat them after you.

3. Guide students as they complete steps 1 through 5 of the Foldable.

4. Have students use the Foldable to practice the vocabulary words independently or with a partner.

networks

Go to connected.mcgraw-hill.com for additional resources.

- Vocabulary Flashcards
- Vocabulary Games
- Graphic Organizers

GO Vocabulary!

Follow these steps to help students construct a vocabulary graphic organizer. Provide students with a circle chart divided into quarters, like the one below. Have students write one vocabulary word from *any* part of Unit 6 in each quarter. Then, have students give their circle chart a title.

Have students answer questions in relation to their graphic organizer. **Ask:**

1. *How is your title related to each word you chose?*

2. *How is each word related to the other three words in your circle chart?*

3. *Is there one word that doesn't fit as well as the others? Explain.*

4. *Change one word in your circle chart. Does this change alter the meaning of the title? What new title could you give your chart?*

constitution	constitution
ratify	ratify
veto	veto
impeach	impeach
amendment	amendment
guarantee	guarantee
fundamental	fundamental
responsibility	responsibility

Primary Sources

Diaries

A diary is one type of primary source. While a diary entry can contain many different types of information, most diary entries are records of a person's day-to-day experiences. Through diaries, we can learn much about what it was like to live long ago. We can even learn more about important events through the eyes of those who lived at that time.

In this unit, you will learn how and why the Founders of our country formed our national government. You will read about how their first plan of government caused many problems. Many people were unhappy, and some people even formed a rebellion. The diary entry on the right was written by someone who lived near the area where a rebellion occurred.

Primary Source

Thursday, the 30th a small snow in the night . . . on Monday last John Bardwell . . . had orders from Shays . . . to have [his company] ready to march. . . .

Monday, the 4th cool towards night snowed . . . John Bardwell marched 40 men with him. . . .

Wednesday, the 6th . . . towards Night orders came . . . for the Militia to be in readiness to march tomorrow to Worcester

Thursday, the 7th . . . Our Militia seemed eager to go . . . I made a speech to them persuading them to be quiet & rest the Matter with [the government]

Friday, the 8th we hear that [General] Shays . . . has took possession of Worcester . . . and has taken [three judges prisoner]

—from the diary of Justus Forward

DBQ Document-Based Questions

Read the diary entries. As you read, complete the following activities.

1. Underline details that describe the writer's environment.
2. Circle details that describe the event the writer experienced and who was involved.

networks
There's More Online!
● Skill Builders
● Resource Library

United States 197

Differentiated Instruction

▶ **ELL** Have students identify difficult words and explain their meaning. Then, ask students to come up with synonyms or a series of keywords in their first language that relate to each problem word. Have students make cards or a graphic organizer to help them practice the difficult terms.

W O R D   P L A Y

Play SWAT! Write or post the words on the board, and divide the class into two teams. One student from each team comes to the board, picks up a fly swatter, and stands with his/her back to the words.

The teacher reads a definition, says, "Go!" and the students turn and quickly try to SWAT the correct word. If both students choose the same word, the fly swatter that is on the bottom gets the point.

networks

Go to connected.mcgraw-hill.com for additional resources.

- Skill Builders
- Resource Library

Primary Sources

Active Teaching

Students should notice that Justus Forward's diary does not contain complete sentences. Rather, it is a compilation of notations in shorthand. Explain to students that diaries, while they are a historical record, were private at the time they were written. They were written for the purposes of the writer, and the writer probably didn't account for the needs of other readers.

Say: *Diary entries are not formal writing. Diary writers might use their own special language, symbols, or code words to record their thoughts. You will have to put on your detectives' hats in order to understand the meaning of each entry.*

Work through each entry as a class. Have students look for key words that help identify what the entries say about:

- the weather or climate,
- the events described, and
- Justus Forward's feelings about the events.

Lesson 1 — Struggles of a New Nation

Essential Question

What is the purpose of government?

What do you think?

_____

_____

_____

_____

Words To Know

Write the definition of each word in your own words.

constitution _____

confederation _____

*conclusion _____

delegate _____

A plan is a set of directions that help people figure out how to do something. There are many reasons to have a plan. Your family probably has an emergency plan, such as how to get out of the house in case of a fire.

Interview a parent or a trusted adult about a plan he or she has. Write his or her answers below.
I interviewed:

Ask: What is your plan for?

Ask: Why do you need your plan?

Ask: What is the most important part of your plan?

198

Making Plans

Plans are an important part of life. Plans can be simple, such as what to eat for dinner. Or, they can be complicated and very important, especially when there are many things to be done.

Governments have many responsibilities. You already know a little about governments.

Make a list of things governments do.

A Plan for Government

Governments serve many purposes. The most important purpose of government is to provide laws. This helps to avoid conflicts and settle disagreements. Governments also provide security for their people. This is why we have police officers and armed forces. Governments must also provide services and supplies that wouldn't be available otherwise. These include building and repairing roads, delivering the mail, and providing money and other aid for those in need. Another function of governments is managing the economy. A government must collect and spend money in order to operate and provide for its people.

Every government in our nation has a plan to help it serve these purposes. This plan consists of a set of laws. There is a special word for a plan for government: **constitution**. Our nation's constitution has an interesting story. In this Lesson, you will learn about that story.

▲ Our nation's Founders had a lot of work to do to set up our government.

Circle the purposes of a constitution. Rewrite them in your own words.

199

Lesson 1

Activate Prior Knowledge

After students have completed their interviews, ask for volunteers to share what they wrote with the class. Discuss the reasons for making each plan and what might happen if a plan did not exist for each goal or reason. Explain that in this lesson, students will learn about our nation's first plan of government and how it didn't meet all of the young nation's needs.

Essential Question
What is the purpose of government?

Have students explain what they understand about the Essential Question. Discuss their responses. Explain that everything they learn in this lesson will help them understand the Essential Question better. Remind them to think about how the Essential Question connects to the unit Big Idea: Rules provide order.

More about the Articles of Confederation   As you read this lesson, remind students that the Articles of Confederation is not a "first draft" of the Constitution. Once the Founders realized the Articles weren't working and couldn't be fixed, they wrote a completely new document: the Constitution.

Active Teaching

Words To Know   Once students have completed the Words to Know activity, have them identify the part of speech to which each vocabulary word belongs. Next, have students come up with a synonym or antonym for each word.

Develop Comprehension

• Have students read page 198 and do the interview activity as homework a few nights before you plan to begin the lesson.

• In order to do the first activity on page 199, students will have to recall information they've learned in prior years. You may choose to do this activity as a class during guided reading to help beginning level students.

networks

Go to **connected.mcgraw-hill.com** for additional resources.

• Interactive Whiteboard Lessons
• Worksheets
• Assessment
• Lesson Plans

Creating a New Government

You've already learned about the Declaration of Independence and the Revolutionary War. There's more to the story of forming the United States. To tell it, we have to go back in time a little bit. Think back to the year 1776 and the Second Continental Congress.

At the same time that the Founders were deciding to break away from Great Britain, they were also deciding what to do afterward. How would they govern the thirteen colonies on their own?

It would be a challenge. The Founders wanted to protect the liberties, or freedoms, that Americans were fighting for. And the colonies didn't yet think of themselves as a single country. In fact, some colonies had already written their own constitutions. No one wanted another too-powerful government telling them what to do, as Britain's Parliament and king had.

Our family is from Connecticut!
We proudly call New Jersey "home."
This family is loyal to South Carolina!
We are Virginians here!

◀ Painter Archibald MacNeal Willard painted "The Spirit of 1776" more than 100 years after the signing of the Declaration of Independence.

1. Think back to what you've learned. What else happened at the Second Continental Congress?

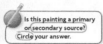
The Declaration of Independence

2. Explain why the colonies didn't want a new government to have too much power.

_____

Is this painting a primary or secondary source? Circle your answer.

The Articles of Confederation

Some thought that the new nation would be more like a friendly group of independent states than a single, united country. The Second Continental Congress set about writing a plan of government, called the Articles of Confederation, around this idea. A confederation is a group of separate governments that agree to help one another.

The Articles of Confederation eventually became the first constitution of the United States of America. It took the Congress seven months to complete, and the country started working according to this plan in 1777. However, the thirteen states still had to **ratify**, or approve and adopt it. The Articles were finally ratified by all the states in 1781. From beginning to end, it took more than four years to make the new government final. And the former colonies were fighting the Revolutionary War at the same time. Imagine that!

The Articles of Confederation ▶

Reading Skill
Analyze Information

Using the above image and what you have read in the text, what patterns or relationships do you notice about the loyalties of Americans at the time of the Revolution?

They were loyal to their states, not the country.

200

201

Active Teaching

Help students understand the difference between state loyalties in the 1770s and state loyalties that Americans hold today.

1. **Ask:** *What country are you a citizen of?*

2. Then, discuss with students the symbols, holidays, and songs with which we express and celebrate our patriotism.

3. Next, **ask:** *What state do you live in?*

4. Discuss with students what it means to be a member of a nation vs. a state. Explain that in the 1770s, residents of each state thought of their state as their nation.

Develop Comprehension
Ask:

1. *Where might you find a list of freedoms that the Founders wanted to protect?* **L1**

2. *What two things did the Founders do at the Second Continental Congress?* **L2**

3. *How do the items listed in the Declaration of Independence relate to the Founders' concerns about power in the new national government?* **L3**

☑ Formative Assessment

Have students show what they've learned about the formation of the United States government. Have students explain why each statement is false.

Say:

1. *Americans were united in their wish to form a new national government.* (false; states felt independent of one another)

2. *The Founders wrote the Articles of Confederation at the Third Continental Congress.* (false; Second Continental Congress)

Use this assessment to monitor student understanding and identify the need for intervention.

Reading Skill

Common Core Standards RI.3 Explain the relationships or interactions between two or more individuals, events, ideas, or concepts in a historical, scientific, or technical text based on specific information in the text.

Analyze Information Ask: *Why do you think each state was not necessarily loyal to the whole country?*

▲ Paper money from Massachusetts

A Small Government

The government set up by the Articles of Confederation was very small and limited in its powers. It was made up of one lawmaking body called Congress. Each state sent at least two representatives to Congress, but each state only had one vote on every matter. The individual states kept most of the power. At first, the Articles of Confederation seemed to meet the needs of the young nation. But as time went on, weaknesses emerged. Read the chart below to learn about some of the effects of these weaknesses.

THINK • PAIR • SHARE
With a partner, pick one effect from the chart. Circle it on your page, then brainstorm reasons why this was a problem.

Weaknesses of the Articles of Confederation	
Cause	**Effect**
The national government had no power to raise money through taxes.	The national government could not • pay off high war debts. • pay lawmakers. • pay soldiers for their service.
The national government had no power to support the national currency.	Each state made its own paper money.
	The value of money was different in each state. Some money was worthless.
The national government had no power to manage trade.	Each state made its own trade laws.
	Merchants never knew which laws to follow.
	Trade slowed, as did economic growth.
The national government had no power to force states to follow national laws.	States did whatever they wanted.
The national government had no power to raise an army.	The nation could not defend itself. Britain and Spain both took advantage of this on the frontier by ignoring U.S. claims to land.

202

Troubles for the New Government

After the Revolutionary War, the new country faced many problems. Congress had borrowed large amounts of money to pay for the war. Now it was unable to collect taxes to repay those debts.

Many state governments also had large debts. To pay off this debt, they increased taxes. Many people and businesses could not afford to pay these taxes and went into debt. Because Congress could not regulate trade, each state made its own trade laws. Some states taxed goods that came from other states or countries. Supplies and goods became more expensive, and people went deeper into debt.

Violence Erupts

When people couldn't pay their debts, they were thrown in jail. Daniel Shays was a military officer in the Revolutionary War. He was now a farmer who was deep in debt. Shays urged others to rebel. He led a group of armed men and across western Massachusetts. They closed courthouses and broke into jails to free debtors. Shays then attacked a federal arsenal, or storage area for weapons.

Shays's Rebellion was quickly stopped by the state militia. However, the rebellion showed many people that the Articles had failed. Wealthy Americans wanted a national government strong enough to protect their property. Farmers wanted a government that could issue paper money that had value.

Shays's Rebellion ▼

1. Why did Daniel Shays rebel?
   He was freeing debtors.

2. Why did people think they needed a new government after the rebellion?
   They felt the government could not provide the protection and money they needed.

203

Lesson 1

Active Teaching

Help students understand the cause-and-effect chart and the implications of the effects on Americans.

1. Explain that each cause is a weakness of the Articles. Each effect was either a problem in and of itself, or it caused further problems.

2. After students have completed the Think-Pair-Share activity, have each pair share their responses with the class.

3. Then, lead a discussion of how students feel when they have too much work to do or when they witness a fight or other confrontation.

4. Help them draw a connection between their feelings of being overwhelmed or afraid, and how the citizens of the United States must have felt.

Page Power

Interact more with the page. Have students:

- label different parts of the image on page 203. Possible labels include: Shays's rebels; militia; courthouse; damage; casualty; etc.

- evaluate Daniel Shays as either a hero or a villain of history and circle sentences that reinforce their evaluation.

- write in the margins their predictions about what might happen next.

Differentiated Instruction

▶ **Approaching** Assist students in drawing connections between the causes of Shays's Rebellion and the weaknesses listed in the chart. Have students locate key words such as *money* and *army* in the text and chart on each page.

▶ **Beyond** Lead students in an analysis of why the weaknesses of the Articles led to problems. Have students create a comic strip or an illustrated flow chart that describes the weaknesses of the Articles.

▶ **ELL** As students read pages 202–203, have them identify unfamiliar or difficult words. Then have them research the definition and one example of each word, writing their notes in the margins.

The Northwest Ordinance

Overall, the Articles were not working. But they did have one lasting success: Congress was able to set up land policies for expanding the country. Many Americans wanted to move west of the Appalachians to search for new land and opportunities. To provide land for these settlers, the Confederation Congress passed the Northwest Ordinance of 1787. This plan created the Northwest Territory out of land north of the Ohio River and east of the Mississippi River.

Settlers poured into the Northwest Territory. They eventually carved out five states under the Northwest Ordinance: Ohio, Indiana, Illinois, Michigan, and Wisconsin.

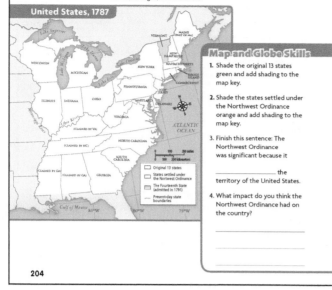

United States, 1787

Map and Globe Skills

1. Shade the original 13 states green and add shading to the map key.

2. Shade the states settled under the Northwest Ordinance orange and add shading to the map key.

3. Finish this sentence: The Northwest Ordinance was significant because it

_____ the territory of the United States.

4. What impact do you think the Northwest Ordinance had on the country?

_____

_____

Calls for Change

The Founders came to the **conclusion** that the Articles had failed. But what should they do about that? This was an urgent matter, indeed. Violence had already become a reality, and more violence could be on the way. Many Americans called for the Articles of Confederation to be changed. A few members of Congress called a special meeting to decide what to do.

The Constitutional Convention

In May 1787, leaders from 12 states convened, or met, in Philadelphia. There, the **delegates** to the Constitutional Convention had to decide the future of their government. A delegate is a person who represents others at an important meeting. They elected George Washington to lead the convention and began a long, difficult discussion. The delegates decided that the Articles were too broken to be saved. Instead, they decided to start over with a new constitution. The fate of the young nation was in their hands.

▲ The Constitutional Convention was held in Pennsylvania's State House in Philadelphia. Today this building is called Independence Hall.

Lesson 1

? Essential Question What is the purpose of government?

_____

_____

_____

_____

_____

_____

Go back to *Show As You Go!* on pages 190–191. ◄◄◄

networks There's More Online!
• Games • Assessment

204   205

Active Teaching

Develop Comprehension
Ask:

1. *What was the name of the land policy that was developed by Congress under the Articles of Confederation?* **L1**

2. *Why was it important?* **L2**

3. *Why was it urgent that the leaders find a solution to the nation's problems under the Articles?* **L2**

4. *What might have happened if the leaders didn't fix the nation's problems?* **L3**

> *Show As You Go!* Remind students to go back to the Unit Opener and complete the activities for this lesson.

Map and Globe Skills

Students should use context clues to fill in the map. Extend students' comprehension of map details.
Ask:

1. *What direction did the U.S. border move with the addition of the Northwest Territory?*

Response to Intervention

? Essential Question
What is the purpose of government?

If . . . students cannot identify the purpose of government

....

Then . . . divide students into eight groups. Assign one group to each page of the lesson. Have each group identify a purpose of government described. Have groups tell the class the purpose they found and lead a class discussion of the roles that governments fill.

Following discussion, allow students to respond to the Essential Question again.

Page Power

Interact more with the page. Have students:

- circle why the Confederation Congress passed the Northwest Ordinance.

- underline what delegates decided to do about the Articles.

Lesson 2 — Writing the Constitution

Essential Question
What are the functions of government?
What do you think?

_____

_____

_____

_____

_____

Have you ever heard or seen the phrase "We the People"? You can find it at the very beginning of our nation's Constitution—the plan for government written at the Constitutional Convention. "We the People" sums up the idea that the government of the United States is run by its people, for its people. This idea is also called popular sovereignty. Read the rest of the Preamble, or beginning words, of the Constitution below.

We the People of the United States, in Order to form a more perfect Union, establish Justice, insure domestic Tranquility, provide for the common defence, promote the general Welfare, and secure the Blessings of Liberty to ourselves and our Posterity, do ordain and establish this Constitution for the United States of America.

Words To Know
Have you heard these words before? Make a guess about what each word means. Then find it in the Lesson.

*persuade _____

federalism _____

appeal _____

impeach _____

Circle one phrase from the Preamble. Then, go to a dictionary to look up any words you don't know. Once you know the meaning of those words, write on the lines what the phrase you circled means.

_____

_____

_____

_____

_____

_____

206

Key Concepts of the Constitution

You might be wondering what happened at the Constitutional Convention. We'll get to that soon, but first you should know about some key concepts, or ideas, that took shape as the Convention went on. Each of these concepts limits the government's power. You see, even as the framers of our government knew that the Articles of Confederation were too weak, they continued to worry about making our government too powerful.

Key Concept	Origin (Where it Came From)
Popular Sovereignty The government is run by its people. The people choose their own leaders.	This idea is also called democracy. The ancient Greeks invented democracy thousands of years ago.
Rule of Law The Constitution is the highest set of laws. No one is above the Constitution. This is also called "Limited Government."	England's plan of government, called the Magna Carta, limited the power of the king or queen, or monarchies.
Separation of Powers Government is divided into three branches. Each branch has a different job to do.	A French writer named Montesquieu wrote about these ideas in the mid-1700s. The delegates decided to try them out.
Checks and Balances Each branch of government has power over the other two branches.	
Federalism The national government and the states share power.	This concept was invented at the Constitutional Convention. The delegates wanted to give the federal government just enough power, and reserve all other powers to the states.
Individual Rights This is the idea that people have rights, which should be protected by their government.	John Locke and other philosophers said people have "natural rights" that cannot be taken away.

Chart and Graph Skills
1. Circle the concept supported by John Locke.

2. Highlight the concept invented by the delegates to the Constitutional Convention.

3. Put a box around the concept that is related to the Magna Carta.

207

Lesson 2

Activate Prior Knowledge

After students have completed the Preamble activity, explain that the Preamble can be thought of as our nation's mission statement. A mission statement outlines the goals and purpose of a group, organization, or nation of people. Lead students in a discussion of what their goals are when they come to school, and write a classroom mission statement from those goals.

Essential Question
What are the functions of government?

Have students explain what they understand about the Essential Question. Discuss their responses. Explain that everything they learn in this lesson will help them understand the Essential Question better. Remind them to think about how the Essential Question connects to the unit Big Idea: Rules provide order.

More About the Preamble The word "defence" appears to be misspelled in the Preamble. Actually, to the Founders this wasn't a misspelling. Until the 1800s, even the most educated of individuals typically spelled words in the way that was common to their region, speech patterns, or personal preference. Noah Webster was the first to undertake the enormous task of standardizing American spellings. He published his first dictionary in 1806.

Active Teaching

Words To Know After students have completed the Words to Know activity, have students read the definitions of the vocabulary words in the text. Then, present students with a list of three or four words or phrases related to each word. Have students identify the word or phrase that does not fit with the rest. Have students explain their choice.

Develop Comprehension
- Ask students to take turns explaining each concept from the chart in their own words.

- As an extension, have students locate Greece, England (Great Britain), and France on a world map or globe. Lead them in a discussion about how ideas get passed from region to region.

Chart and Graph Skills

Read a Table Ask: What concepts did Montesquieu write about? **L1**

Separating the Powers

Discussions at the Constitutional Convention were serious business. The big problem with the Articles of Confederation was that it didn't give the national government enough power. But no one wanted to give any person or group too much power. The representatives decided to separate the powers of government into three branches. The first three articles, or major parts, of the Constitution describe the branches of our government and their powers.

The Legislative Branch

Find it in: Article I of the Constitution
Name: Congress
Most Known For: Making our nation's laws
The Great Compromise: Delegates suggested two different ways to organize Congress. One plan gave small states more power. Another gave large states more power. The delegates argued for weeks, but were finally **persuaded** into a compromise. They combined parts of the two plans. This solution was called the Great Compromise.
How Congress is Organized: Congress has two houses, or parts. In the House of Representatives, the number of members sent by each state is based on a state's population. In the other house, called the Senate, each state has two senators.
Electing Law Makers: The Constitution created a representative government. This means that the people elect, or choose, people to represent them in government. Members of the House of Representatives serve for two years. In the beginning, the state legislatures chose the senators. Today, the people also elect their senators directly. Senators serve for six years.
Writing Laws: A bill is an idea for a new law. To become law, first a bill has to be approved by both houses of Congress. Then the bill goes to the President. Bills about money must always begin in the House of Representatives.
Other Powers: Congress has many other powers. These include the power to collect taxes, control trade with other countries, manage a national currency, and declare war.

THINK • PAIR • SHARE
Work with a partner and use the Internet or other resource to find both an audio and a video recording of different State of the Union addresses. Discuss what the speech tells you about what was happening in the country at that time.

Circle for whom Congress works.

the Senate
the President
(the People)

208

The Executive Branch

Find it in: Article II of the Constitution
Name: The President of the United States
Most Known For: Carrying out, or enforcing, the laws
The Electoral College: Constitutional Convention delegates worried that the people would choose power-hungry leaders, or leaders who couldn't do the job. The delegates created the Electoral College to choose the President. In this system, each state gets one electoral vote for each of its members of Congress.
Signing Bills Into Law: A bill that has been approved by both houses of Congress goes on to the President. The President then has a choice. He or she can sign the bill, making it a law. Or, the President can **veto**, or reject, the bill. If a bill is vetoed, it goes back to Congress. Congress can still pass the law if two-thirds of the members of both houses approve the bill. This is called overriding the veto.
Other Powers: The President serves for four years. The President also is the commander-in-chief of our nation's military and is responsible for signing treaties and appointing government officials.
Kings vs. Presidents: Kings inherit their power, which means they receive their power from their parents. But U.S. Presidents are chosen by—and get their power from—the people.

▲ George Washington was our first President under the Constitution.

Circle for whom the President works.

Congress   the President   (the People)

The Constitution requires the President to report to Congress on the "state of the union" each year. In 1947 Harry Truman was the first President to deliver the State of the Union address on television. ▼

209

Active Teaching

For the Think-Pair-Share activity, you may want to encourage students to research State of the Union addresses during critical times in American history. For example, students can find State of the Union addresses during wartime or those that come in tough economic times, such as during the Great Depression. Encourage students to use the Internet or other resources to better understand what was going on in the country and the world at the time.

Develop Comprehension
Ask:

1. *What was the Great Compromise?* **L1**

2. *For how many years does a member of the House of Representatives serve? A member of the Senate?* **L1**

3. *Which branch of government are the House of Representatives and the Senate part of?* **L1**

4. *What is this branch's major responsibility?* **L2**

5. *What branch of government does the President belong to?* **L1**

6. *How is a king different from a U.S. President?* **L3**

DID YOU KNOW?

Say: *The Great Compromise reflects a struggle between states with large numbers of enslaved people and states with small numbers of enslaved people.*

Page Power

Interact more with the page. Have students:

- do research to find out who their Senators and Representatives are and write their names in the margins on page 208. Have them write the current President's name in the margin on the opposite page.

- <u>underline</u> details in the text that describe the powers of each branch of government.

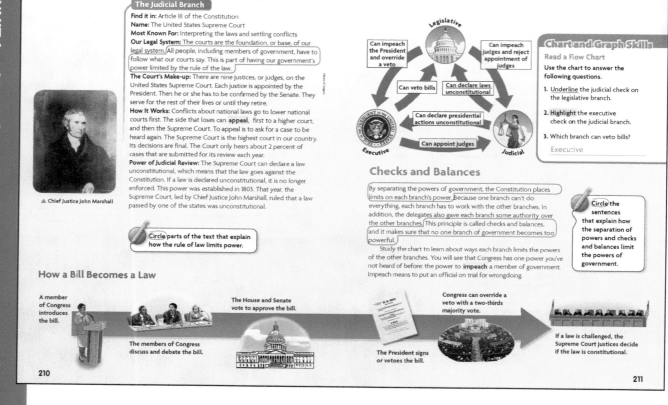

The Judicial Branch

Find it in: Article III of the Constitution
Name: The United States Supreme Court
Most Known For: Interpreting the laws and settling conflicts
Our Legal System: The courts are the foundation, or base, of our legal system. All people, including members of government, have to follow what our courts say. This is part of having our government's power limited by the rule of the law.
The Court's Make-up: There are nine justices, or judges, on the United States Supreme Court. Each justice is appointed by the President. Then he or she has to be confirmed by the Senate. They serve for the rest of their lives or until they retire.
How It Works: Conflicts about national laws go to lower national courts first. The side that loses can **appeal**, first to a higher court, and then the Supreme Court. To appeal is to ask for a case to be heard again. The Supreme Court is the highest court in our country. Its decisions are final. The Court only hears about 2 percent of cases that are submitted for its review each year.
Power of Judicial Review: The Supreme Court can declare a law unconstitutional, which means that the law goes against the Constitution. If a law is declared unconstitutional, it is no longer enforced. This power was established in 1803. That year, the Supreme Court, led by Chief Justice John Marshall, ruled that a law passed by one of the states was unconstitutional.

▲ Chief Justice John Marshall

Circle parts of the text that explain how the rule of law limits power.

Can impeach the President and override a veto
Can veto bills
Can declare laws unconstitutional
Can impeach judges and reject appointment of judges
Can declare presidential actions unconstitutional
Can appoint judges

Legislative
Executive
Judicial

Chart and Graph Skills

Read a Flow Chart

Use the chart to answer the following questions.

1. Underline the judicial check on the legislative branch.

2. Highlight the executive check on the judicial branch.

3. Which branch can veto bills?
   Executive

Checks and Balances

By separating the powers of government, the Constitution places limits on each branch's power. Because one branch can't do everything, each branch has to work with the other branches. In addition, the delegates also gave each branch some authority over the other branches. This principle is called checks and balances, and it makes sure that no one branch of government becomes too powerful.

Study the chart to learn about ways each branch limits the powers of the other branches. You will see that Congress has one power you've not heard of before: the power to **impeach** a member of government. Impeach means to put an official on trial for wrongdoing.

Circle the sentences that explain how the separation of powers and checks and balances limit the powers of government.

How a Bill Becomes a Law

A member of Congress introduces the bill.

The members of Congress discuss and debate the bill.

The House and Senate vote to approve the bill.

The President signs or vetoes the bill.

Congress can override a veto with a two-thirds majority vote.

If a law is challenged, the Supreme Court justices decide if the law is constitutional.

210

211

Lesson 2

Active Teaching

Develop Comprehension

Ask:

1. *Who chooses Supreme Court Justices?* **L1**

2. *What do you think it means to "confirm" a justice?* **L3**

3. *How do cases get to the Supreme Court?* **L2**

Say:

4. *Finish this sentence: By separating the powers of (government) the delegates placed (limits) on each branch's power.* **L2**

5. *Study the chart on page 211. Who can give me an example of one way the legislative branch checks and balances the executive branch? A way the executive branch checks and balances the judicial branch?* **L3**

Repeat number five until you've covered all the ways the branches check and balance each other.

Differentiated Instruction

▶ **ELL** Lesson 2 contains many words that English learners may find difficult, especially if there is no easy translation for the word in their first language. Have students select up to eight words with which they are having difficulty and create an additional vocabulary Foldable—using the instructions found at the beginning of each unit—from a sheet of 8.5" x 11" paper. Have students attach their Foldable to their work text for safe-keeping.

Page Power

Interact more with the page. Have students:

- label the branches of government that are involved in how a bill becomes a law on the flow chart at the bottom of the page.

- write an additional comprehension question in the margin and underline the answer in the text.

Chart and Graph Skills

Read a Flow Chart

Ask:

1. *Looking at the chart, how do you know which power belongs to which branch?* **L2**

2. *Why did the Constitution set up a system of checks and balances?* **L2**

Federalism

You know that problems with the Articles of Confederation proved that the young nation needed a stronger national government. But the delegates still worried that they were making the national government too powerful. They needed a way to balance power between the national government and the states.

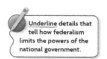
Underline details that tell how federalism limits the powers of the national government.

Federal and State Powers

The delegates designed a system called **federalism**. Under federalism, power is shared between a national government and states. There are certain things that only the national government can do. Other things only the states can do. By creating this system, the delegates hoped that state governments could keep the national government from becoming too powerful.

The national, or federal, government has certain powers and responsibilities. Federal powers mostly relate to the needs of the whole nation, such as declaring war or coining money. "Coining" money is another way of saying "minting" or "printing" money. Other powers are reserved for the states, such as creating public schools or making traffic laws. Some powers are shared between the federal and state governments.

> Explain what federalism is.
>
> Federalism is when power is shared between a national government and states.

▲ A state capitol building

▼ The United States Capitol

212

The chart below gives examples of how power is divided between the federal and state governments. On the blank lines, fill in two more examples for each set of powers. Try to do this without looking back at page 212.

Division of Powers Under Federalism

Federal Powers
- Make treaties with other countries
- Control trade between the states
- Declare war
- Run the postal service
- Coin money
- Settle disputes between the states

A U.S. postal worker ▶

State Powers
- Set up local governments
- Build roads
- Public schools
- Run elections
- Traffic laws
- Make laws that control trade within the state

▲ A public school

Shared Powers
- Set up courts
- Enforce laws
- Collect taxes
- Borrow money
- Maintain parks
- Protect the environment

Why do you think some powers are shared?

_____

_____

Police officers ▶

213

Active Teaching

Develop Comprehension

After students have read page 212, **Ask:**

1. *What state do we live in?*

2. *What powers does a state government have?*

3. *What states are north of us?*

4. *What powers do they have?*

Explain that each of the 50 states all have the same powers within their own borders. Illinois can't control state powers in Georgia, and vice versa. Lead students in a discussion of why the 50 smaller state governments together are able to balance the power of the larger federal government.

More About State Governments Article IV of the U.S. Constitution guarantees to the states a "Republican Form of Government." This means a government in which the citizens choose leaders to make laws and decisions for them. The U.S. Constitution also requires each state to have its own constitution and requires each state to respect the laws and citizens of the other states.

Differentiated Instruction

▶ **Approaching** Allow students to look back at page 212 as they complete the activity on page 213. Have them re-read the page and underline text clues that will help them identify the missing federal and state powers.

▶ **Beyond** Have students analyze the relationship between the division of federal and state powers and the weaknesses of the Articles of Confederation described in Lesson 1. Have them develop a chart, illustration, or short essay that explains this relationship.

▶ **ELL** Read page 212 sentence by sentence with students, helping them understand difficult words. Allow students to draw illustrations for their answers to the activity on page 213.

Amending the Constitution

The delegates to the Constitutional Convention knew their new plan wasn't perfect. They knew the country would grow and that its needs would change over time. So in Article V of the Constitution they laid out the **amendment** process. An amendment is a change or an addition to the Constitution.

There are two parts to the amendment process: proposal and ratification. During the proposal process, supporters of an amendment submit it to the government for review. If the amendment has enough support, it moves on to the ratification, or approval, process. Under the Constitution, there are two ways of proposing an amendment and two ways of ratifying it. Read the flow chart below to learn how it works.

FUN FACTS
There have been 27 constitutional amendments. You will learn more about some of these in Lesson 4.

Amending the Constitution

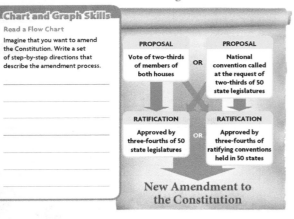

Chart and Graph Skills

Read a Flow Chart

Imagine that you want to amend the Constitution. Write a set of step-by-step directions that describe the amendment process.

_____

_____

_____

_____

_____

_____

PROPOSAL
Vote of two-thirds of members of both houses

OR

PROPOSAL
National convention called at the request of two-thirds of 50 state legislatures

RATIFICATION
Approved by three-fourths of 50 state legislatures

OR

RATIFICATION
Approved by three-fourths of ratifying conventions held in 50 states

New Amendment to the Constitution

214

Review the Constitution

Use information you learned in Lesson 2 to review what you know about the Constitution.

Explain how each concept listed places limits on the powers of the federal government.

Popular Sovereignty: _____

Rule of Law: _____

Separation of Powers: _____

Checks and Balances: _____

Federalism: _____

Lesson 2

? **Essential Question** What are the functions of government?

_____

_____

_____

_____

_____

_____

Go back to *Show As You Go!* on page 190–191. ◄◄◄

networks There's More Online! • Games • Assessment

215

Lesson 2

Active Teaching

Once students have completed page 214, have them begin the activities on page 215. These activities are designed to encourage students to thoroughly review and engage with all of the concepts presented in Lesson 2. Allow them to flip back and forth in their work text as they complete the activities.

Show As You Go! Remind students to go back to the Unit Opener and complete the activities for this lesson.

DID YOU KNOW?

Say: *The 27th Amendment is the most recent amendment. It was ratified in 1992. It makes congressional pay raises take effect in the term after they are passed. This amendment was originally one of the twelve amendments James Madison proposed in 1789. Ten of those twelve amendments became the Bill of Rights.*

Chart and Graph Skills

Read a Flow Chart Make sure that students read the chart starting at the top and then following the arrows.

Ask: *What are the two different ways that an amendment can be proposed?*

Response to Intervention

? **Essential Question**
What are the functions of government?

If . . . students cannot explain how popular sovereignty, rule of law, separation of powers, checks and balances, or federalism limit the powers of the federal government

. . . .

Then . . . first identify which concept students have the most trouble with. Refer students back to the page(s) that cover that topic. Have them read the page, highlighting context clues that will help them understand how the concept limits power. Then have them write a short response in which they describe the concept, its origins and how it limits power.

Following discussion, allow students to respond to the Essential Questions again.

Lesson
3   Convincing the People

Essential Question

How do people make decisions?

What do you think?

_____

_____

_____

_____

_____

_____

_____

Have you ever had an idea that you thought was great, but your friends disagreed? Did you try to win them over? Think of positive ways you can persuade someone to agree to something you want.

_____

_____

Once the Constitution was finished, the delegates had to convince the nation's people that it was a good plan. In Lesson 3, you will learn about what they had to do to get the Constitution ratified.

Delegates signed the Constitution on September 17, 1787. ▼

Words To Know

Look at the words below. Tell a partner what you think you already know about each word.

*debate
guarantee
submit

Signing the Constitution

The delegates to the Constitutional Convention worked for nearly four months. They had decided to keep their meetings a secret, so they kept the windows and doors to the Philadelphia's state house closed and locked. The summer sun made the building a hot and uncomfortable place to work. Delegates held passionate debates over many points in the Constitution. Some delegates even left in protest. By the time the Constitution was finished, everyone was ready to go home. The 39 remaining delegates finally signed the Constitution on September 17, 1787.

More Work to Do

This was not the end of the Constitution's story, however. The delegates needed the states to agree to it, so that the whole country could work together. They decided that in order to make the Constitution official, at least 9 of the 13 states had to ratify it. A long national **debate**, or careful discussion, was about to begin.

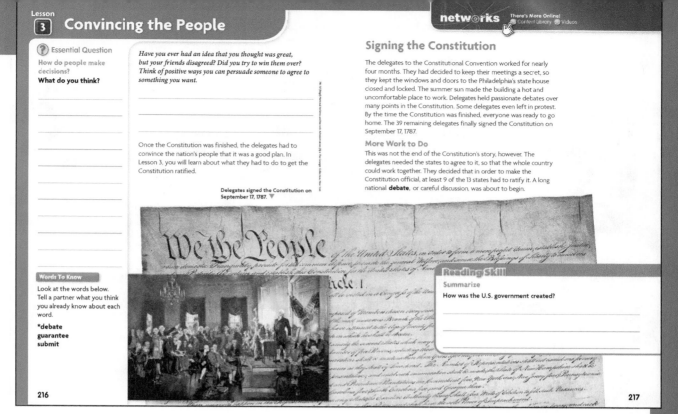

Reading Skill

Summarize

How was the U.S. government created?

_____

_____

216   217

Lesson 3

Activate Prior Knowledge

After students have completed the activity, lead them in a discussion about why being able to persuade people is an important skill to have.

Say: _The ability to respectfully listen to and consider others' opinions is another important skill to have. Together, all these skills ensure that everyone has enough information to make the best decision._

? Essential Question

How do people make decisions?

Have students explain what they understand about the Essential Question. Discuss their responses. Explain that everything they learn in this lesson will help them understand the Essential Question better. Remind them to think about how the Essential Question connects to the unit Big Idea: Rules provide order.

Active Teaching

Words To Know   After students have completed the Words to Know activity, have students write what they think the definition of each word is on another sheet of paper. Then, have students look up the definition in the glossary and write it beneath their definition. Have students attach their word list to their work text for safe keeping.

Develop Comprehension

Ask:

1. _When was the Constitution signed?_ (September 17, 1787) **L1**

2. _Why do you think the delegates wanted to keep their meetings a secret?_ **L3**

Reading Skill

Common Core Standards **RI.2** Determine two or more main ideas of a text and explain how they are supported by key details; summarize the text.

Summarize   Students will need to think back to what they've learned in Lessons 1 and 2 in order to write their summaries. Have students answer "Who," "What," "When," "Where," "Why," and "How" as they relate to the creation of the Constitution.

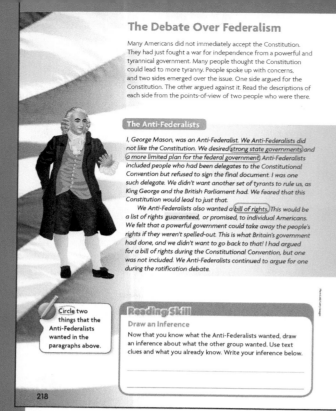

The Debate Over Federalism

Many Americans did not immediately accept the Constitution. They had just fought a war for independence from a powerful and tyrannical government. Many people thought the Constitution could lead to more tyranny. People spoke up with concerns, and two sides emerged over the issue. One side argued for the Constitution. The other argued against it. Read the descriptions of each side from the points-of-view of two people who were there.

The Anti-Federalists

I, George Mason, was an Anti-Federalist. We Anti-Federalists did not like the Constitution. We desired strong state governments and a more limited plan for the federal government. Anti-Federalists included people who had been delegates to the Constitutional Convention but refused to sign the final document. I was one such delegate. We didn't want another set of tyrants to rule us, as King George and the British Parliament had. We feared that this Constitution would lead to just that.

We Anti-Federalists also wanted a bill of rights. This would be a list of rights guaranteed, or promised, to individual Americans. We felt that a powerful government could take away the people's rights if they weren't spelled-out. This is what Britain's government had done, and we didn't want to go back to that! I had argued for a bill of rights during the Constitutional Convention, but one was not included. We Anti-Federalists continued to argue for one during the ratification debate.

> Circle two things that the Anti-Federalists wanted in the paragraphs above.

Reading Skill

Draw an Inference

Now that you know what the Anti-Federalists wanted, draw an inference about what the other group wanted. Use text clues and what you already know. Write your inference below.

_____

_____

218

The Federalists

My name is James Madison, and I was a Federalist. Federalists supported the new Constitution. We felt that making the national government less powerful would lead to problems in the future. And we felt that federalism protected against government tyranny because it reserved powers for the states and divided powers among three government branches. In short, we felt we had spread government powers out among enough people. We were confident that no one could ever become too powerful.

We Federalists also didn't feel the Constitution needed a bill of rights. Many state constitutions already had statements protecting rights. We also thought that listing some rights and not others could allow the government to take away rights that weren't listed. What a mistake that would be!

Federalists worked to preserve the Constitution. Alexander Hamilton, John Jay, and I published several essays. These essays are now called the Federalist Papers. They explained why we felt federalism was a good solution to our nation's problems. Federalism was a new idea, and the Federalist Papers helped many Americans understand how it would work, and why.

Reading Skill

Compare and Contrast

Fill in the Venn diagram below to compare the Anti-Federalist and Federalist views of government.

GLUE FOLDABLE HERE

Anti-Federalists — **Both** — **Federalists**

Did not like Constitution

Strong state governments

Bill of rights

Both: Wanted to protect the people from government tyranny

Supported Constitution

Strong national government

No bill of rights

219

Lesson 3

Active Teaching

> The content that is **boldface and italicized** on pages 218–219 is told in first person from the point of view of each historical figure. Students may need to be reminded of what it means to read a first-person point of view in order to understand these pages.

Page Power

FOLDABLES Interact more with the pages in this lesson. Have students create a Notebook Foldable.

1. Provide each student with a copy of Foldable 6A from the Notebook Foldables section at the back of this book.

2. Have students cut out the Foldable and glue the anchor tab just to the left of the Venn diagram on page 219.

3. On the top flap, have students write one sentence comparing the points of view.

4. On the bottom flap, have students write one sentence contrasting the points of view.

5. On the reverse of the bottom flap, have students choose a side and write one sentence defending their choice.

Differentiated Instruction

▶ **Approaching** Have students work in small groups to fill in their Venn Diagrams. Have students read each paragraph and then stop to fill in the corresponding parts of the diagram.

▶ **Beyond** Have students role play a debate between Mason and Madison. Students should prepare a list of talking points for whichever character they will be representing.

▶ **ELL** Assist students with finding the meaning of these words or phrases: *tyrannical, tyranny, emerged, anti-, spelled out. Tyrannical* and *tyranny* both have the same root and are related to *tyrant*—which students learned in Unit 4. *Emerged* is similar to "formed" or "came about." *Anti-* means "not" or "in opposition to." *Spelled out* is a colloquialism that means "listed."

Reading Skill

Common Core Standards RI.1 Quote accurately from a text when explaining what the text says explicitly and when drawing inferences from the text.

Remind students that when they draw an inference, they combine new information with what they already know.

Ratifying the Constitution

The Federalists' arguments won over many people. Between September 1787 and May 1788, eight states ratified the Constitution. In June 1788, New Hampshire became the ninth state to ratify it. The Constitution officially became the law of the United States.

Anti-Federalists Hold Out

Underline the major obstacle to getting Virginia and New York to ratify the Constitution.

Some people worried that 9 of 13 states wouldn't be enough, though. Of the states that remained, two were the largest in the nation—New York and Virginia. These states had strong groups of Anti-Federalists who fought against ratification. These groups demanded that the Constitution clearly spell out the individual rights of the people. A nation that had won independence from a king would never approve a plan that did not guarantee their liberties, said the Anti-Federalists. Federalists, such as Virginia's James Madison and New York's Alexander Hamilton, feared that the Constitution would fail without the support of these states.

FUN FACTS
Vermont was the first state added to the country under the new plan of government. It became the fourteenth state to ratify the Constitution on January 10, 1791.

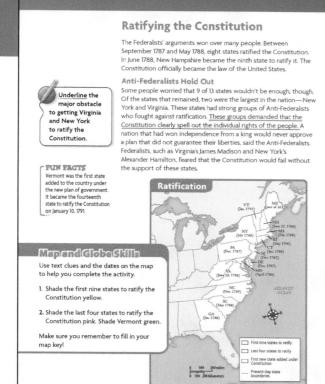

Ratification

Map and Globe Skills

Use text clues and the dates on the map to help you complete the activity.

1. Shade the first nine states to ratify the Constitution yellow.

2. Shade the last four states to ratify the Constitution pink. Shade Vermont green.

Make sure you remember to fill in your map key!

Map key:
- First nine states to ratify
- Last four states to ratify
- First new state added under Constitution
- Present-day state boundaries

◄ New York City celebrated the ratification of the Constitution with a parade.

What did Madison agree to do in order to get Virginia and New York to ratify the Constitution?

Adding the Bill of Rights

To win ratification by Virginia and New York, James Madison agreed to **submit**, or offer for approval, a bill of rights to Congress in the form of Constitutional amendments. He promised the Anti-Federalists that he would work to get the bill approved if they voted to ratify the Constitution.

Each side kept its end of the bargain. Virginia and New York both ratified the Constitution in 1788. James Madison submitted a list of amendments to the House of Representatives in June 1789. The final two states to ratify the Constitution were North Carolina and Rhode Island.

Lesson 3

? **Essential Question** How do people make decisions?

Go back to **Show As You Go!** on pages 190–191. ◄◄◄

 networks There's More Online!
• Games • Assessment

Active Teaching

Have students read and complete pages 220–221 before completing the map activity.

Use the leveled reader, *The Life of Alexander Hamilton*, to extend and enrich students' understanding of Hamilton's contributions to the development of the government of the United States. A lesson plan for this leveled reader can be found on pages T30–T31 at the front of this Teacher Edition.

Show As You Go! Remind students to go back to the Unit Opener and complete the activities for this lesson.

networks

Go to connected.mcgraw-hill.com for additional resources.

- Interactive Whiteboard Lessons
- Worksheets
- Assessment
- Lesson Plans

Map and Globe Skills

Use the historical map students completed to help them understand why New York and Virginia were so important to ratification.

Say: *Imagine that the yellow parts of the map were one country and the pink parts of the map were different countries.*

Ask: *Do you think it is helpful for all parts of a country to be connected? Why or why not?*

Response to Intervention

? **Essential Question**
How do people make decisions?

If . . . students cannot describe how concerns about individual rights led to the creation of the Bill of Rights

....

Then . . . have students complete a cause and effect graphic organizer. To start, have them turn back to page 218 and highlight sentences that include the words "bill of rights." Next, have students turn to page 220 and highlight sentences that include the words "individual rights." Have students use the highlighted text to come up with their cause. Finally, have students reread page 221 to find the effect and complete their graphic organizer.

Lesson 4 — Protecting and Expanding Rights

? Essential Question
How do we protect our rights?
What do you think?

_____

_____

_____

_____

When people have needs or wants, they sometimes make a list. Your parents might make a list of groceries they need. You might make a list of presents you want for your birthday. Lists don't always have to be about things, though. They can be about ideas or tasks. Make a list of three ways you want to be treated by your friends, and give your list a title.

List title: _____

1. _____

_____

2. _____

_____

3. _____

_____

The Bill of Rights

As part of his agreement with the Anti-Federalists, James Madison submitted a list of amendments to Congress. Of those, Congress agreed on 12 and sent them to the states for approval. The amendments were debated in each state, and eventually 10 were ratified. From beginning to end, the process took about a year and a half. The amendments were finally added to the Constitution in December 1791. These first 10 amendments are called the Bill of Rights.

The Bill of Rights wasn't the first document to define the rights of citizens. For example, the British government had a bill of rights, as did many of the state governments. In writing the amendments to submit to Congress, James Madison looked to the Virginia Declaration of Rights. This document had existed since 1776. And it had been written by George Mason—James Madison's Anti-Federalist rival!

The Bill of Rights is part of the Constitution, but it is also talked about as a separate document. The rights that it defines are central to our lives as Americans. When people speak of protecting our liberties or freedoms, often they are talking about freedoms granted by the Bill of Rights.

Underline words that tell you the origins of the Bill of Rights. Circle words that tell you about governments that had similar documents.

Freedom of speech is protected by the Bill of Rights. ▼

222

223

Lesson 4 ———

Activate Prior Knowledge
After students have completed the activity, explain that the Bill of Rights has become an important part of protecting our freedoms.

Say: *You learned why the Bill of Rights came to be in Lesson 3. In Lesson 4, you'll learn how it was written and how it continues to protect our rights today.*

? Essential Question
How do we protect our rights?

Have students explain what they understand about the Essential Question. Discuss their responses. Explain that everything they learn in this lesson will help them understand the Essential Question better. Remind them to think about how the Essential Question connects to the unit Big Idea: Rules provide order.

Clarify Misconceptions
Because the Bill of Rights is often talked about as a singular entity, students may come to assume that it is a cohesive document, like the Constitution or Declaration of Independence. In reality, the Bill of Rights is the name given to the set of 10 amendments approved and added to the Constitution in 1791. Each amendment is separate and self-contained.

Active Teaching ———

Words To Know Once students have completed the Words to Know activity, have them use a dictionary to find the definition and the part of speech to which each vocabulary word belongs. Next, have students come up with a synonym or antonym for each word.

Develop Comprehension
Ask:

1. *Of the 12 amendments originally proposed, how many were ratified?* **L1**

2. *Why did James Madison submit a list of amendments to Congress?* **L2**

3. *Why do you think only 10 amendments were ratified?* **L3**

Protecting Individual Rights

The Bill of Rights begins by protecting **fundamental**, or basic, rights of all U.S. citizens. The First Amendment guarantees five freedoms: freedom of religion, freedom of speech, freedom of the **press**, freedom of assembly, and freedom to petition. *Press* refers to members of the news media, such as reporters and columnists. Many Americans find this to be the most important amendment.

The Second Amendment lists another basic freedom: the right "to keep and bear arms." The Supreme Court has interpreted this to mean two things. First, states have the right to maintain their own militias. And second, governments can pass laws to control, but not prevent, individuals from owning firearms. The Third Amendment prevents the government from forcing people to house soldiers.

> Use text clues to help you fill in the chart below. Draw pictures or symbols in the third column.

Fundamental Rights Under the First Amendment

Freedom of . . .	What it Means	Picture or Symbol
religion	People are free to choose their own system of beliefs or none at all.	
speech	People can say what their political ideas are without fear of punishment by the government.	
press	Newspapers and other members of the media are free to publish news and opinions, even if they are critical of the government.	
assembly	People are free to hold meetings and gather peacefully in groups.	
press	People are free to write to the government about its policies and ask for help without fear of punishment.	

224

Right to Due Process

Just as important as basic freedoms is the right to "**due process** of the law." Due process of the law means the government must follow the rules established by law. The Fourth through Eighth Amendments protect the right to due process.

Due Process Amendments

Fourth Amendment The government cannot search through or take away any property without a specific reason that is approved by a court.

Fifth Amendment The government needs to prove it has a good reason to put someone on trial. A person cannot be tried twice for the same crime, or be forced to be a witness against him- or herself. Property cannot be taken away unless the government pays for it.

Sixth Amendment People have a right to a speedy and public trial by a **jury**. A jury is a group of citizens who decide a court case. Accused people have the right to be **defended** by a lawyer.

Seventh Amendment In lawsuits, people have the right to a trial by a jury.

Eighth Amendment People are protected from high bail and fines. People are protected from cruel and unusual punishment.

> Tell in your own words how the Bill of Rights limits the power of the federal government.

Limiting the Government

The Bill of Rights puts firm limits on the federal government in the Ninth and Tenth Amendments. The Ninth Amendment says that the rights of the people are not limited to what is listed in the Constitution. The Tenth Amendment says that powers not given to the federal government belong to the states or to the people.

If an accused person can't afford a lawyer, then the government has to provide him or her with one. This is guaranteed by the Sixth Amendment. ▶

225

Active Teaching

Have students read page 224 and complete the chart activity before moving on to page 225.

Develop Comprehension
Ask:
1. *What are the five basic freedoms protected by the First Amendment?* **L1**
2. *Choose an amendment and explain how it is important to your life.* **L3**

networks

Go to connected.mcgraw-hill.com for additional resources.

- Interactive Whiteboard Lessons
- Worksheets
- Assessment
- Lesson Plans

✓ Formative Assessment

Have students summarize what they know about the Bill of Rights by writing three facts they have learned. Summaries may include details about fundamental rights, due process, or how the Bill of Rights limits the powers of the federal government. Use this assessment to monitor student understanding and identify need for intervention.

Differentiated Instruction

▶ **Approaching** Have students make a list and number it 1 through 10. As a group or individually, read about each amendment and answer questions that the students may have. Then, have students identify two or three key words for each amendment. Have them affix their list to their work text for safe keeping.

▶ **Beyond** Have students read an article about a current event. To ensure relevance, you may need to preselect an assortment of articles from which students may choose. As students read, they should think about the freedoms protected by the Bill of Rights and identify to which amendment the story most relates. Have students write a short response to the current event, explaining how it relates to the Bill of Rights.

▶ **ELL** For each amendment, have students box any words that they do not recognize. Explain the meaning of these unfamiliar words.

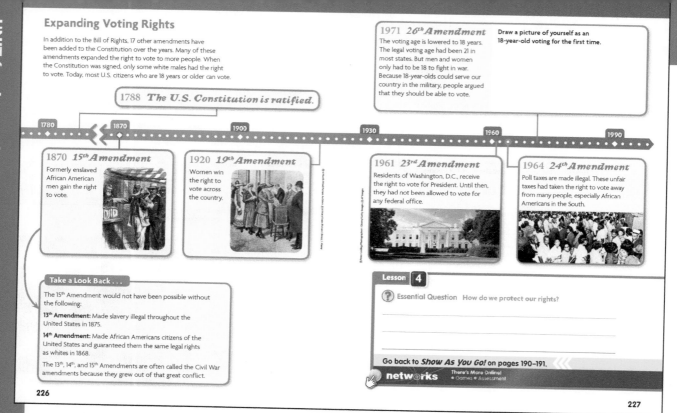

Expanding Voting Rights

In addition to the Bill of Rights, 17 other amendments have been added to the Constitution over the years. Many of these amendments expanded the right to vote to more people. When the Constitution was signed, only some white males had the right to vote. Today, most U.S. citizens who are 18 years or older can vote.

1788 *The U.S. Constitution is ratified.*

1971 26th Amendment
The voting age is lowered to 18 years. The legal voting age had been 21 in most states. But men and women only had to be 18 to fight in war. Because 18-year-olds could serve our country in the military, people argued that they should be able to vote.

Draw a picture of yourself as an 18-year-old voting for the first time.

1870 15th Amendment
Formerly enslaved African American men gain the right to vote.

1920 19th Amendment
Women win the right to vote across the country.

1961 23rd Amendment
Residents of Washington, D.C., receive the right to vote for President. Until then, they had not been allowed to vote for any federal office.

1964 24th Amendment
Poll taxes are made illegal. These unfair taxes had taken the right to vote away from many people, especially African Americans in the South.

Take a Look Back . . .

The 15th Amendment would not have been possible without the following:

13th Amendment: Made slavery illegal throughout the United States in 1875.

14th Amendment: Made African Americans citizens of the United States and guaranteed them the same legal rights as whites in 1868.

The 13th, 14th, and 15th Amendments are often called the Civil War amendments because they grew out of that great conflict.

Lesson 4

? **Essential Question** How do we protect our rights?

Go back to **Show As You Go!** on pages 190–191.

networks There's More Online!
• Games • Assessment

226

227

Lesson 4

Active Teaching

Have students read the introductory paragraph first. Make sure they understand that these amendments are separate from the Bill of Rights. Next have students read the time line entries from left to right across pages 226–227. Discuss each amendment, its date, the associated image, and to whom each amendment extended voting rights. Once students have a sufficient grasp of the evolution of voting rights in our country, have them complete the fill-in activity on page 226.

Develop Comprehension

Say: *The Bill of Rights protects the basic freedoms of all Americans.*

Ask: *Why do you think these amendments were necessary to protect and expand the right to vote?* **L3**

> **Show As You Go!** Remind students to go back to the Unit Opener and complete the activities for this lesson.

Response to Intervention

? **Essential Question**
How do we protect our rights?

If . . . students have difficulty analyzing how voting rights have expanded under the Constitution,

. . . .

Then . . . have students recall what they've learned about who could vote in our nation's early history. Then, have them review pages 226–227 and form a conclusion about who can vote today. Ask students to describe how voting rights have changed over time through amendments to the Constitution.

Following discussion, allow students to respond to the Essential Questions again.

Lesson
5 Active Citizenship

Essential Question

How do citizens participate?
What do you think?

Words To Know

Think of a synonym for each word. A synonym is another word that means the same thing.

responsibility

politics

*inform

Think back to the Constitutional Convention. The delegates had kept their meetings secretive, and no one outside knew what was going on. The citizens of Philadelphia were curious about what was being planned. Benjamin Franklin was a delegate at the convention. As he left the state house on the final day, a woman called out to him. Read their conversation below.

> Well Doctor, what have we got: a republic or a monarchy?

> A republic, if you can keep it.

Republic is the word for the type of government that we have under the Constitution. It is a government in which the people choose representatives to govern for them. What do you think Franklin meant when he said "if you can keep it"?

Civic Responsibilities

All citizens of the United States have civic **responsibilities.** A responsibility is something that people must do because it is their job or duty. These responsibilities are things good citizens do to help keep their city, state, and national governments working effectively.

For example, respecting and obeying the law is one important civic responsibility. By obeying the law, citizens help each other stay safe and healthy. Paying taxes is another civic responsibility. Taxes pay for services and projects that benefit all Americans. Without money from taxes, we wouldn't be able to keep our roads, public buildings, or schools maintained.

Jury Duty

One particular duty of citizens is to serve on juries. You read in Lesson 4 that the Bill of Rights guarantees all citizens the right to a trial by a jury. Juries sit in on a court case, listen to the facts, and then make a decision about whether the accused person is guilty or innocent. Without participation by citizens, it would be impossible for us to have this right, or any other rights at all.

▲ One responsibility of citizenship is to serve on juries.

> Evaluate the importance of civic responsibilities to our democracy. Tell why it is important for citizens to participate.

228

229

Lesson 5

Activate Prior Knowledge

Engage students in a discussion about active citizenship to introduce this lesson.

Ask: *Who has chores to do at home? What do you do? Explain that these chores or jobs are the student's responsibilities.*

Say: *In addition to responsibilities at home, each of you also has responsibilities as a citizen of this nation.*

Then, read aloud the following list of actions:

- Playing in a park
- Voting
- Paying taxes
- Following the law

For each action, ask students to respond with right, responsibility, neither, or both. Student responses will help identify their level of understanding.

Essential Question **How do citizens participate?**

Have students explain what they understand about the Essential Question. Discuss their responses. Explain that everything they learn in this lesson will help them understand the Essential Question better. Remind them to think about how the Essential Question connects to the unit Big Idea: Rules provide order.

Active Teaching

Words To Know Once students have completed the Words to Know activity, have them write one sentence for each word, using it in proper context.

Develop Comprehension
Ask:

1. *What is a civic responsibility? Give an example.* **L1**
2. *How are rights and civic responsibilities related?* **L3**
3. *Why would it be impossible for us to have the right to a jury trial without citizen participation?* **L3**

networks

Go to **connected.mcgraw-hill.com** for additional resources.

- Interactive Whiteboard Lessons
- Worksheets
- Assessment
- Lesson Plans

Political Participation

You've already learned that voting is a right. Did you know it is a civic responsibility too? Good citizens participate in politics. Politics is the process of choosing government leaders and running the government. To participate in politics effectively, good citizens stay informed about public issues and candidates. Then, through voting, they tell the government who they want to represent them and what actions the government should take. Voting is one way that responsible citizens make their voices heard.

Responsible citizens make their voices heard in other ways too. They write letters or e-mails to their government leaders and representatives. This helps government leaders determine the will of the people. Responsible citizens might also sign a petition about an issue that they agree with. Sometimes, responsible citizens participate in marches or protests in support of or against a political idea.

As you read pages 230 and 231, circle ways citizens can participate in the political process. Highlight ways citizens can go beyond their basic responsibilities.

▼ Good citizens exercise their voting rights.

▲ Citizens can sign petitions about issues they agree with.

Going Above and Beyond

Citizens can go above and beyond their basic civic responsibilities. One way to do this is to become a volunteer. As a volunteer, you might work with others on a civic issue, such as a neighborhood watch or a litter clean-up event. Political campaigns are always looking for volunteers as well. They need workers to help convince voters to choose their candidate.

Another way to go above and beyond is to initiate, or begin, changes in laws or public policy. The simplest way to do this is to write to a lawmaker about a problem that exists in your community and propose a solution. In some cities and towns, citizens can initiate a change themselves through a petition. If citizens gather enough signatures from voters, their issue is put up for a vote. If the issue passes, then it becomes law.

Finally, some citizens go above and beyond by becoming public officials. Any citizen who meets some very basic requirements can run for office. Requirements usually include age and residency, which is the place where a person lives. Becoming a government leader is an excellent way to serve your community.

▲ Jerrod W. Holton served his community as a member of the city council. He was only 23 years old when elected!

▲ Citizens of all ages can volunteer to help their community.

Think of a new law for your community. Describe your law and one way you could initiate this change in policy.

_____
_____
_____
_____
_____

230

231

Lesson 5

Active Teaching

Develop Comprehension
Ask:

1. *What are some ways responsible citizens make their voices heard?* **L1**

2. *How can average citizens affect laws and public policy?* **L2**

3. *What qualities do you think would make someone a good public leader? Why?* **L3**

✔ Formative Assessment

After students have read these pages, have them summarize what they know about political participation by writing three facts that they learned. Summary should include some of the following: good citizens stay informed and vote, citizens can write about issues to government officials, people can run for public office, etc. Use this assessment to monitor student understanding and identify the need for intervention.

Differentiated Instruction

▶ **Approaching** Present students with a series of cards that contain these words or images to represent the words: *politics, voting, communicate, petition, march, protest, volunteer, public leader.* First, have students identify what the words have in common. Next, have students select words that relate to basic civic responsibilities. Finally, have students select words relating to civic participation that goes above and beyond. As students select words or images, have them explain their choices. Correct and explain misconceptions as you interact with students.

▶ **Beyond** Have students use the Internet or other resources to find out what kinds of civic participation are available for kids their age in your area. Students should create a poster or other visual aid to inform and stir up interest for the form of civic participation they chose.

▶ **ELL** Review the topics on pages 230–231 and help students define unfamiliar words. Provide or create visuals to represent any words that students still struggle with.

Participation: Then and Now

In the United States, political participation is important for keeping our democracy running. Our tradition of political participation goes all the way back to our country's colonial period. Since then, it has continued to develop into what it is today.

Underline different ways people participate in politics.

The Colonial Era

From the very beginning, white male settlers were able to vote for their leaders in colonial governments. They also participated by speaking up at local meetings. They let their leaders know their wants and needs by writing letters. Letter writing was the main form of communication back then.

As frustrated colonists grew tired of British policies, more people became involved in politics. Colonists held protests, such as the Boston Tea Party. And before declaring their independence, colonists sent a petition to the British government, asking for help one last time.

▲ Only white males had a voice in colonial governments.

Participation by Non-voters

In the colonial era, African Americans—both enslaved and free—and women weren't allowed to vote. A few still found ways to participate in politics. For example, one group of enslaved Africans sent petitions to colonial leaders in Massachusetts. These petitions tried to bring attention to the living conditions of enslaved people. Political participation by groups who couldn't vote was very rare. For many years, women and non-white individuals who tried to participate were usually ignored, discouraged, or even arrested.

Women fought for the right to vote for many years. ▶

232

Participation Today

Citizens today participate in their government in many of the same ways the colonists did. We still vote, protest, and petition. We still write letters and have discussions about issues at local meetings. We also use some new ways, too.

One major difference in participation is in the ways people stay informed. Radio, television, and the Internet all make it easier for citizens to learn about issues. And through e-mail, it's easier than ever to contact representatives. Most government leaders have Web pages, where you can read their opinions on the issues of the day.

You might say that the most important difference of all is in who can participate. Male and female citizens of all races can all participate in our democratic process by voting and speaking out on important issues.

▲ Don't forget to vote!

What is different between political participation in the colonial period and participation today?

new forms of communication;

more people can participate

What is the same?

People still vote, protest,

petition, and write letters.

Lesson 5

? Essential Question How do citizens participate?

_____

_____

Go back to *Show As You Go!* on pages 190–191.

networks There's More Online!
• Games • Assessment

233

Active Teaching

Develop Comprehension

1. *Who could participate in the colonial period?* **L1**

2. *Explain how the ways people participate in politics today have changed from colonial times.* **L2**

3. *Why do you think women and minorities wanted to participate in the colonial period?* **L3**

> *Show As You Go!* Remind students to go back to complete the project on the Unit Opener.

Page Power

FOLDABLES Interact more with the pages in this lesson. Have students create a Notebook Foldable.

1. Provide each student with a copy of Foldable 6B from the Notebook Foldables section at the back of this book

2. Have students cut out the Foldable and glue the anchor tab on page 233.

3. On one flap, have students describe civic participation in the colonial era. On the other flap, have students describe political participation today.

4. Have students use their Foldable to help them understand the ways political participation has changed and how it has stayed the same.

Response to Intervention

? Essential Question
How do citizens participate?

If . . . students have difficulty evaluating the importance of civic responsibilities in American democracy,

· ·

Then . . . have students turn back to page 228. Write the Benjamin Franklin quote on the board and lead students in an analysis of the parts. For example, "If" points to the uncertainty of the idea; "you" points to each citizen's responsibility to participate; "can keep it" points to the idea that a republic is not a self-sustaining system. If the duties of citizens are ignored and neglected, freedom can easily be lost. Explain to students that in the past some republics have fallen apart and crumbled into tyranny. It is each citizen's duty to stay informed and participate in order to maintain freedom.

Following discussion, allow students to respond to the Essential Questions again.

UNIT 6 Wrap Up

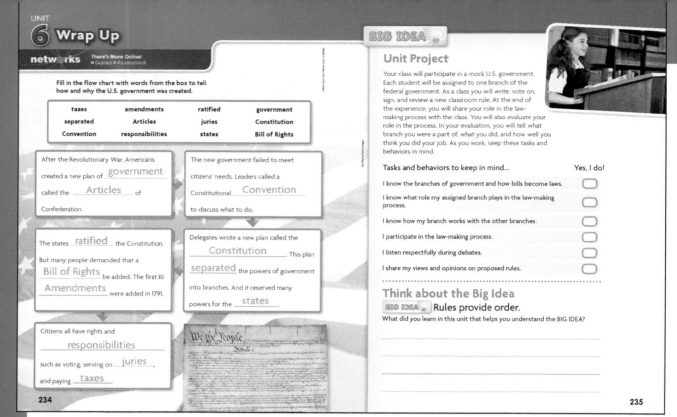

Fill in the flow chart with words from the box to tell how and why the U.S. government was created.

taxes	amendments	ratified	government
separated	Articles	juries	Constitution
Convention	responsibilities	states	Bill of Rights

After the Revolutionary War, Americans created a new plan of **government** called the **Articles** of Confederation.

The new government failed to meet citizens' needs. Leaders called a Constitutional **Convention** to discuss what to do.

The states **ratified** the Constitution. But many people demanded that a **Bill of Rights** be added. The first 10 **Amendments** were added in 1791.

Delegates wrote a new plan called the **Constitution**. This plan **separated** the powers of government into branches. And it reserved many powers for the **states**.

Citizens all have rights and **responsibilities**, such as voting, serving on **juries**, and paying **taxes**

234

BIG IDEA

Unit Project

Your class will participate in a mock U.S. government. Each student will be assigned to one branch of the federal government. As a class you will write, vote on, sign, and review a new classroom rule. At the end of the experience, you will share your role in the law-making process with the class. You will also evaluate your role in the process. In your evaluation, you will tell what branch you were a part of, what you did, and how well you think you did your job. As you work, keep these tasks and behaviors in mind.

Tasks and behaviors to keep in mind...	Yes, I do!
I know the branches of government and how bills become laws.	○
I know what role my assigned branch plays in the law-making process.	○
I know how my branch works with the other branches.	○
I participate in the law-making process.	○
I listen respectfully during debates.	○
I share my views and opinions on proposed rules.	○

Think about the Big Idea

BIG IDEA Rules provide order.

What did you learn in this unit that helps you understand the BIG IDEA?

235

Wrap Up

Flow Chart

Have students complete the activity on page 234 to summarize their understanding of how and why the U.S. government was created.

BIG IDEA Big Idea Project

Read through the project directions and checklist with students. Answer any questions they have and make sure they understand the requirements. Before you start the mock U.S. government activity, review how a bill becomes a law.

- Remind students to use their **Show as You Go!** pages to assist them in completing the project.
- To assess the project, refer to the rubric on the following page.

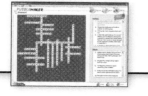

Differentiated Instruction

▶ **Approaching** Have students work on the project in groups or pairs instead of working alone. They may then verbally tell how well they think the class worked.

▶ **Beyond** Explain to students that in the Senate, bills sometimes have riders or earmarks—amendments added to the bill that can be completely unrelated to the original bill. Have students come up with riders to the class rule. Have students try to convince the class to add them to the rule.

▶ **ELL** Have students create a word web for each branch of the government and its role in creating a law. Have them highlight specific vocabulary by extending the web and including a definition or synonym for each word.

Response to Intervention

BIG IDEA Rules provide order.

If . . . students cannot give a substantiated explanation of how rules provide order in society

. . . .

Then . . . have students think of everyday examples of how rules provide order in their lives. Have them think about what would happen if there were no rules.

Name _____ Date _____

Mock Government Experience

4 Exemplary	3 Accomplished	2 Developing	1 Beginning
The student:	**The student:**	**The student:**	**The student:**
☐ knows all three branches of government and all of their associated powers.	☐ knows all three branches of government and most of their associated powers.	☐ knows two of the three branches of government and some of their associated powers.	☐ knows one or none of the branches of government and can only name one associated power.
☐ knows all the steps of how a bill becomes a law.	☐ knows most of the steps of how a bill becomes a law.	☐ knows some of the steps of how a bill becomes a law.	☐ knows one or two steps of how a bill becomes a law.
☐ knows how his or her branch is supposed to interact with the other branches.	☐ mostly knows how his or her branch is supposed to interact with the other branches.	☐ somewhat knows how his or her branch is supposed to interact with the other branches.	☐ has an inaccurate understanding of how his or her branch is supposed to interact with the other branches.
☐ fully participates in the law-making process by listening respectfully to others and offering his or her opinions on the topic at hand.	☐ participates in the law-making process by listening respectfully to others and offering his or her opinions, though he or she sometimes strays off topic.	☐ participates in the law-making process by listening respectfully to others, and offering his or her opinions, though he or she frequently strays off topic.	☐ partially participates in the law-making process by listening to others, or offering his or her opinions; he or she frequently strays off topic.
☐ returns an evaluation that is thoughtful, detailed, and accurate.	☐ returns an evaluation that is mostly thoughtful, detailed, and accurate.	☐ returns an evaluation that is somewhat thoughtful, contains two or three details, and some inaccuracies.	☐ returns an evaluation that is not thoughtful, contains fewer than two details, and many inaccuracies.

Grading Comments: _____

_____

_____

_____

_____

_____

Project Score: _____

Read the passage "How Should the President Be Elected?" before answering Numbers 1 through 6.

How Should the President Be Elected?

by Jennifer Beyer

The United States uses a system called the Electoral College to choose its Presidents. Each state gets one electoral vote for each of its members of Congress. This means that states with more people get more votes.

When voters cast their ballots on Election Day, what they're really doing is choosing for whom all the electors from their state should vote. A presidential candidate who wins a state is supposed to receive all of that state's electoral votes. Because some states get more electoral votes than others, a candidate can sometimes win the Electoral College but lose the popular vote!

Some voters don't think this is fair. When this happened in the year 2000, it started a debate about the Electoral College. Fifth-grade students from across the country were interviewed about this subject. Here's what some of them had to say.

Trevor from Oklahoma
"I think the popular vote should be counted instead of the electoral vote. . . . The Electoral College was developed in the 1700s when the citizens of America were less educated. . . . Americans today have information available . . . from newspapers, magazines, the Internet, TV, and radio. People can make educated decisions about their vote, and we should let them elect their own President."

Matthew from Iowa
"We should keep the Electoral College, but we should change it to make it fairer. We should let the states divide up their electoral vote. For example, if one-fourth of a state's voters pick Candidate A, . . . then Candidate A should get one-fourth of the state's votes. . . . The way it is now, some voters might feel that their vote doesn't count."

Ebony from Florida
"The Electoral College is an easy, simple, organized way to elect the President. The electors . . . are supposed to vote in the Electoral College for the candidate that the majority of people in their state voted for. . . . This system makes sure that the majority of states get the President they want."

236

---

1 What happened in the year 2000?
Ⓐ The Electoral College chose the wrong candidate.
Ⓑ The vote was unfair.
Ⓒ The winning candidate won the Electoral College but lost the popular vote.
Ⓓ The losing candidate won the Electoral College but lost the popular vote.

2 Which person thinks the Electoral College should NOT be changed?
Ⓕ Ebony
Ⓖ Matthew
Ⓗ Trevor
Ⓘ the author

3 Read the sentences from the passage.

> The Electoral College was developed in the 1700s when the citizens of America were less educated. . . . Americans today have information available . . . from newspapers, magazines, the Internet, TV, and radio.

Which statement tells Trevor's feelings about modern Americans?
Ⓐ Americans today are more informed than Americans in the 1700s.
Ⓑ Americans today are less informed than Americans in the 1700s.
Ⓒ Americans today are uninformed.
Ⓓ Americans today have too much information.

4 What is the author's MAIN purpose for writing the passage?
Ⓕ to tell her opinion about the Electoral College
Ⓖ to tell who won the 2000 presidential election
Ⓗ to describe different opinions about the Electoral College
Ⓘ to describe how voting rights have changed over time

5 How does the student from Iowa think the Electoral College should change?
Ⓐ Each vote should count more than it does now.
Ⓑ Each elector should be able to choose whom he or she wants.
Ⓒ Each candidate should get one-fourth of the votes.
Ⓓ Each state should divide up its electoral votes.

6 Read the sentence from the passage.

> The electors . . . are supposed to vote in the Electoral College for the candidate that the majority of people in their state voted for.

What does the word *majority* mean in this passage?
Ⓕ an unknown number
Ⓖ the largest number
Ⓗ the least number
Ⓘ an equal number

237

Test Preparation

Test-Taking Tips

Share these test-taking tips with your students:

- Read each question carefully. If you do not know the answer to a question, skip it and come back to it later. Do not leave any answers blank.

- Answer the question being asked. Read over the question and your answer. Does your response answer what is being asked?

- Check your answers. Reread each question and make sure your answer makes sense. Erase incorrect answers completely.

- Check your answer sheet. For multiple-choice questions, fill in each answer bubble completely. Make sure there are no extra marks on the answer sheet.

Answers

1. C **CCS RI.7**

2. F **CCS RI.3**

3. A **CCS RI.2**

4. H **CCS RI.2**

5. D **CCS RI.7**

6. G **CCS RI.4**

Teacher Notes

UNIT
7 Planner WESTWARD EXPANSION

 **Relationships affect choices.**

Student Portfolio

- ***Show As You Go!***
  Use these pages to introduce the Big Idea. Students record information specific to each lesson. They use these pages to help them plan their Big Idea Project.

netw⚙rks™

- **Group Technology Project**
  Students use 21st century skills to complete a group extension activity of the unit project. Lesson plans, worksheets, and rubrics are available online.

Student Portfolio

- **Big Idea Project**
  Students work with a team to create a board game about westward expansion. The Big Idea Project Rubric is on page 281W.

Reading Skills

Student Portfolio

- **Reading Skill: Integrate Information**
  Pages 240–241. Common Core State Standards RI.6, RI.7, and RI.9

Leveled Readers

Use the leveled reader *Riding the Rails to a New Life* with Lesson 3. Find the lesson plan on pages T30–T31 of your Teacher Edition.

Treasures Connection

Teach this unit with Treasures Unit 3, *When Esther Morris Headed West*, pages 294–307 and Unit 5, *A Historic Journey*, pages 570–573.

Social Studies Skills

Student Portfolio

- **Primary and Secondary Sources: Newspapers**
  Page 245

netw⚙rks™

- **Skill Builders**
  Introduce and teach analyzing primary and secondary sources.

Activity Cards

- **Center for Social Studies Skills Investigation**
  Use the center activity cards to help students explore Primary Sources, Geography, and Citizenship.

FOLDABLES®

Student Portfolio

- Students can create vocabulary Foldables right in their portfolios.

- Additional Foldables templates can be found on pages R34–R42 of your Teacher Edition. See page R33 for instructions.

Assessment Solutions

- **McGraw-Hill networks™**
  Safe online testing features multiple question types that are easy to use and editable.

- **Self-Check Quizzes**

- **Worksheets**

UNIT 7 **At a Glance**

Lesson	Essential Question	Vocabulary
1 Early Expansion	**Why do people take risks?**	pioneer expedition *interpreter
2 The War of 1812	**What do people fight for?**	neutral impressment War Hawks *response
3 The Industrial Revolution	**How do ideas influence choices?**	cotton gin interchangeable parts *application reaper stagecoach steam engine *previous immigrant
4 Internal Struggles	**How do ideas influence choices?**	slave state *balance free state Union
5 The Overland Trails	**Why do people move?**	wagon train manifest destiny overland wagon *conditions forty-niners

*denotes academic vocabulary

Digital Resources

Go to
connected.mcgraw-hill.com
for additional resources:

- Interactive Whiteboard Lessons

- Worksheets

- Assessment

- Content Library

- Lesson Plans

- Skill Builders

- Videos

- Use Standards Tracker on **networks** to track students' progress.

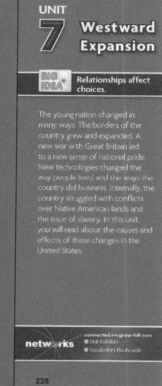

UNIT 7 Westward Expansion

BIG IDEA Relationships affect choices.

The young nation changed in many ways. The borders of the country grew and expanded. A new war with Great Britain led to a new sense of national pride. New technologies changed the way people lived and the ways the country did business. Internally, the country struggled with conflicts over Native American lands and the issue of slavery. In this unit, you will read about the causes and effects of these changes in the United States.

networks connected.mcgraw-hill.com
● Skill Builders
● Vocabulary Flashcards

238

Add the following to the map:

After Lesson 1:
○ Louisiana Purchase
○ Routes of Lewis and Clark

After Lesson 2:
○ Land gained through the Adams-Onis Treaty

After Lesson 3:
○ Erie Canal
○ Major Railways

After Lesson 4:
○ Missouri Compromise Line
○ Trail of Tears

After Lesson 5:
○ Overland Trails
○ Land gained through the Treaty of Guadalupe Hidalgo
○ Gadsden Purchase
○ Complete the Map Key
○ Give the map a title

Show As You Go! After you read the following lessons, complete the map of the United States. Use the checklist on page 238 for suggestions of what to add to your map and map key.

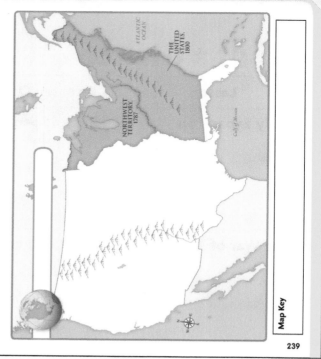

Map Key

239

Introduce the Unit

✓ Diagnostic Assessment

Ask: *What is the farthest away from home you have traveled?*

Call on students to answer. As they give their answers, have them think about the following questions:

- Why did you travel?
- How did you travel? By car? By airplane?
- How was the area different from where you live now?

Say: *Imagine you had to travel all that way by foot or in a slow wagon. How different would the trip have been? What challenges might you have faced? How long would the trip have taken?*

Student responses will help identify their level of understanding early modes of travel in the United States.

Active Teaching

BIG IDEA Relationships affect choices.
Students will use use information from each lesson of this unit to complete the activity on the **Show As You Go** pages.

Explain that at the end of the unit, students will use this map to help complete the Unit Project. Have students fold back the corner of page 239 to make returning to these pages easier.

Differentiated Instruction

▶ **Approaching** Provide students with a list of each territory, as well as when they were acquired. As students read, they can use this list to help them locate details in the text to complete the map.

▶ **Beyond** As students complete each lesson, have them add state boundaries and major cities to the map.

▶ **ELL** Review the following map terms: *key*, *legend*, and *direction*. Discuss these words as homonyms. Provide a graphic organizer, such as the one shown below, to help students define the versions of each homonym.

word		word
definition		definition

Reading Skill

Common Core Standards
RI.6: Analyze multiple accounts of the same event or topic, noting important similarities and differences in the point of view they represent. RI.7: Draw on information from multiple print or digital sources, demonstrating the ability to locate an answer to a question quickly or to solve a problem efficiently. RI.9: Integrate information from two texts on the same topic in order to write or speak about the subject knowledgeably.

Integrate Information

When you integrate information, you combine details from multiple sources. To integrate information effectively, it is a good idea to generate a list of questions that you want to answer about the topic. Then chart information from each source that fits those questions.

If the sources agree on an idea, the information is most likely correct. If the sources disagree, you probably need to check the information in more sources.

Information that connects in each source

Underline details in each source that show how the opening of the Erie Canal affected the United States.

LEARN IT

To integrate information from multiple sources:

- Make a list of questions and chart answers you find in each source.
- Look for connections between the pieces of information.
- Draw a conclusion based on the information in all of the sources.

Source 1

'Tis, that Genius has triumph'd and science prevail's . . .

It is, that the [people] of Europe may see

The progress of mind, in a land that is free

All hail! to a project so vast and [wonderful]!

A bond that can never be [broken] by time

Now unites us still closer, all jealousies [stop]

And our hearts, like our waters, are singled in peace

Source 2

When the Erie Canal opened in 1825, it was an instant success. The man-made waterway linked the West to the Atlantic Ocean. Ports along the Great Lakes and canal grew into large cities. With the ability to ship farm products around the world, farming in the West became profitable. Suddenly, settlers flooded the region. Business boomed thanks to shipping and trade. New York City became the country's largest city in the mid-1800s.

TRY IT

Graphic organizers like the one below help you integrate information. Fill in the chart with the information from both texts on page 240.

Source 1	Source 2
↓	↓

Conclusion

APPLY IT

My Question: How did the opening of the Erie Canal affect the United States?

- Review the steps for integrating information in Learn It.
- Find another source about the opening of the Erie Canal on the Internet.
- Find details in this source that answer the question in Try IT.
- Integrate the information in all three sources to draw a conclusion.

Conclusion:

_____

_____

_____

_____

_____

240

241

Common Core Standards **RI.6** Analyze multiple accounts of the same event or topic, noting important similarities and differences in the point of view they represent. **RI.7** Draw on information from multiple print or digital sources, demonstrating the ability to locate an answer. **RI.9** Integrate information from two texts on the same topic in order to write or speak about the subject knowledgeably.

Reading Skill

Active Teaching

LEARN IT Integrate Information

Say: *When I integrate information from multiple sources, I begin by focusing on the main idea and key details. It's important to look for differences in details between the sources. If there aren't any, then the information is likely correct. If there are differences, I consider if I can trust the sources. I do this by looking for opinions in the details because I know these aren't facts. If I find that too many opinions are involved, I have to find more sources so I can make sure my facts are correct. If I don't need to research more, I analyze the information and draw a conclusion.*

TRY IT Encourage students to try the modeled strategy as they complete the TRY IT activity.

APPLY IT After students have completed the APPLY IT activity, **Ask:**

1. *Were there any opinions in these sources? Explain.* **L2**

2. *What conclusion can you draw about the importance of the Erie Canal?* **L3**

3. *Why is it important to not base your conclusions*

Differentiated Instruction

▶ **Approaching** Review the **LEARN IT** activity as a small group. Do the **TRY IT** activity together. Have students complete the **APPLY IT** activity independently. Regroup to compare and correct.

▶ **Beyond** Prompt students to come up with at least two separate conclusions in the **APPLY IT** activity.

▶ **ELL** Read and summarize the sources together. Lead the students through the **TRY IT** activity. Regroup to compare and discuss student conclusions.

networks

Go to **connected.mcgraw-hill.com** for additional resources:
- Skill Builders
- Graphic Organizers

Words to Know | FOLDABLES

Common Core Standards
RI.4: Determine the meaning of general academic and domain-specific words and phrases in a text relevant to a grade 5 topic or subject area.

The list below shows some important words you will learn in this unit. Their definitions can be found on the next page. Read the words.

pioneer (py • uh • NEER)

expedition (ehks • pih • DIHSH • uhn)

neutral (NOO • truhl)

cotton gin (‹AHT • uhn jihn)

steam engine (STEEM EHN • jihn)

free state (FREE STAYT)

manifest destiny
(MAN • uh • fehst • DEHS • tuh • nee)

overland wagon
(OH • vuhr • land WA • guhn)

The Foldable on the next page will help you learn these important words. Follow the steps below to make your Foldable.

Step 1 — Fold along the solid red line.

Step 2 — Cut along the dotted lines.

Step 3 — Read the words and their definitions.

Step 4 — Complete the activities on each tab.

Step 5 — Look at the back of your Foldable. Choose ONE of these activities for each word to help you remember its meaning:
- Draw a picture of the word.
- Write a description of the word.
- Write how the word is related to something you know.

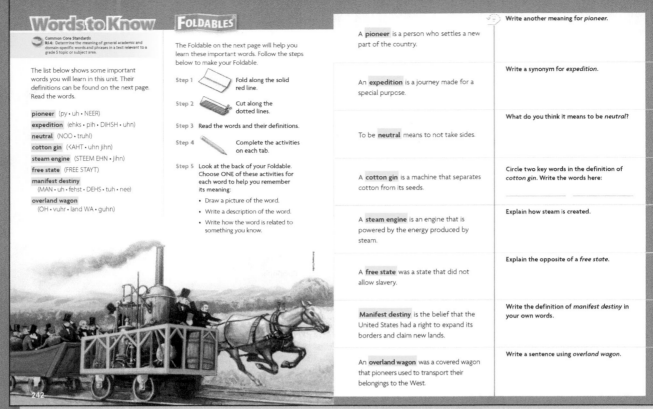

242

A **pioneer** is a person who settles a new part of the country.	Write another meaning for *pioneer*.
An **expedition** is a journey made for a special purpose.	Write a synonym for *expedition*.
To be **neutral** means to not take sides.	What do you think it means to be *neutral*?
A **cotton gin** is a machine that separates cotton from its seeds.	Circle two key words in the definition of *cotton gin*. Write the words here: _____ _____
A **steam engine** is an engine that is powered by the energy produced by steam.	Explain how steam is created.
A **free state** was a state that did not allow slavery.	Explain the opposite of a *free state*.
Manifest destiny is the belief that the United States had a right to expand its borders and claim new lands.	Write the definition of *manifest destiny* in your own words.
An **overland wagon** was a covered wagon that pioneers used to transport their belongings to the West.	Write a sentence using *overland wagon*.

Common Core Standards RI.4 Determine the meaning of general academic and domain-specific words and phrases in a text relevant to a grade 5 topic or subject area.

Words to Know
Active Teaching

FOLDABLES Guide students through the making of their Foldable. Remind students that they are **not** to rip out their Foldable. This will stay in their book as a study guide. Go to connected.mcgraw-hill.com for flashcards to introduce the unit vocabulary.

1. Read the words on the list and have students repeat them after you.

2. Define each word and use it in a sentence for students.

3. Guide students as they complete steps 1 through 5 of the Foldable.

4. Have students use the Foldable to practice the vocabulary words independently or with a partner.

networks
Go to connected.mcgraw-hill.com for additional resources.
- Vocabulary Flashcards
- Vocabulary Games
- Graphic Organizers

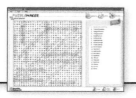

GO Vocabulary!
Use a graphic organizer like the one below to help students make connections to the vocabulary words in this unit.

Say:
Think of other words that will help you remember the meaning of each word. Using this graphic organizer will help you understand each vocabulary word by making connections to what you already know.

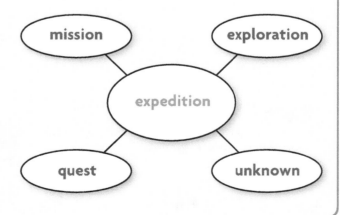

pioneer	pioneer
expedition	expedition
neutral	neutral
cotton gin	cotton gin
steam engine	steam engine
free state	free state
manifest destiny	manifest destiny
overland wagon	overland wagon

Primary Sources

Newspapers

Newspapers are usually printed daily or weekly. They report on current events, or things that have recently happened, on the local, state, national, or world level. To read a newspaper correctly, you need to understand the parts of newspaper articles. These parts are:

- the headline or title
- the dateline (when and where the story took place)
- the by-line, or author's name
- the article or story.

Each newspaper story answers six questions about the topic: Who was involved? What took place? When did the event happen? Where did it happen? Why did it happen? How did it happen?

DBQ Document-Based Questions

Study the newspaper article, then complete the activities.

1. Use different colors or symbols to highlight the answers to the following questions: Who? What? When? Where? Why? How?

2. What did you learn about what happened to Washington, D.C., during the War of 1812?

_____

_____

THE AMERICAN NEWSPAPER
Washington, D.C., August 25, 1814

Dolley Saves the Day!
by Jim Smith

Yesterday the British burned down the White House. They did this as payback for the United States burning down Canada's capital. During the chaos and confusion of the British invasion of Washington, D.C., one person certainly kept her cool. First lady Dolley Madison acted quickly to save what she could from the White House.

Mrs. Madison was able to save important documents, silverware, and other items. The most important thing she saved was a portrait of our first President—George Washington. The frame it was in was too large to carry. So Mrs. Madison used a knife to cut the painting from its frame! Now, the painting will hang in the White House for generations to come.

networks
There's More Online!
● Skill Builders
● Vocabulary Flashcards

245

Differentiated Instruction

▶ **ELL** Have students make a two-column chart. Review each vocabulary word with students. Have students write the word in the left column and write notes or draw pictures to help them remember the meaning of the word in the right column. Have students continue to add notes and pictures to their charts after each word is introduced in the unit.

WORD PLAY

Play Vocabulary Baseball!

1. Divide the class into two teams.

2. Push the desks to the sides of the room. Set up first, second, and third bases, as well as home plate.

3. Have student take turns "at bat." They must give the definition when given the word, state the word when given the definition, or supply the correct word for a close-type sentence.

4. Students may advance to each base if they answer correctly.

5. The first team to score 10 runs wins.

Primary Sources

Active Teaching

Explain that the United States and Great Britain were involved in the War of 1812. Explain that the British stormed Washington, D.C., and set fire to many buildings in the city. At that time, newspapers were one of the few ways for news to travel across the country. As a result, news of the capital's destruction traveled slowly across the country.

Ask: *How does information travel today? How does this compare to how it traveled in the past?*

Bring a current newspaper into class. Organize the students into groups. Have each group choose an article and discuss the six questions: Who? What? When? Where? Why? How?

networks

Go to **connected.mcgraw-hill.com** for additional resources.

- Skill Builders
- Resource Library

Lesson
1 Early Expansion

(?) Essential Question
Why do people take risks?
What do you think?

_____
_____
_____
_____
_____
_____

THINK • PAIR • SHARE *Imagine you are alone in the woods or wilderness where you've never been before. How would you find your way around? What would you do to survive?*

Expanding the Nation

You learned in Unit 6 that in 1787 Congress issued the Northwest Ordinance. It created the Northwest Territory north of the Ohio River and east of the Mississippi River. The ordinance stated that an area became a territory when its population reached 5,000. Territories could apply for statehood when the population reached 60,000. This led to the addition of Ohio, Indiana, Illinois, Michigan, and Wisconsin. The ordinance also pushed Native Americans off their lands, leading to many conflicts.

One important piece of the Northwest Ordinance was the bill of rights for settlers. It guaranteed freedom of religion, and the right to trial by jury. It also banned slavery. This was the first attempt to prevent slavery in the United States.

This law allowed the country to expand in a slow and specific way. Soon, **pioneers** began making the journey west in search of new lives. A pioneer is a person who settles a new part of a country.

Words To Know

Write a number on each line to show how much you know about each word.

1 = I have no idea!
2 = I know a little.
3 = I know a lot.

____ pioneer

____ expedition

____ *interpreter

▼ Early pioneers packed their belongings into Conestoga wagons like this one.

Let's Go West!

In 1790 only about 200,000 settlers lived west of the Appalachian Mountains. By 1820 that number had exploded to nearly 2 million Americans! One reason people were able to settle that land was because of the work of Daniel Boone.

I'm Daniel Boone. I'm from the Pennsylvania countryside. I've spent my whole life learning how to live off the land. So I know my way around the wilderness. The new territory was wild and confusing for some folks. I was hired to find a route from North Carolina to Kentucky. As I made my way west, I discovered a natural passage that led through the Appalachian Mountains. I called this passage the Cumberland Gap.

In 1775 Boone and 30 men began to fix up the trails between the Carolinas and the Northwest Territory. They cleared a road by cutting down trees and clearing brush. This road became the main way people traveled west.

Circle important contributions made by Daniel Boone during the period of westward expansion.

The Wilderness Road, 1770s

Map and Globe Skills

1. Using a dark color, trace the southern edge of the Northwest Territory on the map.

2. The Cumberland Gap passes through which mountain range?

   Appalachian
   Mountains

246

247

Lesson 1

Activate Prior Knowledge

After students have discussed the scenario of being alone in the woods, ask for volunteers to share what they wrote with the class.

Ask:

How do you think people were able to survive over 200 years ago?

(?) Essential Question Why do people take risks?

Have students explain what they understand about the Essential Question. Discuss their responses. Explain that everything they learn in this lesson will help them understand the Essential Question better. Remind them to think about how the Essential Question connects to the unit Big Idea: Relationships affect choices.

Map and Globe Skills

Have students study the map on page 247.
Ask:

Which present-day states were connected by the Wilderness Road?

Active Teaching

Words To Know Once students have *completed* the activity, have them find the words in the lesson and read their definitions. Then, present the students with a list of three to five words or phrases related to each vocabulary word. Have students identify the word or phrase that does not fit with the rest of the group and explain their choice.

Develop Comprehension

The content that is ***boldface and italicized*** throughout the lesson is told in first person from the point of view of historical figures. Students may need to be reminded of what it means to read a first-person point-of-view.

Ask:

1. *What was Boone hired to do in the new territory?* **L1**

2. *Why was the work of Boone and his friends necessary?* **L3**

Jefferson and Louisiana

While the size of the country was changing, so were the politics. In 1800 the United States elected a new President. He was a famous Patriot who changed the boundaries of the United States. This multi-talented writer, inventor, and statesman was Thomas Jefferson.

I was born in Virginia in 1743. I accomplished so much in my life, it's hard to know where to start. You may remember that I wrote the Declaration of Independence. I also wrote Virginia's state constitution and founded the University of Virginia!

In your opinion, which of Jefferson's accomplishments was most important? Why?

_____

_____

_____

▼ The Jefferson Memorial in Washington, D.C.

248

The Louisiana Purchase

Jefferson believed that expanding the United States was essential to its success. In the South, the French port city of New Orleans was an important center of trade along the Mississippi River. In 1803 American representatives in France offered to buy New Orleans for $10 million. To the surprise of the Americans, the French offered to sell the entire Louisiana Territory for $15 million. The purchase nearly doubled the size of the United States.

I was shocked that we got such a tremendous bargain. I mean, look at these numbers—we received almost 525 million acres of land for about 4 cents an acre! But we had a problem: few Americans knew anything about this huge territory. We needed to find out as much about this land as we could. And I knew just the man for the job.

DID YOU KNOW?
The French sold Louisiana to pay for an ongoing war with Great Britain. Napoleon Bonaparte, France's leader, planned to take Louisiana back after they defeated Great Britain. However, France lost the war with Great Britain.

▼ The city of New Orleans before the sale of Louisiana

UNDER MY WINGS EVERY THING PROSPERS

249

Active Teaching

Remind students about the activity on top of page 247. Tell them that as they go through the entire lesson, they should be circling important people and their contributions.

Develop Comprehension
Ask:

1. *How did Jefferson contribute to the westward expansion of the nation?* **L3**

2. *What was so important about the geographic location of New Orleans?* (Since it was at the mouth of the Mississippi River, whoever controlled that land controlled trade in the area.) **L3**

More About Relations with Native Americans The area west of the Appalachians had been home to Native Americans for centuries. In the 1790s, Native American groups joined together to drive white settlers off their lands. President Washington sent the army to Ohio three times to protect settlers. In 1795 Native American leaders in the area signed the Treaty of Greenville to end the fighting. Not all tribes signed the treaty. They did not want to lose their land. Trouble between settlers and Native Americans continued well into the next century.

Reading Skill

Common Core Standards RI.3 Explain the relationships or interactions between two or more individuals, events, ideas, or concepts in a historical, scientific, or technical text based on specific information in the text.

Cause and Effect After students underline the causes of the Louisiana Purchase, have them discuss what they think the effects could be. The text already states that the size of the country doubled.
Ask:

How do you think it would affect the United States today if the amount of land suddenly doubled?

networks

Go to **connected.mcgraw-hill.com** for additional resources.

- Interactive Whiteboard Lessons
- Worksheets
- Assessment

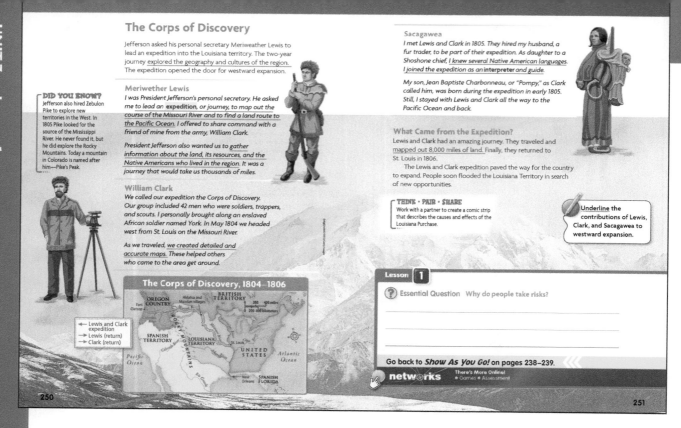

The Corps of Discovery

Jefferson asked his personal secretary Meriweather Lewis to lead an expedition into the Louisiana territory. The two-year journey explored the geography and cultures of the region. The expedition opened the door for westward expansion.

DID YOU KNOW?
Jefferson also hired Zebulon Pike to explore new territories in the West. In 1805 Pike looked for the source of the Mississippi River. He never found it, but he did explore the Rocky Mountains. Today a mountain in Colorado is named after him—Pike's Peak.

Meriwether Lewis
I was President Jefferson's personal secretary. He asked me to lead an **expedition**, or journey, to map out the course of the Missouri River and to find a land route to the Pacific Ocean. I offered to share command with a friend of mine from the army, William Clark.

President Jefferson also wanted us to gather information about the land, its resources, and the Native Americans who lived in the region. It was a journey that would take us thousands of miles.

William Clark
We called our expedition the Corps of Discovery. Our group included 42 men who were soldiers, trappers, and scouts. I personally brought along an enslaved African soldier named York. In May 1804 we headed west from St. Louis on the Missouri River.

As we traveled, we created detailed and accurate maps. These helped others who came to the area get around.

Sacagawea
I met Lewis and Clark in 1805. They hired my husband, a fur trader, to be part of their expedition. As daughter to a Shoshone chief, I knew several Native American languages. I joined the expedition as an **interpreter** and guide.

My son, Jean Baptiste Charbonneau, or "Pompy," as Clark called him, was born during the expedition in early 1805. Still, I stayed with Lewis and Clark all the way to the Pacific Ocean and back.

What Came from the Expedition?
Lewis and Clark had an amazing journey. They traveled and mapped out 8,000 miles of land. Finally, they returned to St. Louis in 1806.

The Lewis and Clark expedition paved the way for the country to expand. People soon flooded the Louisiana Territory in search of new opportunities.

THINK • PAIR • SHARE
Work with a partner to create a comic strip that describes the causes and effects of the Louisiana Purchase.

Underline the contributions of Lewis, Clark, and Sacagawea to westward expansion.

The Corps of Discovery, 1804–1806
- ← Lewis and Clark expedition
- → Lewis (return)
- → Clark (return)

Lesson 1

(?) **Essential Question** Why do people take risks?

Go back to **Show As You Go!** on pages 238–239.

networks There's More Online!
• Games • Assessment

250

251

Lesson 1

Active Teaching

Explain that the group traveled together on the way west. After reaching the Pacific, Lewis and Clark split up so they could explore more territory. Have students locate this place on the map.

Develop Comprehension
Ask:

1. Who was York? **L1**

2. What were Jefferson's goals for the expedition? **L2**

3. Why would traveling with a Native American interpreter have been helpful to the expedition? **L3**

4. Why would the group travel together when heading west and then split up on the way back? **L3**

> **Show As You Go!** Remind students to go back to the Unit Opener and complete the activities for this lesson.

Differentiated Instruction

▶ **Approaching** As a group, list the significant individuals who impacted westward expansion. Have students find the answers to these questions for each person: What did he or she do? When did he or she do it? Why was what he or she did important? How did it affect westward expansion?

▶ **Beyond** Have students research other people who influenced westward expansion in the library or on the Internet. Allow time for students to present this information to the class.

▶ **ELL** Have students identify unfamiliar or difficult words and research the definitions, writing their notes in the margins.

Response to Intervention

(?) **Essential Question** Why do people take risks?

If . . . students cannot identify why people take risks,
. . . .

Then . . . take students back to pages 249–251. Discuss what was gained from the Louisiana Purchase and the journey of Lewis and Clark.
Ask: How do you know if something is worth the risk? Following discussion, allow students to respond to the Essential Question again.

Lesson 2
The War of 1812

(?) **Essential Question**
What do people fight for?
What do you think?

_____

_____

_____

_____

Have you experienced friends or family members having a disagreement? Did you try to stay out of it? Or did you get involved? What happened?

_____

_____

_____

On the Brink of War

While Jefferson expanded the country, he also dealt with the war between France and Great Britain. The United States tried to stay **neutral**, or not take sides in the war. Americans continued to trade with both countries. This angered both the British and the French. Warships from both countries stopped American merchant ships at sea and took their goods. The British also forced American sailors to serve on British ships. This practice, called **impressment**, enraged Americans.

To protect American ships and lives, an angry Congress passed the Embargo Act in 1807. The act closed all American ports. It also prevented trade in American waters. Though it was meant to hurt Great Britain and France, the law actually weakened the American economy. As the United States continued to remain neutral, its relationship with France and England worsened.

Many Americans were forced to serve in the British Navy

Words To Know

Write the definition of each word in your own words.

neutral _____

_____

impressment _____

_____

*response _____

_____

GLUE FOLDABLE HERE

252

June 1812   **Networks News**   Special Edition

WAR DECLARED!

A Call to Arms

Conflict seemed to be on the horizon. In 1810 a new group was elected to Congress. They were called "**War Hawks**" because they wanted to go to war with Great Britain.

Many War Hawks were settlers from areas west of the Appalachian Mountains. Native Americans in that area wanted settlers to stop taking their lands. A Shawnee chief named Tecumseh tried to unite all western tribes to fight against these settlers. The British provided support and supplies to Tecumseh and other Native Americans in the area. This angered War Hawks.

As Speaker of the House, Henry Clay led War Hawks in Congress.

Underline events that led to the War of 1812.

"Mr. Madison's War"

In June 1812 Congress declared war on Great Britain. President James Madison signed the declaration.

Not all Americans supported the war. New England merchants depended on trade with Great Britain. The Embargo Act had damaged their businesses, and they feared the war would cause more problems with trade. Many Americans wanted to settle their problems with Great Britain peacefully. Many New Englanders called the war "Mr. Madison's War." Today, this war is known as the War of 1812, although it lasted several years.

How did the economy contribute to the start of the War of 1812?

Americans tried to continue trading with both France and England. When trade stopped, the economy failed.

253

Lesson 2

Activate Prior Knowledge

After students have completed the activity, ask students if the disagreement ever came back up, or if the same people disagreed about something else at a later time. Remind them that the United States and Great Britain had just finished fighting a war in 1781.

Say:

Much like a disagreement among families or friends, countries can sometimes come into conflict again after reaching a peace agreement.

Explain that in this lesson, students will see how the United States and Great Britain struggled to keep the peace.

(?) **Essential Question What do people fight for?**

Have students explain what they understand about the Essential Question. Discuss their responses. Explain that everything they learn in this lesson will help them understand the Essential Question better. Remind them to think about how the Essential Question connects to the unit Big Idea: Relationships affect choices.

Active Teaching

| Words To Know | After students have completed |

the Words to Know activity, have them locate each word in the text and read its definition. Then, have students divide up into groups and use each word in a sentence.

Develop Comprehension
Ask:

1. *What was the Embargo Act of 1807?* **L1**
2. *Why were the War Hawks so eager to go to war?* **L2**

Page Power

FOLDABLES Interact more with the page. Have students create a Notebook Foldable to keep track of major events during the War of 1812, including causes and effect of the war.

1. Provide students with Foldable 7A from the Notebook Foldables section at the back of this book.

2. Have students construct the Foldable and glue its anchor tab where indicated on page 252.

3. Have students complete a time line of events leading to, during, and at the end of the War of 1812.

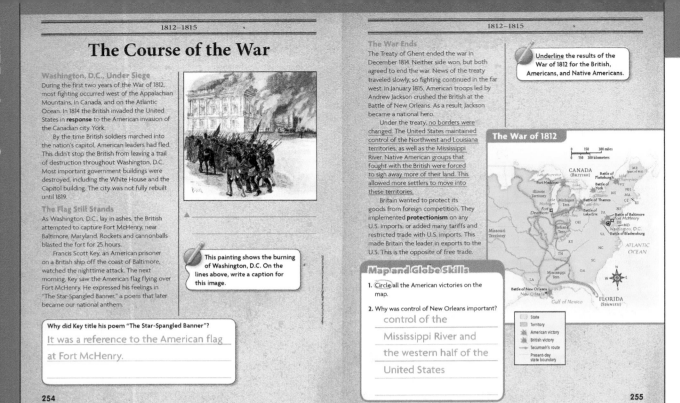

Lesson 2

Active Teaching

Have students imagine what it would have been like to be one of the people who lived close enough to hear the bombing of Fort McHenry all night long. What assumptions would have been made about the fate of the fort and the soldiers protecting it?

Develop Comprehension

Ask:

1. What did the British soldiers do to Washington, D.C., in 1814? **L1**

2. What emotions do you suppose people felt when day broke and they saw the American flag still standing at Fort McHenry? Explain how this led to the creation of the national anthem. **L1**

3. Why did the Battle of New Orleans occur after the war? **L2**

4. Why was maintaining control of the Mississippi River important? **L3**

Use the Leveled Reader, *Florida Becomes a State*, to enrich student understanding of the results of the War of 1812. A lesson plan for the leveled reader can be found on pages T32–T33 at the front of this Teacher Edition.

Differentiated Instruction

▶ **Approaching** Have students work with a partner to create a sequencing chart that covers key events in the War of 1812. Their charts should include the events leading up to and including the attack on Fort McHenry.

▶ **Beyond** Have students write a list of Frequently Asked Questions (FAQs) about the War of 1812 and how it led to the creation of the national anthem. Challenge them to find out why Francis Scott Key was on board a British ship at the time (*negotiating the release of a prisoner*) and how many different stanzas the song actually has (*four*).

▶ **ELL** Pair students with a native English speaker and have partners express the meaning of the first stanza of "The Star-Spangled Banner" in their own words.

Map and Globe Skills

Ask:

1. Which battles took place in Canada? **L1**

2. Why would the British want to capture New Orleans? **L3**

1812–1819

Write your own headline for pages 256–257.

"The War Ends" or similar

National Pride

The War of 1812 had many effects on the young nation. Before the war, much of the world had considered the United States a trouble-making British colony. The war showed that the United States was a nation willing and able to defend itself.

For the first time since the Revolutionary War, Americans felt a strong sense of national pride. Those who had been against the war lost power in government. The lack of major political divisions created a feeling of unity among Americans. This period became known as the "Era of Good Feelings."

The Adams-Onis Treaty

Along with a sense of pride came a desire to expand the country's borders. In 1818 Andrew Jackson was sent to Georgia to stop a conflict with Native Americans. Instead, Jackson invaded Florida, a Spanish colony. Jackson took over Spanish settlements and removed the Spanish governor from power.

Spain didn't want to start a war with the United States. In 1819 the two countries signed the Adams-Onis Treaty. In the agreement, Spain sold Florida to the United States. In return, the United States gave up its claim to Texas west of the Sabine River.

Reading Skill

Cause and Effect

Use the chart to identify the causes and effects of the War of 1812.

Causes	Effects
• Impressment • Embargo Act, 1807 • Tecumseh • War Hawks	• National Pride • Gained Florida • U.S. gave up Texas

256

1823

▶ President Monroe and his cabinet members discuss the Monroe Doctrine.

Underline the ways the War of 1812 changed how the United States dealt with foreign countries.

Dealing with Foreign Countries

The War of 1812 made people in the United States feel like they were as powerful as Great Britain, Spain, and France. This feeling was challenged by issues in Latin America. Many of the former European colonies there had recently declared independence. In response, some European countries formed an alliance and planned to regain control of the area.

President James Monroe did not want European powers so close to the United States.

In 1823 he issued the Monroe Doctrine. It stated that the United States would not allow European powers to start new colonies in the Americas. In return, the United States would not involve itself in existing European colonies or issues in Europe.

The doctrine's authors saw it as a way for the United States to oppose colonial powers. Americans would later use it to expand the borders of the United States even further.

Lesson 2

(?) **Essential Question** What do people fight for?

_____

_____

Go back to *Show As You Go!* on pages 238–239. ◀◀◀

netw⊙rks There's More Online!
• Assessment • Games

257

Active Teaching

Have students use information from pages 252–257 in order to fill out the chart on page 256. Allow them to flip back and forth in their work text as they complete the activities.

Develop Comprehension
Ask:

1. *What was the name given to the time period after the war?* **L1**

2. *How did the United States gain Florida?* **L1**

3. *How was the Monroe Doctrine a long-term effect of the War of 1812?* **L2**

◀◀◀ Remind students to go back to the Unit Opener and complete the activities for this lesson.

netw⊙rks

Go to connected.mcgraw-hill.com for additional resources.

- Interactive Whiteboard Lessons
- Video
- Assessment
- Lesson Plans

Reading Skill

Common Core Standards RI.3 Explain the relationships or interactions between two or more individuals, events, ideas, or concepts in a historical, scientific, or technical text based on specific information in the text.

Cause and Effect To help students identify the cause and effect relationships of the war, begin with the effects, and ask them to find the causes. Explain to students that in text, effects are often called out directly, making them easier to find in the text. Identifying the cause of each effect is simply a matter of working backward.

Response to Intervention

(?) **Essential Question** What do people fight for?

If . . . students cannot explain what people fight for,

. . . .

Then . . . refer students back to pages 252–253 to review the causes of the War of 1812. Tell students that "what people fight for" doesn't have to only be a reference to war. Have students work in small groups to discuss what is important to them and what they would be willing to do to protect those things.

Following discussion, allow students to respond to the Essential Question again.

Lesson 3 — The Industrial Revolution

? Essential Question

How do ideas influence choices?

What do you think?

_____
_____
_____
_____
_____

Words To Know

Add a suffix to the end of each word to make it plural.

cotton gin _____

*application _____

reaper _____

interchangeable part _____

stagecoach _____

Think about the different kinds of technology you use everyday. Which item is most important to you? What would life be like if you didn't have that item anymore?

_____
_____

A World of New Technology

Until the early 1800s, most families made the items they needed, such as tools and clothes, by hand. Then came a period of rapid invention, when machines began to do the work people once did. This period of invention is called the Industrial Revolution. During this time, new machines and new ideas changed the way people worked, traveled, and lived.

The Industrial Revolution greatly affected the market economy of the United States. In Unit 4, you learned that in a market economy, people decided what goods to make and how much to sell their goods for. Because of the advancements made during the Industrial Revolution, businesses were able to make more goods and sell them at reduced cost. This also meant that more people could afford to buy goods than ever before.

Eli Whitney: Inventions and Innovations

In 1793 Eli Whitney built a **cotton gin** to remove seeds from cotton. The gin, which is short for "engine," could clean more cotton in a few minutes than a whole team of workers could clean by hand in a day. The cotton gin made cotton the most important cash crop in the South.

A cotton gin ▶

In 1801 Whitney had another important idea that would change the way goods were made—**interchangeable parts**. These are pieces made to fit any specific tool or machine. A barrel for one rifle would fit another rifle of the same type, for example. Whitney's idea had many **applications**, and allowed guns, tools, and other products to be made faster and at a lower cost.

Textile Mills

New inventions, such as the double-sided needle, sewing machines, and spinning machines, made it faster and easier to make cloth and clothing. People no longer had to do the whole process by hand. Soon, large factories called textile mills began producing more cloth than ever before. Mills were built near swift rivers. The rushing water turned a large wheel in the factory, which powered the machines. Most mills were built in the North, since that was where the country's known fast-moving rivers were located at that time.

Francis Cabot Lowell was one person who prospered from these inventions. In 1813 he built a textile mill in Waltham, Massachusetts. Lowell's business partners later built several textile mills as well as a town, called Lowell, for the workers. By 1850, Lowell had more than 10,000 workers. Many were young women who left home to work in the town of Lowell.

Workers weaving cloth in a Lowell textile mill ▼

Explain how the Industrial Revolution affected the market economy of the United States.

American _____
businesses grew. _____
More people _____
worked, earned _____
more money, _____
and bought _____
more.

Lesson 3

Activate Prior Knowledge

After students have completed the activity, have students brainstorm new technologies they would like to see made in the future. Ask students to make a guess on when they think such a technology might be possible. Point out that the technologies we take for granted today would seem completely out-of-this-world to people in the 1800s.

? Essential Question

How do ideas influence choices?

Have students explain what they understand about the Essential Question. Discuss their responses. Explain that everything they learn in this lesson will help them understand the Essential Question better. Remind them to think about how the Essential Question connects to the unit Big Idea: Relationships affect choices.

More about the start of the Industrial Revolution Samuel Slater learned to build textile mills while in England. He brought these trade secrets to Pawtucket, RI, where he built America's first factory: a mill with spinning machines powered by water. He had trouble finding workers, so he built a town. Everyone who lived there, including women and children, worked in jobs related to the mill. Other factory owners used his factory as a model.

Active Teaching

Words To Know After students have completed the Words to Know activity, have students write what they think the definition of each word is on another sheet of paper. Then, have students look up the definition in the glossary and write it beneath their definition. Have students attach their word list to their work text for safe keeping.

Develop Comprehension

Ask:

1. *In what ways did inventions impact life in the mid-1800s?* **L3**

2. *How did the expansion of the textile industry change life?* **L2**

Farming Improves

The Industrial Revolution was not limited to manufacturing. The reaper and better plows greatly improved farming during the Industrial Revolution.

The Reaper

In 1832 Cyrus McCormick invented the **reaper**. A reaper is a machine with sharp blades to cut grain. The reapers could harvest four times as much grain as people working by hand in the same amount of time.

The Mechanical Plow

Farmers had traditionally used hand tools to plant seeds. The first horse-drawn mechanical plow was invented in 1797 by Charles Newbold. His iron plow made planting seeds much quicker and easier.

John Deere's Plow

In 1837 John Deere improved the mechanical plow by adding a steel blade. This blade was better able to cut through tough soil. The blade was also polished so that mud would not stick to it.

Reading Skill

Draw Conclusions

How did new farming equipment impact farming?

Farming was easier

What were the effects of these improvements?

With easier farming tools and
techniques, farmers grew more

260

New Forms of Transportation

Farming wasn't the only area where improvements brought changes. Transportation also changed quickly. As more people moved westward, the demand for safer, easier, and faster forms of transportation increased. Suddenly, connecting the West and the East Coast became a priority.

Underline details explaining how improvements to roads impacted the United States.

The Road to Better Travel

In the early 1800s, most people traveled in large, horse-drawn carriages called **stagecoaches**. At the time, the best roads in the United States were paved with rocks or logs. Most others were narrow dirt trails that were full of potholes and tree stumps. When it rained, these roads became muddy, and horses and wagons were slowed down or became stuck. Even on a good day, travel on these roads was slow.

In 1811 the federal government began construction on the National Road. This road stretched from Cumberland, Maryland, to Vandalia, Illinois. The National Road was made of stone and gravel. It connected the East Coast with what was then the West. Businesses could now move more goods and move them faster. The National Road also made it easier for people to settle new lands in the West.

GLUE FOLDABLE HERE

GLUE FOLDABLE HERE

How did improved roads help businesses?

261

Active Teaching

Point out to students that inventions can either create a new product or improve an existing one. In the case of the plow, John Deere improved upon the problems of the existing plow.

Develop Comprehension

Ask:

1. *What was a reaper used for?* **L1**

2. *How was Deere's plow an improvement over the Newbold plow?* **L2**

3. *How did the improvements to the National Road compare to roads that we travel on today?* **L3**

Reading Skill

Common Core Standards RI.1 Quote accurately from a text when explaining what the text says explicitly and when drawing inferences from the text.

Remind students that when they draw a conclusion, they use stated information to figure out ideas that are unstated. In this case, students must think about how improvements in farming technology benefitted the economy.

Page Power

FOLDABLES Interact more with the pages in this lesson. Have students create a Notebook Foldable to help them take notes about improvements in transportation discussed in this lesson.

1. Provide each student with a copy of Foldable 7B from the Notebook Foldables section of this book.

2. Have students cut out the Foldable and glue each anchor tab next to the image as shown.

3. On the left flap, have students write "Transportation Over Land" at the top of the flap. On the right flap, have them write "Transportation Over Water." Beneath each heading, have students list types of transportation discussed in the lesson.

4. On the inside of each flap, have students write additional details about related travel improvements.

netw rks

Go to **connected.mcgraw-hill.com** for additional resources.

- Interactive Whiteboard Lessons
- Worksheets
- Assessment
- Lesson Plans

Rolling on the River

Until the early 1800s, people and goods were also moved on flatboats that traveled on rivers. These boats were pushed downstream by hand with long poles. Traveling upstream was a much tougher job!

River travel improved quickly with the **steam engine**. A steam engine uses compressed steam to power a motor. It produces more power than a team of horses and can pull heavier loads. In 1807 Robert Fulton designed a boat powered by a steam engine. His steamboat traveled 150 miles in 32 hours. Boats without steam engines took 4 days to make the same trip.

These steamboats had one major problem: most rivers don't connect with each other. To solve this problem, people built canals. Canals use a system of locks to raise and lower the water level. In 1825 the Erie Canal was opened. It connected Lake Erie with the Hudson River and the Atlantic Ocean.

DID YOU KNOW?
The success of the Erie Canal caused a rush of canal-building in the 1820s. These canals helped people move more quickly to the West. It wouldn't be long before the United States would need even more land.

The Erie Canal was a huge success. Goods were shipped more quickly between the East and the Midwest. The canal connected Midwest goods with the Atlantic Ocean, making it easier to trade with foreign countries. Trade boomed, and New York City became the country's largest and most important port.

Reading Skill

Use Visuals Examine the diagram of the lock. Then answer the questions.

1. Why were locks necessary? to connect rivers

2. How did canals improve transportation and trade?
Allowed goods to travel faster

262

The Iron Horse

Within a few years, a new steam-powered invention made canals less important. People had traveled by railroad for years, but on early railroads, horses pulled coaches over iron rails. In 1814 British inventor George Stephenson built the first train powered by a steam engine. These new trains were nicknamed "iron horses."

In 1830 Peter Cooper, an American merchant, built a small locomotive he named *Tom Thumb*. At first, few people believed a locomotive could move without horses. A Baltimore stagecoach company challenged Cooper and his locomotive to a race against a horse-drawn carriage. Although this train lost the race, trains won in the end. Railroads soon became the main form of transportation in the United States.

The combination of canals and railroads made shipping goods quicker and cheaper than **previous** methods. As a result, businesses sold goods at lower prices, which meant more people could afford them.

▲ Tom Thumb racing a horse-drawn carriage

FUN FACTS
Trains provided Americans with one of their first chances at tourism. Passengers took tours of new lands in the West. Granted, at first only the wealthy could afford to ride trains.

Explain why railways were located near rivers or large ports.

Railways, 1800s

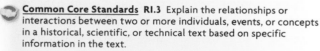

263

Lesson 3

Active Teaching

After students have read page 263, Ask:

1. *Why were flatboats not the most efficient way to travel on rivers?* **L2**

2. *What was a steam engine?* **L1**

3. *How did it improve travel?* **L2**

4. *Why did the steam locomotive make canal travel less important?* **L3**

Reading Skill

Common Core Standards RI.3 Explain the relationships or interactions between two or more individuals, events, or concepts in a historical, scientific, or technical text based on specific information in the text.

Use Visuals Have students work in pairs to analyze the diagram and write a description for each section. Allow time for pairs to share their descriptions and compare.

Explain to students that many railroads ultimately connected to port cities on the East Coast. This made it possible for goods to then be shipped overseas.

Differentiated Instruction

▶ **Approaching** Have students work in pairs to make a 3-column table to record information about the different types of improvement: *roads, canals,* and *railroads.*

▶ **Beyond** Have students create an illustrated time line of improvements to transportation in the early 1800s. Students can extend their time lines to cover more modern forms of transportation, including automobiles, airplanes, and space shuttles.

▶ **ELL** Have students look at the images on pages 261–263 and read the descriptions of the new improvements in transportation. Have students use what they have read in the text to draw a picture of an improved method of transportation and write a description of it in their own words.

More About the Erie Canal When Dewitt Clinton, the governor of New York, wanted to build the Erie Canal, people thought he was crazy. They referred to the project as "Clinton's Folly." However, the canal encouraged thousands of pioneers to move to the Midwest. Boats carried their supplies west and moved their crops back east. For 50 years, the Erie Canal was the most important commercial route in the United States.

Highlight the effects of the telegraph and the Pony Express.

Better Communication

New inventions also helped people communicate much faster. Samuel Morse began working on an invention called the telegraph in 1832. The telegraph sent messages using electricity. It could send a message in a matter of minutes, compared to waiting weeks for letters to arrive in the mail. Telegraph messages were a series of clicks and sounds that stood for letters and numbers. By 1844, the first telegraph line connected Washington, D.C., to Baltimore, Maryland.

▶ **DID YOU KNOW?**
By 1861, there were over 67,000 miles of telegraph lines across the country.

A telegraph machine ▼

The Pony Express

It took a while for telegraph lines to reach the western United States. In the meantime, people needed a faster way to send and receive messages. In April 1859 the Leavenworth & Pike's Peak Express Company was created. The company employed mail carriers who traveled on horseback along a trail that was nearly 2,000 miles long. Because carriers rode horses, the service was referred to as the Pony Express. The Pony Express was in operation until late October 1861, when telegraph lines finally reached the West Coast.

A Pony Express rider passes crews installing telegraph poles ▼

264

The Growth of Cities

With better communication, new jobs, and new ways to get from place to place, cities grew quickly during the Industrial Revolution. In 1820 only about 700,000 people lived in all of the cities in the United States. By 1840, urban populations totalled almost 1.8 million people.

You learned earlier that some of this growth happened when people moved from rural areas in search of work. Others came in search of a better life too. **Immigrants**, mostly from Europe, came to find new job opportunities or to seek fortunes. An immigrant is a person who moves to and lives in a country in which he or she was not born. Almost all immigrants entered the nation through port cities like New York City, Boston, and New Orleans. Some immigrants moved westward, but many remained in the cities on the East Coast.

Yet another reason for the growth of cities was the Industrial Revolution itself. Cities sprung up around factories and along rail routes. Roads and railroads connected cities around the country. These routes also made moving to and trading with areas in the West easier. As more and more people moved westward, the boundaries of the United States began to change and take the form they have today.

Reading Skill Main Idea and Key Details (Circle) the main idea of this text passage and underline key details that support it.

//////// GLUE FOLDABLE HERE ////////

Lesson 3

? **Essential Question** How do ideas influence choices?

_____
_____
_____
_____
_____

Go back to *Show As You Go!* on pages 238–239. ◀◀

networks There's More Online!
• Games • Assessment

265

Active Teaching

Have students look at the image of the Pony Express rider on page 264.

Ask: *What do you see in this picture?* Make sure students note that around the Pony Express rider, people are putting up telegraph poles and wires.

Ask:
1. *How were telegraphs responsible for the end of the Pony Express?* (Once the lines made it out to the West, the Pony Express was not necessary.) **L2**

>>> *Show As You Go!* Remind students to go back to the Unit Opener and complete the activities for this lesson.

Reading Skill

Common Core Standards RI.2 Determine two or more main ideas of a text and explain how they are supported by key details; summarize the text.

Main Idea and Key Details After students read page 265,
Ask:
How did the Industrial Revolution fuel the growth of cities?

Page Power

FOLDABLES Provide students with Foldable 7C from the Notebook Foldables section at the back of this book. Have students glue the anchor tab above the Essential Question box on page 265. Students will compare and contrast how two technological advances (industry, travel, or communication) affected people's decision to move west.

Response to Intervention

? **Essential Question**
How do ideas influence choices?

If . . . students cannot describe how ideas influence choices,

. . . .

Then . . . take students back to pages 258–259 and read about life before the Industrial Revolution and about the start of factories.
Ask: *What sort of job opportunities do you think women had before the establishment of Lowell? How do you think the building of new factories affected the amount of options people in the United States had for jobs?*

Following discussion, allow students to respond to the Essential Question again.

Lesson 4 Internal Struggles

Essential Question
How do ideas influence choices?
What do you think?

Have you ever had to compromise with someone? What did you give up? What did you receive?

_____

_____

_____

The Nation Begins to Divide

By the late 1700s, feelings about slavery began to change in the United States. The economies, cultures, and attitudes of the North and South were very different.

Large cities and new factories were growing quickly in the North. Immigrants flooded the United States to fill factory jobs. By 1804 all Northern states had outlawed slavery.

In the South, the economy had not changed much. The plantation system was still the main way of life. On large farms, hundreds of enslaved Africans worked without pay. Most Southerners worked on small farms, and not all had slaves. However, the plantation owners were the wealthiest and had the most political power.

Enslaved workers use a cotton gin ▼

Words To Know
Tell a partner what you think you know about these words.

slave state

*balance

free state

Union

266

The Missouri Compromise 1820 (map)

Compromise for Missouri

As the United States expanded west, many wondered if slavery would expand as well. In 1819 Missouri applied for statehood as a **slave state**, a state in which slavery is allowed. At the time, the nation had a **balance** of 11 slave states and 11 **free states**, or states in which slavery was not allowed. Letting Missouri enter the Union as a slave state would give slave states more votes in the Senate.

Congress argued over Missouri for a year. In 1820 Senator Henry Clay from Kentucky came up with the Missouri Compromise. Under this plan, Missouri was added as a slave state. Maine, which had been part of Massachusetts, became a free state. The compromise stated that, in the future, slavery would not be allowed in any states north of Missouri's southern border.

This compromise was only a temporary solution. As the United States continued to expand, new compromises and decisions had to be made.

Map and Globe Skills

1. Was slavery allowed in Alabama?

   Yes

2. Which state entered the Union as a free state under the Missouri Compromise?

   Maine

Reading Skill
Cause and Effect Underline the causes and circle the effects of the Missouri Compromise.

267

Lesson 4

Activate Prior Knowledge

Explain to students that in this unit they will learn about two situations in which the United States had to reach compromise.

Ask:

What makes a compromise work? Why might a person not want to compromise? What happens when people are unable to compromise?

Essential Question
How do ideas influence choices?

Have students explain what they understand about the Essential Question. Discuss their responses. Explain that everything they learn in this lesson will help them understand the Essential Question better. Remind them to think about how the Essential Question connects to the unit Big Idea: Relationships affect choices.

More About the Missouri Compromise Many feared that the Missouri Compromise was a temporary solution that only postponed the problems with the issue of slavery. President John Quincy Adams said, "I take it for granted that the present question is a mere preamble—a title page to a great tragic volume."

Active Teaching

Words To Know Once students have completed the Words to Know activity, have them use a dictionary to find the definition and the part of speech to which each vocabulary word belongs. Next, have students come up with a synonym or antonym for each word.

Develop Comprehension
Ask:

1. _How many slave states and free states were in the United States when Missouri applied for statehood?_ **L1**

2. _How did the Missouri Compromise help keep the balance between slave and free states?_ **L2**

Map and Globe Skills

Point out to students that at the time of the Missouri Compromise, territories within the Louisiana Territory were just starting to gain statehood.

The Age of Jackson

Prior to 1824, only wealthy men were allowed to vote. Then, new laws were passed that allowed all white men age 21 or older to vote. This wave of new voters helped elect a "common man" as President—Andrew Jackson.

Andrew Jackson: Biography

▲ Andrew Jackson

Born: March 15, 1767
Early Life: Jackson was born in rural South Carolina. At age 13, he worked as a courier during the Revolutionary War. He later became a lawyer. Jackson earned fame as a general during the War of 1812.
Crisis in South Carolina: During Jackson's Presidency, lawmakers in South Carolina threatened to leave the **Union** if they were forced to collect a new federal tax on imported goods. A union is a group of states joined together.

Jackson sent troops and warships to South Carolina to enforce collection of the tax. The tax was collected and the crisis passed. People accused Jackson of acting more like a king than a President.

Primary Source

Political Cartoons

Political cartoons express an artist's opinion about people or events. Often, the image exaggerates details in a humorous or ridiculous way. The title, labels, or details will help you identify and understand the opinion being expressed.

Many people were outraged that President Jackson would order military action against his own people over taxes. In fact, it reminded them of events that happened before the Revolutionary War. They felt Jackson had violated their rights and was acting more like a king than President.

Circle the parts of the political cartoon that support this opinion of Jackson.

268

Indian Removal Act, 1830–1840

Trail of Tears

Lands and Routes of Native American Relocation
- Cherokee
- Chickasaw
- Choctaw
- Seminole
- Muscogee
- Present-day boundary
- City

Conflicts Over Land

In the early 1800s, many Native Americans in the Southeast, such as the Cherokee, lived peacefully with their white neighbors. Their right to their homeland had been guaranteed by treaties signed with the United States government.

As settlers continued to move to the West and Southeast, the demand for land increased. This sometimes led to conflicts with Native Americans.

The Indian Removal Act
President Jackson and some of his supporters believed that Native Americans should leave their lands in the Southeast and allow settlers to live there. In 1830 Congress passed the Indian Removal Act. This act forced Native Americans to move to an area called the Indian Territory, in parts of present-day Oklahoma.

The Cherokee believed this act was unfair. They sued the state of Georgia to stop the government from forcing them out of their homeland. Eventually, the case went to the United States Supreme Court. The Court ruled in favor of the Cherokee. President Jackson, however, refused to obey the ruling.

Map and Globe Skills

1. In which states did the Cherokee originally live?

   Georgia, Alabama,
   Tennessee

2. Describe the route of the Seminole.

   across Gulf of Mexico

DID YOU KNOW?
In 1821 a Cherokee named Sequoyah developed the first written Native American alphabet. It took him 12 years to create this alphabet. It has 86 letters!

269

Active Teaching

Have students read pages 268–269 before they do the Primary Sources activity on page 268.

Develop Comprehension
Ask:
1. *How did Jackson take care of the crisis in South Carolina?* **L1**
2. *Why was the Indian Removal Act passed?* **L1**
3. *Why was Jackson considered a "common man"?* **L3**

Primary Source

Political Cartoons Andrew Jackson believed the President should be strong and do what was best for ordinary people. As a result, he was considered to be a "man of the people."
Ask: *How did the people's opinion of Jackson change? Why did it change?*

Map and Globe Skills

Point out to students that the Seminole arrow on the map travels over water.
Ask: *Why were there so many routes?*

Differentiated Instruction

▶ **Approaching** As students read, have them underline or circle different aspects of Jackson's personality and presidency. Have them work in pairs and use this information to complete the Primary Source activity.

▶ **Beyond** Have students create their own political cartoon. They can either create one that covers the content in their book or research a current issue. They should label their cartoon and write descriptions of the cartoons.

▶ **ELL** Have students scan the text for words that describe conflicts involving Jackson. Then they should analyze the cartoon to see if these ideas are represented in the image. Have students write other words that come to mind as they look at the image.

networks

Go to **connected.mcgraw-hill.com** for additional resources.
- Interactive Whiteboard Lessons
- Worksheets
- Assessment
- Lesson Plans

The Trail of Tears

In May 1838, General Winfield Scott and 7,000 federal troops arrived at the Cherokee capital. Scott threatened to use force if the Cherokee didn't leave. He told the Cherokee that they were surrounded and escape was impossible. The Cherokee knew that fighting would lead to their destruction.

Filled with sadness and anger, Cherokee leaders gave in, and the 800 mile march to the Indian Territory began. Around 2,000 Cherokee died in camps waiting for the move to begin. About another 2,000 died along the way from starvation, disease, and harsh weather conditions. This journey became known as the Trail of Tears.

> **How did the westward movement of settlers affect Native Americans in the Southeast?**
>
> They died from disease, starvation, and
> harsh weather.

The Seminole Fight Back

The United States also tried to relocate the Seminole, who lived in Florida. In 1832 some Seminole leaders signed a treaty with the United States agreeing to relocate. However, others refused and retreated south into the Everglades.

Led by a man named Osceola, the Seminole who decided to stay fought against United States troops. Osceola eventually was captured, but the Seminole continued to fight. The Seminole wars would last nearly 50 years and cost the United States $40 million. A few hundred Seminole survived and remained in the Everglades.

> **Explain how westward expansion affected Native Americans.**
>
> Lost homelands,
> Lost culture,
> Lost lives

▲ Osceola

PrimarySource

Quote

This primary source describes what one soldier saw along the trail.

> "[In] May 1838 . . . I saw helpless Cherokee arrested and dragged from their homes. . . . I saw them loaded like cattle or sheep into six hundred and forty-five wagons and starting toward the west. . . . Many of the children rose to their feet and waved their little hands good-by to their mountain homes, knowing they were leaving them forever."

–A section from *Story of the Trail of Tears* by John G. Burnett, published in 1890

How did John Burnett feel about the way Native Americans were relocated? Circle the words and phrases that led to your answer.

_____

_____

270

Lesson 4

(?) **Essential Question** How do ideas influence choices?

_____

_____

_____

_____

_____

Go back to **Show As You Go!** on pages 238–239. ◀◀◀

netw⚹rks There's More Online!
• Assessments • Games

271

Lesson 4

Active Teaching

Have students use the information on pages 269–271 to answer the question on page 271 about how westward expansion affected Native Americans.

Develop Comprehension
Ask:

1. *What was the Trail of Tears?* **L1**

2. *Who was Osceola?* **L1**

3. *How does Burnett's story help you understand the Trail of Tears?* **L3**

◀◀◀ Remind students to go back to the Unit Opener and complete the activities for this lesson.

Primary Source

Quote After students finish reading the quote,
Ask:

What do you think about the way people were treated on the Trail of Tears?

Differentiated Instruction

▶ **ELL** As students read the primary source, have them circle unfamiliar words in the text and write their definitions in the margins.

Response to Intervention

(?) **Essential Question**
How do ideas influence choices?

If . . . students have difficulty understanding how ideas influence choices,

. . . .

Then . . . have students read about President Jackson's feelings toward Native Americans and the Indian Removal Act on page 269. Remind students that the idea of manifest destiny led to many Americans feeling a sense of entitlement toward expanding borders in North America. Then bring up a personal example about how choices are limited.
Say: *Imagine you want to go see a movie. When you get to the theater, you find out that it is rated "PG-13." This means that people have deemed the movie unacceptable for someone your age to watch. This idea affects your choice of movie.*

Following discussion, allow students to respond to the Essential Question again.

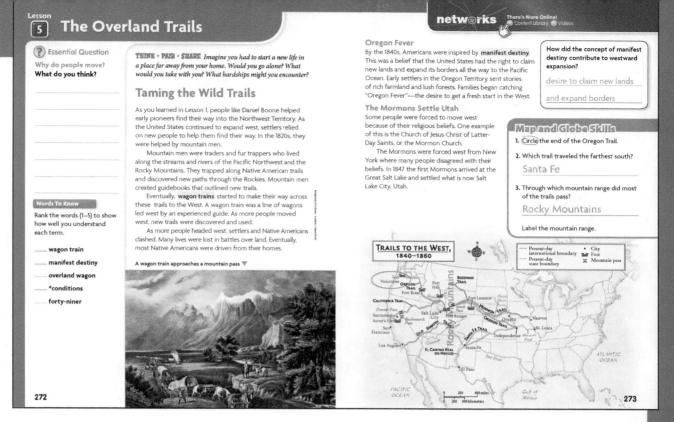

Lesson 5
The Overland Trails

Essential Question
Why do people move?
What do you think?

THINK • PAIR • SHARE *Imagine you had to start a new life in a place far away from your home. Would you go alone? What would you take with you? What hardships might you encounter?*

Taming the Wild Trails

As you learned in Lesson 1, people like Daniel Boone helped early pioneers find their way into the Northwest Territory. As the United States continued to expand west, settlers relied on new people to help them find their way. In the 1820s, they were helped by mountain men.

Mountain men were traders and fur trappers who lived along the streams and rivers of the Pacific Northwest and the Rocky Mountains. They trapped along Native American trails and discovered new paths through the Rockies. Mountain men created guidebooks that outlined new trails.

Eventually, **wagon trains** started to make their way across these trails to the West. A wagon train was a line of wagons led west by an experienced guide. As more people moved west, new trails were discovered and used.

As more people headed west, settlers and Native Americans clashed. Many lives were lost in battles over land. Eventually, most Native Americans were driven from their homes.

Words To Know
Rank the words (1–5) to show how well you understand each term.

___ wagon train

___ manifest destiny

___ overland wagon

___ *conditions

___ forty-niner

A wagon train approaches a mountain pass ▼

272

Oregon Fever
By the 1840s, Americans were inspired by **manifest destiny**. This was a belief that the United States had the right to claim new lands and expand its borders all the way to the Pacific Ocean. Early settlers in the Oregon Territory sent stories of rich farmland and lush forests. Families began catching "Oregon Fever"—the desire to get a fresh start in the West.

The Mormons Settle Utah
Some people were forced to move west because of their religious beliefs. One example of this is the Church of Jesus Christ of Latter-Day Saints, or the Mormon Church.

The Mormons were forced west from New York where many people disagreed with their beliefs. In 1847 the first Mormons arrived at the Great Salt Lake and settled what is now Salt Lake City, Utah.

How did the concept of manifest destiny contribute to westward expansion?

desire to claim new lands

and expand borders

Map and Globe Skills
1. Circle the end of the Oregon Trail.
2. Which trail traveled the farthest south?
Santa Fe
3. Through which mountain range did most of the trails pass?
Rocky Mountains

Label the mountain range.

TRAILS TO THE WEST, 1840–1860

273

Lesson 5

✓ Diagnostic Assessment
Before beginning the lesson, administer a short quiz about pioneers moving west. There are some terms and concepts in this lesson that students may be familiar with. Before students open their book, show them a picture of a covered wagon. **Ask:** *What is this?*

Students should indicate familiarity with each term by holding up fingers with

1 = I know very little about this

2 = I know some about this

3 = I know a lot about this

If any student knows that it is a covered wagon, ask where they have seen one before. Many may answer that they have seen them in books or movies.

Student responses will help identify their level of understanding.

? Essential Question   Why do people move?

Have students explain what they understand about the Essential Question. Discuss their responses. Explain that everything they learn in this lesson will help them understand the Essential Question better. Remind them to think about how the Essential Question connects to the unit Big Idea: Relationships affect choices.

Active Teaching

Words To Know   Once students have completed the Words to Know activity, have them write one sentence for each word, using it in context.

Develop Comprehension
Ask:
1. *Where did the Mormons eventually settle in 1847? (Salt Lake City, Utah)* **L1**
2. *What were the benefits of wagon trains?* **L2**
3. *Why do you think mountain men help pioneers?* **L3**
4. *Why do you think people in the United States started to believe in manifest destiny?* **L3**

Map and Globe Skills

Ask:
1. *Where did the California Trail begin and end?* **L1**
2. *Why were there so many different trails to the West?* **L2**

LIFE ON THE OVERLAND TRAILS

One of the most popular overland trails was the Oregon Trail, which stretched from Independence, Missouri, to western Oregon. It was a long, hard journey of 2,000 miles. It took nearly six months to reach Oregon! Read these pages to find out what the trip was like for a typical family.

Men were responsible for driving the oxen, repairing the wagon, hunting, and protecting their families.

Women cooked, set up camp, and managed supplies. They also cared for and educated their children along the way.

Children helped around camp. They gathered "buffalo chips," dung left by bison. These "chips" were used as fuel for fires.

Settlers used **overland wagons** called prairie schooners. Wagons had to carry everything a family would need for the journey, as well as what they would need once they got to their new home. Label these items on the schooner shown to the left:

weapons	tools	medicine	seeds
books	meat	pans	spare wagon parts

People found strength in numbers on wagon trains. This helped in the event of animal attacks or conflict with Native Americans.

274

Pioneers often used guidebooks they purchased from mountain men or at one of the many stops or forts along the trail. However, these guidebooks weren't always reliable and didn't accurately describe **conditions** on the trails.

As pioneers headed west, unpredictable weather often greeted them. Sometimes, violent storms popped up with little warning. Pioneers had to scramble to make sure their belongings weren't damaged in the storms. As they approached the Rocky Mountains, pioneers had to deal with freezing temperatures and snow storms.

The trails were not always smooth. As pioneers headed west, they had to deal with rocky terrain and rough trails. Sometimes they would have to repair broken wheels. Pioneers had to deal with plants, vegetation, and wildlife with which they were not familiar. Pioneers had to figure out how to get around or through deep rivers. Some pioneers altered their wagons to float across the river like a boat.

Draw a hardship faced by pioneers on the trails. Underline details in the text that help you.

Should include one of the following:
- rough/dangerous trails
- death/sickness
- weather
- attacks
- no supplies

275

Lesson 5

Active Teaching

Develop Comprehension
Ask:
1. *How long did a typical journey to Oregon take?* **L1**
2. *What problems could be caused by an unreliable guidebook?* **L2**
3. *How might encountering unfamiliar weather, terrain, vegetation, and animals present problems for pioneers?* **L3**

Page Power
Interact more with the page. Have students:
- provide speech bubbles for what the people may be saying or thinking as they journey west.
- underline different hardships people faced as they moved west.

Differentiated Instruction

▶ **Approaching** As students read this spread, have them underline hardships that pioneers faced as they traveled west. Students should then use their notes to help them do the drawing activity on page 275.

▶ **Beyond** Have students create a story that features the family on page 274. They should use separate pieces of paper to make a comic book that tells the life story of the family. Student comic books should include the reasons why the family is moving, details of their journey, and what their life is like once they reach their destination.

▶ **ELL** Read the instructions for the activities on pages 274 and 275 sentence-by-sentence with students, helping them understand difficult words.

The War with Mexico

Instead of moving west, some people settled in an area of the Southwest that belonged to Mexico. Eventually, the demands and needs of these settlers led to war with Mexico.

Americans Settle in Texas

In 1821 Mexico won its independence from Spain. At that time, Mexico's northern areas included present-day Texas, New Mexico, and California.

During those years, few people lived in this huge area. To keep the area under Mexican control, Mexico's government offered land and citizenship to Americans who settled in Texas. By 1835, about 25,000 Americans lived in the area. Many of these Americans didn't want to live in Mexico. They complained about Mexican laws. They also wanted slavery, which was illegal in Mexico, to be legal.

Texas Goes to War

Texans went to war with Mexico in December 1835. After a year of fighting, Texans voted to join the United States. They adopted a constitution and made slavery legal.

The U.S. Congress felt that allowing Texas to join the Union might lead to war with Mexico. Instead, Texas became an independent country—the Republic of Texas. It was also known as the Lone Star Republic.

The United States Goes to War

In 1845 Texas joined the Union. However, the United States and Mexico disagreed over the southern border of Texas. Later that year, President James Polk offered to buy the Mexican territories of California and New Mexico for $30 million. When Mexico refused, Polk ordered General Zachary Taylor to march through Texas to the Rio Grande. Fighting broke out with Mexican soldiers in April 1846. As a result, the United States declared war on Mexico.

Fighting continued until 1847, when U.S. troops captured the Mexican capital, Mexico City. The Mexican government signed the Treaty of Guadalupe Hidalgo in February 1848. Under this treaty, Mexico sold Texas to the United States for $15 million. The treaty also included land in much of the Southwest.

In December 1835, a force of 500 Texans attacked the town of San Antonio. Within days, they had control of the Alamo, a Spanish fort. Three months later, the Mexicans recaptured the Alamo after a two-week battle. ▶

Map and Globe Skills

Which present-day states had their borders expanded in 1853?

Arizona,

New Mexico

How did the War with Mexico help the United States achieve the idea of manifest destiny?

Borders extended

completely from

coast to coast.

DID YOU KNOW?

In 1853 the United States paid Mexico $10 million for the Gadsden Purchase. This strip of land included the southern edge of present-day Arizona and New Mexico. With this purchase, the nation reached its present size (not including Alaska and Hawaii).

Land Acquired from Mexico, 1845–1853

276

277

Active Teaching

Explain to students that the text on this spread is presented like a horizontal time line.

Ask:

1. *When did Mexico win independence from Spain?* **L1**

2. *Why was Congress hesitant to allow Texas to join the Union at first?* **L1**

3. *Why did the United States end up going to war with Mexico?* **L2**

Map and Globe Skills

Ask:

1. *How did the United States acquire the southern portions of present-day Arizona and New Mexico?* (Gadsden Purchase) **L1**

2. *Why do you think the Rio Grande serves as a border between Texas and Mexico?* **L3**

More About Texas In December 1835, a force of 500 Texans attacked the town of San Antonio. Within days, they took control of the Alamo, a Spanish mission that had been made into a fort. In March of the following year, Mexican forces recaptured the Alamo after an almost two-week battle. All of the Americans in the Alamo were killed. This did not stop the Texans. In fact, the brave efforts at the Alamo became a rallying cry! A month later, the Texan forces surprised a much larger Mexican force at San Jacinto near present-day Houston. The Texans charged the Mexican forces, yelling, "Remember the Alamo!" The Texans won the battle in less than 20 minutes.

▲ Miners often searched for gold in rivers, using pans to separate the gold from pebbles and sand.

California Joins the Union

As a result of the War with Mexico, the United States gained possession of California. Soon, a large flood of people would move to California in hopes of making a fortune.

Gold Fever in California

In January 1848, a man named James Marshall saw something glittering in the American River outside the town of Sacramento, California. What he saw was gold. Marshall tried to keep the discovery a secret, but the news quickly spread.

Over the next year, thousands of miners came to search for gold in the area. Prospecting, or exploring for gold, required only a few tools and the willingness to work hard. It was difficult work, and few people struck it rich.

> **How did the discovery of gold in California influence boundary changes in the United States?**
>
> The population increased as people came in search of gold. This led to a new state.

278

The idea of sudden wealth drew thousands of people to California. So many people came that the period became known as the Gold Rush. By May 1849, more than 10,000 wagons had crossed the continent to reach California. In that year alone, more than 80,000 people arrived in California from around the world. Because these people came to California in 1849, they became known as "**forty-niners**."

The Thirty-First State

By 1850, there were enough people in California to apply for statehood. Settlers wanted courts, land and water laws, mail delivery, and other government services. On September 9, 1850, President Millard Fillmore signed a law that made California the thirty-first state to enter the Union.

▲ Miners used pans such as this one to find gold.

> **How did California becoming a state fulfill the idea of manifest destiny?**
>
> It gave the country a new state on the West Coast. The country's border now stretched to the Pacific Ocean.

Lesson 5

(?) **Essential Question** Why do people move?

_____

_____

_____

_____

Go back to *Show As You Go!* on pages 238–239. ◀◀◀

netw◯rks **There's More Online!**
• Assessment • Games

279

Lesson 5

Active Teaching

After reading these pages, remind students of early Spanish explorations in the Americas.

Say:

The Spanish came to the Americas looking for riches. Explain what happened once they got here. How do the experiences of the Spanish conquistadors compare to the Gold Rush in California?

Develop Comprehension

1. *Who was John C. Fremont?* **L1**

2. *What happened after people learned about James Marshall's discover?* **L1**

3. *What effect did the forty-niners have on California?* **L2**

>>> Remind students to go back to the Unit Opener and complete the activities for this lesson.

Response to Intervention

(?) **Essential Question** **Why do people move?**

If . . . students have difficulty understanding why people move,

. . . .

Then . . . start a class discussion.

Ask: *Has your family ever had to move? If so, why?*

Have students work in pairs to make a chart listing all of the possible reasons they could think of for why their family would have to move.

Following discussion, allow students to respond to the Essential Question again.

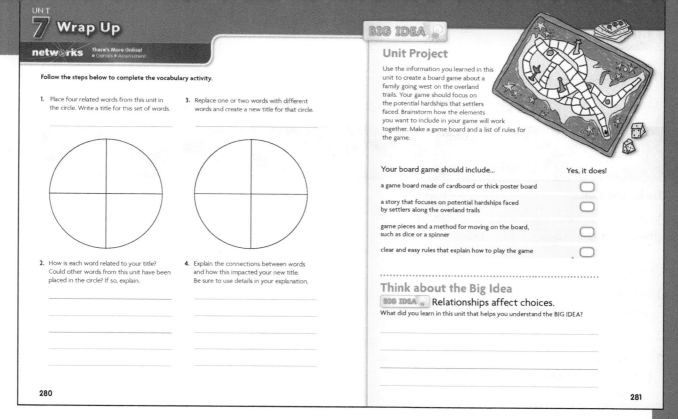

UNIT 7 Wrap Up

networks There's More Online!
• Games • Assessment!

Follow the steps below to complete the vocabulary activity.

1. Place four related words from this unit in the circle. Write a title for this set of words.

3. Replace one or two words with different words and create a new title for that circle.

2. How is each word related to your title? Could other words from this unit have been placed in the circle? If so, explain.

4. Explain the connections between words and how this impacted your new title. Be sure to use details in your explanation.

280

BIG IDEA

Unit Project

Use the information you learned in this unit to create a board game about a family going west on the overland trails. Your game should focus on the potential hardships that settlers faced. Brainstorm how the elements you want to include in your game will work together. Make a game board and a list of rules for the game.

Your board game should include...	Yes, it does!
a game board made of cardboard or thick poster board	☐
a story that focuses on potential hardships faced by settlers along the overland trails	☐
game pieces and a method for moving on the board, such as dice or a spinner	☐
clear and easy rules that explain how to play the game	☐

Think about the Big Idea

BIG IDEA Relationships affect choices.

What did you learn in this unit that helps you understand the BIG IDEA?

281

Wrap Up

Vocabulary

Have students complete the activity on page 280. You may want to provide several copies of the circles so that students can swap out different words in the activity.

BIG IDEA Big Idea Project

- Read through the project directions and checklist with students.
- Answer any questions students may have about the project.
- Remind students to use their **Show As You Go!** pages to assist them in completing the project.
- To assess the project, refer to the rubric on the following page.

networks

Go to connected.mcgraw-hill.com for additional resources.
- Games
- Assessment
- Group Technology Projects

Differentiated Instruction

▶ **Approaching** Students should work in pairs to write an outline for their game rules are. Students may use gameboards and pieces from existing board games to help.

▶ **Beyond** Have students make decks of cards to play with the game. The cards should include positive and negative effects on the players. These cards should affect gameplay and the story. For example, a broken wagon wheel might make you lose a turn. Other cards may make players move back or forward certain spaces.

▶ **ELL** Students may explain their instructions for their games exhibit orally rather than in writing.

Response to Intervention

BIG IDEA Relationships affect choices.

If . . . students cannot give a substantiated explanation of the Big Idea,

Then . . . organize students into pairs. Send each pair to a different Lesson in the Unit. Have them find examples of how different relationships among groups and different situations led to either a limiting of choices or new potential choices. Allow time for a class discussion.

Following discussion, allow students to respond to the Big Idea again.

Name _____ Date _____

Westward Expansion Game Rubric

4 Exemplary	3 Accomplished	2 Developing	1 Beginning
The board game:	**The board game:**	**The board game:**	**The board game:**
☐ clearly describes hardships faced by pioneers on the overland trails	☐ describes hardships faced by pioneers on the overland trails	☐ describes a hardship faced by pioneers on the overland trails	☐ does not describe any hardships faced by pioneers on the overland trails
☐ includes clearly written game instructions	☐ includes written instructions	☐ includes poorly written or incomplete instructions	☐ does not have clearly written instructions
☐ is fun and easy to play	☐ is easy to play	☐ is playable	☐ is difficult to play
☐ is very interesting to look at and very appealing to players	☐ is interesting to look at and appealing to players	☐ is not interesting look at	☐ is not interesting to look at

Grading Comments: _____

_____

_____

_____

_____

_____

_____

_____

_____

_____

_____

Project Score: _____

Read the passage "The City of Lowell" before answering Numbers 1 through 8.

The City of Lowell

by Donnie Tadele

In 1810 Francis Cabot Lowell visited some textile factories in Great Britain. A textile factory is a place where workers turn cotton into cloth. At the time, Britain made it illegal to export machines or machine parts. During his visit, Lowell memorized how the machines in the factory worked.

In 1813 Lowell built a textile factory in Waltham, Massachusetts. All stages of cotton-making—from spinning cotton into thread to weaving thread into cotton—happened under one roof.

Lowell died in 1817. His business partners later built several textile mills along the Merrimack River in Massachusetts. They also built a town, called Lowell, around the factories for workers to live in. Workers used half of their pay to live in the houses owned by the mills. Lowell was the first planned town in the United States.

By 1850, Lowell had more than 10,000 workers. Many of them were young women, sometimes called "Mill Girls." The company hired mainly women and children because they would work for lower wages than men. However, the women still made more money than they could working on farms. They signed one-year contracts agreeing to work 13-hour days, six days a week.

❶ What is this passage mostly about?

Ⓐ how the British protected their factory secrets

Ⓑ how the Lowell mill started and functioned

Ⓒ working conditions in Lowell mills

Ⓓ how many hours Mill Girls worked

❷ How long were the contracts that mill workers signed?

Ⓕ 13 hours

Ⓖ 6 days

Ⓗ 1 year

Ⓘ 13 years

❸ Read the sentence from the passage.

At the time, Britain made it illegal to export machines or machine parts.

What does the word *illegal* mean in this passage?

Ⓐ to be free

Ⓑ to be against the law

Ⓒ to be encouraged

Ⓓ to be expensive to buy

❹ Along what river was the city of Lowell built?

Ⓕ the Massachusetts River

Ⓖ the Waltham River

Ⓗ the Lowell River

Ⓘ the Merrimack River

❺ In what city did Lowell build his first factory?

Ⓐ Lowell

Ⓑ Great Britain

Ⓒ Waltham

Ⓓ Merrimack

❻ Which two words from the passage have the SAME meanings?

Ⓕ factory, workers

Ⓖ cotton, cloth

Ⓗ women, children

Ⓘ wages, pay

❼ What happened in 1813?

Ⓐ Lowell built a textile factory in Waltham.

Ⓑ Lowell died.

Ⓒ Lowell had more than 10,000 workers.

Ⓓ Lowell traveled to Great Britain.

❽ Which of the following was NOT part of the experience for workers in Lowell, Massachusetts?

Ⓕ 13-hour work days

Ⓖ living in houses owned by the mill

Ⓗ exporting British machine parts

Ⓘ six-day work weeks

282

283

Test Preparation

Test-Taking Tips

Share these test-taking tips with your students:
Focus on checking your answers

- Do not leave any questions blank.
- If you do not know the answer:
  - reread the passage.
  - skip the question and come back to it later.
  - make your best guess.
- Check your answer sheet:
  - Erase incorrect answers completely.
  - Fill in the answer bubble completely.
  - Make sure you have not made any stray marks.

Answers

1. B **CCS RI.2**

2. H **CCS RI.1**

3. B **CCS RI.4**

4. I **CCS RI.1**

5. C **CCS RI.1**

6. I **CCS RI.4**

7. A **CCS RI.3**

8. H **CCS RI.1**

UNIT
8 Planner SLAVERY AND EMANCIPATION

 **BIG IDEA** 💡 **Conflict causes change.**

Student Portfolio

- *Show As You Go!*
  Use these pages to introduce the Big Idea. Students record information specific to each lesson. They use these pages to help them plan their Big Idea Project.

netw⊕rks™

- **Group Technology Project**
  Students use 21st century skills to complete a group extension activity of the unit project. Lesson plans, worksheets, and rubrics are available online.

Student Portfolio

- **Big Idea Project**
  Students work with a team to create a museum exhibit about the Civil War. The Big Idea Project Rubric is on page 331W.

Reading Skills

Student Portfolio

- **Reading Skill: Fact and Opinion**
  Pages 286–287. Common Core State Standards RI.4

Leveled Readers

Use the leveled reader *The Gullah: Then and Now* with Lesson 2. Find the lesson plan on pages T32–T33 of your Teacher Edition.

Social Studies Skills

Student Portfolio

- **Primary and Secondary Sources: Charts and Graphs.** Page 291

netw⊕rks™

- **Skill Builders**
  Introduce and teach analyzing primary sources.

Activity Cards

- **Center for Social Studies Skills Investigation**
  Use the center activity cards to help students explore Primary Sources, Geography, and Citizenship.

FOLDABLES®

Student Portfolio

- Students can create vocabulary Foldables right in their portfolios.

- Additional Foldables templates can be found on pages R34–R42 of your Teacher Edition. See page R33 for instructions.

Assessment Solutions

- **McGraw-Hill networks™**
  Safe online testing features multiple question types that are easy to use and editable.

- **Self-Check Quizzes**

- **Worksheets**

UNIT 8 At a Glance

Lesson	Essential Question	Vocabulary	Digital Resources
1 King of Cotton and the Spread of Slavery	How can two areas that belong to the same country grow apart?	slave state free state Missouri Compromise tariff	Go to **connected.mcgraw-hill.com** for additional resources:
2 Heading Toward War	What happens when people cannot agree on an issue?	abolitionist debate treason	• Interactive Whiteboard Lessons
3 The War Begins	What were the North and South willing to fight for?	secede civil war Anaconda Plan draft total war	• Worksheets • Assessment • Content Library
4 The War Rages On	How did the North's goals change?	Emancipation Proclamation Gettysburg Address	• Lesson Plans • Skill Builders
5 The War Ends	Why did the war end?	malice assassination	• Videos • Use Standards Tracker on **networks** to track students' progress.

*denotes academic vocabulary

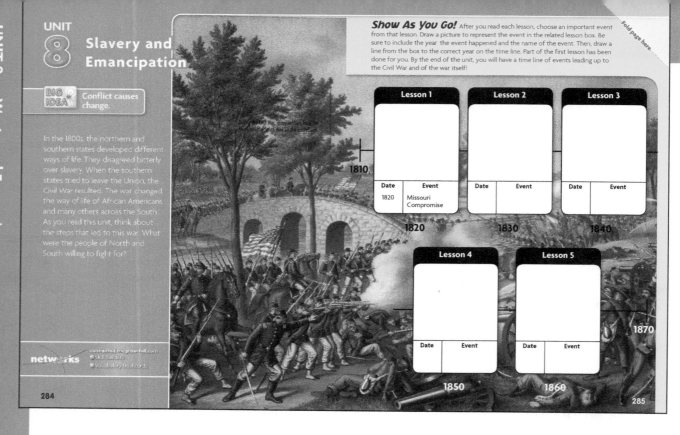

BIG IDEA — Conflict causes change.

In the 1800s, the northern and southern states developed different ways of life. They disagreed bitterly over slavery. When the southern states tried to leave the Union, the Civil War resulted. The war changed the way of life of African Americans and many others across the South. As you read this unit, think about the steps that led to this war. What were the people of North and South willing to fight for?

netw⌂rks
connected.mcgraw-hill.com
• Skill Builders
• Vocabulary Flashcards

284

Show As You Go! After you read each lesson, choose an important event from that lesson. Draw a picture to represent the event in the related lesson box. Be sure to include the year, the event happened and the name of the event. Then, draw a line from the box to the correct year on the time line. Part of the first lesson has been done for you. By the end of the unit, you will have a time line of events leading up to the Civil War and of the war itself!

Fold page here.

Lesson 1

Date	Event
1820	Missouri Compromise

Lesson 2

Date	Event

Lesson 3

Date	Event

1810

1820 · 1830 · 1840

Lesson 4

Date	Event

Lesson 5

Date	Event

1850 · 1860

1870

285

Introduce the Unit

✓ Diagnostic Assessment

Ask: *What do you know about the Civil War in the United States?*

Call on students to answer. As they give their answers, have them think about the following questions:

- Why might the war have started?
- How might the war have begun?
- Where might the war of been fought?

Say: *Imagine you were in a war. What would you be willing to fight for? What would you not be willing to fight for? What challenges might you face? How long will the war last?*

Active Teaching

BIG IDEA — Conflict causes change.
Students will use information from each lesson of this unit to complete the activity on the **Show As You Go!** pages.

Explain that at the end of the unit students will use this time line to help complete the Unit Project. Have students fold back the corner of page 285 to make returning to these pages easier.

Differentiated Instruction

▶ **Approaching** Provide students with a sample time line with other times and events listed on it so they understand how they work. As they review these samples, have them make a time line up of events that have happened in their own lives.

▶ **Beyond** As students complete each lesson, have them add more dates and events to the time line.

▶ **ELL** Review the following time line terms: *date, event,* and *time line*. Discuss these words and how they are important to this activity. Let them ask further questions about these words.

word	word
definition	definition

Reading Skill

Common Core Standards
RI.4 Determine the meaning of general academic and domain-specific words and phrases in a text relevant to a grade 5 topic or subject area.

Fact and Opinion

When people write about events, they often include both facts and opinions. Facts are statements that can be proven true. Opinions state feelings and beliefs. Opinions cannot be proven true or false. Being able to distinguish facts from opinions will help you understand what you read in social studies.

LEARN IT

- Facts can be checked and proven true.
- Opinions are personal views. They cannot be proven true or false.
- Clue words such as *think, felt, believe,* and *it seems* often state opinions.
- Now read the passage below. Look for facts and opinions.

The Underground Railroad

Fact
After traveling 90 miles, she reached the free soil of Pennsylvania.

Opinion
I felt like I was in heaven.

In 1849 Harriet Tubman heard that she and other enslaved workers on her Maryland plantation were to be sold farther south. Tubman believed that life there would be more difficult. She fled from the plantation in the middle of the night. After traveling 90 miles, she reached the free soil of Pennsylvania. She later said, "I felt like I was in heaven."

286

TRY IT

Complete the chart below. Fill in the chart with two facts and two opinions from the paragraph about the Underground Railroad.

Fact	Opinion

How did you figure out which phrases were facts and which were opinions?

_____

_____

APPLY IT

- Read the paragraph below. Complete the chart that lists two facts and opinions from the paragraph.

Ulysses S. Grant was Lincoln's best general and he seemed fearless. Lincoln decided to put Grant in charge of the entire Union army. He hoped Grant would bring the ugly war to an end.

Grant had two major goals. First, he planned to destroy Lee's army in Virginia. After that, he planned to capture Richmond, the capital of the Confederacy.

For 40 days, from April to June 1864, Grant battled Lee again and again across Virginia. Finally, Grant surrounded Lee in Petersburg, and put the city under siege. In the end, Grant captured Richmond. But he wasted the lives of thousands of Union troops. The Confederacy would have fallen without Grant's attacks.

Fact	Opinion

287

Reading Skill

Active Teaching

LEARN IT Fact and Opinion

Have students read the passage.

Ask: *Why is the distance Tubman traveled to Pennsylvania a fact?* (It can be proven true.)

What was Tubman's opinion about reaching freedom? (She "felt like [she] was in heaven.")

TRY IT
Have students fill in the blank sections of the fact and opinion chart on their own. (Fact: Tubman traveled 90 miles when she escaped from slavery; Opinion: She said freedom felt like being in heaven.)

APPLY IT
After students have completed the APPLY IT activity, have students work individually to find one more fact and one more opinion in the paragraph. Then have them explain how they decided which was a fact and which was an opinion. (Possible facts: Tubman escaped in 1849; she was enslaved in Maryland; she escaped in the middle of the night; she fled because she did not want to be sold farther south; Opinion: slaves' lives in the Deep South were harder than in Maryland; Difference between fact and opinion: Facts can be proven true, while opinions are feelings or beliefs that cannot be proven

Differentiated Instruction

▶ **Approaching** Review the LEARN IT activity as a small group. Do the TRY IT activity together. Have students complete the APPLY IT activity independently. Regroup to compare and correct.

▶ **Beyond** Prompt students to come up with at least two separate fact and opinion charts in the APPLY IT activity.

▶ **ELL** Read and summarize the sources together. Lead the students through the TRY IT activity. Regroup to compare and discuss student conclusions. compare and discuss student conclusions.

networks

Go to **connected.mcgraw-hill.com** for additional resources:
- Skill Builders
- Graphic Organizers

Words to Know

Common Core Standards
RI.4 Determine the meaning of general academic and domain-specific words and phrases in a text relevant to a grade 5 topic or subject area.

The list below shows some important words you will learn in this unit. Their definitions can be found on the next page. Read the words.

Missouri Compromise (muh • ZUHR • ee KOM • preh • meyz)

abolitionist (ab • uh • LISH • uh • nist)

secede (sih • SEED)

civil war (SIV • uhl wawr)

draft (DRAFT)

Emancipation Proclamation (ee • man • sih • PAY • shuhn prok • luh • MAY • shuhn)

Gettysburg Address (GET • iz • burg uh • DRES)

assassination (uh • sas • uh • NAY • shuhn)

FOLDABLES

The Foldable on the next page will help you learn these important words. Follow the steps below to make your Foldable.

Step 1 — Fold along the solid red line.

Step 2 — Cut along the dotted lines.

Step 3 — Read the words and their definitions.

Step 4 — Complete the activities on each tab.

Step 5 — Look at the back of your Foldable. Choose ONE of these activities for each word to help you remember its meaning:
- Draw a picture of the word.
- Write a description of the word.
- Write how the word is related to something you know.

The Battle of Shiloh convinced North and South that the Civil War would be long and difficult.

288

Definition	Activity
The **Missouri Compromise** was an agreement in 1820 that allowed Missouri and Maine to enter the Union and divided the Louisiana Territory into areas allowing slavery and areas outlawing slavery.	What does a *compromise* aim to achieve?
An **abolitionist** was a person who wanted to end slavery in the United States.	Circle two key words in the definition of *abolitionist*. Write the words here: _____ _____
To **secede** is to withdraw from the Union.	Write an antonym for the word *secede*.
A **civil war** is an armed conflict between groups within one country. In the United States, it was the war between the Union and the Confederacy from 1861 to 1865.	Write a sentence using the term *civil war*.
A **draft** is the selecting of persons for military service or some other special duty.	Why would people be selected for military service?
The **Emancipation Proclamation** was an official announcement issued by President Abraham Lincoln in 1862 that led to the end of slavery in the United States.	What other term is related to this term? Write the word here:
The **Gettysburg Address** was a speech made by President Abraham Lincoln at the site of the Battle of Gettysburg in 1863.	What is another word for the word *address* as used in this term?
Assassination is the murder of an important person.	Write a synonym for the word *assassination*.

Common Core Standards RI.4 Determine the meaning of general academic and domain-specific words and phrases in a text relevant to a grade 4 topic or subject area.

Words to Know

Active Teaching

FOLDABLES Have students use the Foldable on these pages to gain a deeper understanding of the vocabulary in this unit.

1. Go to connected.mcgraw-hill.com for flashcards to introduce the unit vocabulary to students.

2. Read the words on the list on page and have students repeat them after you.

3. Guide students as they complete steps 1–5 of the Foldable.

4. Have students use the Foldable to practice the vocabulary words independently or with a partner.

networks

Additional resources are found at **connected.mcgraw-hill.com**.
- Vocabulary Flashcards
- Vocabulary Games
- Graphic Organizers

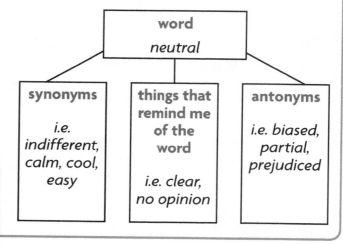

GO Vocabulary!

Use the concept map graphic organizer below to help students gain a deeper understanding of the academic vocabulary.

word
neutral

synonyms
i.e. indifferent, calm, cool, easy

things that remind me of the word
i.e. clear, no opinion

antonyms
i.e. biased, partial, prejudiced

Missouri Compromise	Missouri Compromise
abolitionist	abolitionist
secede	secede
civil war	civil war
draft	draft
Emancipation Proclamation	Emancipation Proclamation
Gettysburg Address	Gettysburg Address
assassination	assassination

Primary and Secondary Sources

Charts and Graphs

Charts arrange information in rows and columns so that data can be compared easily. Graphs use visuals to display information that can be given in the form of numbers. Sometimes charts and graphs are used together to give different information about the same subject. When that is done, you can use the information in both to draw conclusions about that subject.

In this unit, you'll learn about the Civil War fought between the North and the South. Both sides expected to win the war.

DBQ Document-Based Questions

The chart and graph shown here help you compare the North and the South. Then answer the questions below.

1. Why did the North have more troops?

_____

_____

2. Why was iron an important resource?

_____

_____

3. Based on the chart and graph, which side do you think had a better chance to win the war? Why?

_____

_____

Human Resources, Civil War

	Troops	Population
Union States	2,000,000	23,000,000
Confederate States	800,000	9,000,000

Economic Resources, Civil War

■ Union States
■ Confederate States

networks
There's More Online!
• Skill Builders
• Vocabulary Flashcards

291

Primary Sources

Differentiated Instruction

▶ **ELL** Use the word web graphic organizer below to help students gain a deeper understanding of the vocabulary. Write the vocabulary word in the center and related words in the other ovals.

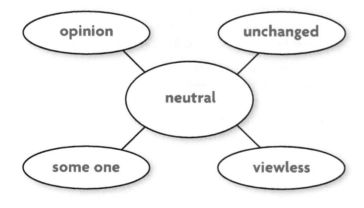

Active Teaching

Begin by discussing that graphics allow people to see patterns in statistical information at a glance.

Ask: *Why is the table of human resources easier to read than a paragraph?* (Students may point out that the graph shows only the numbers and that is easy to see their relationship.) **L2**

Explain that there are many types of chart and graphs. The bar graph here shows the relationship between information, like the North and the South. The chart compares the human resources used by both the North and the South during the war.

Develop Comprehension

1. *What conclusion can you draw by looking at the economic resources graph?* (The North had far more resources.). **L3**
2. *Which resource did the Union States have less of?* (grain production). **L3**

WORD PLAY

1. Have students place vocabulary words on a 3 x 3 grid.
2. Define the words one at a time. Do not say the words.
3. As students recognize a definition, they should mark or cover it on their card.
4. The first to get a Bingo wins the round.

networks

Additional resources are found at **connected.mcgraw-hill.com**.

• Vocabulary Flashcards   • Vocabulary Games

Lesson 1 King Cotton and the Spread of Slavery

? Essential Question

How can two areas that belong to the same country grow apart?

_____

_____

_____

_____

_____

Have you ever had a disagreement with someone you were close to? How did you settle the issue?

_____

_____

_____

_____

_____

The hot climate and moist soil of the South were perfect for growing cotton. In the 1800s it became the most important cash crop in the South. By the 1830s, Southerners called this crop "King Cotton."

Plantation owners used enslaved Africans to work in cotton fields. Many owners grew wealthy from selling cotton harvested by enslaved workers. It was sold mainly to Great Britain, where factories made the cotton into cloth.

Cotton plants weakened the soil. Planters needed more land, so they moved west. Cotton fields spread across Tennessee, Alabama, Mississippi, and, eventually, across the Mississippi River to Arkansas and Texas.

Circle the reason that plantation owners planted cotton.

Words To Know

Pick the symbol that shows how much you know about the meaning of each word below. Draw the symbol next to the word.

? = I have no idea!
▲ = I know a little.
♆ = I know a lot.

____ slave state

____ free state

____ Missouri Compromise

____ tariff

▼ The cotton gin removed the seeds from cotton bolls.

Cotton Rules the South

Enslaved Population Grows

The growth of cotton as a cash crop and the movement to the west created a need for more enslaved workers. In 1806 Congress passed a law that said no enslaved people could be brought into the United States after 1808. This law did not bring an end to slavery. The population of enslaved people continued to grow because the children of enslaved people were also enslaved. In addition, planters often brought enslaved people into the country from Caribbean islands illegally.

Southern Economy

The economy of the South was built on the labor of these enslaved workers. The wealthiest Southerners owned large areas of land and held hundreds of enslaved workers. Most Southern farmers planted crops on small pieces of land. They did not have enslaved workers. Even so, both plantation owners and owners of small farms depended on cotton.

Farmers grew food for the plantations, repaired roads, and built wagons. When the cotton was harvested, some farmers earned money transporting crops to Southern ports by wagon.

▼ Cotton was the most important cash crop in the Southern economy during the 1800s.

Reading Skill

Fact and Opinion

What is a fact about cotton?

_____

_____

292   293

Lesson 1

Activate Prior Knowledge

After students have thought about the question alone about a disagreement, ask for volunteers to share what they wrote with the class.

Ask: *How do you think disagreements are best solved? What if they are between entire countries?*

? Essential Question How can two areas that belong to the same country grow apart?

Have students explain what they understand about the Essential Question. Discuss their responses. Explain that everything they learn in this lesson will help them understand the Essential Question better. Remind them to think about how the Essential Question connects to the unit Big Idea: Conflict causes change.

Reading Skill

Common Core Standards RI.4 Determine the meaning of general academic and domain-specific words and phrases in a text relevant to a grade 4 topic or subject area.

Fact and Opinion After students have answered the question about cotton, have them underline more facts they find within this lesson. Have them discuss why they are facts.

Ask: *How do you think our world would be today without the introduction of cotton?*

Active Teaching

Words To Know Once students have completed the activity, have them find the words in the lesson and read their definitions. Then, present the students with a list of three to five words or phrases related to each vocabulary word. Have students identify the word or phrase that does not fit with the rest of the group and explain their choice.

Develop Comprehension

The content that is ***boldfaced and italicized*** throughout the lesson is told in first person form the point of view of historical figures. Students may need to be reminded of what it means to read a first-person **point-of-view**.

Ask:

1. *What are the advantages and disadvantages of a compromise?* **L2**

Political Balance

As you read in unit 7, in 1819 Missouri applied to be admitted to the Union as a slave state. At the time, the nation had 11 slave states and 11 free states. Northern states wanted to keep the political balance in Congress. Letting Missouri enter the Union as a slave state would upset the balance in Congress. Slave states would have more votes in the Senate than free states.

Both sides argued over Missouri for a year. Finally, Senator Henry Clay of Kentucky suggested the Missouri Compromise. Under this plan, Missouri was admitted as a slave state. Maine, which had been part of Massachusetts, became a separate, free state. The compromise stated that, in the future, slavery would not be allowed in any new states north of Missouri's southern border.

Map and Globe Skills

1. Circle the state of South Carolina. What kind of state was it?

2. Which states made up a larger area of the United States— slave states or free states?

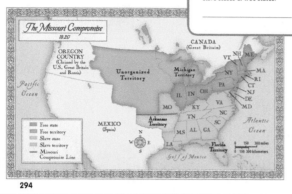

The Missouri Compromise 1820

Free state
Free territory
Slave state
Slave territory
Missouri Compromise Line

Economic Differences

Slavery was not the only issue that divided the North and South. The regions had important economic differences. Cotton was "king" in the South. Even people who did not grow cotton worked in some way to help bring it to market.

Unlike the South, the Northern economy was based on industry. These industries did not use enslaved workers. This led states in the North to outlaw slavery. In 1777 Vermont became the first state to outlaw slavery. Then, in 1804, New Jersey became the last Northern state to outlaw slavery.

In the North, men, women, and even children worked in factories making cloth, iron tools, rope, and other products. These factories were small compared to those of Great Britain. Also, British factories used new technology to make many of the same products more cheaply. This meant that they could sell their products to Americans at prices lower than those charged by U.S. manufacturers.

Lower prices made it difficult for the smaller, American factories to compete with British factories. American businesses that could not sell their products, which were more costly, failed. As a result, business owners asked Congress to pass tariffs, or special taxes on goods coming into the United States. Tariffs raised the prices of foreign-made products and helped American industries. In 1828 Congress passed tariffs on British goods, which pleased Northern business owners.

1. Put a box around the sentence that explains why American business owners wanted tariffs.
2. Circle around the phrase that shows their opinion when the tariff was passed.

294

295

Active Teaching

Tell students that the map on the page shows the balance of power between Northern and Southern states in 1820.

Develop Comprehension
Ask:

1. *How did the Missouri Compromise keep the balance between slave and free states?* (Missouri was admitted as a slave state and Maine as a free state, keeping the number of slave and free states equal.) **L2**

2. *What issues led to tension between the North and the South?* (Possible answers include slavery, tariffs, and states' rights.) **L2**

More about Southerners Some Southerners claimed that "robber barons" treated factory workers worse than enslaved people on a plantation. Some Northerners though that the Southern "slave power" was anti-democratic and stuck in the past.

Map and Globe Skills

Have students study the map.
Ask:

1. *What does being an "Unorganized Territory" mean?*
2. *Draw a line where slavery would not be allowed any more due to the Missouri Compromise.*

networks

Go to **connected.mcgraw-hill.com** for additional resources:
- Interactive Whiteboard Lessons
- Worksheets
- Assessment

Tariffs Divide States

The new tariffs angered people in the South. Owners of small farms complained that tariffs raised the prices of imports, or goods brought into the country. In fact, imported goods often cost more anyway. The tariffs also angered plantation owners. High tariffs meant that British manufacturers sold fewer goods in the United States. Fewer sales meant that Great Britain had less money to buy cotton. This hurt Southern exports, or goods shipped out of the country.

Speaking Out Against Congress

Southerners believed the tariffs threatened their way of life. Senator John C. Calhoun of South Carolina spoke out against the tariffs. He claimed that Congress was trying to destroy the Southern economy. He said that Congress was using tariffs to force the South to end the use of enslaved workers.

Calhoun said that the Constitution gave states the right to ignore the laws passed by Congress if those laws hurt the state. Many Americans, including President Andrew Jackson, strongly disagreed with Calhoun. They thought that allowing states to decide which federal laws to obey could destroy the Union.

Jackson sent U.S. forces to South Carolina to enforce the tariffs. This use of federal troops caused even greater anger in the South. It would eventually be one cause of the bloodiest war in United States history.

▲ Senator John C. Calhoun of South Carolina

Reading Skill

Fact and Opinion

Why did John C. Calhoun speak out against tariffs?

_____

_____

Complete the chart to compare the North and South.

	North	South
Basis of economy		
View on slavery		
View of tariffs		

Lesson 1

? Essential Question How can two areas that belong to the same country grow apart?

_____

_____

_____

Go back to *Show As You Go!* on pages 284–285! «

 networks There's More Online!
• Games • Assessment

Lesson 1

Active Teaching

Explain that tariffs increased tension between the North and the South. Ask students what they think would have happened if people had accepted Calhoun's idea that states could ignore federal laws. What effect might this have had?

Develop Comprehension

Ask:

1. *Why did the new tariffs anger the people in the South?* (They raised the price of imports.) **L2**

2. *What did the high tariffs mean?* (They meant that British manufacturers sold fewer goods in the U.S.) **L2**

3. *What was one cause of the war?* (Jackson sending U.S. forces to South Carolina to enforce the tariffs.) **L2**

« *Show As You Go!* Remind students to return and record information they learned from this lesson.

Differentiated Instruction

▶ **Approaching** As a group, list the differences from the chart. Have students find answers to these differences by rereading the lesson. Ask: What was the North's economy like? What was their view on slavery? What was their view on tariffs? Then ask the same questions about the South.

▶ **Beyond** Have students research why Henry Clay was called the "Great Compromise".

▶ **ELL** Ask students what the difference in view might be between the North and the South. Write their answers in front of the class.

Response to Intervention

? Essential Question How can two areas that belong to the same country grow apart?

If . . . students cannot identify how two areas can grow apart,
. . . .

Then . . . take students back to pages 292–297. Discuss why the tariffs were so high and how this angered people in the South.

Ask: *How do you know when you have angered somebody?*

Following the discussion, allow students to respond to the Essential Question again.

Lesson 2 — Heading Toward War

? Essential Question

What happens when people cannot agree on an issue?

What do you think?

_____

_____

_____

_____

What happens when two people disagree on an issue and that issue keeps coming up again and again? What effect does that have on how they feel about each other? What effect does it have on their ability to settle the issue? Write your responses below.

_____

_____

_____

_____

_____

_____

Words To Know

Pick the symbol that shows how much you know about the meaning of each word below. Draw the symbol next to the word.

? = I have no idea!
▲ = I know a little.
★ = I know a lot.

____ abolitionist

____ debate

____ treason

Between 1820 and 1860, no issue divided the United States more than slavery. Some people said slavery was morally wrong. Others claimed it was necessary to preserve their way of life.

▲ Harriet Beecher Stowe, author of *Uncle Tom's Cabin*

▲ Sarah Moore Grimké

▲ Angelina Emily Grimké

The Fight over Slavery

By the 1830s, many Americans wanted to abolish, or end, slavery. These people were called **abolitionists.**

Among the abolitionists were two sisters who grew up in South Carolina—Angelina and Sarah Grimké. Angelina said the abolition of slavery was

"a cause worth dying for."

One abolitionist leader was William Lloyd Garrison of Massachusetts. In 1831 he founded *The Liberator*, an abolitionist newspaper. In 1833 Garrison founded the American Anti-Slavery Society.

Another well-known person who spoke out against slavery was Frederick Douglass. He was born into slavery. After escaping Douglass gave speeches about his early life. He also published an anti-slavery newspaper, *The North Star.*

In 1852 Harriet Beecher Stowe wrote *Uncle Tom's Cabin.* Her novel described a cruel slaveholder's treatment of enslaved people. This book turned many people against slavery.

Frederick Douglass

Reading Skill

Fact and Opinion

Was Angelina Grimké's statement a fact or an opinion? Why do you think so?

_____

_____

298

299

Lesson 2 —————————➤

Activate Prior Knowledge

After students have completed the activity, ask students if they have ever disagreed on something with someone that keeps coming up again and again. Remind them that the Lincoln believed that the United States could only survive by deciding whether slavery was legal or not.

Say: *Much like a disagreement among friends or family, countries or states can sometimes come into conflict again.* Explain that in this lesson, students will see how the issue of slavery affected the United States.

? Essential Question What happens when people cannot agree on an issue?

Have students explain what they understand about the Essential Question. Discuss their responses. Explain that everything they learn in this lesson will help them understand the Essential Question better. Remind them to think about how the Essential Question connects to the unit Big Idea: Conflict causes change.

Reading Skill ——————————

Common Core Standards RI.4 Determine the meaning of general academic and domain-specific words and phrases in a text relevant to a grade 4 topic or subject area.

Fact and Opinion After students answer the question in the Reading Skill box, have them discuss why they thought the statement was a fact or opinion.

Ask: *What do you think might happen to slavery if everyone believed this was a fact?*

Active Teaching ——————

Words To Know After students have completed the Words To Know activity, have them locate each word in the text and read its definition. Then have students divide up into groups and use each word in a sentence.

Develop Comprehension
Ask:

1. *What are some examples of issues on which compromise is possible?* **L2**

2. *Why was compromise not a good solution to the issue of slavery?* **L2**

net works

Go to **connected.mcgraw-hill.com** for additional resources:

• Interactive Whiteboard Lessons
• Worksheets
• Assessment

A Route to Freedom

In the 1830s, enslaved people, free African Americans, and white abolitionists started the Underground Railroad. This was a secret network of trails, river crossings, and hiding places which helped people escape slavery. Many railroad terms had double meanings on this network. Enslaved people who decided to escape were called *passengers*. *Conductors* helped enslaved people escape. The houses where passengers could eat and rest were called *stations*.

Jermain Loguen was one of the many sucessful conductors on the Underground Railroad. He had escaped from slavery and wanted to help other people gain their freedom. His home in Syracuse, New York, became a well-known station. Harriet Tubman, who had escaped slavery herself, was a famous conductor who led many others North to freedom.

> Circle around the word that explains why this network was called the *Underground* Railroad.

▼ Many people who escaped slavery headed North on the Underground Railroad.

Compromise Leads to Violence

Congress tried to settle the slavery issue with compromises. As new territories applied to enter the Union, however, slavery continued to divide lawmakers and the American people.

Compromise of 1850

The U.S. victory in the 1846–1848 war with Mexico brought large areas of land under U.S. control. In 1849 California applied to join the nation as a free state. This would change the balance of 15 free and 15 slave states.

As in 1820, neither side wanted the other to gain control in the Senate. Southern lawmakers refused to admit California. In the end, Congress agreed to the Compromise of 1850. This allowed California to enter the Union. In return, Congress passed the Fugitive Slave Law. This law forced Americans to return escaped enslaved people to the person who had held them, or go to jail. Many Northerners were angered by this law.

▼ The Compromise of 1850 included several parts. Put a check mark in the column showing which side, North or South, you think gained from key parts of the agreement. If you think neither side won, put the check mark in the last column.

Action	Which Side Gained?		
	North	South	Neither
California is admitted as a free state.			
New law makes it easier to catch slaves who escape to North.			
The sale of slaves will no longer take place in Washington, D.C.			
New Mexico and Utah will be free or slave depending on what their people want.			

300

301

Lesson 2

Active Teaching

Have students imagine what it would be like to be a part of the Underground Railroad, either as a passenger or a conductor. Why were both jobs important to the operation? Why did they choose which person they wanted to be? Share with the class. Tell students to write a message using Underground Railroad code words. Message might refer to the Drinking Gourd (North Star); Promised Land (Canada); stockholders (people who donated money); or parcels (escapees). Have students exchange papers and decode their partner's message.

Develop Comprehension

Ask:

1. *What was the Underground Railroad?* (A secret network of trails, river crossings, and hiding places which helped people escape slavery.) **L1**

2. *What was the difference between passengers and conductors in the Underground Railroad?* (Passengers were the enslaved people and Conductors helped them escape.) **L2**

3. *How did the Fugitive Slave Law help California become a state in the Union?* (California wanted to be a free state and this was its way of allowing it to be.) **L3**

4. *In which direction did people escape slavery?* (From the South to the North.) **L2**

More About Frederick Douglass As a child, Douglass overheard his slaveholder tell his wife not to teach him to read because literate enslaved people became unmanageable. "At that moment," he wrote in his autobiography, "I understood the path from slavery to freedom."

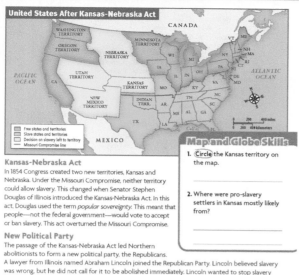

United States After Kansas-Nebraska Act

Free states and territories
Slave states and territories
Decision on slavery left to territory
Missouri Compromise line

Kansas-Nebraska Act

In 1854 Congress created two new territories, Kansas and Nebraska. Under the Missouri Compromise, neither territory could allow slavery. This changed when Senator Stephen Douglas of Illinois introduced the Kansas-Nebraska Act. In this act, Douglas used the term *popular sovereignty*. This meant that people—not the federal government—would vote to accept or ban slavery. This act overturned the Missouri Compromise.

New Political Party

The passage of the Kansas-Nebraska Act led Northern abolitionists to form a new political party, the Republicans. A lawyer from Illinois named Abraham Lincoln joined the Republican Party. Lincoln believed slavery was wrong, but he did not call for it to be abolished immediately. Lincoln wanted to stop slavery from spreading to new states.

Map and Globe Skills

1. Circle the Kansas territory on the map.

_____

2. Where were pro-slavery settlers in Kansas mostly likely from?

_____

_____

Reading Skill

Fact and Opinion

What opinion did abolitionists have about the Kansas-Nebraska Act?

_____

_____

"Bleeding Kansas"

After the passage of the Kansas-Nebraska Act, many Southerners moved to Kansas. They came to vote under popular sovereignty. Northern abolitionists also responded by moving to Kansas. Suddenly, armed settlers supporting both sides of the issue flooded the area.

Violence broke out in 1856 when settlers who favored slavery burned the town of Lawrence, Kansas, which did not allow slavery, to the ground. A few days later, abolitionist John Brown and his sons killed five Southerners. Newspapers began to describe the territory as "Bleeding Kansas." The violence in Kansas did not become all-out war, but it was a preview of events to come.

This image shows the first fighting that broke out in "Bleeding Kansas." Write a caption for the image.

_____

_____

_____

302

303

Active Teaching

Have students use the information from the pages to complete a caption for the image. Allow them to reread the text in order to complete this task.

Develop Comprehension

Ask:

1. *What did Stephen Douglas mean by "popular sovereignty?"* (The people of Kansas and Nebraska could decide whether their state was slave or free.) **L2**

2. *What effect did the passage of the Kansas-Nebraska Bill have on Kansas?* (Pro- and anti- slavery settlers began moving to the state; after their conflict erupted into violence, the territory became known as "Bleeding Kansas.") **L3**

3. *What was the new political party formed from the passage of the Kansas-Nebraska Act?* (Republican Party) **L1**

Map and Globe Skills

Ask:

1. *How may free states were there after the Kansas-Nebraska Act?* (19) **L1**

2. *How many states had "free choice" on whether they were a free state or slave state?* (4) **L2**

Differentiated Instruction

▶ **Approaching** Have students work with a partner to write the definitions of the Kansas-Nebraska Act and "Bleeding Kansas".

▶ **Beyond** Challenge students to find out more about how Northerners resisted the Fugitive Slave Law.

▶ **ELL** Work with students to make a word web of words related to *fugitive*.

networks

Go to **connected.mcgraw-hill.com** for additional resources:
- Interactive Whiteboard Lessons
- Worksheets
- Assessment

A Nation Divided

By 1857 the United States was close to breaking apart. Many Americans wondered whether the country could survive half slave and half free.

In 1857 a case about the rights of enslaved people came before the United States Supreme Court. It was the case of *Dred Scott v. Sandford.* Dred Scott was an enslaved person bought by a doctor in Missouri, a slave state. The doctor moved his household to Illinois, a free state, and then to the Wisconsin Territory, where slavery was banned by the Northwest Ordinance of 1787.

Years later, the doctor and his household returned to Missouri. When the doctor died, Scott said he was a free man because he had lived on free soil. Eleven years later, the Supreme Court refused to free Scott. Chief Justice Roger Taney wrote that enslaved people could be

> "bought and sold, and treated as an ordinary article of merchandise."

The court's decision meant that enslaved workers could be taken anywhere, even free states, and remain enslaved.

In 1857 most Northerners didn't want to abolish slavery in the South. They just did not want slavery in new territories. This issue would soon become important in a political campaign.

▲ Dred Scott

What were the issues dividing the country after the *Dred Scott* decision?

_____

_____

_____

What could leaders do to settle the disagreement between North and South?

_____

_____

_____

Lincoln Against Douglas

In 1858 two candidates from the Senate from Illinois attracted national attention. Abraham Lincoln, a Republican, ran against Stephen Douglas, a Democrat, for the Senate. Compared to the popular Douglas, Lincoln was unknown.

The two candidates held seven **debates**, or public discussions, on political issues. The three-hour debates drew crowds as large as 15,000 people. The candidates argued over many issues, but the issue of slavery drew the most attention.

Although Douglas disliked slavery, he refused to speak out against it. He believed popular sovereignty was the way to resolve the disagreement over slavery. Douglas tried to paint Lincoln as a reckless abolitionist.

Lincoln believed that slavery was wrong for a nation founded on freedom. In a speech during the campaign, Lincoln said,

> "This government cannot endure permanently half slave and half free."

Lincoln received more votes than Douglas in the election. At that time, state legislatures chose Senators for the state. The Democrats held more seats in the Illinois legislature, and they picked Douglas, a Democrat. In the end, the campaign helped Lincoln. Republicans from the North and the Midwest agreed that he would be a good presidential candidate.

Reading Skills

Fact and Opinion

1. Write one fact about the Lincoln-Douglas campaign.

_____

_____

2. Write one opinion about that campaign.

_____

_____

Lesson 2

Active Teaching

Tell students that the illustrations show three people who influenced the debate over slavery. Ask them what they think the quotation in bold type means. Have students use the information on the pages to complete the questions.

Develop Comprehension
Ask:

1. *Who was Dred Scott?* (He was an enslaved person who sued to win his freedom and lost.) **L1**

2. *Why did the Dred Scott decision anger Northerners?* (The Supreme Court said enslaved people were property and could be taken into free states.) **L2**

3. *Why didn't Stephen Douglas take a stand against slavery?* (He was afraid that Southerners would not vote for him.) **L2**

4. *How did debating Douglas help Lincoln?* (Even though Lincoln lost the election, people thought he should run for president.) **L3**

Reading Skill

 Common Core Standards RI.4 Determine the meaning of general academic and domain-specific words and phrases in a text relevant to a grade 4 topic or subject area.

Fact and Opinion After students write one fact and one opinion about the Lincoln-Douglas campaign, have students write a paragraph comparing Lincoln's beliefs about slavery with Douglas's beliefs.

More About the Dred Scott Decision Chief Justice Taney's decision might have been influenced by his anger at Northern abolitionists. He had freed his own enslaved workers and decided in favor of the captives who rebelled on the Amistad. However, he hoped a ruling against Dred Scott would end the controversy over slavery. Instead, it angered Northerners and is considered by some to be the worst Supreme Court decision ever.

At the Edge of War

By 1859, many Americans feared that war would soon tear the nation apart. There seemed to be no way to avoid violence.

For John Brown, there was no compromise on slavery. The fierce abolitionist had been a conductor on the Underground Railroad in New York. He was also involved in the violent events in "Bleeding Kansas." In 1859 Brown tried to start a revolt among enslaved people. He planned to attack an army arsenal in Harpers Ferry, Virginia. Brown then planned to give the weapons to enslaved people who he believed would rise up against plantation owners. On October 16, Brown and a small force captured the arsenal. Enslaved people nearby did not join him or revolt against the slaveholders. Two days later, U.S. soldiers, commanded by Colonel Robert E. Lee, recaptured the arsenal. Brown was convicted of **treason**, or betraying one's country, and hanged. His raid struck fear across the South.

Two Views

1. How would southerners react to John Brown's raid? Why?

_____

_____

_____

2. How would northerners react to John Brown's raid? Why?

_____

_____

_____

Slave and Free States by 1860

Free state
Slave state

Map and Globe Skills

1. Circle the slave states that shared a border with free states.

2. Write a number to finish this sentence:
   In 1860 the United States had _____ slave states.

Lesson 2

? **Essential Question** What happens when people cannot agree on an issue?

_____

_____

_____

Go back to *Show As You Go!* on pages 284–285!

networks
There's More Online!
• Assessments • Games

Active Teaching

Have students use the information on the pages in order to answer the questions on the pages. Allow them to flip back and forth in their work text as they complete the activities.

Develop Comprehension
Ask:

1. *What did John Brown hope to accomplish by raiding Harpers Ferry?* (He wanted to start a revolt of enslaved people.) **L2**

2. *What were the effects of John Brown's raid?* (Students might note that the raid failed and Brown was executed, but Southerners feared more attacks might come.) **L2**

> *Show As You Go!* Remind students to return and record information they learned from this lesson.

Map and Globe Skills

Explain that the United States Congress tried to keep a balance of free and slave states. That balance continued until 1858. Have students count the number of free states by 1860 (17). Explain that many Southern states were upset that the balance had shifted to the North and that they had less power in the U.S. Congress.

Response to Intervention

? **Essential Question** What happens when people cannot agree on an issue?

If . . . students cannot explain what happens when people cannot agree,

....

Then . . . refer students back to pages 298-307 to review the causes of the friction between the North and the South. Have students work in small groups to discuss what is important to them and what they would be willing to fight for.

Following the discussion, allow students to respond to the Essential Question again.

Lesson 3 — The War Begins

networks There's More Online! Content Library Videos

Essential Question
What were the North and South willing to fight for?

What did the people of the North and of the South want in 1860?

_____

_____

_____

_____

_____

Words To Know

Pick the symbol that shows how much you know about the meaning of each word below. Draw the symbol next to the word.

? = I have no idea!
▲ = I know a little.
★ = I know a lot.

_____ secede

_____ civil war

_____ Anaconda Plan

_____ draft

_____ total war

308

The Election of 1860

In the presidential election of 1860, Abraham Lincoln ran as the Republican candidate. Stephen Douglas ran as a Democrat. Two other candidates also joined the race. Only Lincoln took a stand against slavery in the new territories. Southern lawmakers warned that if Lincoln won, they would **secede**, or withdraw, from the Union.

In November 1860, Lincoln was elected. In December South Carolina seceded from the Union. By February six more states had seceded. They established the Confederate States of America, also called the Confederacy. Mississippi Senator Jefferson Davis did not agree with secession but he accepted his state's decision to secede. In 1861 he became president of the Confederacy.

▲ Jefferson Davis was the Senator of Mississippi.

First Shots Fired

In the spring of 1861, Confederate troops seized several U.S. Army arsenals in the South. Fort Sumter, an island arsenal in the harbor of Charleston, South Carolina, refused to surrender. The commander asked the federal government for more supplies and weapons. Before supplies could arrive, Confederate guns fired on the fort on April 12, 1861. The Civil War had begun. A civil war is a war among people who live in the same country.

In the beginning, leaders in both the North and South thought the **Civil War** would last about two months. Some soldiers even feared the war would be over before they had a chance to fight.

The First Battle of Bull Run

The first major battle of the Civil War was fought on July 21, 1861. It took place at a stream called Bull Run, near the town of Manassas, Virginia. Manassas is located between Washington, D.C., and Richmond, Virginia. Richmond was the capital of the Confederacy. That day, sightseers followed the Union troops. Many expected to watch a rapid Union victory. They hoped Richmond would then fall quickly. What they saw instead was bloodshed and death.

For hours, Union soldiers attacked the line of Confederate soldiers but could not break through.

With the battlefield littered with bloody bodies, fresh Southern troops arrived by railroad. Soon, Northern troops retreated in panic. Frightened soldiers and panicked sightseers fled to Washington, D.C. The South had won the first major battle of the war.

Reading Skill
Fact and Opinion
What opinion did leaders on both sides share at the beginning of the war?

_____

_____

_____

▼ The Civil War began with an attack by Confederate artillery on Fort Sumter in Charleston, South Carolina, on April 12, 1861.

309

Lesson 3

Activate Prior Knowledge

After students have completed the activity, have students make predictions on what this lesson might be about by the title "The War Begins." Remind students that the North called the conflict the _War of the Rebellion_, while the South called it the _War Between the States_ and the _War for Southern Independence_.

? Essential Question What were the North and South willing to fight for?

Have students explain what they understand about the Essential Question. Discuss their responses. Explain that everything they learn in this lesson will help them understand the Essential Question better. Remind them to think about how the Essential Question connects to the unit Big Idea: Conflict causes change.

More about Stonewall Jackson
Stonewall Jackson proved himself a master of tactics at many battles. After he was accidently shot by his own sentries, General Lee said, "He has lost his left arm; I have lost my right." Jackson's death from his wounds weakened the South's morale and ability to fight.

Active Teaching

Words To Know After students have completed the Words To Know activity, have them write what they think the definition of each word is on another sheet of paper. Then, have students look up the definition in the glossary and write it beneath their definition. Have students attach their word list to their work text for safe keeping.

Develop Comprehension

Ask:

1. _Why was Lincoln's election a step toward war?_ (His opposition to expanding slavery prompted seven Southern states to secede.) **L2**

2. _How do you think people felt when they realized the war would not be over quickly?_ **L2**

3. _If you had lived near Manassas in 1861, how would you have felt before the fighting started?_ **L2**

Strengths and Weaknesses

Many Southerners believed they would win the war because they had a stronger military tradition than the North. Southern generals had more experience. Confederate soldiers had grown up riding horses and hunting. Large numbers of Southerners volunteered to fight. They were eager to protect their homes and way of life.

Northerners were also brave fighters, but many lived in cities where the military tradition was not as strong as it was in the South. Even so, Northerners believed they would win simply because they had more people, industry, and money than the South.

THE CONFEDERACY

STRENGTHS	WEAKNESSES
• It planned a defensive war, which is easier for the military to win.	• It had less than half the population of the North, and one-third were enslaved people.
• A third of the nation's officers joined the Confederate Army, including Robert E. Lee, the most respected general in the army.	• The South had less money to support the war effort than the North.
• It had a strong military tradition, with 7 of the nation's 8 military schools located in the South.	• The South had only one factory producing cannons and no major factory for making gunpowder.
• Southerners were more skilled in shooting, hunting, and riding.	• The South had half as many miles of railroad track as the North, making it difficult to get food, weapons, and other supplies to troops.
• Soldiers began preparing for war before the attack on Fort Sumter.	

1. What do you think was the greatest strength of the South? Why?

_____

_____

2. What do you think was the biggest weakness of the South? Why?

_____

_____

THE UNION

STRENGTHS	WEAKNESSES
• In 1861 the North had more than twice the population of the South.	• Union troops fought mostly in Southern areas, where people were defending their homes.
• More than three-quarters of U.S. Navy officers came from the North, and 90 percent of the navy stayed with the North.	• Long supply lines made it difficult for Union troops to move quickly.
• About 80 percent of U.S. factories were in the North.	• Many Northern soldiers came from areas where there was little military tradition.
• The majority of railroads were in the North.	• Most Union soldiers had little military training.
• Almost all firearms were manufactured in the North.	• Union armies would have to take control of most of the South in order to bring it back into the Union.
• Northern farms grew more food than Southern farms.	

1. What do you think was the greatest strength of the North? Why?

_____

_____

2. What do you think was the biggest weakness of the North? Why?

_____

_____

310 311

Active Teaching

Point out the different organization of text on these pages. Ask them how the organization helps them compare the armies of the North and South.

Develop Comprehension
Ask:

1. *Why did the North think their side would win?* (Although the South had a strong military tradition, the North had more resources.) **L2**

2. *Why did the South think their side would win?* (They had a strong military background.) **L2**

3. *How evenly matched were the two sides at the beginning of the war?* (Students may say that each side had advantages that could prove decisive, including the South's fighting on home soil and the North's greater resources.) **L3**

Reading Skill

 Common Core Standards RI.5 Compare and contrast the overall structure (e.g. chronology, comparison, cause/effect, problem/solution) of events, ideas, concepts, or information in two or more texts.

Compare and Contrast Remind students that when they compare and contrast something they look at both similarities and differences. Students will compare and contrast the strengths and weaknesses of the Union (the North) and the Confederacy (the South).

More About "Johnny Reb" The slang term for a Confederate soldier was "Johnny Reb" (short for rebel). Southern soldiers usually fought in groups of 100 men. Some volunteered because they wanted to preserve slavery. Many wanted the adventure of going to war. Most, however, wanted to protect their homes.

More About "Billy Yank" Ordinary Union soldiers were nicknamed "Billy Yank" (short for Yankee). Like Southern soldiers, they wanted adventure and fought to preserve American ideals. However, they hoped to keep the country together.

networks

Go to **connected.mcgraw-hill.com** for additional resources:
- Interactive Whiteboard Lessons
- Worksheets
- Assessment

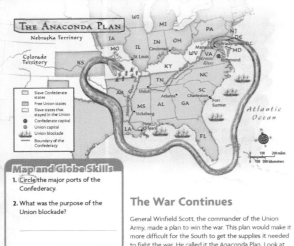

THE ANACONDA PLAN

Nebraska Territory

Colorado Territory

Legend:
- Slave Confederate states
- Free Union states
- Slave states that stayed in the Union
- ● Confederate capital
- ● Union capital
- Union blockade
- Boundary of the Confederacy

0 100 200 miles
0 100 200 kilometers

1. Circle the major ports of the Confederacy.

2. What was the purpose of the Union blockade?

_____

_____

The War Continues

General Winfield Scott, the commander of the Union Army, made a plan to win the war. This plan would make it more difficult for the South to get the supplies it needed to fight the war. He called it the Anaconda Plan. Look at the map of the **Anaconda Plan** on this page.

The Anaconda Plan

An anaconda is a giant snake that strangles its prey. This is exactly what General Scott wanted to do to the South. Scott's Anaconda Plan had three parts. First, Northern ships would blockade, or cut off, Southern seaports. Without trade, the South would be unable to buy weapons and supplies. Second, the North would take control of the Mississippi River. This would divide the South and prevent Confederates from using the river to move supplies. In the final part of the plan, Union troops would invade the South, squeezing the region from both the east and the west.

The South's Strategy

While the North worked on its Anaconda Plan, the South prepared to defend its homeland. Jefferson Davis, president of the Confederacy, knew that a Union blockade of Southern ports could destroy the Confederate economy. Davis also knew that Great Britain and France needed Southern cotton. He believed British ships would break the Union blockade. Davis soon realized he was wrong. Europe had a surplus of cotton in the 1860s. Also, the British and French did not want to get involved in a foreign war.

The Battle of Shiloh

The number of casualties, or people killed and wounded, at Bull Run shocked people on both sides. However, those numbers were slight compared to those at the Battle of Shiloh in Tennessee. There, on April 6, 1862, Confederate forces under General Albert Sidney Johnston surprised Union forces commanded by General Ulysses S. Grant.

Most of the soldiers had never seen battle. The South pushed back one Union position after another. At one spot along a sunken road, bullets buzzed through the air. This place became known as "The Hornet's Nest."

The next day, dead bodies covered the bloody battlefield. The Union troops were near defeat. Suddenly, more Union forces arrived. The tired Confederates could not hold off a fresh Union attack. The North won at Shiloh, but both sides paid a heavy price. Twice as many Americans died in this single battle as died in the entire American Revolution. Shiloh showed both sides that the war would be long and bloody. Never again would people go sightseeing at the scene of a battle. What they had seen was too terrible.

Reading Skill
Fact and Opinion

How did opinions about the war change after the Battle of Shiloh?

_____

_____

_____

_____

_____

▼ Twice as many Americans were killed at Shiloh as were killed in the American Revolution.

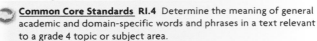

Lesson 3

Active Teaching

After students have read the pages and analyze the elements of Scott's Anaconda Plan.

Develop Comprehension
Ask:

1. *What were the three parts of Scott's Anaconda Plan?* (blockade Southern ports, control the Mississippi River, and invade from the east and the west) **L2**

2. *What is an anaconda?* (a giant snake that strangles its prey) **L1**

3. *Why did Davis's plan to get foreign help fail?* (Europe had other sources of cotton, and the British and French did not want to spend money to help.) **L2**

Map and Globe Skills

Have students study the map.
Ask:

1. *Whose plan is the Anaconda Plan? How can you tell?* (the North's; the snake surrounds the area the north was going to attack in the south) **L1**

2. *What does the red line stand for?* (It is the boundary dividing the north and the south.) **L2**

3. *What do the encircled stars mean on the map key?* (the capitals) **L1**

Reading Skill

Common Core Standards RI.4 Determine the meaning of general academic and domain-specific words and phrases in a text relevant to a grade 4 topic or subject area.

Fact and Opinion   To help students find the answer to the fact and opinion question on the page, have them reread the last paragraph. Would everyone have the same opinion? Why or why not? Why would opinions change after the first battle of the war?

More About "Johnny Shiloh"   Before his tenth birthday, Johnny Clem ran away from home to join the Union army. He began his career as the youngest drummer boy ever to serve, and retired a Major General. He was sometimes called "Johnny Shiloh," but his monument at Arlington National Cemetery identifies him as "The Drummer Boy of Chickamauga."

A New Kind of War

The Civil War was different from earlier American wars because it reached beyond battlefields. Farms and cities were burned. People were terrorized. Some historians call the Civil War the first **total war**. In a total war, each side strikes against the economic system and civilians of the other. Civilians are people who are not in the armed forces. In total war, entire populations are pulled into the conflict.

Unrest

At first, excitement about the war made many in the North and the South eager to join the fight. As the war dragged on, the death toll rose. Both sides had to use a **draft**. A draft is the selection of people who must serve in the military. Draft riots broke out in many Northern cities.

New Technology

Technology transformed the way the Civil War was fought. Railroads and telegraphs changed the way generals made battlefield decisions. Technology also made the Civil War more deadly than earlier wars. Rifles could fire bullets longer distances and with greater accuracy. Land mines were used to surprise and kill the enemy. Iron-covered battle ships, called ironclads, made wooden ships seem outdated overnight because cannon balls simply bounced off the hard metal sides.

The Confederates built the first ironclad ship, the CSS *Virginia*, formerly the USS *Merrimack*. To counter this new threat, the Union built the ironclad USS *Monitor*. On March 9, 1862, the two ironclads fought off the Virginia coast. Neither ship could sink the other. Still, it was a victory for the North because they kept their blockade in place. One month later, the Union captured the port of New Orleans. Continuing the Anaconda plan, Union ships began to sail up the Mississippi River. Soon, the Union Navy controlled the river.

After the battle of the ironclads, "*Monitor* fever" swept the nation. Ironclad railroad cars were manufactured. With their thick armor plates and cannons, they were similar to modern tanks. Both sides also experimented with land mines, torpedoes, and submarines.

The South tried many ways to break the Union blockade of its ports. One Confederate, Horace L. Hunley, invented a submarine to sink warships. On February 16, 1864, the CSS *H.L. Hunley* sank the USS *Housatonic* near the Port of Charleston. Soon after the attack, however, the *Hunley* also sank. It may have been damaged during the blast. Even though the mission was a success, the port remained under Union control. The Union's ability to cut off the South's supplies would have a significant effect on the outcome of the Civil War.

Reading Skill
Fact and Opinion

Take the part of a soldier of the North or South. Write a diary entry about the experience of the war. Include at least one fact and one opinion.

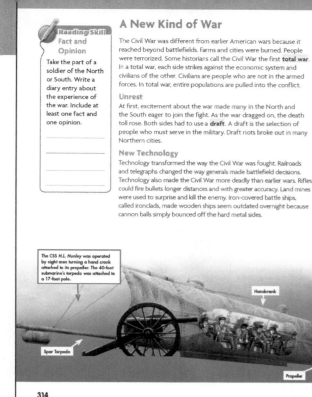

The CSS *H.L. Hunley* was operated by eight men turning a hand crank attached to its propeller. The 40-foot submarine's torpedo was attached to a 17-foot pole.

Handcrank

Spar Torpedo

Propeller

314

Lesson 3

 Essential Question What were the North and South willing to fight for?

Go back to *Show As You Go!* on pages 284–285.

net**works**
There's More Online!
• Games • Assessment

315

Active Teaching

Have students look at the image of the CSS H.L. Hunley. Based on this illustration, what is one reason the Civil War was considered "a new kind of war?"

Develop Comprehension
Ask:

1. *What are some examples that show why the Civil War is called a total war?* (Civilians were targeted; farms and cities were burned.) **L1**

2. *How did the first Confederate submarine get its name?* (It was named for its inventor, Horace L. Hunley.) **L1**

> ***Show As You Go!*** Remind students to return and record information they learned from this lesson.

Reading Skill

 Common Core Standards RI.4 Determine the meaning of general academic and domain-specific words and phrases in a text relevant to a grade 4 topic or subject area.

Fact and Opinion After students read the pages,

Ask: *What was the most important strength of each side of the Civil War? Write your opinion on a separate sheet of paper.*

Response to Intervention

 Essential Question What were the North and the South willing to fight for?

If . . . students cannot explain what the North and South fought for,

. . . .

Then . . . refer students back to pages 308–315 to review what the North and South were fighting for. Have students work in small groups to discuss what is important to them and what they would be willing to fight for.

Ask: *What were the strengths and weaknesses of the North? What were the strengths and weaknesses of the South? How did these strengths and weaknesses come into play with the war?*

Following the discussion, allow students to respond to the Essential Question again.

Lesson 4 | The War Rages On

Essential Question
How did the North's goals change?

What did the North want in 1862? What did the South want in 1862?

_____

_____

_____

_____

_____

Words To Know
Pick the symbol that shows how much you know about the meaning of each word below. Draw the symbol next to the word.

? = I have no idea!
▲ = I know a little.
★ = I know a lot.

_____ **Emancipation Proclamation**

_____ **Gettysburg Address**

Battle of Antietam

For months, Lincoln wanted to make an announcement that would change the purpose of the Civil War. He needed to do it after a Union victory. That victory finally came on September 17, 1862, the bloodiest day in American history.

After winning several battles in Virginia, Robert E. Lee's Confederate army marched north into Maryland in September 1862. Lee planned to continue east and surround Washington, D.C. The Confederates encountered the Union army at Antietam Creek near Sharpsburg, Maryland, on September 17. When the fighting ended that day, nearly 6,000 Confederate and Union soldiers were dead and another 17,000 were seriously wounded. The Union had won the battle. Many people questioned the purpose of so much bloodshed.

Lincoln's Important Announcement

Five days after the Battle of Antietam, Lincoln issued the **Emancipation Proclamation**. This document stated that on January 1, 1863, all enslaved people in the Confederacy were emancipated, or freed. It did not apply to slave states that had stayed in the Union—Delaware, Kentucky, Maryland, and Missouri.

The Emancipation Proclamation was an executive order based on powers given to the President by the Constitution. Lincoln hoped it would give Union troops a new sense of purpose, weaken the South and, eventually, help the North win the war.

Public Opinion Changes

The Emancipation Proclamation changed ideas about the reasons for fighting the Civil War. Now the fighting was about more than Southern independence or saving the Union. It was also about slavery and freedom.

Reading Skill
Fact and Opinion

What opinion do you think enslaved people had about the Emancipation Proclamation? Why?

_____

_____

DID YOU KNOW?
Early in the Civil War, Lincoln's goal was to keep the Union together. Later he decided to use the **Emancipation Proclamation** to change public views and the course of the war.

The Emancipation Proclamation

Lesson 4

Activate Prior Knowledge

Explain to students that in this lesson they will learn about the turning point of the Civil War.

Ask: *What are goals? How do people meet their goals? Why are they important to have? What happens if you do not meet your goals? What happens if you do meet your goals?*

Essential Question How did the North's goals change?

Have students explain what they understand about the Essential Question. Discuss their responses. Explain that everything they learn in this lesson will help them understand the Essential Question better. Remind them to think about how the Essential Question connects to the unit Big Idea: Conflict causes change.

More About Frederick Douglass on Emancipation In *Life and Times* (1881), Douglass wrote that the Emancipation Proclamation "was the turning point in the conflict between freedom and slavery. A death blow was then given to the slaveholding rebellion."

Active Teaching

Words To Know After students have completed the Words To Know activity, have them write what they think the definition of each word is on another sheet of paper. Then, have students look up the definition in the glossary and write it beneath their definition. Have students attach their word list to their work text for safe keeping.

Reading Skill

Common Core Standards RI.4 Determine the meaning of general academic and domain-specific words and phrases in a text relevant to a grade 4 topic or subject area.

Fact and Opinion After students read the pages,

Ask: *Do you think the Emancipation Proclamation was an important document? Why or why not?*

On The Battlefield

Lincoln's Emancipation Proclamation encouraged thousands of free African Americans to join the Union Army and Navy. The Governor of Massachusetts asked an experienced officer and abolitionist, Robert Gould Shaw, to organize one of the first African American fighting forces.

In February 1863, Shaw began training the 54th Massachusetts Colored Regiment at Camp Meigs, Massachusetts. This regiment included the two sons of Frederick Douglass. It became known as "The Fighting 54th."

On July 18, 1863, the 54th Regiment attacked Fort Wagner, South Carolina. Many soldiers from the 54th died in the fighting that ended in a Union defeat. In spite of the loss, the soldiers of the Fighting 54th proved their bravery. Harriet Tubman, who helped care for the wounded, later described the battle:

"And then we saw the lightning, and that was the guns; and then we heard the thunder, and that was the big guns; and then we heard the rain falling, and that was the drops of blood falling; and then we came to get in the crops, it was dead men that we [gathered]."

Although they were not treated as equals of white soldiers off the battlefield, they fought with courage in battle. By the end of the war, nearly 200,000 African Americans had joined the Union forces.

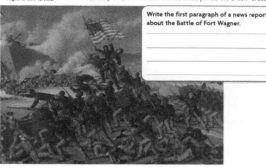
The Fighting 54th attacked Fort Wagner in South Carolina.

> Write the first paragraph of a news report about the Battle of Fort Wagner.

▲ Ulysses S. Grant watched his troops march into Vicksburg, Mississippi.

After the battle ... one [naturally wants] to do as much to [stop] the suffering of an enemy as a friend.
—ULYSSES S. GRANT

The Fall of Vicksburg

One goal of the Anaconda Plan was for the Union to gain control of the Mississippi River. General Ulysses S. Grant achieved this goal in July 1863, when Union troops took control of Vicksburg, Mississippi.

For months, the city had been under siege by Grant's forces. In a siege, a military force surrounds a city and cuts off its supplies. Grant's artillery pounded Vicksburg for weeks. Lack of food forced some people to eat rats! Finally, the city fell on July 4, 1863. Grant was sickened by the sight of thousands of casualties after the battle. Later, Grant wrote:

The victory gave the Union control of the Mississippi River. More importantly for the Union, the Confederacy was now split in two. The Anaconda Plan was almost complete.

> Circle around the name of the city that General Grant targeted.

318

319

Active Teaching

Have students read the pages before they do their news report.

Develop Comprehension

Ask:

1. *How did the Union army change after the Emancipation Proclamation?* (African Americans were allowed to fight.) **L1**

2. *Why was the fall at Vicksburg such a blow to the South?* (The Union controlled an important transportation route and the Confederacy was divided.) **L2**

3. *What did the Union victory win them?* (control of the Mississippi River) **L1**

More About Fighting for Freedom About 180,000 African Americans fought with the Union forces. They made up about one-tenth of the federal army. One of the 24 African American Medal of Honor winners was Sgt. Major Christian Fleetwood, who wrote: "A double purpose induced me and most others to enlist, to assist in abolishing slavery and to save the country from ruin."

Differentiated Instruction

▶ **Approaching** Have students use the map on page 312 to explain why capturing Vicksburg was an important part of Grant's plan.

▶ **Beyond** Tell students that the quotation on this page is from Grant's *Memoirs*. Encourage students to go online and use the Internet to find other interesting quotations or facts about the war.

▶ **ELL** Place students in groups of two. Ask students to explain the Emancipation Proclamation to each other.

networks

Go to **connected.mcgraw-hill.com** for additional resources:

- Interactive Whiteboard Lessons
- Worksheets
- Assessment

The Turning Point

1. Draw a box around the sentence that identifies General Lee's goal in moving north.
2. Draw a box around the sentence that explains the impact of the Battle of Gettysburg.

By the spring of 1863, Lee's army had defeated the Union in several battles. In June Lee decided to take the war north again. His army marched through towns in southern Pennsylvania looking for badly needed supplies, especially shoes.

On July 1, 1863, Lee's army met Union troops under General George Meade in the small farm town of Gettysburg, Pennsylvania. Neither army had planned to fight there, but the nation would soon learn of the bloody Battle of Gettysburg. For three days, the armies fought each other. Ground was taken and lost, but neither side was able to win.

On July 3, 1863, with the Confederate ammunition running low, Lee ordered General George Pickett to charge the Union lines. Confederate soldiers formed lines about a mile wide and half a mile deep. They began what came to be called "Pickett's Charge." More than 12,000 troops ran almost one mile across an open field into cannon and rifle fire from Union troops. More than 6,000 men were killed and wounded in that attack. Lee was forced to retreat. The line of wagons carrying wounded soldiers back to Virginia was 17 miles long.

In all, about 51,000 soldiers were killed or wounded at the Battle of Gettysburg. It was the bloodiest battle ever fought in North America. Union victories at Gettysburg and Vicksburg turned the war in favor of the North.

▼ Thousands of Confederates died during Pickett's Charge. More than 51,000 men in all were killed or wounded at Gettysburg.

320

The Gettysburg Address

In November 1863, Lincoln gave a short speech at Gettysburg to dedicate a cemetery for dead Union soldiers. When he finished, the audience was silent. Lincoln thought his speech was a failure but the people were silent out of respect for the powerful words. The **Gettysburg Address** is known as one of the greatest speeches in American history. Read it in the Primary Source feature.

Primary Source

The Gettysburg Address

"Four **score** and seven years ago our **fathers** brought forth on this continent, a new nation, **conceived** in Liberty, and **dedicated** to the **proposition** that all men are created equal.

Now we are engaged in a great civil war, testing whether that nation, or any nation so conceived and so dedicated, can long endure. We are met on a great battle-field of that war. We have come to dedicate a portion of that field, as a final resting place for those who here gave their lives that that nation might live. It is altogether fitting and proper that we should do this.

But, in a larger sense, we cannot dedicate—we can not **consecrate**—we can not **hallow**—this ground. The brave men, living and dead, who struggled here, have consecrated it, far above our poor power to add or detract. The world will little note, nor long remember what we say here, but can never forget what they did here.

It is for us the living, rather, to be dedicated here to the unfinished work which they who fought here have thus far so nobly advanced. It is rather for us to be here dedicated to the great task remaining before us—that from these honored dead we take increased devotion to that cause for which they gave the last full measure of devotion—that we here highly resolve that these dead shall not have died in vain—that this nation, under God, shall have a new birth of freedom—and that government of the people, by the people, for the people, shall not perish from the earth."

—Abraham Lincoln • Gettysburg, Pennsylvania 1863

score times twenty
fathers forefathers or ancestors
conceived formed
dedicated set apart for a special purpose
proposition intention or plan
consecrate set apart as holy
hallow consider holy

WRITE ABOUT IT
What reasons did Lincoln give for continuing the war?

321

Lesson 4

Active Teaching

Have students give their ideas about what a "turning point" is and what it means in a war. Have them read the pages and see if the information can help them figure out the turning point of the Civil War.

Develop Comprehension
Ask:

1. *Why did General Lee take the risk of ordering General Pickett to charge?* (He wanted to end the two-day battle, and his army was getting low on ammunition.) **L1**

2. *Which battles were most important in giving the advantage to the North?* (Vicksburg and Gettysburg) **L1**

3. *How did Lee have to change his plans after Gettysburg?* (He had to retreat instead of taking the battle to the North.) **L2**

> **Show As You Go!** Remind students to return and record information they learned from this lesson.

Primary Source After students have a chance to read Lincoln's Gettysburg Address,

Ask:

1. *What was the occasion at which Lincoln delivered the Gettysburg Address?* (He spoke at the dedication of a cemetery for the dead soldiers Union in 1863.) **L1**

2. *What do you think is the most important message of Lincoln's speech?* (Students may note that Lincoln said that the war was fought to preserve American democracy, that the best way to honor the dead was to finish the job of protecting freedom and self-government, or that it was time to live up to the promise of equality in the Declaration of Independence.) **L2**

3. *Why do you think that Lincoln's address is considered one of the great documents of American history?* (Students may note that both the writing and the ideas are powerful, or that Lincoln summarized American democratic ideals.) **L3**

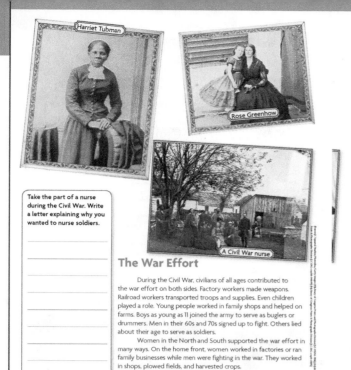

Harriet Tubman

Rose Greenhow

A Civil War nurse

Some women took dangerous jobs as spies or nurses near the front lines. Rose Greenhow served as a Confederate spy. Before being caught, she directed a group of spies from her home in Washington, D.C. After getting information about Union plans, she sent coded messages to the Confederate army. Greenhow also traveled to Europe to gain financial support for the South.

Harriet Tubman, the well-known conductor on the Underground Railroad, served the Union as a spy, scout, and nurse. Clara Barton served on the battlefield, bringing food, medicine, and supplies to the wounded. In 1881 she founded the American Red Cross.

Match the person in the left column with the activity in the right column.

Abraham Lincoln	Helped wounded soldiers as a nurse
Clara Barton	Captured Vicksburg
Robert E. Lee	Spied for Union army
Harriet Tubman	Led 54th Massachusetts
Robert Gould Shaw	Led Confederate troops
Ulysses S. Grant	Issued Emancipation Proclamation

Take the part of a nurse during the Civil War. Write a letter explaining why you wanted to nurse soldiers.

The War Effort

During the Civil War, civilians of all ages contributed to the war effort on both sides. Factory workers made weapons. Railroad workers transported troops and supplies. Even children played a role. Young people worked in family shops and helped on farms. Boys as young as 11 joined the army to serve as buglers or drummers. Men in their 60s and 70s signed up to fight. Others lied about their age to serve as soldiers.

Women in the North and South supported the war effort in many ways. On the home front, women worked in factories or ran family businesses while men were fighting in the war. They worked in shops, plowed fields, and harvested crops.

Women also helped the military. They cared for wounded soldiers, sewed uniforms, and made tents and ammunition.

Lesson 4

? Essential Question How did the North's goals change?

Go back to *Show As You Go!* on pages 284–285!

networks
There's More Online!
• Assessments • Games

322

323

Active Teaching

Have students look at the images of the women of the Civil War.

Ask:

1. *What is an example of how civilians helped the war effort?* (Students may note that children helped with work or enlisted as bugle boys or drummers; older men signed up to fight; women did jobs men were not available to do and also served on the battlefield as spies, nurses, and even soldiers.) **L1**

2. *How do you think the Civil War changed people's ideas about what women could do?* (Like African American soldiers, women proved that they could do more than anyone had expected. The war gave them new opportunities to work outside the home in factories and in professions like nursing.) **L2**

More About Home Front: North Few areas in the North were invaded, but life changed. Nearly 100,000 women took jobs in factories to earn income. Others took over farming duties. Northern women who became nurses found new professional opportunities.

More About Home Front: South Four out of five white men were in the army. Women filled the gap, from running plantations to making ammunition in factories. The lack of labor caused economic hardship, as food and goods were in short supply.

Response to Intervention

? Essential Question How did the North's goals change?

If . . . students cannot explain how the North's goals changed,

. . . .

Then . . . refer students back to pages 316-323 and read about the turning point of the Civil War. Have them explain why civilians had to join in the fight.

Ask: *What jobs do you think women were doing before the Civil War?*

Following the discussion, allow students to respond to the Essential Question again.

The War Ends

? Essential Question
Why did the war end?
What do you think?

_____

_____

_____

_____

Why were the battles of Vicksburg and Gettysburg important?

_____

_____

_____

_____

Words To Know

Pick the symbol that shows how much you know about the meaning of each word below. Draw the symbol next to the word.

? = I have no idea!

▲ = I know a little.

★ = I know a lot.

_____ malice

_____ assassination

Ulysses S. Grant was a strong general who had won important victories in the West. In 1864 Lincoln put Grant in command of the entire Union army. He hoped Grant would bring the war to an end.

Grant had two major goals. He wanted to destroy Lee's army in Virginia, and he wanted to capture Richmond, Virginia, the Confederate capital. For 40 days, from April to June 1864, he battled Lee's army.

▼ Richmond, Virginia, lay in ruins after the war.

The Final Battles

The number of dead and wounded in these battles was enormous. At the Battle of Cold Harbor, Grant lost 7,000 men in about an hour. The Union army was so much larger than the Confederate army that it was able to continue its attacks.

Finally, Grant reached Petersburg, a key railroad center south of Richmond. From there, he hoped to capture Richmond. Lee could not leave Petersburg. If he did, Grant would have a clear path to Richmond. With Lee trapped, Grant put Petersburg under siege for 10 grim months.

People wondered if the war would ever end. Some Northerners wanted to let the Confederacy secede. Many blamed President Lincoln for continuing the fight to keep the Union together. As a result, Lincoln felt he had little hope of winning reelection in 1864.

The Battle of Cold Harbor ▼

Reading Skill

Fact and Opinion

What opinion did some Northerners have about Lincoln's handling of the war?

_____

_____

Lesson 5

Activate Prior Knowledge

After students have completed the activity, have them share their reasons they wrote for why the battles of Vicksburg and Gettysburg were important. Remind students that the Civil War was a total war.

Ask: *If you had lived in 1864, how would you have responded to someone who argued that Lincoln should let the South secede?*

? Essential Question Why did the war end?

Have students explain what they understand about the Essential Question. Discuss their responses. Explain that everything they learn in this lesson will help them understand the Essential Question better. Remind them to think about how the Essential Question connects to the unit Big Idea: Conflict causes change.

Active Teaching

Words To Know Once students have completed the activity, have them find the words in the lesson and read their definitions. Then, present the students with a list of three to five words or phrases related to each vocabulary word. Have students identify the word or phrase that does not fit with the rest of the group and explain their choice.

Develop Comprehension

The content that is ***boldfaced and italicized*** throughout the lesson is told in first person from the point-of-view of historical figures. Students may need to be reminded of what is means to read a first person point-of-view.

Ask:

1. *What was Grant hired to do in 1864?* (Grant was put in command of the entire Union army.) **L1**
2. *What were Grant's two goals?* (To destroy Lee's army and to capture Richmond, Virginia.) **L1**

Sherman's March

General William Tecumseh Sherman now led Union forces in the West. Following the Anaconda Plan, he marched his troops across Tennessee and Georgia to squeeze the South. Sherman believed that the North needed to launch a total war, which would break the South's fighting spirit. He told his men to destroy anything of value to the enemy. Sherman's soldiers terrorized the South. They burned crops and buildings. They destroyed railroads and factories. They even killed livestock and left the animals for vultures.

In September 1864, Sherman captured and burned Atlanta, Georgia, which was one of the South's largest cities and a railroad center.

Sherman's 60,000-man army cut a path that was 60 miles wide and 300 miles long across Georgia to the city of Savannah on the Atlantic Coast. Union forces took Savannah in December. From there, the army marched into South Carolina—the state some people blamed for starting the war. Many cities in Sherman's path were left in ashes. One soldier said:

"Here is where treason began and... here is where it shall end!"

Map and Globe Skills

1. Circle the battles that took place in 1864.
2. Where did General Sherman go after Savannah?

_____

_____

Battles of the Civil War

Robert E. Lee surrendered to Ulysses S. Grant at Appomattox Court House in Virginia.

1. Draw a box around the sentence that explains why General Lee surrendered.
2. Draw a box around the sentence that explains why General Grant let Lee's men keep their horses.

The South Surrenders

With the fall of Atlanta, it seemed the end of the war was finally in sight. Northerners began to regain confidence in Lincoln and his ability to lead the Union to victory. In November 1864, voters reelected him.

In March 1865, Grant was closing in on Lee at Petersburg. After the Union siege, Confederate soldiers defending the city were near starvation. On April 2, Lee took his army west, hoping to find food and gather more Confederate troops. As a result, Petersburg fell. The next day, Richmond, the Confederate capital, also fell. Lee knew that more killing would be meaningless. The war was over.

On April 9, 1865, Lee surrendered to Grant at Appomattox Court House in Virginia. Grant did not take any prisoners. Instead, he offered Lee generous terms. For example, Lee and his soldiers were allowed to return to their homes. They could also keep their horses to help with the spring plowing.

After Lee's surrender, Jefferson Davis fled to the deep South, where he hoped to keep the Confederacy alive. On May 10, 1865, he was captured in Georgia. Davis was later imprisoned for two years in Virginia.

326

327

Active Teaching

Discuss the effects of Sherman's march to the sea.

Develop Comprehension
Ask:

1. Which is easier to understand: a list of states that voted for Lincoln, or the map on this page? (Students will probably say that the map makes it easier to see at a glance how many states supported Lincoln.) **L1**

3. What changed people's opinion of Lincoln? (When they began to hope that the war would end soon, they did not want to switch leaders.) **L2**

> **Show As You Go!** Remind students to return and record information they learned from this lesson.

More About Sherman of War Critics said that Sherman's "scorched earth" policy was brutal. Sherman defended his tactics by saying, "War is cruelty. There is no use trying to reform it. The crueler it is, the sooner it will be over." The general believed that if he proved to Southerners that their government could not protect them, they would give up the fight.

Map and Globe Skills

Ask:

1. Who won the battle of Gettysburg? (Union) **L1**
2. What direction did General Sherman march? (Southeast, then Northeast) **L2**

Differentiated Instruction

▶ **Approaching** Have students use the map to explain how Sherman's march completed Grant's Anaconda Plan.

▶ **Beyond** Ask students to find out why it was important for Sherman's troops to live off the land.

▶ **ELL** Have students find pictures of Sherman's march and describe them.

networks

Go to **connected.mcgraw-hill.com** for additional resources:
- Interactive Whiteboard Lessons
- Worksheets
- Assessment

Lincoln Is Shot

Lincoln did not want to punish the South. In his second inaugural address, he encouraged Americans to put away their **malice**, or desire to harm, with these words: "with malice toward none, with charity for all."

Less than a week after Lee's surrender, Lincoln was watching a play at Ford's Theater in Washington, D.C. Suddenly a gunshot rang out. John Wilkes Booth had shot the President. The next morning, April 15, 1865, Lincoln died. Abraham Lincoln's **assassination** shocked the nation. Assassination is the murder of an important leader. The poet Walt Whitman expressed the country's sadness:

O CAPTAIN! my Captain! our fearful trip is done; The ship has weather'd every [storm], the prize we sought is won; . . .

—WALT WHITMAN

▼ Abraham Lincoln's funeral procession passed through several states on its way to Springfield, Illinois.

328

Troops Return Home

At the end of the war, the South had few farms left in working condition. Troops returned not only to the property that had been destroyed, but also to a way of life that had ended. In the South, one of every four white men had been killed. Two-thirds of its wealth had been lost. It would take many years for the South to recover. One Confederate soldier, returning home to Richmond, wrote:

"I shall not attempt to describe my feelings. The city [is] in ruins. . . . With a raging headache and a swelling heart I reach my home, and here the curtain falls."

The Union had survived, but the cost of the Civil War had been huge. The North's victory ended slavery for millions of African Americans. At the same time, it left the South in ruins. United once again, the nation faced the task of rebuilding the South.

> Take the part of a Union or Confederate soldier. Write a letter to your parents saying what you think the Civil War meant for the United States.
>
> _____
> _____
> _____
> _____

Lesson 5

(?) **Essential Question** Why did the war end?

_____
_____
_____
_____

Go back to *Show As You Go!* on pages 284–285.

networks There's More Online!
• Assessment • Games

329

Lesson 5

Active Teaching

Have children finish the lesson by reading these pages. Then ask them to complete the letter home on page 329. Allow them to flip back and forth in their work text as them complete the letter. Have volunteers share their letters with the class.

Develop Comprehension

Ask:

1. *What event made Lee decide to surrender?* (After Richmond fell, Lee knew the war could not be won.) **L1**

2. *How did Grant treat Lee at Appomattox?* (Grant treated Lee with respect and offered generous surrender terms.) **L2**

3. *What challenges did leaders face after the war?* (They had to reunite the nation and rebuild the South, which had lost one-quarter of its white males and most of its wealth.) **L3**

Response to Intervention

(?) **Essential Question** Why did the war end?

If . . . students cannot explain why the war ended,

. . . .

Then . . . refer students back to pages 324–329 and read about the turning point of the Civil War. Have them explain why civilians had to join in the fight.

Ask: *Why did Lincoln say he would show "malice toward none"?*

Following the discussion, allow students to respond to the Essential Question again.

UNIT 8 Wrap Up

networks There's More Online!
• Games • Assessment

Read the names in the box and the speech bubbles below. Decide which person from the years leading to and during the Civil War would have made each statement. Write the name of the person below the speech bubble.

| John C. Calhoun | Robert E. Lee | Harriet Beecher Stowe |
| Frederick Douglass | Abraham Lincoln | Harriet Tubman |

I led an army of the Confederacy and had to surrender at Appomattox Court House.

_____

I wrote a book that stirred the North against slavery.

_____

I escaped slavery and then returned south to lead others to freedom.

_____

I argued that high tariffs were unfair to the people of the South.

_____

I escaped from slavery and then joined the abolitionists trying to end it.

_____

I worked to reunify the country and set the end of slavery as a goal of the Civil War.

_____

330

Unit Project

A museum has hired you and a partner to create an exhibit about an event before or during the Civil War. Make the exhibit about one of the events you leared about in this unit. Before you begin working, look back at **Show as You Go!** on pages 284–285 to review your notes. Read the list below to see what kind of material should be included in your museum exhibit. As you work, check off each item as you include it.

Your museum exhibit should...	Yes, it does!
include text that describes what happened during the event and why the event was important.	☐
include at least one image that supports your text.	☐
include research from primary sources.	☐
include research from secondary sources.	☐
be neat and legible.	☐
be interesting to look at and appealing to visitors.	☐

Think about the Big Idea

BIG IDEA Conflict causes change.

What did you learn in this unit that helps you understand the BIG IDEA?

_____

_____

_____

331

Wrap Up

Vocabulary

Have students complete the activity on page 330 to summarize their understanding of how and why the Civil War was fought.

 Big Idea Project

Read through the project directions and checklist with students. Answer any questions they have and make sure they understand the requirements. Before you start the museum activity, review the events of the Civil War.

- Remind students to use their **Show As You Go!** pages to assist them in completing the project.
- To assess the project, refer to the rubric on the following page.

networks

Go to connected.mcgraw-hill.com for additional resources:
- Games
- Assessment
- Group Technology Projects

Differentiated Instruction

▶ **Approaching** Have students work on the project in groups or pairs instead of working alone. They may then verbally tell how well they think the class worked.

▶ **Beyond** Have students find out more about a particular battle in the Civil War and write a one-page report on it. Have them include pictures they find on the Internet and share the report with the class.

▶ **ELL** Have students create a word web for each famous person in the Civil War and their role in the war. Have them highlight specific vocabulary by extending the web and including a definition or synonym for each word.

Response to Intervention

BIG IDEA Conflict causes change.

If . . . students cannot give a substantiated explanation of how conflict causes change

Then . . . have students think of everyday examples of how conflict causes change in their lives. Have them think about what would happen if there was no change.

Name _____ Date _____

Civil War Museum Exhibit

4 Exemplary	3 Accomplished	2 Developing	1 Beginning
The museum exhibit:	**The museum exhibit:**	**The museum exhibit:**	**The museum exhibit:**
☐ clearly describes one of the events of the Civil War	☐ describes one of the events of the Civil War	☐ describes part of an event of the Civil War	☐ does not describe part of an event of the Civil War
☐ includes multiple colorful images	☐ include at least one image	☐ includes poorly researched image	☐ does not include images
☐ includes research from primary and secondary sources	☐ includes research from primary sources only	☐ includes research from secondary sources only	☐ does not includes research from primary or secondary sources
☐ is very neat, legible, and interesting to look at	☐ is neat, legible and interesting to look at	☐ is not neat or legible, but interesting to look at	☐ is not neat or legible, or interesting to look at

Grading Comments: _____

_____

_____

_____

_____

_____

_____

_____

_____

_____

_____

_____

Project Score: _____

Read the passage "The Impact of the Civil War" before answering Numbers 1 through 8.

The Impact of the Civil War

by Trudi Park

The human cost of the Civil War was high. Tens of thousands of men died in battle or from disease. Many who were wounded had their lives changed. The Civil War also had lasting social, economic, and political effects on the United States. Both the North and the South experienced effects from the war.

The war helped push the North further toward an economy based on industry. The North needed to produce huge amounts of material for its armies during the war. Soldiers needed uniforms, supplies, and equipment. Trains were needed to move those supplies and soldiers. Northern industry met those needs. After the war, industries continued to grow. Companies made iron and steel to build railroads stretching across the continent. Others packed and shipped meat or other food.

The biggest change in the South was the end of slavery. Millions of African Americans were suddenly free. They looked for long-lost family members and went to school. They began to work for wages and hoped to own land. A few years after the war, African American men gained the right to vote. They began to win elections and take part in governing their states.

Many parts of the South were badly damaged by the war. People needed many years to rebuild homes and businesses. Business leaders changed the economy of the South to produce other goods besides cotton.

1 What is the passage mostly about?
Ⓐ the suffering caused by the war
Ⓑ the many effects of the war
Ⓒ changes resulting from the end of slavery
Ⓓ economic growth in the North

2 What does the passage mean by the "human cost" of the war?
Ⓕ the loss of life and the suffering
Ⓖ the money needed to fund the war
Ⓗ the economic changes
Ⓘ the social changes

3 Read the sentence from the passage.

The North needed to produce huge amounts of material for its armies during the war.

What does the word *material* mean in this sentence?
Ⓐ cloth and paper
Ⓑ iron and steel
Ⓒ uniforms and supplies
Ⓓ farms and businesses

4 Based on the passage, in which area did the North have the greatest changes?
Ⓕ daily life
Ⓖ economy
Ⓗ politics
Ⓘ society

5 What was a major industry in the North after the war?
Ⓐ textiles
Ⓑ telegraph
Ⓒ construction
Ⓓ railroad

6 What group experienced the most change from the war?
Ⓕ workers in northern cities
Ⓖ farmers in the South
Ⓗ African Americans in the South
Ⓘ political leaders in the North

7 What was one way that the lives of African Americans changed?
Ⓐ being paid for their work
Ⓑ having families
Ⓒ wanting to be free
Ⓓ hoping to have their own land

8 What major task did people in the South face?
Ⓕ rebuilding homes and businesses
Ⓖ finding new crops to grow
Ⓗ building railroads
Ⓘ starting iron and steel industries

Test Preparation

Test-Taking Tips

Share these test-taking tips with your students:
Focus on checking your answers

- Do not leave any questions blank.
- If you do not know the answer:
  - reread the passage.
  - skip the question and come back to it later.
  - make your best guess.
- Check your answer sheet:
  - Erase incorrect answers completely.
  - Fill in the answer bubble completely.
  - Make sure you have not made any stray marks.

Answers

1. **B** **CCS RI.2**

2. **F** **CCS RI.4**

3. **C** **CCS RI.4**

4. **G** **CCS RI.4**

5. **D** **CCS RI.4**

6. **H** **CCS RI.4**

7. **C** **CCS RI.4**

8. **F** **CCS RI.4**

Reference Section

Geography and You

Geography is the study of Earth and the people, plants, and animals that live on it. Most people think of geography as learning about cities, states, and countries, but geography is far more. Geography includes learning about land, such as mountains and plains, and bodies of water, such as oceans, lakes, and rivers.

Geography includes the study of how people adapt to living in a new place. Geography is also about how people move around, how they move goods, and how ideas travel from place to place.

R1

Dictionary of Geographic Terms

1 **BAY** Body of water partly surrounded by land

2 **BEACH** Land covered with sand or pebbles next to an ocean or lake

3 **CANAL** Waterway dug across the land to connect two bodies of water

4 **CANYON** Deep river valley with steep sides

5 **CLIFF** High steep face of rock

6 **COAST** Land next to an ocean

7 **DESERT** A dry environment with few plants and animals

8 **GULF** Body of water partly surrounded by land; larger than a bay

9 **HARBOR** Protected place by an ocean or river where ships can safely stay

10 **HILL** Rounded, raised landform; not as high as a mountain

11 **ISLAND** Land that is surrounded on all sides by water

12 **LAKE** Body of water completely surrounded by land

13 **MESA** Landform that looks like a high, flat table

14 **MOUNTAIN** High landform with steep sides; higher than a hill

15 **OCEAN** Large body of salt water

16 **PENINSULA** Land that has water on all sides but one

17 **PLAIN** Large area of flat land

18 **PLATEAU** High flat area that rises steeply above the surrounding land

19 **PORT** Place where ships load and unload goods

20 **RIVER** Long stream of water that empties into another body of water

21 **VALLEY** Area of low land between hills or mountains

R3

United States: Political

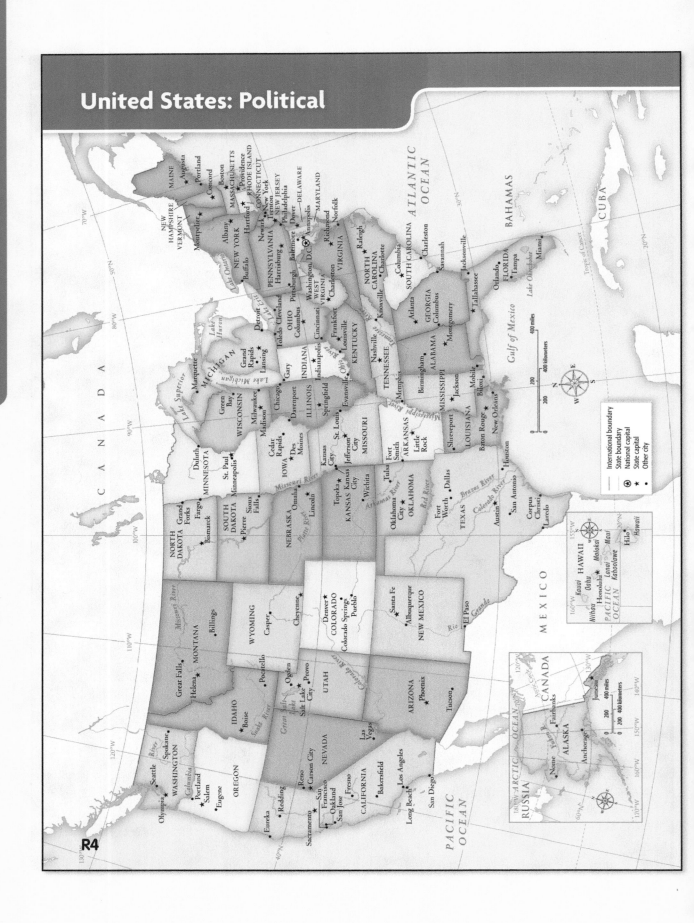

United States: Physical

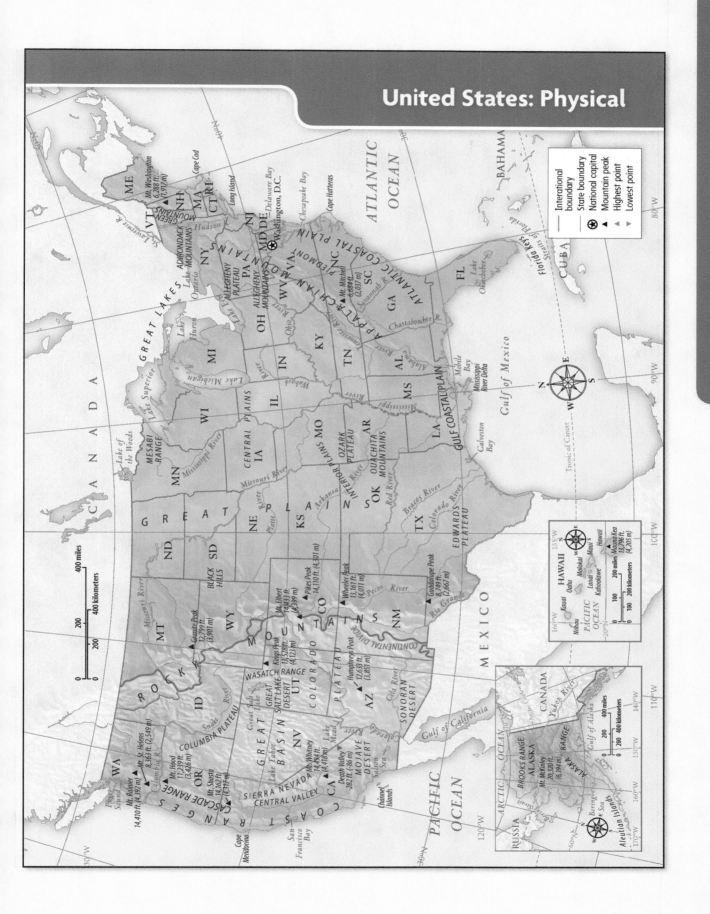

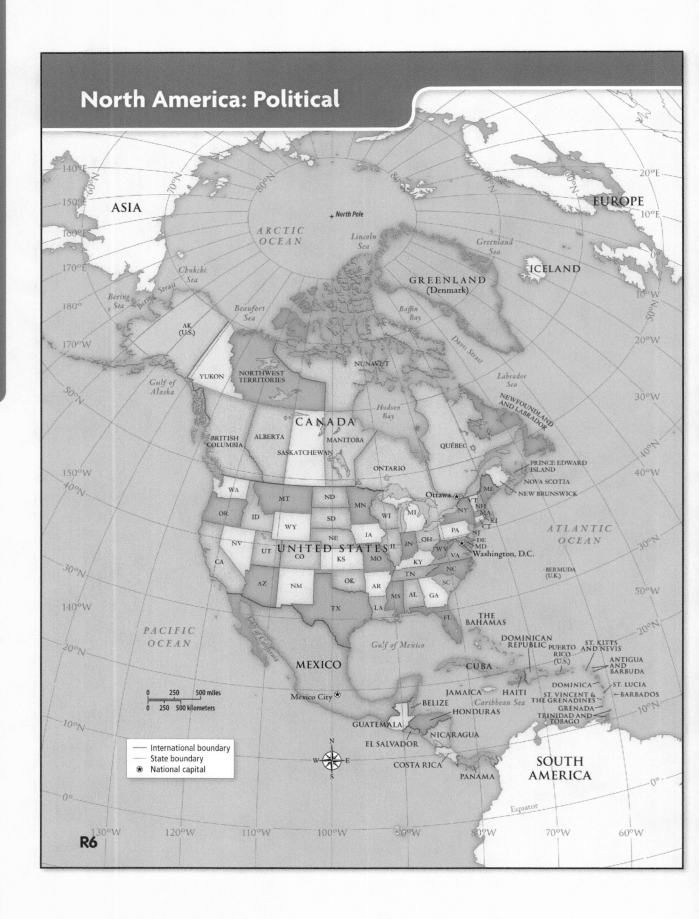

North America: Political

ASIA

ARCTIC OCEAN

+ North Pole

Lincoln Sea

Greenland Sea

EUROPE

ICELAND

GREENLAND (Denmark)

Chukchi Sea

Bering Strait

Bering Sea

Beaufort Sea

Baffin Bay

Davis Strait

AK (U.S.)

Gulf of Alaska

YUKON

NORTHWEST TERRITORIES

NUNAVUT

Labrador Sea

NEWFOUNDLAND AND LABRADOR

BRITISH COLUMBIA

ALBERTA

SASKATCHEWAN

CANADA

MANITOBA

ONTARIO

Hudson Bay

QUÉBEC

PRINCE EDWARD ISLAND

NOVA SCOTIA

NEW BRUNSWICK

WA

OR

ID

MT

WY

ND

SD

MN

WI

MI

NE

IA

Ottawa ⊛

ME

VT

NY

NH
MA
RI
CT

PA

ATLANTIC OCEAN

NV

UT

CO

UNITED STATES

KS

IL

IN

OH

WV

VA

NJ
DE
MD

Washington, D.C. ⊛

CA

AZ

NM

OK

MO

KY

TN

NC

SC

BERMUDA (U.K.)

PACIFIC OCEAN

Gulf of California

TX

AR

MS

AL

GA

LA

FL

THE BAHAMAS

Gulf of Mexico

DOMINICAN REPUBLIC

PUERTO RICO (U.S.)

ST. KITTS AND NEVIS

MEXICO

CUBA

ANTIGUA AND BARBUDA

Mexico City ⊛

JAMAICA

HAITI

Caribbean Sea

DOMINICA

ST. LUCIA

ST. VINCENT & THE GRENADINES

BARBADOS

BELIZE

HONDURAS

GRENADA

TRINIDAD AND TOBAGO

GUATEMALA

NICARAGUA

EL SALVADOR

SOUTH AMERICA

COSTA RICA

PANAMA

Equator

| 0 | 250 | 500 miles |
| 0 | 250 | 500 kilometers |

―― International boundary
―― State boundary
⊛ National capital

N
W   E
S

140°E
150°E
160°E
170°E
180°
170°W
160°W
150°W
140°W
130°W
120°W
110°W
100°W
90°W
80°W
70°W
60°W

20°E
10°E
0°
10°W
20°W
30°W
40°W
50°W

80°N
70°N
60°N
50°N
40°N
30°N
20°N
10°N
0°

R6

North America: Physical

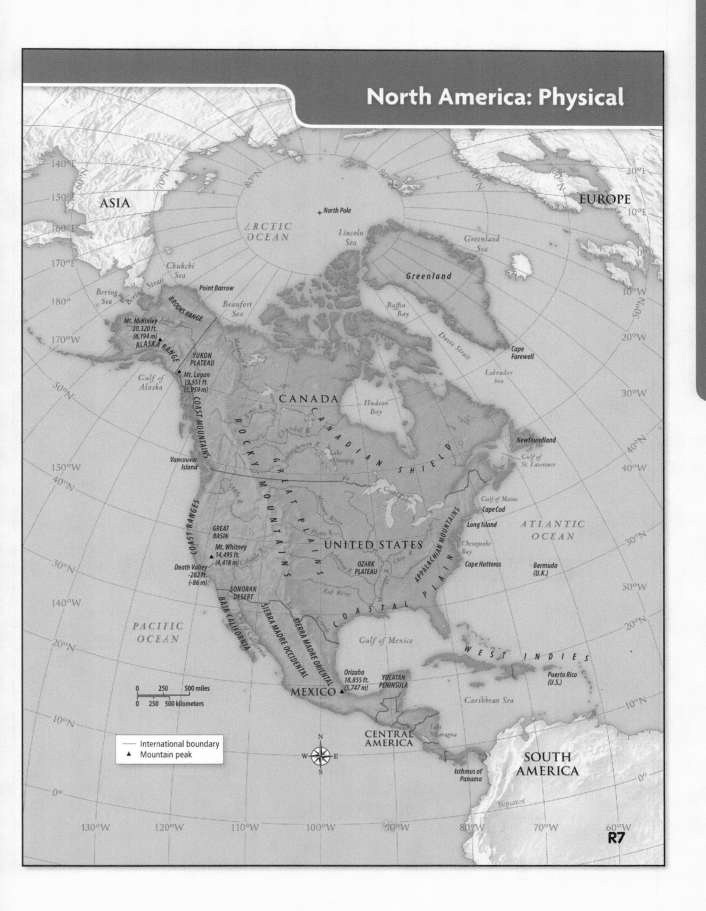

ASIA

EUROPE

North Pole

ARCTIC OCEAN

Lincoln Sea

Greenland Sea

Chukchi Sea

Point Barrow

Beaufort Sea

Baffin Bay

Greenland

Bering Sea

Bering Strait

BROOKS RANGE

Mt. McKinley 20,320 ft. (6,194 m)

ALASKA RANGE

Yukon

Gulf of Alaska

YUKON PLATEAU

Mt. Logan 19,551 ft. (5,959 m)

Davis Strait

Cape Farewell

Labrador Sea

COAST MOUNTAINS

CANADA

Hudson Bay

ROCKY

CANADIAN SHIELD

Churchill R.

Saskatchewan R.

Lake Winnipeg

Newfoundland

Gulf of St. Lawrence

Vancouver Island

COAST RANGES

MOUNTAINS

GREAT

Missouri River

Great Lakes

Gulf of Maine

Cape Cod

Long Island

ATLANTIC OCEAN

GREAT BASIN

Mt. Whitney 14,495 ft. (4,418 m)

Platte R.

PLAINS

Arkansas R.

Ohio R.

OZARK PLATEAU

UNITED STATES

Chesapeake Bay

APPALACHIAN MOUNTAINS

Cape Hatteras

Bermuda (U.K.)

Death Valley -282 ft. (-86 m)

Colorado R.

Red River

Mississippi R.

SONORAN DESERT

BAJA CALIFORNIA

PACIFIC OCEAN

Gulf of California

SIERRA MADRE OCCIDENTAL

SIERRA MADRE ORIENTAL

COASTAL

PLAIN

Rio Grande

Gulf of Mexico

WEST INDIES

Puerto Rico (U.S.)

Orizaba 18,855 ft. (5,747 m)

YUCATÁN PENINSULA

MEXICO

Caribbean Sea

0   250   500 miles
0   250   500 kilometers

CENTRAL AMERICA

Lake Nicaragua

SOUTH AMERICA

Isthmus of Panama

Equator

— International boundary
▲ Mountain peak

N
W   E
S

R7

World: Political

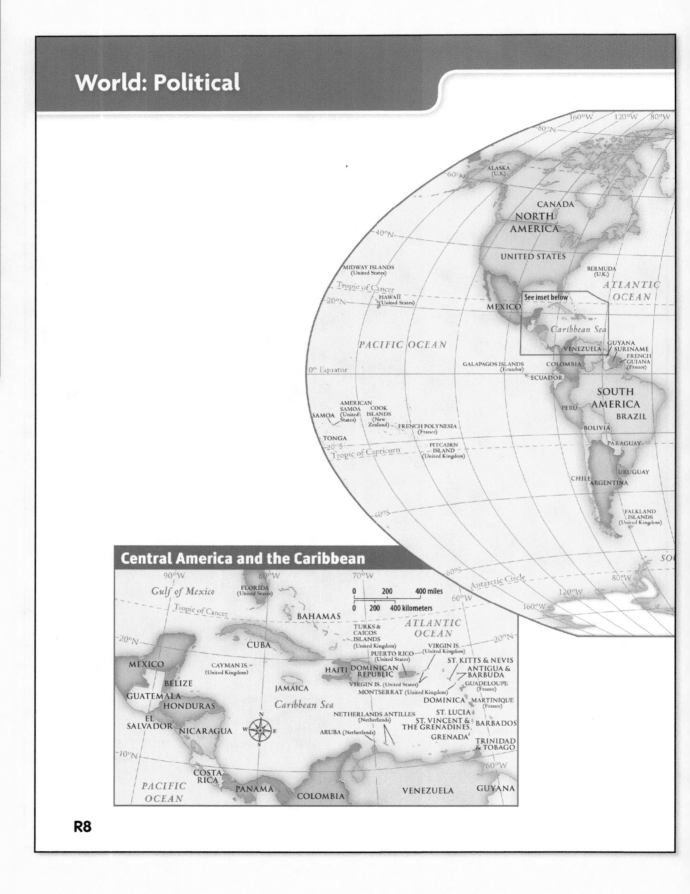

Central America and the Caribbean

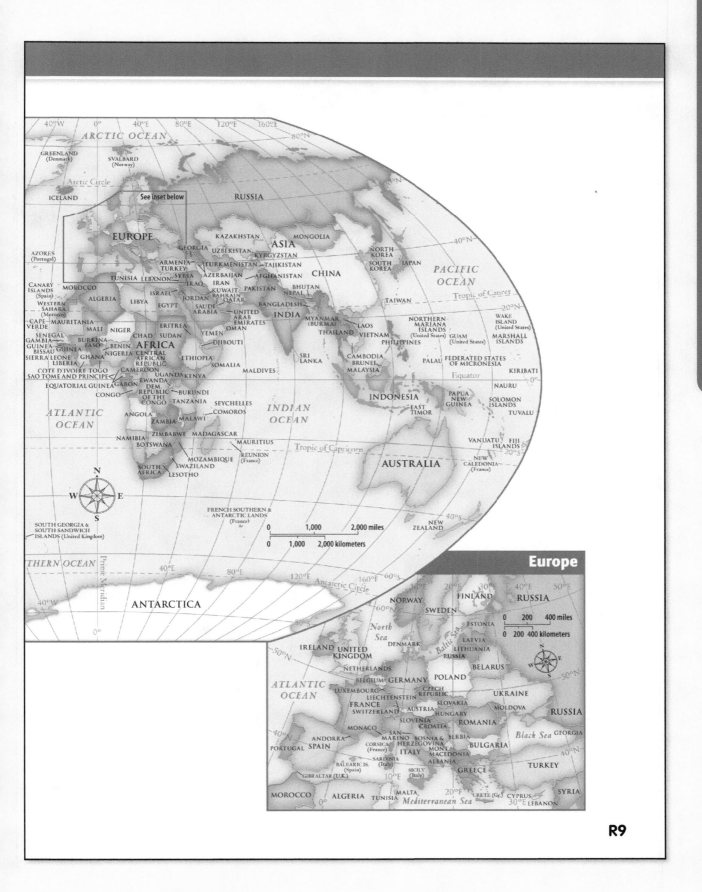

World: Physical

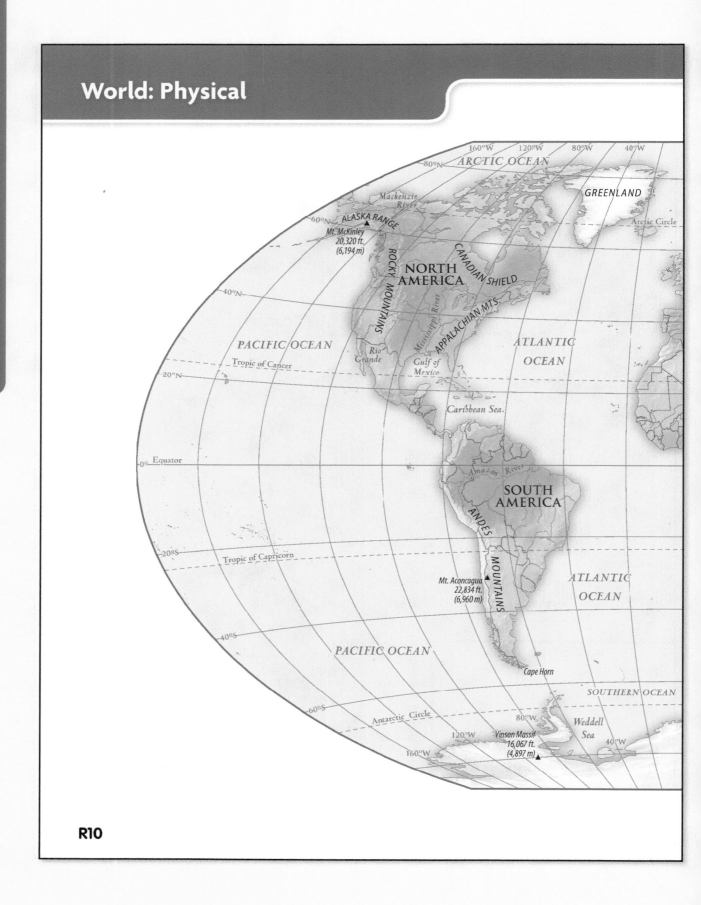

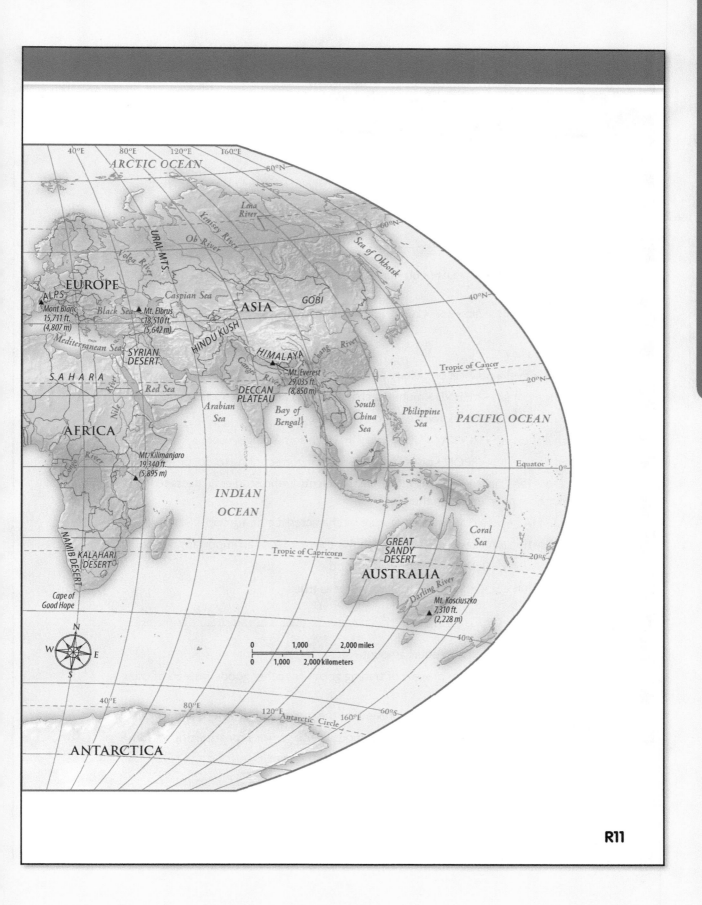

ARCTIC OCEAN

40°E 80°E 120°E 160°E 80°N

60°N

Lena River

Yenisey River

Ob River

URAL MTS.

Volga River

Sea of Okhotsk

EUROPE

ALPS
Mont Blanc
15,711 ft.
(4,807 m)

Black Sea Mt. Elbrus
18,510 ft.
(5,642 m)

Caspian Sea

ASIA

GOBI

40°N

HINDU KUSH

Mediterranean Sea

SYRIAN
DESERT

HIMALAYA

Chang River

Tropic of Cancer

20°N

SAHARA

Red Sea

Ganges River

Mt. Everest
29,035 ft.
(8,850 m)

DECCAN
PLATEAU

Nile River

Arabian
Sea

Bay of
Bengal

South
China
Sea

Philippine
Sea

PACIFIC OCEAN

AFRICA

Congo River

Mt. Kilimanjaro
19,340 ft.
(5,895 m)

Equator 0°

INDIAN
OCEAN

NAMIB DESERT

KALAHARI
DESERT

Tropic of Capricorn

GREAT
SANDY
DESERT

Coral
Sea

20°S

Cape of
Good Hope

AUSTRALIA

Darling River

Mt. Kosciuszko
7,310 ft.
(2,228 m)

N
W   E
S

0   1,000   2,000 miles
0   1,000   2,000 kilometers

40°S

40°E   80°E   120°E   160°E   60°S
Antarctic Circle

ANTARCTICA

Glossary

This Glossary will help you to pronounce and understand the meanings of the vocabulary terms in this book. The page number at the end of the definition tells where the term first appears. Words with an asterisk (*) before them are academic vocabulary words.

 A

abolitionist (ab • uh • LISH • uh • nist) was a person who wanted to end slavery in the United States

absolute location (ab • soh • LOOT loh • KAY • shuhn) the exact location of any place on Earth

act (akt) a law

ally (AL • eye) a political or military partner

amendment (uh • MEHND • muhnt) a change or addition to the Constitution

appeal (uh • PEEL) to ask for a case to be heard again

*application (ap • lih • KAY • shun) a way in which something is used

*appropriate (uh • RPOH • pree • uht) the right or correct thing to do; proper

*archaeologist (ahr • kee • AH • luh • jihst) a scientist who studies artifacts to learn about how people lived in the past

*aspect (AS • pehkt) a particular feature or characteristic of a group

assassination (uh • sas • uh • NAY • shuhn) is the murder of an important person

assembly (uh • SEHM • blee) a lawmaking body

*assume (uh • SOOM) to take for granted or as true

 B

*balance (BA • luhnts) an equal amount

barter (BAHR • tuhr) the process of trading goods for other goods, instead of using money

blockade (blah • KAYD) a barrier preventing the movement of troops and supplies

boycott (BOY • kaht) to refuse to buy goods or use services for a specific reason

C

canyon (CAN • yuhn) a deep valley with steep sides

*characteristic (kare • ihk • tur • IHS • tihk) a quality that belongs to a person, thing, or group

*chart (CHAHRT) a document that shows where things are, such as stars

charter (CHAHRT • tuhr) an official document giving a person permission to do something, such as settle in an area

civilization (sihv • ih • lih • ZAY • shun) a culture that has developed complex systems of government, education, and religion

*claim (KLAYM) to declare ownership of something, such as land

*civil war ((SIV • uhl wawr) is an armed conflict between groups within one country. In the United States, it was the war between the Union and the Confederacy from 1861 to 1865

*code (COHD) a set of rules or laws

*common (KAH • muhn) often found

*conclusion (kuhn • KLOO • zhuhn) a well-thought out judgment or decision

*condition (kuhn • DIH • shuhn) the state something is in

*conduct (kun • DUHKT) to direct or lead an event, such as a ceremony

confederacy (kuhn • FEHD • ur • uh • see) a union of people who join together for a common purpose

*consequence (KAHN • suh • kwehns) the result of an action, an effect

constitution (kahn • stuh • TOO • shuhn) a plan for government

contiguous (kuhn • TIH • gyuh • wuhs) land that is connected by shared borders

cotton gin (KAH • tuhn JIHN) a machine that separates cotton from its seeds

covenant (KUH • vuh • nuhnt) a contract or agreement

culture (kuhl • CHUR) the beliefs, traditions, and language of a group of people

D

debate (dih • BAYT) to discuss all points of view

debt (DEHT) the condition of owing something, such as money, to someone

*defend (dih • FEHND) to argue in favor of a person, action, or point of view

R13

Glossary

delegate — fundamental

delegate (DEH • lih • guht) a person who represents others at an important meeting

*demand (dih • MAND) to ask for with authority

desert (dih • ZUHRT) to run away or to leave someone in their time of need

*develop (DEE • vehl • uhp) to create over a period of time

*discuss (dih • SKUHS) to talk about

*distort (DIHS • tort) to stretch, twist, or bend out of shape

diversity (duh • VUR • suh • tee) a condition of having a great difference or variety among people or things

draft (DRAFT) is the selecting of persons for military service or some other special duty

due process (DOO PRAH • sehs) the idea that the government must follow the rules established by law

E

Emancipation Proclamation (ee • man • sih • PAY • shuhn prok • luh • MAY • shuhn) was an official announcement issued by President Abraham Lincoln in 1862 that led to the end of slavery in the United States

empire (ehm • PY • ur) a large area of different groups of people controlled by one ruler or government

*employ (ihm • PLOY) to hire or use

enslave (in • SLAYV) to force a person to work with no pay and without the freedom to leave

expedition (ehks • pih • DIH • shuhn) a journey for a specific purpose

F

federalism (FEH • duh • ruh • lih • zuhm) a system of government in which power is shared between a national government and states

forty-niner (FOR • tee NY • nuhr) a person who moved to California in 1849 in search of gold

free state (FREE stayt) a state where slavery was banned

frontier (FRUHN • tihr) the name given by colonists to the far end of a country where people are just beginning to settle

fundamental (fuhn • duh • MEHN • tuhl) basic

R14

Glossary

geographer — jury

G

geographer (GEE • ahg • ruh • fur) a person who studies geography

Gettysburg Address (GET • iz • burg uh • DRES) was a speech made by President Abraham Lincoln at the site of the Battle of Gettysburg in 1863

guarantee (gehr • uhn • tee) a promise

H

hogan (HOH • gihn) a dome-shamed Navajo dwelling

I

immigrant (ihm • IH • grihnt) a person who lives in a country in which he or she was not born

impeach (ihm • PEECH) to put an official on trial for wrongdoing

impressment (ihm • PREHS • mihnt) the British practice of capturing American sailors and forcing them to serve on British ships

indentured servant (ihn • DEHN • shuhrd SUHR • vuhnt) a person who worked for someone in colonial America for a set of time in exchange for the voyage across the Atlantic Ocean

inflation (ihn • FLAY • shuhn) a rapid rise in the price of goods

*influence (ihn • FLU • ihns) to change or affect someone or something

*inform (ihn • FORM) to tell

*intent (ihn • TEHNT) the main goal or reason for doing something

interchangeable part (ihn • tur • CHAYNJ • ih • buhl PAHRT) parts of a product built to a standard size so that they can be easily replaced

*interpreter (IHN • tur • prih • tur) a person who changes words from one language into another

*intersect (IHN • tur • sehkt) to meet and cross at one or more points

irrigation (eer • ih • GAY • shuhn) to supply with water by using artificial means

J

jury (JUR • ee) a group of citizens who decide a court case

R15

Glossary

kachina — Missouri Compromise

K

kachina (kuh • CHEE • nuh) spirits that Pueblo people believe bring rain, help crops grow, and teach people how to live

L

latitude (LA • tuh • tood) imaginary lines on Earth that go from east to west and show a location's distance from the Equator

lodge (LAHJ) a home made of logs covered with grasses, sticks, and soil, which Native Americans of the Plains used when living in their communities

longhouse (lahng • HOWS) a home shared by several related Iroquois families

longitude (LAHN • juh • tood) imaginary lines on Earth that go from north to south and show a location's distance from the Prime Meridian

Loyalist (LOY • uh • lihst) a colonist who supported Great Britain during the American Revolution

M

manifest destiny (MA • nuh • fehst DEHS • tuh • nee) the belief that the United States had a right to expand its borders west to the Pacific Ocean and south to the Rio Grande

market economy (MAHR • kuht ih • KAH • nuh • mee) a type of economy in which individual producers decide what goods or services to sell, based on available resources and demand

mercenary (MUHR • suh • nehr • ee) professional soldiers from other countries

merchant (MER • chuhnt) a person who makes his or her living by buying and selling goods

migrate (MY • grayt) to move from one place to another

militia (muh • LIH • shuh) a group of volunteer soldiers who fight only in an emergency

missionary (MIH • shuh • nehr • ee) a person who tries to persuade people to accept new religious beliefs

Missouri Compromise (muh • ZUHR • ee KOM • preh • meyz) was an agreement in 1820 that allowed Missouri and Maine to enter the Union and divided the Louisiana Territory into areas allowing slavery and areas outlawing slavery

R16

navigable — proclamation

N

navigable (nav • IH • guh • buhl) deep and wide enough for ships to travel on or through

navigation (nah • vih • GAY • shuhn) the science of finding direction and getting ships from place to place

neutral (NOO • truhl) not expressing strong opinions or feelings; not connected with either side in a war

nomad (NOH • mad) a person that moves from place to place and doesn't have a permanent home

O

occupation (ah • kyuh • PAY • shuhn) the work that a person does in order to earn a living; a job

overland wagon (OH • vuhr • lahnd WA • guhn) wagons that pioneers used to carry all of their possessions along the trails to the West

P

Patriot (PAY • tree • uht) a colonist who supported the colonies' fight for independence in the American Revolution

persecution (puhr • sih • KYOO • shuhn) the act of causing someone to suffer because of their beliefs

*persuade (puhr • SWAYD) to win over with words

pilgrim (pihl • gruhm) a person who travels to a place for religious reasons

pioneer (PY • uhn • eer) a person who settles a new part of the country

politics (PAW • luh • tihks) the process of choosing government leaders and running the government

potlatch (PAWT • lach) a special Native American celebration in the Pacific Northwest at which guests, not hosts, receive gifts

prairie (prehr • EE) flat or gently rolling land covered mostly with grasses and wildflowers

press (PREHS) members of the news media, such as reporters and columnists

*previous (PREE • vee • uhs) coming before, earlier

*primary (PRY • mehr • ee) first; main

proclamation (prah • kluh • MAY • shuhn) an official announcement

R17

Glossary

profit — teepee

profit (PRAH • fuht) the money made on goods or services that is more than the cost of production

profiteering (prah • fuh • TIHR • ihng) to charge high prices for goods that are in demand during a war or emergency

proprietor (pruh • PRY • uh • tuhr) a person who owns property or a business

R

ratify (RA • tuh • fy) to approve and adopt

reaper (REE • pur) a machine that cuts grain for harvesting

relative location (REH • luh • tihv loh • KAY • shuhn) the location of a place in relation to other landmarks

repeal (rih • PEEL) to cancel something, such as a law

*response (rih • SPAHNS) something that is done as a reaction to something else

responsibility (rih • spahn • suh • BIH • luh • tee) something that people must do because it is their job or duty

S

secede (sih • SEED) is to withdraw from the Union

slash-and-burn (SLASH UHND BUHRN) to cut and burn trees to clear land for farming

slave state (SLAYV STAYT) a state where slavery was allowed

slavery (SLAY • vuh • ree) the practice of owning people and forcing them to work without pay

spy (SPEYE) a person who secretly watches people or things in order to get information

stagecoach (STAYJ • kohch) a large carriage pulled by horses that was used to carry passengers

steam engine (STEEM EHN • jihn) a machine that uses steam from boiling water to create power

submit (sub • MIHT) to offer for approval

T

*technique (tehk • NEEK) a way, or method, of doing something

teepee (TEE • pee) a cone-shaped tent made from animal hides and wooden poles used by Native Americans of the Plains

R18

Glossary

territory — War Hawks

territory (tehr • IH • tor • ee) an area of land that is under a country's control and protection, but is not part of the country

tolerate (TAH • luh • rayt) to allow something to be or be done without trying to stop it

totem pole (TOH • tuhm POHL) a log that is carved and then painted with symbols, called totems, of animals or people

*translate (trans • LAYT) to change words from one language into another language

treaty (TREE • tee) an agreement between nations, such as for peace

tributary (trihb • YOO • tehr • ee) a river or stream that flows into a larger river or lake

*typically (TIH • pih •klee) what is normal or expected of a certain place, person, situation

tyrant (TY • ruhnt) a person who uses power in a cruel or unjust way

U

union (YOON • yuhn) a group of states or nations that are ruled by one government or that agree to work together

V

veto (vee • toh) to reject a bill

W

wagon train (WA • guhn TRAYN) a line of wagons led west by an experienced guide

wampum (WAHM • puhm) polished beads made from shells strung or woven together and used in gift-giving and trading by Native Americans

War Hawks (WAWR HAHKS) members of Congress that supported the war against Great Britain during the War of 1812

R19

Index

This index lists many topics that appear in the book, along with the pages on which they are found. Page numbers after a *c* refer to a chart or diagram, after a *g* to a graph, after an *m* to a map, after a *p* to a photograph or a picture, and after a *q* to a quotation.

Index

Civil War — Cotton gin

Index

Index

Index

Index

New Amsterdam — Pony Express

R28

P

R30

Index

USS Monitor —Yorktown, battle of

Notebook Foldables®

Strategies for using your Elementary Social Studies Program

- Help students organize information.
- Engage students further with the text.
- Provide an opportunity for enrichment and extension.

How to Construct Notebook Foldables®

Provide students with a copy of the template that corresponds to the activity you wish to teach. Then, direct students to:

1. **Fold** the anchor tab(s) and the information tabs where indicated on the template.
2. **Glue** the anchor tab(s) to the page where indicated.
3. **Cut** the Foldable to separate the information tab(s).

Once students have constructed their Notebook Foldables®, have them complete the activity as described in the Teacher Edition.

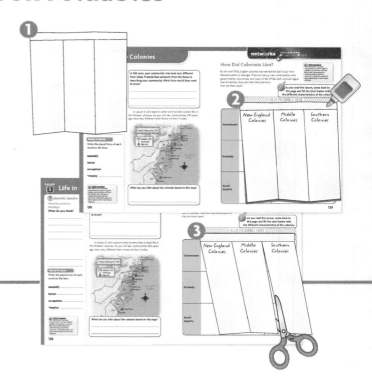

Notebook Foldables® by Dinah Zike

This best-selling book from Dinah Zike features adaptations of her Foldables® specially designed to fit into composition books, spiral notebooks, binders, and even Big Books. The book comes with reproducible graphics and instructions on how to create these modified Foldables® using regular paper. You'll be amazed at the hundreds of full-color examples found throughout the book! This book contains 129 pages complete with templates and a complimentary CD for easy customization and insertion of your own text and graphics.

For more information on this or other Dinah Zike products, visit www.dinah.com or call 1-800-99DINAH.
ISBN-10: 1-882796-27-6

Fold and glue **BEFORE** cutting!

Notebook Foldable® 1A—Use with Unit 1 Lesson 2, page 20.

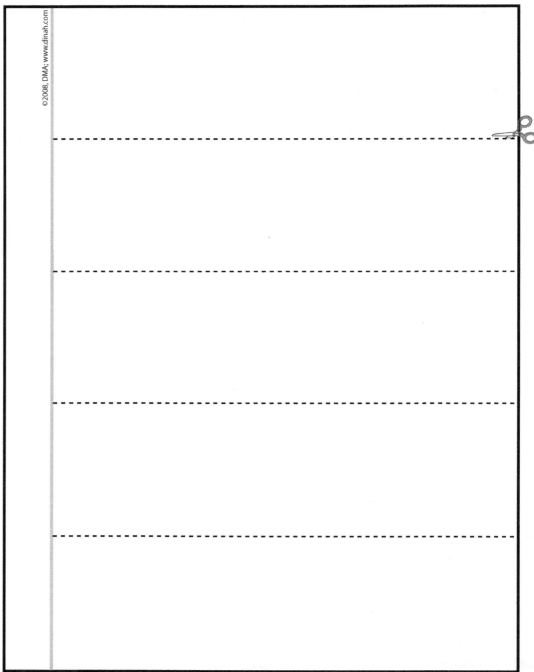

©2008, DMA; www.dinah.com

Fold and glue __BEFORE__ cutting!

Notebook Foldable® 2A—Use with Unit 2 Lesson 1, page 49.

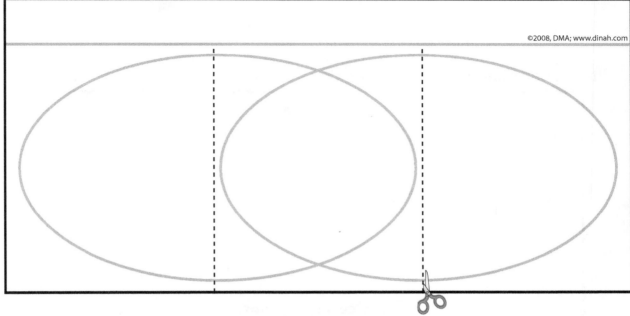

©2008, DMA; www.dinah.com

Notebook Foldable® 2B—Use with Unit 2 Lesson 4, page 59.

©2008, DMA; www.dinah.com

Fold and glue BEFORE cutting!

Notebook Foldable® 3A—Use with Unit 3 Lesson 1, page 83.

Astrolabe

Orienteering Compass

Sextant

Fold and glue BEFORE cutting!

Notebook Foldable® 4A—Use with Unit 4 Lesson 5, page 129.

©2008, DMA; www.dinah.com

New England Colonies	Middle Colonies	Southern Colonies

Unit 4 Notebook FOLDABLES®

Fold and glue BEFORE cutting!

Notebook Foldable® 4B—Use with Unit 4 Lesson 6, page 141.

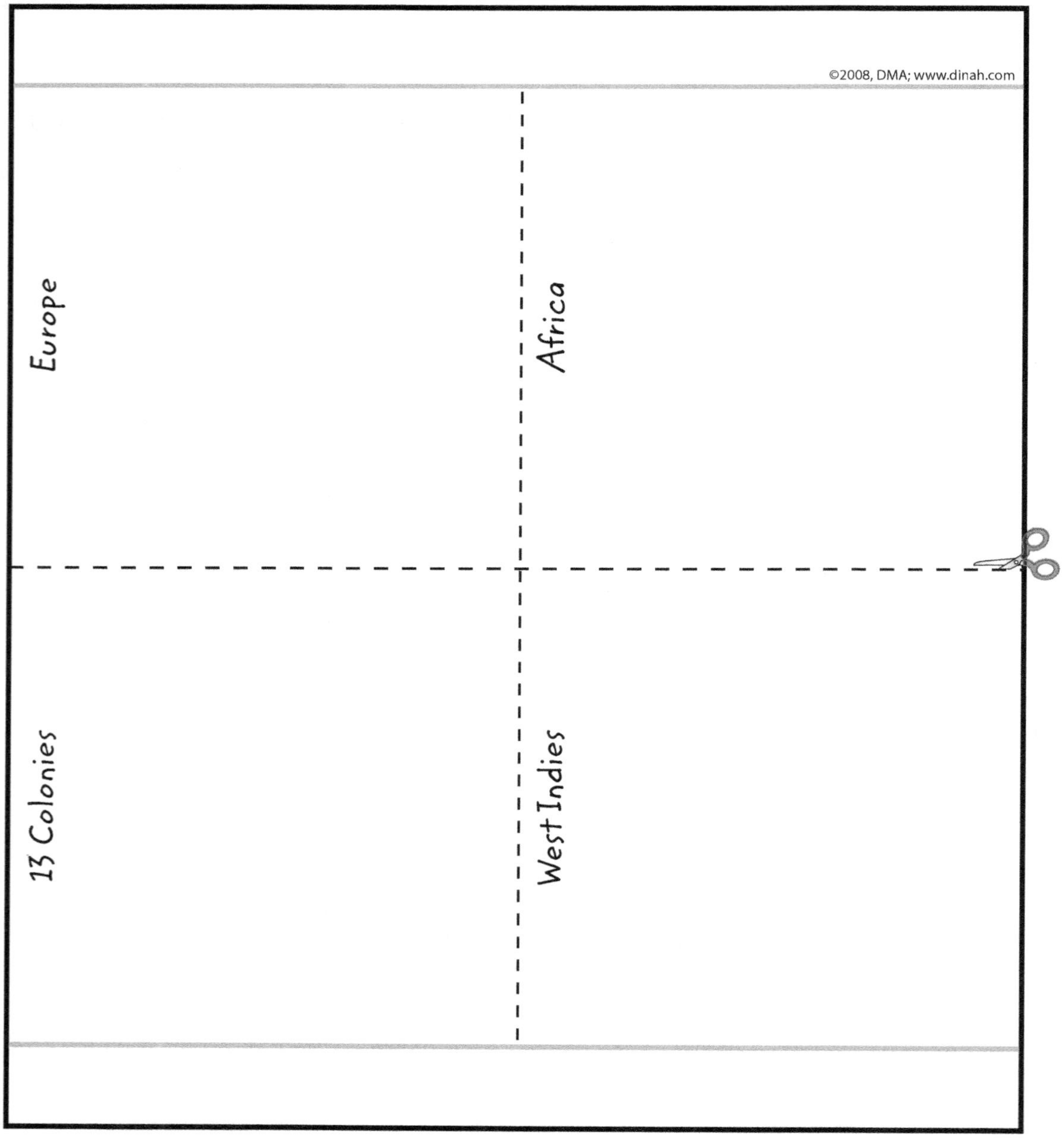

©2008, DMA; www.dinah.com
Europe
Africa
13 Colonies
West Indies

Fold and glue BEFORE cutting!

Notebook Foldable® 5A—Use with Unit 5 Lesson 2, page 168.

Undecideds

- -

Loyalists

- -

Patriots

©2008, DMA; www.dinah.com

Notebook Foldable® 5B—Use with Unit 5 Lesson 3, page 173.

©2008, DMA; www.dinah.com

Red Coats

©2008, DMA; www.dinah.com

Patriots

Fold and glue BEFORE cutting!

Notebook Foldable® 6A—Use with Unit 6 Lesson 3, page 219.

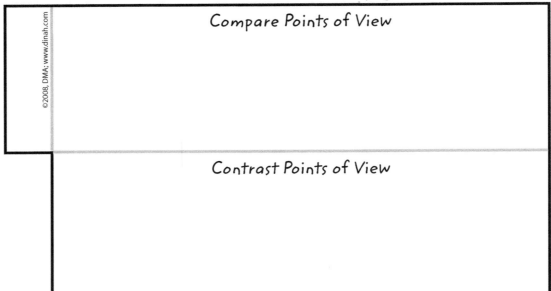

©2008, DMA; www.dinah.com

Compare Points of View

Contrast Points of View

Notebook Foldable® 6B—Use with Unit 6 Lesson 5, page 233.

©2008, DMA; www.dinah.com

Colonial Era

Today

Fold and glue
BEFORE cutting!

Notebook Foldable® 7A—

Use with Unit 7 Lesson 2, page 252.

©2008, DMA; www.dinah.com

Fold and glue BEFORE cutting!

Notebook Foldable® 7B—Use with Unit 7 Lesson 3, page 261.

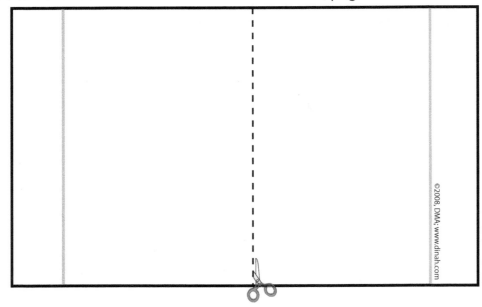

©2008, DMA; www.dinah.com

Notebook Foldable® 7C—Use with Unit 7 Lesson 3, page 265.

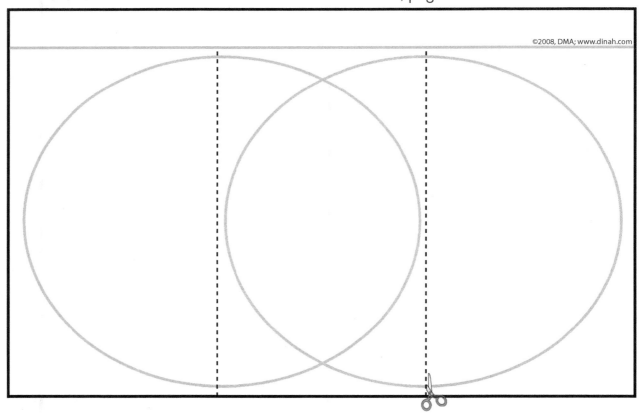

©2008, DMA; www.dinah.com